Komé – Kribi

Rescue Archaeology Along the Chad–Cameroon
Oil Pipeline, 1999–2004

Africa Magna Verlag

Komé – Kribi

Rescue Archaeology Along the Chad–Cameroon
Oil Pipeline, 1999–2004

Philippe Lavachery, Scott MacEachern,
Tchago Bouimon & Christophe Mbida Mindzie

Journal of African Archaeology   Monograph Series 4

Journal of African Archaeology Monograph Series

The Journal of African Archaeology Monograph Series is a supplement to the Journal of African Archaeology.
It offers a platform for more extensive contributions such as research monographs, refereed conference proceedings
and other collections.

Series Editors: Peter Breunig, Katharina Neumann
                       Goethe-Universität Frankfurt
                       Archäologie & Archäobotanik Afrikas
                       Grüneburgplatz 1
                       60323 Frankfurt am Main
                       Germany

Copy Editors: Richard Byer, Germany
                       Gabriele Franke, Germany

Publisher: Africa Magna Verlag
                       Altkönigblick 83
                       60437 Frankfurt am Main

Design & typesetting: Sonja Magnavita

Graphical assistance: Barbara Voss

Print: Druckhaus « Thomas Müntzer » GmbH, Bad Langensalza

Printed in Germany

Bibliografische Information der Deutschen Bibliothek

Die Deutsche Bibliothek verzeichnet diese Publikation in der Deutschen Nationalbibliografie;
detaillierte bibliografische Daten sind im Internet über http://dnb.ddb.de abrufbar.

ISBN: 978-3-937248-14-1

Foreword – Republic of Cameroon
Ministry of Culture (MINCULT)

When in 2001, the first earth moving equipment started the trench for the Chad/Cameroon Pipeline from Kome in Chad towards Kribi on the Cameroon coast; very few people, except for the experts, could expect the archaeological findings contained in the present book. This scepticism was associated with an old myth existing since the 19th century in Europe that excluded the African equatorial forest area from the main historical trends. According to the theorists of that period, it was the world of "darkness". This undertaking started with little serenity amongst stakeholders.

The Chad/Cameroon Pipeline and the archaeological vestiges are two symbols that recall for the first, the notion of modernity, circulation, prosperity, and for the second, the image of the remote past. Considered in the endless dilemma of history, the first builds itself on the second, or better still, the first exhumes the second. Generally speaking, construction works (quarries, earthworks, roads, railways, buildings, and gas and oil pipelines) always cause the destruction of the vestiges in the subsoil. The preventive archaeology permits to rescue an important part of these vestiges. Any information gathered from these excavations always enriches the knowledge of the past. This is the case with the Chad/Cameroon Pipeline.

In Cameroon, this is the second example after the Bertoua/Garoua-Boulai (BGB) road construction project that permitted to protect an important archaeological heritage. The quantity and the variety of the archaeological vestiges discovered along the Chad/Cameroon Pipeline transect of 900 km length in the Cameroonian territory with more than three hundred archaeological sites revealed, already show the archaeological potentialities of our subsoil.

From the scientific stand point, these discoveries proved what was suspected until then, that people, likely hunters and gatherers, had been living in the heart of the dense forest in Southern Cameroon as early as the 5th millennium before our era. These also confirm the emergence of the settlement of the sedentary villages in between the southern border of Adamawa plateau in the North and the coastal region in the Southern part of Cameroon, already known in Yaoundé area at the end of the 2nd millennium BC. Besides, there is also evidence of the emergence of iron smelting civilizations since the last millennium before our era, until the Christian era. These new data substantially enrich our knowledge of Central Africa history and Cameroon archaeological heritage. The latter is stored in a curation facility located at Ekounou, Yaoundé in Cameroon, where it will be valued during exhibitions and scientific publication.

Although statistics concerning archaeology on the whole territory are not yet available, the numerous upcoming or ongoing infrastructure projects in the country (roads, hydroelectric dams, quarries, large farms, logging activities, various constructions, etc….) may favour progress in the same vein, just like the Chad/Cameroon Pipeline. It may be worth noting that the sites of the famous figurines of Nok made of terracotta, bronze made heads of Ife, and the bronzes of Igbo Ukwu in Nigeria, were discovered during similar civil works. Hence the need to reinforce awareness campaigns towards public and private promoters of large scale infrastructure projects on the importance of the archaeological heritage preservation.

Finally, the publication of the present book on the archaeological findings along the Chad/Cameroon Pipeline emphasizes the strong will of both the Republic of Cameroon and the Republic of Chad to integrate the cultural heritage aspect into any infrastructure work, be it, essentially economical. In fact, this is one of the missions of the Cameroon Ministry of Culture to ensure the protection, the conservation, the enrichment and the promotion of cultural heritage, in accordance with the global objectives set forth during the Earth Summit held in Rio de Janeiro, Brazil in 1992, concerning the implementation of sustainable development, desirable to preserve the human being, his environment and his social identity.

Ama Tutu Muna
Minister of Culture

Foreword – Republic of Cameroon
Pipeline Steering & Monitoring Committee (PSMC)

The Chad/Cameroon Pipeline is the first large-scale infrastructure project implemented in Cameroon, after promulgation of Law n° 96/12 dated 5th August 1996, defining the framework for environmental management.

In compliance with this law, as well as with the World Bank guidelines relating to environmental management, the Environmental Management Plan (EMP) of the Chad/Cameroon Pipeline has given particular attention to the archaeological aspect of this infrastructure, of which the potential impacts from the construction works had been previously identified, on the sacred sites, grave sites and other archaeological sites along the pipeline right-of-way. The Cameroon Administration through the Ministry in charge of Culture had to ensure the effective mitigation of these impacts.

To this end, the Pipeline Steering and Monitoring Committee (PSMC), an inter ministerial structure set-up by a decree of the President of the Republic of Cameroon on 7th July 1997, to liaise with the Cameroon Administration and the Pipeline companies such as Cameroon Oil Transportation Company (COTCO), operator of the Pipeline in Cameroon. The PSMC has facilitated the administrative monitoring and technical control of the archaeological aspects of this infrastructure, by the Ministry in charge of Culture.

Thanks to such follow-up carried out by the Ministry in charge of Culture with professionalism, as well as to the straightforward collaboration with COTCO, the archaeological resources identified along the pipeline route were well managed and are listed in this book.

It is worth noting that beyond the publication of this book, the achievement of the Chad/Cameroon Pipeline Project were beneficial to Cameroon, notably with respect to the improvement of knowledge regarding the history of the areas crossed by the pipeline in particular, and Cameroon in general. In the archaeological field, an experience has been acquired in the administrative monitoring and technical control of the cultural heritage aspects of large-scale projects.

Besides and in respect of the strengthening of the archaeological resources management capacities, an equipped archaeological reserve in which artefacts from the Chad/Cameroon Pipeline are stored, has been upgraded at Ekounou, Yaoundé in Cameroon, on the behalf of the Ministry in charge of Culture.

I wish to seize this opportunity to thank all the stakeholders for their active involvement in the archaeological aspect of the Chad/Cameroon Pipeline, notably, the Cameroonian Administration, COTCO, the World Bank, Non Governmental Organizations (NGOs), the local populations, as well as the several scientists from Cameroon, Chad and elsewhere. This involvement permitted not only to immortalize through this book the findings of the archaeological survey along the Pipeline route, but also to know more about Cameroon history.

Adolphe Moudiki
Executive General Manager /
President of the Pipeline Steering & Monitoring Committee

Foreword – Republic of Chad

A few years ago, the southern part of Chad and more specifically the oilfield basin of the eastern Logone, were represented as *terra incognita* on the archaeological map of Chad. In other words, until the present survey, no researcher had been really interested in the history and the civilization of the peoples inhabiting this part of the Extreme South of Chad. Let's point out that a few travellers revealed details about the iron smelting activities and the rare sites of that area. According to their background and to the extent of their specialization, the later had been concerned with the identification of some forges and blacksmiths.

It is a pity that the archaeological and technological aspects of the stone blocks cuttings, the ceramic production, metals and metallic objects did not arouse the same interest. Hence, concerning iron as raw materials, many hypotheses have been built, and sometimes theories of diffusion in which the research of production sites, itineraries and stops of the migrants, gave way to thoughtless conjectures. The rare studies of the history of southern Chad mainly dealt with the colonial and postcolonial periods. The pre-colonial period remained unknown, with respect to the chronological stages and the knowledge of the peoples and their civilizations.

This book on the archaeology of Southern Chad aims at completing and enriching some historical aspects of this area in particular and Chad in general.

The research focused on this part of Chad continued over several consecutive surveys thanks to the permanent support of the Government of Chad, Esso-Chad and the World Bank.

To consider all periods of Chadian history, an important role must be given to the particularly rich and original archaeology.

The research undertaken has not covered entirely this part of Chad, but it appears that the results are sufficiently enlightening to enable their exhaustive publication without further delay. This decision has been largely motivated by Chadians and Cameroonians willing to know the history of their past civilization and their origin. We believe that these pages can permit Chadians to have a better knowledge of the history of their country. This information collected on the main excavated sites can enable them to reflect on their history and to present it from a Chadian point of view.

The four contributors to this summary have however one certainty: that the next step shall be the development of a 'veritable archaeology of Chad', which will no longer be only a juxtaposition 'of regional archaeologies'.

In order to do an in depth study of the archaeology or the history of Chadian regions, Chadians must collaborate with researchers from Cameroon (as it is the present case), Nigeria, Niger, Libya, Sudan and Central African Republic as different civilizations extended and are spreading across the boundaries of these countries.

Thus designed, in its diverse views and in the scope imposed by the very extent of this topic, this book is intended for a large public, literate or not, as well as for tourists willing to be informed on the cultural sites of the country and the civilizations which they will not miss to come across during their travels.

Of course, this book is particularly valuable for the well informed reader or the student willing to improve on their archaeological knowledge who will find it a complete work instrument.

Lucienne Nodjiadjim Dillah
Minister of Cultural and Artistic Development

Foreword

Cameroon Oil Transportation Company (COTCO) & Chad Oil Transportation Company (TOTCO)

During the construction of the Chad/Cameroon Pipeline, one of our major concerns was to protect and to preserve the cultural sites located along the 1070 kilometres of the survey corridor through the forests and savannas, from coastal south Cameroon towards the high savannas in Southern Chad. After what appears nowadays as the most extensive archaeological survey ever conducted in Central Africa, researchers from Cameroon, Chad and other countries have largely documented the sites and discoveries until then unknown.

On behalf of COTCO and TOTCO, I have the pleasure to present to the public this book: *Komé–Kribi: Rescue Archaeology Along the Chad–Cameroon Oil Pipeline, 1999–2004*. This work is the result of an intense archaeological survey reminding us that for centuries, several generations practising the rituals of their ancestral customs have inhabited the areas called nowadays, Cameroon and Chad.

On these same sites where one can still find indigenous peoples in their natural habitat, this extensive quest for archaeological, linguistic and historical data was rendered effective by the construction of the Chad/Cameroon Pipeline, of which the contribution on the cultural plan eventually extends well beyond the known socio-economic benefits.

Through the descriptions of sites, hundreds of artefacts and a lot of other data carefully written in this book: *Komé–Kribi: Rescue Archaeology Along the Chad–Cameroon Oil Pipeline, 1999–2004*, the latter to a certain extent, pays tribute to the peoples of Cameroon and Chad and to their cultures. I consider this work a contribution to the protection of the ancient heritage of these peoples, and therefore express the wish to see it given the same recognition as other means and instruments that may help today to improve the management of Chad and Cameroon cultural heritage.

Indeed, the discoveries presented in this book open another view on the historical knowledge that we have had until now about the peoples of this part of Central Africa.

Peter Matthys
General Manager of COTCO and TOTCO

Contents

List of figures

List of tables

List of maps

Preface

How can one not be impressed by the importance of the work and the extent of the results presented here.

A few years ago, as the first rumours of the construction of a pipeline that would link new oilfields in southern Chad with the Cameroonian coast began to circulate, the small scientific community working in this area realised the exceptional opportunities of such a project.

When it was confirmed that such a gigantic project would involve the construction of a pipeline 1070 km long, corresponding to the distance from Paris to Rome, the possibility of such a transect, crossing a crucial area at the very hinge of the continent, stirred the imagination of researchers.

This transect would traverse this "Africa in miniature", the nation of Cameroon, from the dry northern savannas to the lush forests of the Atlantic littoral, crossing an area where different linguistic groups live together today and not far from the cradle of the Bantu languages, an area that must have witnessed the first steps of an expansion that continued to the Indian Ocean and Southern Africa.

Between the dream and this book, about fifteen years elapsed. The launching of the project was complex and delicate, but once started, everything progressed very quickly. The exploratory surveys began in March 1999 in Chad, and the monitoring of the project ended in September 2003. In less than four years, our archaeological knowledge of these key areas for the entire history of Africa has increased spectacularly.

The following pages give the details of what has been achieved. Several aspects of these results are especially significant.

First, concerning the collaboration between the stakeholders: officials of both countries involved and particularly the Ministries in charge of culture, the Cameroonian, Chadian and Western archaeologists as well as their universities and attached institutes, the pipeline companies COTCO and TOTCO, themselves resulting from gradually evolved partnerships between several oil companies, and, finally the lenders and especially the World Bank.

To cooperate, to understand each other and finally to have such a disparate group working together is all

the more remarkable, as they hardly had any experience of this type of joint project. Even though, at the beginning, ignorance of the expectations and the habits of some parties caused some misunderstandings, the collaborative work, the resources made available for that work, and a desire to maintain dialogue on behalf of the parties permitted them to meet these challenges. Here is the result, in your hands. It is quite conclusive.

The possibility of cooperation between such different partners, each of them having their own objectives and points of view, open up new perspectives for archaeological research in Africa. This is the first significant benefit.

Owing to the immensity of Central Africa, the density of its vegetation and the fact that few human and material resources have been allocated to its archaeological research so far, archaeological discoveries from the beginning of the colonial period have largely resulted from infrastructure projects: roads, bridges, railways, plantations, housing estates-subdivisions. Systematic surveys are still very rare, as are excavations of sites.

For more than a century, large infrastructure projects have therefore been windfalls for improving our archaeological knowledge, even though until recently the archaeologist would come afterward, taking advantage of access opened in the bush or forest and of the exposure of archaeological sites by bulldozers and road graders, hoping that a part of the site thus exposed had been protected so as to provide the possibility of a thorough excavation and not only a salvage operation.

Thus, the famous Obobogo site, in the suburbs of Yaoundé, discovered during a road survey in 1941, was rediscovered during recent works, almost forty years later. The systematic excavations organized there prior to construction in the area were able to unearth the remains of a former village, which proved to be the oldest at that time in Central Africa. Characterized by large pits and a very distinctive type of ceramics, this Oboboguian was thereafter the subject of several research projects. In addition, thanks to road upgrades during subsequent years, many sites of the same type were discovered and studied around Yaoundé and in its vicinity by Cameroonian researchers.

However, the archaeologists still came after the bulldozers. This was particularly upsetting because in the West, for several decades already, a new kind of archaeology had developed, and was experiencing significant growth, multiplying the number of archaeological discoveries and offering jobs to many young professionals. This salvage archaeology, also called "preventive archaeology", generated its own methods. It expanded in the general context of increasing efforts in Europe and in America towards the preservation and the improvement of the cultural heritage.

In the Anglo-Saxon world more especially, this so-called "Cultural Heritage Management" (CHM), experienced a significant development.

Therefore, there was no excuse to still behave in Africa in a way that was no longer acceptable in the West! For this reason, important lenders began recently to develop statutory provisions that require a systematic accounting of the impact of development projects, notably with respect to the cultural heritage. In the same vein, the concerned African states have gradually set forth appropriate laws under the impulse of their own researchers and technical experts. The "Chad Export Project" (CEP) and this work marvellously illustrate the results of such concerns.

In parallel, large companies are now aware that their role is not restricted to the pursuit of profits, and that they have social responsibilities, often at a global scale. Thus, issues of "Corporate Social Responsibility" (CSR) play an increasing role in managers' concerns today; not only are they afraid of being criticized, but also because by assuming larger responsibilities, the company wins a new legitimacy, a pride that impregnates its own culture and that strengthens the feeling of membership of its employees.

Both CHM and CSR, working together on an operation of this kind, and of which this book is the result, open up new and promising perspectives. Therefore, this publication must also mark a turning point.

But by thus gradually developing its activities on many different levels, salvage archaeology must also adapt itself to these new contexts. It must pay attention to local, social, cultural, economic and scientific realities. It must be able to respond to the requests and priorities of the inhabitants and the local officials of the areas involved. In rich countries, where the amount of archaeological research is already significant, the strategy is especially to detect sites before construction work starts, as is reflected by the term "preventive archaeology". Hence, to the greatest extent possible, the goal is to avoid sites, or otherwise to examine them preliminarily.

On the other hand, in areas where archaeological knowledge remains very incomplete and where other priorities mean that available resources are often insufficient, large construction projects still appear more as an opportunity than a threat. One of the merits of the local directors of CEP is to have understood very quickly that it was necessary to adapt their intervention to this particular context and even better, to go farther with this logic and contribute to the strengthening of local archaeological capabilities. Thus, additional resources were made available in order to complete analyses and radiocarbon chronologies, to build a laboratory and to support young researchers. In addition to these efforts, this publication very well illustrates that this kind of intervention should not only be limited to the analysis of sites, but must be considered to a larger context.

Appearing very soon after the end of the project (which should also be praised), with research still underway and a number of doctoral theses in progress thanks to this gigantic project, this book gives us a first view of the extent of the archaeological discoveries. They are explained in detail in the following pages.

Having led archaeological researches in this part of Africa for more than 35 years, I may in any case confirm that there will now be a "before" and an "after" the pipeline.

Our knowledge of the area has increased tremendously thanks to the discovery of about 472 sites, 110 of which must be considered as important and the availability of about 60 radiocarbon dates.

In Chad, the approximately 170 sites discovered have enriched our knowledge of an area that until now had remained quite unknown to archaeologists. If we may wonder at the rarity of Stone Age sites, we may also note the presence of significant iron-smelting activity, with important sites appearing about 2000 years ago, followed by occupations that allows us to construct a preliminary cultural sequence extending to modern populations.

In Cameroon, the 302 sites discovered have also generated valuable information that will guide research in the years to come. The quite variable number of sites discovered in different sectors along the pipeline provides for the first time details of human densities according to period and region.

For the Stone Age, the quite variable and scattered data confirm that people have occupied modern forest areas since the Middle Stone Age.

For the Iron Age, the abundance of the findings has delimited a series of regional cultural ensembles. In the north, these data fill a gap in our knowledge. They demonstrate the existence of two successive cultural stages, the first beginning during the first centuries AD.

In the south, the discoveries along the pipeline permit us to distinguish three zones of occupation, and confirm that the Iron Age starts in this part of Cameroon during the last millennium BC.

Thanks to the pipeline, the spatiotemporal limits of the main archaeological unit, which very likely correspond to occupation by the ancestors of the present populations, are further explained as one reads the following pages.

So, in an exemplary way, the construction of this pipeline shows that preparing a better future can also enlighten a past still very much unknown. More than ever, and literally, the future is rooted in the past. Let's therefore be delighted!

Pierre de Maret
Université Libre de Bruxelles

Acknowledgements

The work described in this book has been undertaken under the aegis of the Chad Export Project. The authors would like to acknowledge the very valuable assistance provided by the Minister of Culture of the Republic of Cameroon, the Minister of Cultural and Artistic Development of the Republic of Chad, the Pipelines Steering and Monitoring Committee (Cameroon), the staff of the Ministry of Culture (Cameroon), the staff of the Ministry of Cultural and Artistic Development (Chad), the University of Yaoundé I, the University of N'Djamena, TOTCO, COTCO, EEPCI and ExxonMobil Corporation. The authors wish to thank the Chadian, Cameroonian and expatriate archaeologists who have been central to this research in the field and in the laboratory: Professor Joseph-Marie Essomba, Raymond Neba'ane Asombang, Martin Elouga, Richard Oslisly, Alain Froment, Gosdé Bedoum, Roseline Betouguéda, Remy Dzou Tsanga, Bienvenu Gouem Gouem, Pierre Kinyock, Jérémie Man-Nangou, Jean Mbairo, Moussa Wayor, Clison Nangkara, Olivier Nkokonda, Yves Onana Onana, Kainba Baidi Ouang-Namou Ouangtoua, Pierre Tada, Pazeu Teyabé and Desiré Yegba. We would also like to acknowledge in particular the support and interest of a number of Project staff: Grant Batterham, Ellen Brown, Ed Caldwell, Jacky Gruat, Ulrich Sellier, Elizabeth Kostiuk, Pandora Snethkamp and Joey Tucker, Moctar Djamil, Dingamyo Mbao, Brigitte Lehman, Celine Mbaissouroum and Jeannette Moral. Finally, we would like to thank the staff of Africa Magna Verlag for all of their assistance, and Dr. James Denbow and an anonymous reviewer for their helpful comments.

October 2008

1 – INTRODUCTION

Between 1999 and 2004, a cultural heritage management program, involving a large amount of archaeological field research, took place in those areas of Chad and Cameroon scheduled to be impacted by construction work associated with the Chad Export Project (CEP, or the Project). This Project involved construction of oil extraction facilities in southwestern Chad, an oil pipeline running to the Atlantic coast of Cameroon, and a marine terminal off the Cameroonian coast at Kribi (*Map 1*). It was undertaken by a consortium of international oil companies led by Exxon, with involvement of the World Bank Group and the governments of Chad and Cameroon. The Environmental Management Plan (EMP) for the Project included a significant archaeological component. This research resulted in the discovery and prioritization of almost 500 archaeological sites in this area of Central Africa (*Maps 2* and *3*), as well as in mitigation of construction impacts on significant sites, analysis of materials recovered and development of the cultural heritage management (CHM) infrastructure in both countries.

One vital element in any such initiative involves dissemination of research results: to be truly useful, information must be made available to interested parties beyond the program principals directly involved — in this case, Chad Export Project personnel, CHM professionals involved with the Project, and representatives of the governments of Cameroon and Chad and the World Bank. Such interested parties might in these circumstances include interested citizens of Chad and Cameroon, other cultural heritage managers and professional archaeologists in Central Africa and beyond, and the wider public interested in African history and prehistory. Far too often after the publication of the results of CHM archaeological projects, such publications vanish into an ever-expanding 'gray literature', where reports are held by writers and clients, but are almost impossible for other professionals (and still less interested citizens) to access (see for example AUGER 1989; LATTANZI 1999). This problem is especially critical in regions like Africa, where resources for both CHM and archaeological research are generally in short supply and where very little is known about the culture history of vast areas of the continent — including some areas in which Project research was undertaken. In such regions, it is vital not merely to successfully complete a thorough and careful cultural heritage management program, but to make the results of that program generally available for public and professional consumption.

The necessity for a comprehensive scientific publication, both summarizing the archaeological results and their implications for future archaeological research in Central Africa more widely, was recognized by the management of the Chad Export Project, by the World Bank personnel conducting Project oversight, and by the national governments of Cameroon and Chad. Initial reports of this CHM program were published in archaeological journals in 2005 (LAVACHERY *et al.* 2005a, 2005b), but such short introductory reports could not hope to reflect the full range of archaeological activities of the Project. It was decided in a meeting of the principal actors in Brussels in February 2006 that the most appropriate form for such a publication would be a book-length academic monograph, written by the archaeologists who worked on and carried out oversight of the program, peer-reviewed and disseminated by a publisher specializing in Africanist archaeology.

This book is the result of that meeting and of those efforts. It is important to African archaeology on a number of different levels. In the first place, it describes the largest integrated CHM program ever undertaken in sub-Saharan Africa, spanning two countries, seven years (to date) and a very large amount of territory. Given the growing importance of CHM initiatives in African cultural heritage protection, and the well-known challenges of integrating heritage management and academic archaeological approaches (KING 2005), this Project and its results may serve as an important illustration of the potentials and the challenges of such initiatives (for accounts of other African CHM initiatives and broader discussions, see for example S.K. MCINTOSH 1993; DEACON 1999; BRANDT & HASSAN 2000; CAMPBELL 2000; KINAHAN 2000; MABULLA 2000; MITCHELL 2000; MACEACHERN 2001a; DELNEUF, ASOMBANG & MBIDA 2003). The coordination of research efforts in two different countries is extremely unusual for such a program in Africa, and the implications of that requirement will be further considered in later chapters of this book.

Second, the Chad Export Project CHM effort is probably the largest single archaeological project ever undertaken in Central Africa, and one of the largest ever undertaken in sub-Saharan Africa. The construction effort associated with the Project involved installation of a pipeline along a right-of-way that stretched from the oilfield areas of southern Chad to the Atlantic coast of Cameroon. Archaeological survey, construction monitoring and data recovery took place along the full length of that right-of-way. This provided Project CHM personnel with a unique chance to examine prehistoric cultural variability along a continuous transect almost 1100 kilometers long, extending through what are now a variety of ecological and cultural zones and including regions that are central to our understanding of cultural developments in Africa during the Holocene, and to a lesser extent along road surveys also associated with the Project. This is a very unusual situation in archaeological research, which tends to be associated with specific sites or quite restricted regions and where the chance to compare the remains of human activity over many hundreds of kilometers is extremely rare. In particular, this transect cuts across what would have been the wave front of cultural change associated with the 'Bantu Expansion' — a phenomenon whose characteristics have certainly been debated, but that definitely changed the face of sub-Saharan Africa as we know it (see *Chapters 3* and *4* for further consideration of this phenomenon).

This monograph cannot hope to give a comprehensive description of every discovery associated with the Chad Export Project archaeological research. A very large number of sites were found, some CHM fieldwork continues to take place in Chad (see *Chapter 5*), and an important amount of material remains to be analyzed. Research and publication sparked by Project efforts continues and will continue into the future, not as a formal CHM program but as the result of initiatives by various archaeologists working in Chad and Cameroon. In this book, we hope instead to give a broad overview of prehistoric cultural diversity in the areas where the Project CHM work took place, with particular attention paid to changes along the linear survey areas described above. The text is thus primarily descriptive on a site level. We also wish to examine in some detail the legislative and regulatory structure that defined the Project's cultural heritage management program, hoping that such an examination will prove useful for archaeologists and heritage management professionals contemplating such programs in Africa in the future. We will be extremely pleased if this CHM program serves as a useful precedent to such professionals, in arguing for an expansion of CHM initiatives on the African continent.

Structure of the text

The text is broadly divided into two parts: (1) a set of introductory and descriptive chapters that set out the environments (regulatory, natural, cultural and archaeological) within which the Project CHM effort took place; and (2) a set of descriptive and synthetic chapters (with appendices) that set forth the results of that effort. *Chapter 2* provides a general description of the Chad Export Project, as well as consideration of the legislative and regulatory structures that defined the Project CHM program. *Chapter 3* provides background data on the natural environments encountered in the Project area and their potential effects upon human occupation, as well as on modern cultural, ethnic and linguistic variability in the region. The latter is vital, in that it is very influential in providing archaeologists with the modern analogies that we use in interpreting ancient cultural remains. *Chapter 4* is a summary of the archaeological, historical, linguistic and palaeoenvironmental

information previously available for this part of Central Africa. For some parts of the region (the area around Yaoundé, for example) more data are available than for others (all of southwestern Chad). *Chapter 5* provides information on the objectives and organization of the CEP cultural heritage management programs in Cameroon and Chad, on the ways in which data from both countries were amalgamated, and particularly on research methodologies and the procedures used for determining the significance of archaeological sites located. This will place this project in the context of cultural heritage management initiatives both within and beyond Africa.

Chapters 6, 7 and *8* constitute the descriptive core of the book. *Chapter 6* provides a comparative examination of site patterning across the Project area as a whole, in both Cameroon and Chad. This includes a discussion of the broad characteristics of the sites themselves (including their chronological and geographical distributions, as well as the types of sites encountered) and the prioritizations and treatments extended to different sites in the Project area as a whole. *Chapters 7* and *8* include systematic descriptions of sites and archaeological materials located in the course of CEP archaeological research, in Chad and Cameroon respectively. This involves the description of site inventories for all sites located in the region, more detailed considerations of site distributions, and a brief description of a number of sites judged to be archaeologically significant that were the focus of sustained research. Condensed descriptions of excavations and artifact variability are also included in these two data chapters. The more geographically restricted area of Project activity in southwestern Chad is covered as a single unit. For Cameroon, in contrast, where fieldwork took place over almost 900 linear kilometers of the pipeline right-of-way, the description is separated into two parts, roughly corresponding to the environmental and cultural divide between the wooded savannas of east-central Cameroon (referred to as Cameroon North) and the tropical forests of the southwest and the Atlantic littoral (referred to as Cameroon South).

In *Chapter 9*, the authors interpret these sites in the context of known Central African history, with particular attention paid to (1) the chronological data, derived from comparative artifact typologies and radiocarbon dating that is the foundation of regional cultural history, and (2) data on economies and environmental variation through time, which will help us understand how people adapted to Central African environments in the late Pleistocene and Holocene. The final section of the book, *Chapter 10*, includes a summary of interpretations and recommendations for further archaeological work in the area. A section of appendices at the end of the work provides tabular data on site characteristics across the Project survey area in both Chad and Cameroon.

2 – PROJECT STRUCTURE AND REGULATORY BASIS

Background to the Chad Export Project

The ultimate goal of the Chad Export Project is petroleum extraction from oilfields in the Doba area of southwestern Chad and the export of this petroleum to international markets. The Project involved the construction of oilfield and support facilities in the Doba area, a 1070-kilometer pipeline with accompanying pumping facilities running from Doba in Chad through eastern and southern Cameroon to the Atlantic coast, and a marine terminal off the Cameroonian coast at Kribi. The construction phase of the Project was essentially completed as of mid 2004.

The Chad Export Project is the largest construction project ever undertaken in Central Africa, and will probably continue to hold that status for some time in the future. The scale of construction activities associated with the Project had the potential for significant damage to the cultural heritage resources of both Cameroon and Chad. Because of this, the Environmental Management Plan developed by the Chad Export Project included a substantial cultural heritage management component, comprising an archaeological program that was itself one of the largest archaeological efforts undertaken in this part of Africa to date. Fieldwork along the pipeline right-of-way constituted the longest continuous archaeological transect ever undertaken in Africa, allowing researchers to examine cultural diversity at a local scale over more than one thousand kilometers in a variety of different environments. In this chapter, we examine the institutional and legal structures within which this cultural heritage management program took place.

Overall organization of the Chad Export Project: host countries and institutions

The Chad Export Project has been the result of extensive collaboration between a consortium of oil companies, the World Bank Group and the national governments of Chad and Cameroon. This project structure was adapted to the complexities of oil exploration and production in this area of Central Africa. Exploratory efforts resulted in the identification of oil reserves in Chad in the mid-1970s. In 1988, the national government of Chad and a consortium of multinational oil companies signed an agreement giving that consortium exploration and oilfield development rights in southern Chad (CHAD/CAMEROON DEVELOPMENT PROJECT 2003) as well as exploration rights in other parts of the country. This agreement marked the beginning of the Chad Export Project and laid out the framework for environmental protection and heritage management that

would eventually cover the archaeology program in Chad and in Cameroon. Changes in consortium partnership ultimately resulted in the composition of the consortium as it exists today, with ExxonMobil as the operator, along with Petronas and Chevron.

While exploration and development of the oilfields were to take place in southern Chad, the export of these resources required the involvement of Cameroon, specifically with the construction of a pipeline across that country to an oil terminal to be located on the Atlantic coast near Kribi. Between 1996 and 1998, bilateral agreements between Cameroon and Chad, and internal adoption of legislation permitting pipeline construction in Cameroon, resulted in the establishment of a project framework in Cameroon parallel to that in Chad, which was, as in Chad, to cover among many other elements environmental protection and heritage management.

The World Bank Group and the European Investment Bank participated in the Project by consenting to provide loans to the two governments. The goals of the World Bank Group, along with the other members of the consortium and the national governments of Cameroon and Chad, were in general to maximize the positive impacts and minimize the negative impacts of the Project. To this end, the World Bank Group also worked with the other partners to provide essential expertise and supervision in a number of different areas of project planning and execution, including: (a) assistance with the development of environmental and socioeconomic management plans; (b) evaluation of project compliance with the Environmental Management Plan through the period of project execution; and (c) capacity-building measures for the institutions in Chad and Cameroon involved in ensuring national supervision and control of the project.

The consortium conducted its activities through three companies created specifically for Project purposes. An ExxonMobil subsidiary, Esso Exploration and Production Chad, Inc. (EEPCI) was designated as operator of the Project and was responsible for oil exploration, for development of the oilfields in southern Chad and for transportation of the oil to international markets. Two other companies, Tchad Oil Transportation Company S.A. (TOTCO) and Cameroon Oil Transportation Company S.A. (COTCO), were responsible for the construction, operation and maintenance of the oil pipeline itself in Chad and Cameroon respectively. Through their involvement with TOTCO and COTCO, the two host countries hold shares in the Project; they thus play a management role, with representatives on the Board of Governors of both companies.

Archaeological work on the cultural heritage management program was to a great degree coordinated and supported through those three companies, with different arrangements for research support (under the umbrella of the overall EMP) depending upon where the archaeological research was actually being undertaken. This complex Project management structure, and the fact that work was taking place simultaneously in two different countries, each of which legitimately wished to make independent decisions about their separate cultural heritage, necessitated parallel CHM organizations, interacting but working separately in both countries. The fact that the infrastructure (local researchers, conservation and analysis facilities, storage areas, legislation and so on — see below) available to support archaeological/CHM research was quite different in Cameroon and Chad also warranted such an organization. The overall cultural heritage management organization and the relationship between the archaeological programs developed in Cameroon and in Chad will be examined in *Chapter 5*.

The organization of oil extraction

The scope of construction work

The principal Project goals in Chad include the development of three separate oil fields, the Komé, Miandoum, and Bolobo oil fields. About one billion barrels of oil will be produced over the 25- to 30-year life of the Project. Project components in the Oilfield Development Area (OFDA) include: (1) approximately 300 production wells and 25 water reinjection wells; (2) a gathering system to transport produced oil (connection pipelines); and (3) an Operations Center (OC) located in the Komé field, consisting of the Central Treatment Facility (CTF), an airstrip, housing for personnel, and a power plant to serve Project needs.

The transportation system, both in Chad and in Cameroon, includes: (1) a 1069 km long, 760 mm diameter underground pipeline; (2) an originating pump station (PS I) located near the CTF in Chad; (3) two intermediate pump stations (PS II and PS III) located along the pipeline route in Cameroon (Dompta and Belabo), occupying 36 ha (including an airstrip); (4) a pressure-reducing station (PRS) close to the Atlantic coast crossing of the pipeline (Kribi), occupying 5 ha; and (5) an undersea pipeline roughly 11 km long, ending at a Floating Storage and Offloading (FSO) vessel offshore of Kribi, Cameroon (***Map 4***). All these facilities (except the undersea pipeline) necessitated substantial earthmovement during construction, with a high risk of disturbing archaeological sites.

Onshore pipeline construction of concern to archaeologists involved a number of different steps: (1) the temporary clearing of a strip of land, typically approximately 30 m wide, along the pipeline route (clearing); (2) the leveling of the pipeline easement (grading); (3) the excavation of a ditch to accommodate the pipeline (trenching); (4) the installation of the pipe in the trench; (5) the backfilling of the trench; and (6) the rehabilitation of the cleared area along the pipeline route (reclamation). In addition, approximately 475 km of road were also improved, 35 km of new road constructed and a new bridge across the Mbéré River built at the Chad-Cameroon border. Other Project facilities include four permanent storage yards at the ports of Douala, Ngaoundal, Ngoumou and Komé, and eight temporary yards and a landing strip at various locations along the pipeline right-of-way between Douala and Komé.

The Oilfield Development Area

In the Oilfield Development Area, approximately 1080 ha were needed for facilities and their related infrastructure. Approximately 300 producing wells will eventually be located in the Komé, Bolobo and Miandoum fields. There will be ten field manifolds within the Komé field, three within the Miandoum field, and three within the Bolobo field. For the wells and manifolds located at the southern and northern ends of the Komé field, two field pump stations (KP-1 and KP-2) will pump the production fluids to the Komé gathering station. No field pump station was required in the Miandoum field. Two gathering stations were built (in Komé and Miandoum) to receive production from individual wells via field manifolds and field pump stations. An approximately 3200 m long airfield was constructed at Komé to provide air transport during construction and subsequent operations. A laterite road was constructed to connect the Operations Center facilities to the Moundou-Sahr road at Bébédjia. The Operations Center facilities were also connected to field facilities and well sites by upgrading existing laterite roads or building new laterite roads.

Construction of OFDA facilities took place over a period of about 2.5 years. The first year focused on the preparation of the major sites, including construction of the initial well pads and roads, construction of the construction camp, site preparation for the airfield, and site/foundation work for the production facilities. During the second year, the construction effort centered on the major plants, including the CTF, the power plant, PS 1 and the Miandoum gathering station. The majority of the flow lines, manifolds, and overhead electrical power lines were also erected during this time. A number of site preparation operations required archaeological monitoring, including clearing, grubbing, grading and excavation as well as the development of borrow pits for construction materials, such as sand, gravel and laterite. After the completion of site preparation activities, archaeologists monitored the trenching for the underground utilities and flow lines, and the foundation excavations. Field pipeline activities followed the same general construction techniques used for the main export pipeline (see below).

Although pipeline and facilities construction was largely completed by the end of 2003, development work in the OFDA will continue for the foreseeable future, and it is likely that more archaeological sites will be found in the course of that work. Because the heritage management program is thus continuing at a much smaller scale, we have decided that a somewhat arbitrary cut-off date of January 1, 2004 will be used to determine the choice of material covered in this book. The results of further archaeological fieldwork will be presented in periodic reports to be submitted to journals of Africanist archaeology.

Pipeline construction

An overall land easement width of 30 m was required for the construction of the pipeline. This included room for the ditch, for storage of sediment and material, and for a temporary road to transport machines and material. Additional land easement widths were necessary at locations with steep slopes, the shore crossing (50 m), and other terrain features such as river crossings (60 m). The pipeline was built with two major spreads or construction units, each carrying out the full range of construction operations. Pipeline construction was undertaken from moveable construction base camps (one for each construction spread). Each base camp was located close to the land easement and supported pipeline construction activities for a distance of approximately 60 to 80 km. There were only two base camps in full operation at any one time. Each camp relocated periodically to provide construction support and logistical functions over the entire pipeline corridor. After the land easement was surveyed and staked to identify the centerline, it was prepared for construction by clearing and grading. Clearing included the removal of aboveground vegetation and rocks to the side of the land easement. Any trees and large shrub debris that needed to be removed were felled and stockpiled alongside the land easement. Grading included the leveling of the right-of-way to enable the passage of construction and transport of machines and equipment.

The pipeline trench was centered on a line approximately 10 m from one side of the 30 m land easement. This provided 10 m width for storing ditch spoil, and up to a 20 m working area for construction equipment and pipe assembly. The ditch was excavated mechanically, and the length of the ditch opened at any one time generally did not exceed 20 km. Dimensions of the trench generally ranged from 1.2 to 1.4 m in width and 1.8 to 2.2 m in depth. Backfill material was returned to the ditch and crowned on top of the ditch to compensate for future settling. Excess backfill material was spread over graded sections of the land easement. A minimum of 1 m of soil cover was added on top of the pipeline. Cover was greater at road intersections, river crossings, and near pump stations. When solid rock was encountered, blasting was required and a minimum of 0.5 m of cover was provided.

A portion of the smaller shrub vegetation moved to the side of the land easement was conserved and spread over the land easement after construction was completed to help control erosion, serve as mulch, and provide a source of seed for re-vegetation. In agricultural areas, the topsoil was removed, stockpiled, and eventually re-spread over the graded area. Topsoil that was removed for subsequent reuse was stored within the land easement in a manner allowing retrieval during cleanup operations for redistribution over the graded area. Cleanup and restoration of the land easement was achieved once backfilling and compaction were completed.

National resources: people, institutions and equipment

Cameroon

There are a number of active Cameroonian archaeologists, most associated with the Université de Yaoundé. The archaeology program at that university, directed by Professor Joseph-Marie Essomba, has produced a number of researchers who have obtained their doctorates and who now direct fieldwork initiatives, especially in the south of the country. Two of these archaeologists, Drs. Christophe Mbida and Raymond Asombang, at present occupy administrative positions in the Cameroonian Ministry of Culture, where their duties include oversight on issues that might impact the cultural patrimony of Cameroon, as well as being involved in research programs. In addition, there is a small number of students with archaeological field experience at the Université de Yaoundé. There are also a number of foreign archaeologists, primarily of European and Canadian origin, who are involved in long-term research in different parts of the country. However, researchers working in the country in the mid-/late-1990s had relatively little experience with cultural heritage management programs and procedures, since these are carried out mainly in North America.

Before the beginning of the CHM program associated with the Chad Export Project, no facilities for archaeological analysis or storage conforming to UNESCO norms existed in Cameroon. Very limited laboratory and storage facilities were available at the Université de Yaoundé, and there existed (and still exists) a serious lack of even basic equipment needed for archaeological survey, excavation and analysis. In addition, no facilities for related technical analyses (radiocarbon or thermoluminescence dating laboratories, reference collections for faunal or floral analysis and so on) exist in Cameroon. All such analyses of material from Cameroon are at present undertaken in facilities outside the country.

Chad

Only one Chadian researcher works as a professional archaeologist at this point. Dr. Tchago Bouimon is a member of the faculty of the Université de N'Djamena, conducts his own fieldwork, and oversees archaeological research taking place in Chad. The number of non-Chadian archaeologists working in Chad is comparatively much smaller than in Cameroon. Most of their research has been undertaken in the northern, Saharan and Sahelian, regions of the country. A number of Dr. Tchago's students have some experience in archaeological fieldwork. Researchers working in this country again had almost no experience with cultural heritage management programs.

As in Cameroon, no facilities for archaeological analysis or storage conforming to UNESCO norms existed in Chad before the beginning of the Project work. There is limited storage space for artifacts in the Musée National in N'Djamena, and extremely limited space for the examination of artifacts was available at the university. As in Cameroon, there is a severe lack of the equipment necessary for undertaking archaeological research. No facilities for technical analyses were available in the country; such work was in all cases done outside Africa.

The regulatory basis for the protection of cultural patrimony: national legislation and international accords

There are a number of regulatory instruments relevant to the management of cultural properties discovered in Cameroon and Chad during the course of the Project. These include both pertinent national heritage laws, international conventions concerning heritage protection, agreements between the national governments of Cameroon and Chad and the Chad Export Project, as well as requirements put in place by the World Bank

for projects of this type. This section will also describe commitments that have been made in other documents relating to the management of cultural properties.

Cameroon

Most of these data are taken from the Project's *Environmental Management Plan — Cameroon Portion* (Appendix E — Management Plan For Cultural Properties) (CHAD EXPORT PROJECT 1999a). In Cameroon, management of the cultural patrimony, including archaeological sites, is controlled by Law No. 91/008 of July 30, 1991 entitled "On the Protection of the Cultural and Natural Heritage of the Nation", which provides a process for the registration and protection of important cultural properties. This law requires that the managers of development projects must notify the relevant authorities (in this case the Ministry of Culture) of any significant discoveries of cultural properties, and that provisions must be made for the evaluation and protection of such properties.

The Republic of Cameroon is also a signatory to a number of international conventions concerning the protection of cultural properties. These include:

(1) the Third ACP (African-Caribbean-Pacific countries) — EEC (now European Community) Convention, ratified at Lomé on December 8, 1984 (Part II, Title VIII, Chapter 3, Article 127 of that Convention addresses issues of cultural heritage preservation and promotion);

(2) the UNESCO Convention on the Means of Prohibiting and Preventing the Illicit Import, Export and Transfer of Ownership of Cultural Property of 1970; and

(3) the UNESCO Convention Concerning the Protection of the World Cultural and National Heritage of 1972.

Chad

In Chad, the management of the cultural patrimony, including archaeological sites, is controlled by Law No. 14–60 of November 2, 1960 stating "…pour objet la protection des monuments et sites naturels, des sites et monuments de caractère préhistorique, archéologique, scientifique, artistique ou pittoresque, le classement des objets historiques ou ethnographiques et la réglementation des fouilles…" (UNESCO 2002). This legislation establishes the concept of a list of classified monuments and sites for which preservation is necessary, and of a commission to control development of sites on that list. It states that any archaeological excavation undertaken must obtain permission from the national government. Chad is also a signatory to the following international conventions concerning the protection of cultural properties:

(1) the Third ACP (African-Caribbean-Pacific countries) — EEC (now European Community) Convention, ratified at Lomé on December 8, 1984 (Part II, Title VIII, Chapter 3, Article 127 of that Convention addresses issues of cultural heritage preservation and promotion); and

(2) the UNESCO Convention Concerning the Protection of the World Cultural and National Heritage of 1972.

World Bank and UNESCO conventions

There are a number of legal and regulatory instruments related to the identification and management of cultural properties directly affected by the Project. The relevant World Bank policy document covering cultural properties is Operational Policy Note 11.03 (World Bank 1986). For the purposes of the Project, the definition of cultural properties followed that set forth in that policy note, which states:

"The United Nations term "cultural property" includes sites having archaeological (prehistoric), paleontological, historical, religious, and unique natural values. Cultural property, therefore, encompasses both remains left by previous human inhabitants (for example, middens, shrines, and battlefields) and unique natural environment features such as canyons and waterfalls. . . ."

The World Bank's general policy regarding cultural properties, as set out in Note 11.03, is to assist in their preservation and to seek to avoid their elimination, stating specifically:

"(a) The World Bank normally declines to finance projects that will significantly damage non-replicable cultural property. . . . (b) In some cases, the project is best relocated in order that sites and structures can be preserved, studied, and restored intact *in situ*. In other cases, structures can be relocated, preserved, studied, and restored on alternate sites. Often, scientific study, selective salvage, and museum preservation before destruction is all that is necessary. Most such projects should include the training and strengthening of institutions entrusted with safeguarding a nation's cultural

patrimony. Such activities should be directly included in the scope of the project, rather than being postponed for some possible future action…".

The most comprehensive document giving direction on the management of cultural patrimony prepared for the World Bank is probably World Bank Technical Paper 62, entitled *The management of cultural property in World Bank-assisted projects* (GOODLAND & WEBB 1987). The Technical Paper describes types of projects needing cultural property components, including large-scale earth moving projects. Project cultural property components may in these cases include:

(1) "…Project design or siting change…

(2) Archaeological or palaeontological study or salvage…

(3) Restoration and preservation of historical and religious structures…

(4) Preservation of 'tribal' sacred sites…

(5) Preservation of sites of natural uniqueness… [and]

(6) Training and institution building…." (GOODLAND & WEBB 1987: 18–21)

Archaeological or palaeontological study or salvage, and preservation of 'tribal' (more accurately phrased as 'indigenous') sacred sites, were the two primary areas of effort in this Project, with training and institution building a significant secondary concern. The majority of cultural properties in the Project area were expected to be archaeological sites, and indeed that was the case. The Technical Paper describes the sequence of steps to be taken in the management of archaeological sites in broad terms (GOODLAND & WEBB 1987: 19):

(a) "… regional reconnaissance survey; mapping and sampling of all sites; literature survey . . .

(b) evaluation of sites in or near the project area to determine their relative scientific importance and potential for preservation, possibly including a test-pit to help date surface collections; evaluation may form a triage in which (i) some sites can be abandoned with no further study and no significant loss to the nation, (ii) some sites are studied or recorded and then abandoned, and (iii) some sites merit special protection or removal;

(c) determination of the impact of the proposed economic development project on such sites;

(d) preservation of significant sites in place, to the extent project design allows or can be modified to allow it;

(e) excavation and retrieval of data from sites likely to be affected;

(f) maintenance, preservation, and study of significant sites and representative artifacts; and

(g) preparation, publication, and dissemination of scientific reports."

The concerns and procedures described in Technical Paper 62 were important in determining management procedures for the Project's cultural heritage management program.

Project documentation and requirements

Cultural heritage management issues are also dealt with in a number of Chad Export Project documents.

Environmental Management Plan – Cameroon Portion, Volume 1

Chapter 2, socio-economic topic 7, 'Sacred and cultural sites', discusses agreements between the Republic of Cameroon and COTCO with regard to the identification and management of cultural and sacred sites. It treats a broad range of procedures that are integrated in the general organizational strategy of the Project. It notes among these that during construction and extraction phases, the Project will notify "… appropriate Republic of Cameroon authorities if archaeological, historical, or palaeontological sites are discovered as per legislative requirements.".

Environmental Management Plan – Cameroon Portion, Volume 3

The Cameroonian Compensation Plan, section 5.5.5, describes the types of sacred sites that the Project expects to discover, and the type of compensation envisaged for these sites. The list includes sacred sites, burials and cemeteries.

Environmental Management Plan – Chad Portion, Volume 1

Chapter 2, socio-economic topic 7, 'Sacred and cultural sites', discusses agreements between the Republic of Chad and EEPCI/TOTCO with regard to the identification and management of cultural and sacred sites. It treats a broad range of procedures that are integrated in the general organizational strategy of the Project. It notes among these that during construction and

extraction phases, the Project will notify "… appropriate Republic of Chad authorities if archaeological, historical, or palaeontological sites are discovered as per legislative requirements.".

Environmental Management Plan – Chad Portion, Volume 3

The Chadian Compensation Plan, section 5.5.5, describes the types of sacred sites that the Project expects to discover, and the type of compensation envisaged for these sites. The list includes sacred sites, burials and cemeteries.

Job Specification Coordination Procedure (JSCP), Section 29

JSCP, section 29, sub-section 5.11, page 2903, states: "If sites of archaeological value are discovered during construction, Contractor shall leave the archaeological findings undisturbed and shall immediately report the event to Esso. Esso will instruct the Contractor how to proceed."

Management Plans for Cultural Properties: guidelines for field procedures

Both the *Environmental Management Plan – Chad Portion* (Volume 1, Appendix C) and the *Environmental Management Plan — Cameroon Portion* (Volume 1, Appendix E) contain Management Plans for Cultural Properties, which outline the procedures to be used for the management of cultural properties that might be impacted by activities associated with the Chad Export Project. These documents provide the broad guidelines for the protection of cultural properties in the course of cultural heritage management activities for the Project. The Chadian and Cameroonian Management Plans are structured in the same way. They contain:

(1) a description of the steps to be taken for the identification and management of cultural resources;

(2) a background literature search on cultural properties in the Project area of the country covered in the Management Plan (including previous archaeological research and geological environments in the area);

(3) a summary of the different classes of cultural properties likely to be encountered during Project activities in that country;

(4) a summary of World Bank guidelines and national legislation covering the protection of cultural properties, along with a summary of resources available for the protection in that country;

(5) a summary of procedures to identify cultural resources based on preliminary Project survey work already undertaken;

(6) a discussion of Site Treatment Plans and mitigation monitoring, as well as of techniques to be employed to minimize impacts to cultural properties;

(7) a discussion of data recovery methods (including field data collection methods and laboratory/curation techniques) to be used on cultural properties encountered during Project activities; and

(8) a list of standards for documentation and reporting of cultural properties encountered during Project activities.

Of these different elements, background literature research, discussions of cultural properties likely to be encountered during Project activities, and summaries of relevant national legislation are of course specific to the particular national Management Plan for Cultural Properties. All other elements, and especially the standards and procedures to be used in the mitigation of impacts upon cultural property, are the same in both the Chadian and Cameroonian Master Plans. Two very significant topics covered in the Management Plans were criteria for site prioritization and criteria for mitigation procedures during Project activities. These are further described in *Chapter 5*.

Permit procedures and ownership of cultural resources

Cameroon

The Ministry of Culture of the Republic of Cameroon is responsible for the issuing of permits for non-academic archaeological research (for both survey and excavation) in the country (permits for academic research are issued by the ministry in charge of scientific research). Any artifacts or samples removed from the country for technical analysis (radiocarbon dating, faunal analysis, anthracological analysis, and so on) usually require a temporary loan permit to be obtained from the Ministry of Culture. All cultural materials recovered in the course of the Project in Cameroon are considered to be the property of Cameroon, as part of the cultural patrimony of the country.

Chad

The Ministry of Higher Education, Scientific Research and Professional Development of the Republic of Chad is responsible for the issuing of permits for archaeological research (for both survey and excavation) in the country. Any artifacts or samples removed from the country for technical analysis (radiocarbon dating, faunal analysis, anthracological analysis, and so on) usually requires a temporary loan permit to be obtained from the Ministry of Culture. All cultural materials recovered in the course of the Project in Chad are considered to be the property of Chad, as part of the cultural patrimony of the country.

The articulation of these legislative and regulatory requirements with the structure of the CEP cultural heritage management program will be considered in *Chapter 5*, which describes the different management plans in Cameroon and Chad, site definition and prioritization, and archaeological impact mitigation procedures. The following *Chapters 3* and *4* provide background information on natural and cultural environments and on prehistoric cultural patterning in the study area.

3 – Natural and human environments in the Chad Export Project study area

Physical environments: climate, geomorphology and vegetation

The nature of the Chad Export Project, with development of oilfield facilities in southwestern Chad and construction of an oil transport system to the Atlantic coast of Cameroon, meant that archaeological fieldwork and monitoring activities took place along a transect of Central Africa that was approximately 1070 km long. More extensive fieldwork was done in the Oilfield Development Area (OFDA) in Chad and at sites where support facilities were to be built in both Chad and Cameroon. As would be expected, the spatial extents of the Project meant that archaeological fieldwork and monitoring were undertaken in a variety of different topographies and environments, from the Sudano-Guinean woodlands of the Doba area of Chad through the dissected escarpment north of the Mbéré River valley to the humid tropical forests near Kribi on the Atlantic coast (*Map 5*).

Such environmental variability has a number of implications for the results of a cultural heritage management program focused upon archaeological resources. The visibility of archaeological remains, and the taphonomic processes acting upon such remains, may be quite different in such diverse environments. This is especially the case given that erosional and depositional contexts varied significantly along the pipeline right-of-way, leading to significant differences in the probability of discovery of archaeological sites of different ages and/or characteristics. We would also obviously expect that cultural adaptations through such a range of different physical environments would be equally diverse, in terms of cultural boundaries and human adaptation. While the antiquity of the sites identified depends mostly on the history of the peopling and the geomorphology of a given region, past and present cultures are bound to vary tremendously on such a large geographical scale.

In this section, we briefly discuss the different environments encountered in the course of the Project cultural heritage management program, and especially in the OFDA and along the pipeline right-of-way. For simplicity, we have divided the region into three separate zones. These roughly correspond to geomorphologically and/or environmentally different regions, as will be seen below. The first two zones also reflect the presence of the international boundary between Chad and Cameroon. The distinction between the two regions in Cameroon does not precisely correspond to the two Project construction zones, Spread 1 and Spread 2, the boundary line for which was Kilometer Post (KP) 647 at Ewankang, just east of Nanga Eboko. The Lom River is just over 100 km further to the northeast at KP 539.

Chad: Komé to the Mbéré River

Geomorphology

This zone extends from the OFDA to the border with Cameroon on the Mbéré River. Most of this zone is the southernmost extension of the Lake Chad Basin (Pias 1970b; Kusnir 1995) and comprises a set of flat pediplains mantled with the eroded ferrallitic soils (oxisols) characteristic of much of this area of Central Africa, with some seasonally inundated soils along river valleys and in some other low-lying areas. These seasonal and one permanent (the Lim River) watercourses, which provide a variety of resources to local populations, often have a low relief and only a minor degree of incision into surrounding sediments. Between KP 0 and KP 30, and thus through most of the OFDA, one encounters deep clay soils probably resulting from lacustrine/riverine transgressions during the Holocene, with older sediments only rarely exposed. Granitic and lateritic ridges protrude from these sediments and provide the only exposures where sub-recent and older occupations may be located on the surface. There is no significant rifting, and the exposure of intact pre-Quaternary sediments appears to be minimal.

From KP 30 to KP 80, southwest of Kagopal, soils are characterized by thin duricrusts, as extensive reworking and erosion has exposed underlying laterites. On the edges of ridges in this area, the lateritic crust is often broken, leaving crests covered with fragmented laterite and deeper soils at the bottom of the slopes. Along the southwestern extremity of the pipeline right-of-way in Chad, between Baibokoum and the Mbéré River, the terrain begins to rise toward the eastern edges of the Adamawa Plateau in Cameroon. Small, isolated massifs of crystalline metamorphic rocks (especially gneiss) protrude above the sediments of the surrounding plains. Rivers run significantly more quickly in deeper valleys in this region, resulting in the frequent exposure of bedrock and older sediments.

The Project pipeline right-of-way and the OFDA are generally located in environments of sediment accumulation, with massive and poorly differentiated soils sometimes found to a depth of more than three meters. Under these conditions, we would expect that most archaeological sites discovered will date to relatively recent times, and the vast majority will probably be mid-/late-Holocene in date. Isolated, reworked and redeposited artifacts dating from the Late or Middle Stone Age may be encountered, but intact sites dating from these periods will be extremely rare. It is possible that Neolithic and Iron Age sites will be encountered in any part of the survey area, but their visibility and preservation will critically depend upon local processes of deposition and erosion.

Climate and vegetation

The pipeline right-of-way in Chad and the OFDA are found within Sudano-Guinean environments, with wooded savannas and gallery forests along permanent and seasonal watercourses (PIAS 1970a). According to WWF Terrestrial Ecosystem nomenclature, this zone corresponds to East Sudanian savanna (see ***Map 5***) The average temperature is 28ºC, the average rainfall is between 950 and 1350 mm/year, with a single dry season lasting from November to April. Primary tree species are *Isoberlinia doka*, *Anogeissus leiocarpus*, and *Terminalia* spp., with some occurrences of Sudanic species, including *Khaya senegalensis* and *Acacia* spp., while the seasonal grasses include *Eragrostis* and *Hyparrhenia*. In addition, there is a significant suite of tree species that are either planted or encouraged by local people; these include néré (*Parkia biglobosa*), shea (*Vitellaria paradoxa*), mango (*Mangifera indica*), *Acacia albida* and tamarind (*Tamarindus indica*) (BLENCH 2000). The occurrence of these trees away from present-day settlements is one indication of human occupation in the relatively recent past. Narrow gallery forests exist along the seasonal watercourses running through the area; higher moisture levels in these areas support trees and shrub species with strong Guinean affinities, including *Anthocleista oubangiensis*, *Diospyros* spp. and *Acacia caffra*.

The plant cover changes dramatically through the seasons. During the dry season, progressive desiccation and the burning of grass for field clearance and fertilization eventually lead to a near-total exposure of the ground surface. When the first rains arrive in April or May, the recovery of grasses and tree species is very rapid, with some grasses encountered in extensive, thick stands to a height of 3–4 m. Seasonality of archaeological survey is thus an important element in predicting site visibility. There is less seasonal variability in gallery forests and in marshes. These areas do not dry out as quickly during the dry season, and they are rarely burned. A variety of animal species concentrates in these latter areas during the dry season, and (along with the plants found in those areas) may form an important food source for local communities during that period. The entire area has been heavily impacted by human exploitation especially through various forms of shifting agriculture, with extensive burning, field clearance, fallowing and grazing throughout the Project study zone.

Cameroon North: the Mbéré River to the Lom River

Geomorphology

Much of this area lies along the southern edge of the Adamawa Plateau. This plateau, with an average altitude of 1100 m asl, divides the slightly lower (600–900 m asl) Southern Cameroonian Plateau from the lowlands of northern Cameroon and Chad. As noted above, the Mbéré River, running along the border between Cameroon and Chad and then along the Cameroon–CAR border, actually flows into the Lake Chad Basin to the north. Its valley forms part of the Cretaceous rift complex that dominates the topography of this area of Central Africa (SÉGALEN 1967; COMMISSION DU BASSIN DU LAC TCHAD 1968; FAIRHEAD & GREEN 1989). The Pangar and Lom rivers, further to the southwest, contribute to the Sanaga River basin and thus flow towards the south. The degree of sedimentary accumulation between seasonal watercourses and along these rivers is again quite remarkable, albeit with major areas of ferrallitic soils and lateritic ridges. All these rivers have a significantly faster flow than those in Chad (see above), and their valleys are more deeply incised. They are often bordered by rocky inselbergs and hills, which are subject to high levels of erosion. Consequently, bedrock and more ancient sedimentary layers are often exposed on the surface.

The pipeline right-of-way runs for about 70 km along the northern edge of the Mbéré River Valley, between 1 and 5 km parallel to the north of the escarpment edge. This area of the pipeline right-of-way, between the communities of Dompla and Belel, is highly dissected by erosional channels trending north to south off the edge of the escarpment down to the Mbéré River. These are occupied by seasonal watercourses during the rainy season, with substantial areas of inundation at their bottom that remain swampy through the dry season. Slopes in some of these areas are extremely abrupt and unstable. This yields a topography dominated by erosional exposures along the sides of these channels and zones of substantial though periodic sediment accumulation along their bottoms, with isolated and limited areas of internal plateau between them. The nature of this terrain had a significant effect both upon the conduct of the right-of-way survey in 2001 and upon the nature of the cultural material recovered (see *Chapter 8*).

Between Meiganga and the Lom River, the topography grades fairly gradually into the Southern Cameroonian Plateau, with a landscape of rolling uplands interspersed with permanent and seasonal watercourses. Relief is, in general, quite gradual; there are very few of the abrupt hills and inselbergs encountered to the northeast near the border with Chad. Again, this area is characterized by deeply weathered, ferrallitic soils with frequent laterite crusts on top of granitic bedrock. Under these circumstances, the exposure of archaeological materials depends very much upon the particular balance of sediment deposition and erosion in any one location. In general, though, this area resembles the pipeline right-of-way in Chad more than along the Mbéré River escarpment, and in most cases we may expect that only quite recent sites will not be deeply buried in sediments.

Climate and vegetation

As with the Project area in Chad, the region between the Mbéré and the Lom rivers is part of the Sudano-Guinean environmental zone (WWF Terrestrial Ecosystem zone is Northern Congolian forest-savanna mosaic, see *Map 5*) The average annual precipitation is approximately 1400–1600 mm/year, increasing from northeast to southwest. A single rainy season may extend from March to November, but the rains are usually concentrated between May and October. Most of this area is characterized by wooded savanna, dominated by *Daniella oliveri* (especially north of the Mbéré River Valley, along the southern edge of the Adamawa Plateau), *Terminalia* spp., *Lophira lanceolata*, and *Burkea africana* (LETOUZEY & FOTIUS 1985). Seasonal grasses again include *Eragrostis* and *Hyparrhenia* spp. As in Chad, watercourses are bordered by more closed gallery forests and plant species with Guinean affinities, including *Aubrevillea kerstingii* and *Khaya grandifoliola*. In the northern part of this region, the seasonal cycle and deliberate burning lead to drastic differences in plant cover and in the degree of soil surface visibility through the year, as it does in Chad. Further to the south, these influences are not as noticeable.

From the Lom River to approximately 50 km east, local environments are characterized by a deciduous-forest/savanna mosaic, dominated by *Terminalia glaucescens* and with tree cover increasing toward the Lom. This is a transitional zone between the Sudano-Guinean wooded savannas to the north and east and the Guinean forest zones found further to the southwest along the pipeline right-of-way, between the Lom and the Atlantic coast of Cameroon. In general, the northern part of this area is more heavily impacted by human activity than is the region closer to the Lom River, areas of which are protected environmental reserves. Logging, both legal and illegal, is becoming increasingly important east of the Lom, however, and is a dominant economic activity west of the river.

Cameroon South: from the Lom River to Ebomé

Geomorphology

The zone between the Lom River and Ebomé includes two primary geological ensembles: the Southern Cameroonian Plateau and the Coastal Plain. The Southern Cameroonian Plateau, from the Lom River (KP 539) to Lolodorf (KP 965), is about 600 m asl in average altitude, descending from its contact with the Adamawa Plateau (at 900 m asl) to the east and to the south (500 m asl) to its contact with the Coastal Plain (SÉGALEN 1967). Although the area is a plateau complex in overall extent, on a more detailed scale it is made up of a very large number of hills, some of substantial size (in the region of Yaoundé, for example), and intervening valley drainages, the latter often associated with hydromorphic soils. Archaeological survey work was in some cases quite complicated in these regions, given the difficult nature of the terrain and the substantial ground cover (see *Chapter 8*).

The Coastal Plain in the area of Kribi is actually another low plateau (falling gradually in altitude from approximately 400 m asl east of Lolodorf to sea level at Kribi) with a rocky coastline. This region is part of the broader Atlantic Basin, which includes the Sanaga River Basin (with tributaries such as the Lom and Pangar rivers) that originates from the Adamawa Plateau and reaches the Atlantic coast west of Edéa, as well as smaller river basins like those of the Nyong (crossing the pipeline right-of-way at KP 907), the Lokoundjé (crossings at KP 946 and 1006) and the Kienké (crossing at KP 1062).

The bedrock substrata through this region are composed of metamorphic rocks, such as gneiss, schists and micaschists, and soils that derive from the erosion of the bedrock are most widespread. Red ferrallitic clay soils are most frequent on the Southern Cameroonian Plateau, while yellow clays are commonest in the Coastal Plain. Despite the relatively dense plant cover on these soils, their proportions of organic material are usually quite low. These soils cover deep lateritic crusts, sometimes found just below surface and usually with an interface that includes red-yellow clays, fragments of quartz and laterite rubble. Mechanical erosion is not as dominant as it is in some areas further to the northeast along the pipeline right-of-way (as north of the Mbéré River), because of the substantial plant cover, but these soils have been subjected to a very large degree of chemical weathering. When trees are felled, through logging or for agricultural needs, for example, the thin clay soils are washed away and the iron crusts are exposed. In that case, erosion proceeds far more quickly.

Climate and vegetation

The region between the Lom River and Yaoundé has two rainy (March–June and September–November) and two dry seasons (December–February and July–August). The average annual rainfall varies from 1500 mm/year to 2000 mm/year from north to south, and the average yearly temperature is about 23.5°C. Between Yaoundé and the coastal region of Kribi, the average temperature increases (to 27°C at Kribi) and the area is very wet. The annual rainfall climbs to approximately 2900 mm/year at Kribi, and the rains are distributed throughout the year (Amou'ou Jam *et al.* 1985).

The vegetational regime through this region is similarly complex. The area between the Lom River (KP 539) and Batchenga (KP 795) is broadly described as semi-deciduous forest, but in fact it is characterized by a mosaic of forest patches (dominated by *Sterculiaeceae* and *Ulmaceae*), wooded savanna (with *Terminalia glaucescens*, *Anona sengalensis* and *Bridelia ferruginia* as the important tree species) and areas of cleared and fallow land with isolated, relict stands of forest (Letouzey & Fotius 1985). The area around Yaoundé, from Batchenga (KP 795) to Ngoumou (KP 875), is by far the most populated zone of the right-of-way and correspondingly shows the greatest evidence of human impact on the environment, especially through erosion and clearance activities. This stretch of the pipeline easement is characterized by a mixed forest environment (WWF Terrestrial Ecosystem zone is Northwestern Congolian lowland forest, see *Map 5*), a mosaic of isolated patches of semi-deciduous forest, along with cultivated fields and fallows.

The wettest stretch of the pipeline easement, through the Coastal Plain, is covered by Guinean-Congolese rainforest and specifically by Atlantic littoral forest (WWF Terrestrial Ecosystem zone is Atlantic Equatorial coastal forest, see *Map 5*), which extends 194 kilometers from north of the town of Ngoumou (KP 875) to the coast at Ebomé (KP 1069). This zone is characterized by moist tropical evergreen forest vegetation, dominated by Caesalpiniaceae and especially *Dialium pachyphyllum* and *Anthonotha fragrans*. Since the pipeline for the most part follows the old Kribi – Lolodorf road, which has created a corridor of penetration into the forest, vegetation is often more or less disturbed by the farming and logging activities of local farming communities. Primary forest is then replaced by secondary forest, characterized by very thick underbrush. In general, surface visibility is low throughout this zone, except in areas cleared by human activity, either through farming or because of the clearance and construction activities associated with the Project.

The physical environment of the pipeline easement is extremely varied and, as such, presents very different conditions for CHM work and especially archaeological survey and site discovery. In terms of proportions of the area under study, wooded savanna is the most frequent environment along the right-of-way, with approximately 46 % of the area falling within this vegetation type. Semi-deciduous forest is also important (28 %) as is Atlantic littoral forest (18 %), while mixed forest (7 %) is restricted to the Yaoundé area. Whereas the flat plains of the southernmost Lake Chad Basin in southwestern Chad with their sparsely wooded savanna vegetation could not be expected to yield sites older than the mid-/late-Holocene, the dissected escarpments and hills at the edge of the Adamawa Plateau in southern Chad and northern Cameroon are ideal for the discovery of Stone Age occurrences, especially during the dry season. However, the thinness and fragility of soils in these areas will frequently have negative consequences on the integrity of sites, since such soils are very vulnerable to erosion. The more humid forested zones of southern Cameroon present another problem, as the heavy vegetation cover made archaeological survey very difficult before the start of the Project construction activities.

Cultural diversity in the study area

From a culture-historical point of view, one of the most interesting aspects of the Project activities is that those activities provide a continuous transect across Central Africa, a transect almost 1100 km long and in large part running through areas previously almost unknown archaeologically. As noted at the beginning of the chapter, we would expect this geographical extent of Project activities and its attendant environmental variability to be accompanied by a corresponding diversity in the ancient human adaptations and cultural systems that would form the primary subject matter of the cultural heritage management program. We also expect such ancient cultural diversity in part because the modern cultural diversity throughout this area is quite significant. Economic activities and material culture toolkits, the bases of archaeological research, were similarly variable, with foragers, pastoralists, Sudanic and tropical forest farmers and urbanites all living in close proximity to the areas in which research took place. Along the pipeline transect, researchers encountered communities where people identified themselves ethnically in dozens of different ways, and Project activities took place through territories occupied by speakers of at least fifteen different languages (DIEU & RENAUD 1983; SUMMER INSTITUTE OF LINGUISTICS 2006).

The cultural diversity of modern communities in the research area also has significant implications for our interpretations of regional history. We cannot assume cultural continuity between past and present societies in the research area, and must take account of the historical ruptures and hiatuses of both the prehistoric and historic periods (DOZON 1985; JEWSIE-WICKI 1989; VANSINA 1990; STAHL 1993, 1999). Indeed, archaeological data (see *Chapter 4*) indicate that the prehistory of the Project area exhibited as much dynamism and cultural change as can be seen in more recent times. At the same time, the characteristics of modern societies in a region may still provide a source for analogies useful in interpreting the traces of ancient occupations discovered in the course of CHM work (DAVID & KRAMER 2001; MACEACHERN 2004). This will especially be helpful when regional histories are otherwise little known, and thus where researchers have relatively few data to work with, and also when the majority of sites located date from the last few centuries — as is the case for sites discovered in the course of Project work.

There is a variety of different ways in which cultural variability throughout this area could be analyzed: through examination of economies and/or material culture, of ethnic identities or of linguistic affiliations, for example (DE VOS & ROMANUCCI-ROSS 1975; FISHMAN 1989). The archaeological implications of these different kinds of human identities are quite variable (HODDER 1982; STAHL 1991; ADELBERGER 1995; GOSSELAIN 1999; MACEACHERN 2001c; BROOKS 2002). For archaeological purposes, one might argue that the consideration of regional distributions in material culture (especially ceramics) would be most useful, but unfortunately only rather limited data on those distributions exist in this part of Central Africa. We will thus consider cultural variability in the Project area primarily as an expression of linguistic and ethnic identities. In these terms, the area as a whole can be divided into two subregions: a northern region, where Central Sudanic and Adamawa-Ubangian languages are predominantly spoken, and a southern area, where Bantu-speaking populations are found.

The 'Bantu Expansion'

Consideration of linguistic affiliations also reminds us of the fundamental importance of this region in the patterning of modern African languages across most of Africa south of the Equator. The most striking historical phenomenon associated with the Project area is usually known as the 'Bantu Expansion', the process(es) through which Niger-Congo languages of the Bantu group came to be spoken across most of Central, eastern and southern Africa. The term is somewhat unfortunate, as it is highly unlikely that this language spread occurred as a single process spanning half a continent and many millennia. There is a great deal of debate about the broad mechanisms of this phenomenon, about whether it involved a spread of human populations speaking early Bantu languages or the progressive adoption of those languages by pre-existing African communities (or both), whether other cultural systems (iron technologies or agriculture, for example) spread along with Bantu languages, about the exact routes and sequences of the expansion, and so on (see for example BOUQUIAUX *et al.* 1980; VANSINA 1990, 1995; HOMBERT & HYMAN 1999; EHRET 2001).

There is in particular a debate about the possible archaeological signals of the 'Bantu Expansion', and whether archaeologists should expect to see traces of this expansion process in the archaeological record (EGGERT 1992; BLENCH 1993b; LAVACHERY 1998; EHRET 2001; see also BELEZA *et al.* 2005; EGGERT 2005; BLENCH 2006). There is, however, virtual unanimity that the geographical origins of this phenomenon lay in the Grassfields region of northwestern Cameroon and adjacent areas of Nigeria, and that from this area, early precursors of modern Bantu languages expanded towards the south and southeast, toward the edges and eventually into the tropical forests of Central Africa. Linguistic estimates for the timing of that initial expansion are imprecise, but it is likely that it dated to the mid-Holocene, probably to about 5000 years ago (BOUQUIAUX *et al.* 1980; BASTIN *et al.* 1983; HOMBERT & HYMAN 1999).

The transect of the Project pipeline right-of-way, running from southwestern Chad to the Atlantic, crosses the area of the initial phases of the 'Bantu Expansion', at a distance of roughly 200 kilometers from the Grassfields region around Bamenda (*Maps 2* and *3*). As noted above, there is a good deal of debate on the nature of the expansion as a whole, and it is extremely likely that this term encompasses a whole series of different linguistic and demographic processes that have taken place over approximately 4000 years. We should thus not necessarily expect to find straightforward, unequivocal archaeological evidence of the early stages of this process in the course of Project CHM fieldwork. At the same time, the existence of a continuous program of archaeological survey and excavation across the region where the early phases of the 'Bantu Expansion' took place offers an unparalleled opportunity to examine cultural and technological systems in place in this part of Central Africa during the mid-/late-Holocene, systems which may well have played a role in stimulating a spread of language and culture that changed the face of Africa as we know it today.

The northern zone: Komé to Belabo

The northern zone is roughly equivalent to the Chadian and northern Cameroonian environmental zones described above, and to the comparable areas of Project research detailed in *Chapters 7* and *8*. The vast majority of people in these zones are subsistence farmers in Sudano-Guinean wooded savanna and woodland environments, with sorghum and millet as the traditional staple crops. These populations (as almost all of the peoples living along the pipeline right-of-way) lived in pre-colonial times in societies where political authority was quite decentralized, with villages and village clusters being the most common focus of ethnic and social identities. The Fulfulde and Arabic spoken by transhumant and resident pastoralists are languages intrusive from further north and attest to the recent movement of those peoples into the area.

Central Sudanic-speaking populations
Central Sudanic-speaking populations belong to the Nilo-Saharan language family, of which they represent the southwestern branch and one of its latest offshoots (BLENCH 1993b; BENDER 2000; MALHERBE 2000). Nilo-Saharan is the second largest language phylum of Africa (after Niger-Congo) and is also the most differentiated internally, indicating a very ancient history on the continent (EHRET 1993). Central Sudanic groups live in Chad, Congo, Central African Republic, Uganda and Sudan. Most of the indigenous populations living along the pipeline right-of-way between the OFDA and the southeastern edge of the Adamawa Plateau speak dialects (Mbay Doba, Ngambay and Kaba) of the same language, Sara (CABOT 1965; SUMMER INSTITUTE OF LINGUISTICS 2006). The others speak Adamawa-Ubangian languages (see below). These communities have a strong sense of belonging to the Sara culture as a whole.

As is implied above, social and political identities among Sara populations have frequently been strongly localized, at the community level and at the level of lineage groups within different communities (BROWN 1983; MAGNANT 1986). At the same time, important degrees of political centralization existed among Sara populations in the pre-colonial period, under the political and ritual leaders designated as *mbang* (AZEVEDO 1982). This process of centralization was probably greatest among the Sara populations of Bédaya, where the *mbang* exercised a considerable amount of power over multiple communities in the region and was advised and supported by a complex administrative apparatus. Sara oral traditions identify more than 20 *mbangs* of Bédaya who ruled in succession. Within Sara communities, ritual experts play a significant role in regulating relations between the natural and supernatural worlds and in adjudicating community disputes. In some cases, this latter role can extend to relations between communities as well.

Much of the area of the Sara territory within which Project archaeological activities took place is subject to seasonal flooding, and the percentage of cultivable land is thus relatively low. Sara populations in the area seem to have adapted to these local environmental conditions through tactics of settlement dispersal and mobility during the late pre-colonial and early colonial period (Djarangar, *pers. comm.* 2007). These settlement patterns may well explain aspects of the recent archaeological assemblages found in this zone (see *Chapter 7*). A contributing element to this settlement patterning may have been the slave raiding by the Fulbe from Adamawa region attested to in Sara oral histories through the 19th century at least (BROWN 1983, 1996: 26–27; BURNHAM 1996: 9–23). We do not, however, know whether that settlement mobility (and the violence that may have gone along with it) was characteristic of earlier periods as well; the concentrations and characteristics of iron-working and other sites dated to approximately a millennium ago indicate that it may be a more recent feature of regional culture history.

Adamawa-Ubangian-speaking populations
Adamawa-Ubangian languages constitute an ancient branch of the Niger-Congo language family, which is the largest language grouping found in Africa today and indeed the largest language phylum in the world (WILLIAMSON & BLENCH 2000). Niger-Congo languages make up three-quarters of all languages in Africa, dominating the continent over the area between Senegal, Kenya and South Africa. Of all the Niger-Congo sub-groups, the Adamawa-Ubangian languages are perhaps the least well known. The populations speaking these languages live in eastern Nigeria, Cameroon, and Chad, at the latitude of the Adamawa Plateau and the Ubangi River Basin, as well as in the Central African Republic, northern Democratic Republic of Congo and southwestern Sudan, with isolated communities also found in Congo.

Available historical linguistic data (DAVID 1982a; SAXON 1982) indicate that the survey area in eastern Cameroon and Chad also lies close to the area of differentiation and subsequent expansion of the Adamawa-Ubangian language family, probably after the third millennium BC. The eastward spread of Ubangian-speaking communities through the northern Central African Republic and into the Democratic Republic of Congo and Sudan was a regionally important element in the establishment of present cultural configurations in this part of Central Africa, comparable on a smaller scale to the expansion of Bantu languages further to the south. But we do not know the extent to which the survey area was directly involved in that expansion. The vast majority of Adamawa-Ubangian peoples are subsistence farmers, utilizing a system of shifting agriculture extensively supplemented by hunting, fishing and gathering. Dominant crops are sorghum, millet and maize, with a wide variety of smaller-scale crops also grown in different areas. The shifting agricultural system led to relatively high settlement mobility in the historical period, with the prevalence of slave raiding by Fulbe from Adamawa also contributing to that mobility, as well as in some cases to the concentration of political and military power in the hands of certain individuals — an extremely important change in communities that had up to that point been broadly egalitarian (COPET-ROUGIER 1987). In this, their history resembles that of many of their Central Sudanic-speaking Sara neighbours.

Adamawa-Ubangian populations in the Project area belong to a number of ethnic/linguistic groups, and there is sometimes significant academic disagreement about the detailed linguistic affiliations of these groups. Along the southern Adamawa Plateau, one encounters communities where Karang Laka and related languages (including Pana, Nzakambay, and Kuo) are spoken (CABOT 1965; BOYD 1989; MALHERBE 2000; SUMMER INSTITUTE OF LINGUISTICS 2006) that are classified in the Adamawa branch of the Adamawa-Ubangian family. These populations were often politically associated with neighbouring Sara groups, but their languages are actually most closely related to Mbum. They are to be found in the Project area in the Logone Oriental Province in Chad, in the northern provinces of Cameroon and also in the northern part of the Central African Republic. Other communities in Cameroon along the pipeline speak closely related Adamawa languages, known as Eastern Mbum, Karé/Kali and Gbete. By far the most numerous among these groups (approximately 50,000), the Mbum populations are most frequently found in the area around Touboro and close to the Mbéré River frontier in Chad, while Karé/Kali-speaking populations inhabit the Belel area and the Gbete are settled in the northern part of the Belabo Sub-Division. According

to their oral traditions, Mbum populations have inhabited parts of the Adamawa Plateau for many centuries, and consider themselves the first settlers of this region (FARAUT 1981; MOHAMMADOU 1990).

The Gbaya language is, on the other hand, part of the Ubangian branch of the Adamawa-Ubangian family. Gbaya-speaking populations are settled over a vast region in the Central African Republic and Cameroon, with the pipeline right-of-way in the extreme northwest of this distribution. Gbaya communities occupy large parts of the southeastern Adamawa Province, reaching as far north as southern Touboro district but concentrated around the town of Meiganga (BURNHAM 1980). Gbaya populations are agriculturalists, cultivating primarily manioc and maize, as well as some sorghum and millet. Hunting and gathering are also significant traditional activities, with the balance between agriculture and foraging changing according to specific economic circumstances. In pre-colonial times, settlement mobility was quite high among Gbaya populations. Like many of their neighbours in this area, the Gbaya have a highly decentralized sociopolitical system, although centralization of power in the hands of charismatic leaders could and did take place in the dangerous circumstances of the 19th century, when Fulbe leaders from Adamawa extended their hegemony away from the boundaries of the plateau to the south and east (COPET-ROUGIER 1987; MOUKTAR BAH 1993). Gbaya historical tradition says that the first Gbaya settlers in Cameroon came from the Ubangi River basin in what is now the Central African Republic, from the early 19th century onwards (BURNHAM *et al.* 1986).

The southern zone: Belabo to the Atlantic

The southern zone is roughly equivalent to the southern Cameroonian environmental zone described earlier. The great majority of people living in this area are again subsistence farmers, but in this case in semi-deciduous tropical forest and moist evergreen tropical forest environments, with manioc, yams and other tubers, along with various tree species, as important crops. The main exception to this economic focus (besides, of course, the inhabitants of the towns and cities along the pipeline right-of-way) are the Bakola-Bagyeli/Pygmy hunter-gatherers found in small numbers between Yaoundé and the Atlantic coast. The southern area of the pipeline right-of-way, from Belabo to the Atlantic coast at Kribi, is inhabited almost entirely by Bantu-speaking populations. Only the Vute groups, of which the southernmost villages intermingle with settlements of Bantu-speaking peoples in the Nanga Eboko-Mbandjock stretch of the pipeline right-of-way, speak non-Bantu languages. But even Vute is classified as a Bantoid language (Dieu & Renaud 1983; Summer Institute of Linguistics 2006) and closely related to the more specific Bantu grouping within the Niger-Congo phylum.

Bantu-speaking farming and fishing populations
The Bantu languages are spoken by more than 200 million people in Africa today, between Nigeria, Somalia and South Africa and across over nine million square kilometers of savannas and forests. They constitute by far the largest branch of the Benue-Congo language family, a branch of the Niger-Congo phylum. The Beti-Fang (also known as Yaoundé-Fang) group is a large ensemble of languages, corresponding to Guthrie's A70 language group, spoken over the greater part of southern Cameroon and northern Gabon (Guthrie 1971; Dieu & Renaud 1983; Williamson & Blench 2000; Summer Institute of Linguistics 2006). All these languages can be divided into three ensembles: Beti, Bulu and Fang. In Cameroon, these language groupings have been standardized to some degree by evangelization: Beti by the Catholic Church and Bulu by a variety of different Protestant Churches.

These languages are partially mutually intelligible (and so their status as languages vis-à-vis dialects is sometimes rather unclear), although ethnic distinctions between their speakers are significant. Thus, from east to west along the pipeline right-of-way, nine Beti-Fang languages are spoken. There is no actual frontier between these modes of speech: differences accumulate from village to village without intercomprehension being broken (Laburthe-Tolra 1977; Dieu & Renaud 1983; Summer Institute of Linguistics 2006). In the Lom-et-Djérem Division, Bobili/Bebele groups gather around Belabo while Eki-speaking populations inhabit the district of Diang, just west of Belabo. Mvele speakers (Bamvele) can be found in the east of the Méfou Divison (Nanga Eboko) and Ewondo populations are settled in the rest of the Méfou and in the Mfoundi Division (in the region of Yaoundé). Eton groups inhabit the Lékié Division, with the Manguissa sub-group centered in the Saa Sub-Division, east of the capital. Isolated villages of Fang-speaking groups can be found in the Océan Division, between Lolodorf and Kribi, along the Yaoundé–Kribi road. Bulu populations are settled close to the south of the pipeline right-of-way; the northernmost Bulu villages are to be found in the north of the Nyong-et-Mfoumou Division and the south of the Upper-Sanaga Division.

Traditional slash-and-burn agriculture is still the main economic activity among Beti-Fang populations (Bahuchet 1996). The abundance of precipitation allows a year-long farming system with several harvests and varied crops (tubers, vegetables and fruit trees), an agro-ecological situation that has probably changed very little in its general characteristics through the last three millennia. The introduction of New World crops like maize and manioc and the effects of market systems upon gendered agricultural production (Guyer 1984) have probably changed the system in detail, however. Recently, the area between Nkoteng and Mbandjock has witnessed a significant transformation of agricultural practices, as industrial plantations of sugar canes appeared. Fishing and hunting continue to be carried out on a limited scale, although large game has become rare in heavily populated areas such as the Nanga Eboko-Yaoundé section of the pipeline right-of-way.

Populations speaking Basaa languages inhabit the Nyong-et-Kelle and Sanaga Maritime Divisions, as well as a sizeable part of the Nkam and Wouri (Douala) Divisions. Again, these languages are very closely related, with substantial intercomprehension, and correspond to Guthrie's A40 group (Guthrie 1971; Dieu & Renaud 1983; Summer Institute of Linguistics 2006). Communities speaking the Mvumbo and Mabi dialects of Ngumba, in Guthrie's A80 group, but identifying themselves as Kwasio ethnically, inhabit the western part of the Océan Division. Mvumbo villages are scattered along the Kribi–Lolodorf road, where they are mixed with Fang settlements, while Mabea groups speak Mabi in Kribi (Ardener 1956; ORSTOM/IRCAM 1966; Dieu & Renaud 1983; Summer Institute of Linguistics 2006).

While Basaa-speaking and Mvumbo populations pursue socioeconomic adaptations almost identical to those of Beti-Fang groups living in similar forested environments, Mabea populations are coastal, with economic activities focused primarily on sea and river fishing (Bahuchet 1996). In this, they resemble neighbouring Batanga groups. Batanga populations inhabit the coastal regions of the Océan Division, north and south of the town of Kribi. The languages spoken by these Batanga groups correspond to the A32 ensemble in Guthrie's classification (Guthrie 1971). In Batanga communities, sea fishing is usually the province of men, while both men and women engage in river fishing. Fishing is carried out all year long, but the most favorable season is November–December.

Bantoid-speaking populations
As noted above, the only non-Bantu Niger-Congo language encountered on the pipeline right-of-way southwest of Belabo is Vute spoken by Babute populations. Babute communities inhabit the southern part of the Haute-Sanaga Division, between Nanga Eboko

and Mbandjock (Siran 1980, 1981). Economically, these communities resemble neighboring populations found along the Project right-of-way in this area, but they are strongly matrilineal, in contrast to most other groups of the region. The history of Babute relations with regional Fulbe states through the 19th century is an extremely complicated one, as is the case for many of the communities in this region usually described as 'acephalous' or without concentrated sociopolitical power, and the Babute appear to have participated in the expansion of the *lamidat* of Banyo in a variety of different ways (Gausset 1998).

Bantu-speaking foragers:
Bagyeli/Bakola/Pygmy populations

Pygmies live in small villages in the forest near the pipeline right-of-way, between Kribi and Lolodorf. This settlement pattern is somewhat different from the system of mobile camps used by Baka Pygmies in southeastern Cameroon, and by Efe and related Pygmy populations in eastern Central Africa. These villages are found in forest areas between the axes of settlement of other populations, such as Kwasio- and Fang-speaking agricultural communities (Joiris 1994; Ngima Mawoung 2001). Their language, Gyele, is closely related to the Ngumba language spoken by their Kwasio neighbors, but very different from the Ngabaka languages of the Ubangian group spoken by the Baka Pygmy populations to the east (Malherbe 2000; Summer Institute of Linguistics 2006). As in the rest of Central Africa, Pygmy groups speak languages closely related to those of their agricultural neighbors. However, it has been shown that all the Pygmy populations of Central Africa share common words related to hunting, gathering and honey collection in the forest, words that are not found in Niger-Congo or Nilo-Saharan languages (Bahuchet 1993a). These words may be the remnants of a language or group of languages that these populations shared before they encountered farmers speaking Bantu or other languages, from whom they adopted the languages that they use today.

Bagyeli/Bakola Pygmy populations are tropical foragers, who traditionally got most of their resources from the rainforest (Ngima Mawoung 2001). They also obtained cultivated food, iron tools, pottery and other artifacts from Kwasio farmers, in exchange for products of their hunting and gathering expertise. In addition to these economic exchanges, very close social relations existed between these forager communities and neighboring Kwasio groups. In a general sense, this involves the asymmetric relations between Pygmies and farmers that have sometimes been described as 'client-patron' relations in other parts of Central Africa, and which have proven ethnographically controversial. Bagyeli/Bakola individuals provide labor for Kwasio individuals in a relationship that has persisted for generations. Kwasio men marry Bagyeli/Bakola women (but not the reverse) and they share a common clan structure (Ngima Mawoung 2001, but note that this source is oriented toward Kwasio views of the relationship). Rights to forest resources in this area are patterned by a complex system of kinship and residential criteria involving multiple Bagyeli/Bakola and Kwasio communities (Biesbrouck 1999), although this system — along with the traditional social relations with Kwasio farmers — has to some extent broken down with the advent of commercial logging, cash cropping and other forms of commercial forest exploitation from the 1950s onwards.

There is a long and complex history of interaction between foraging and agricultural populations in this part of Central Africa, and it is likely that the characteristics of relationships between those different groups have changed considerably through time (Vansina 1990; Bahuchet 1993b; Blench 1999; Klieman 2003a). Significant geographical variability in these relations also exists. We thus cannot simply extend modern ethnographic sources backward in time for more than a few centuries in order to interpret archaeological traces of foraging or farming activities in this region. It is likely that subsistence strategies associated with both economic systems were rather different in earlier times than are such systems today.

4 – Background to prehistoric cultural patterning in the Chad Export Project study area

Introduction

Before the initiation of the CHM program detailed in this book, little was known about prehistoric cultural processes in many of the areas where construction related to the Chad Export Project took place. The available data were concentrated in particular parts of the Project area, especially the area around Yaoundé, while the prehistory of most of the rest of the pipeline right-of-way was much less known. Moreover, for reasons of taphonomy and because of the organization of previous archaeological research, only certain site types and periods were represented in the available archaeological data. Thus, for example, the 'pit sites' (see below) associated with prehistoric sedentary communities in the region around Yaoundé are certainly well known, though perhaps not well understood, but little was known about other site types in the same area at the same time, or about any site types in the same area from other periods. This project has certainly not solved this problem, although it demonstrates some advantages in consistent methodologies employed over a survey transect of more than a thousand kilometers.

The interpretation of archaeological occurrences is obviously in part conditioned by researchers' previous understanding of past cultural processes in the study area, and thus by the available data on those processes. This chapter thus examines two different topics. In the first place, it provides a survey of previous research in areas close to the Project area of interest. This focuses upon archaeological data, although historical and linguistic data, where available, are briefly examined. For convenience, this survey is divided into the same three zones used to partition the discussion of environmental diversity in *Chapter 3*. In the second place, it provides an overview of archaeological understanding of culture history in this region prior to Project research, as an orientation to the following descriptive and interpretative chapters.

Previous archaeological research in southwestern Chad

The prehistory of Chad is not well known in general, and most of the archaeological research that has been done in that country has taken place either in the Lake Chad Basin or especially in the Borkou-Ennedi-Tibesti (BET) region in northern Chad (Treinen-Claustre 1982; Tillet 1983). There has been almost no research undertaken in the Province of Logone Oriental, within which the OFDA, the Chadian section of the Project pipeline and the present CHM project took place. Three sources of information are potentially relevant to a consideration of pre-colonial cultural processes in this area: archaeology, historical linguistics and historical sources both oral and written. Available historical linguistic data, especially on the differentiation and subsequent expansion of the Adamawa-Ubangian language, were described in the last chapter. There has been rather little study of the details of that expansion, especially in comparison with the far better known expansion of Bantu languages to the south and southwest.

The only archaeological work within the study area undertaken before the present CHM work was a very preliminary survey undertaken by French researchers (Courtin 1962, 1963) in the early 1960s. For the most part, that survey was concentrated between Doba and Sarh, but material tentatively associated with pre-Iron Age communities was located at Goré, north of Doba, and near Mbaibokoum. At Goré, prehistoric polished stone axes were being used in Sara rainmaking rituals (a common practice in West and Central Africa), while caves with some cultural materials tentatively assigned to the Neolithic (see below for a discussion on this terminology) were found along the slopes of Mount Zlia, just west of Mbaibokoum. This material is interesting, but either lacks provenance or is found in geomorphological contexts (inselberg caves) not encountered along the pipeline right-of-way or in the OFDA around Komé. Elsewhere in southern Chad, Tillet (1978) undertook a preliminary survey in the Mayo Kebbi Province, as a follow-up to the work of Courtin, during the mid-1970s. This research established the probability of occupations in that area through the late Pleistocene and early Holocene, but most of the lithic materials located were not in cultural context. The most important site located, Mont Werdjé, is near Fianga and probably Neolithic in cultural affiliation. In addition, other sites dating to the Palaeolithic and Neolithic were discovered at Gamba-Toubouri, in the Fianga area, and at Mombaroua, between Binder and Léré.

There are some data available on contiguous cultural areas to the north and east in Chad, and on regions now incorporated within Cameroon and the Central African Republic. We can thus to some degree base our expectations of archaeological occurrences within this area on finds in neighbouring regions. Ethnohistorical and archaeological investigations of the Iron Age in southern Chad were undertaken by one of the authors of this volume in the late 1980s and early 1990s (Tchago 1994). This research did not extend into the Logone Oriental Province, but was done throughout Logone

Occidental, Mayo-Kebbi, Tandjile and Moyen-Chari, among various Sara populations, and thus provides a guide to the material one might expect to find in research in the study area. It should be noted (TCHAGO 1994: 90) that no lithic materials (or more generally no materials dating to before the Iron Age as identified by the author) were located in the course of this survey — although the survey was not designed to locate such sites. This, combined with the results of Tillet's research mentioned above, may imply that some of the scattered stone tools located by Courtin were primarily in secondary contexts, perhaps displaced by fluvial activity. Abundant evidence of Iron Age habitation and iron-processing sites was, on the other hand, located throughout the area under study. Habitation sites were in many cases quite large and involved significant accumulation of anthropic sediments. TCHAGO (1994: 81–183) located both pit and gallery mines, where iron ore was extracted from lateritic sediments, and smelting sites with furnaces, slag heaps and forges, where the ore was processed into iron tools. In many cases, these processing sites were adjacent to habitation areas. Given ethnohistorical data (TCHAGO 1994: 250–255) indicating that Logone Oriental was a center of iron production as well, such sites might be expected within the study area.

A number of archaeological projects close to the survey area in both Cameroon and the Central African Republic have also provided data on cultural remains that might be encountered in the OFDA and along the pipeline right-of-way. In the Central African Republic, work in the area around Bouar, between 70 km and 200 km southwest of the survey area, has uncovered a set of megalithic sites, clusters of standing and horizontal stones arranged on low earthen mounds and called *tazunu* in local languages. They are associated with areas now occupied by Mbum, Kara and Gbaya populations (DAVID 1982b; VIDAL 1992; ZANGATO 1999). Several hundreds of these *tazunu* are now known, and they appear to be funerary monuments, although not all of the excavated examples contain burials. They date to between *ca* 1000 BC and approximately the middle of the second millennium AD. The existence of these monuments, and their association with single burials when any such burials are found, may imply some degree of social stratification in this part of Central Africa during this period.

It is possible that the distribution of *tazunu* extends into Cameroon as well, since MARLIAC (1973) located two standing stones, identified as a *tazunu*, at Djohong, near the town of Meiganga in the Mbéré River valley, about 15 kilometers east of the pipeline right-of-way. The granite outcrops from which the standing stones in this *tazunu* are formed exist along the southwestern

section of the oil pipeline right-of-way in Chad and in adjacent areas in Cameroon. ASOMBANG (2004: 295) does not consider the presence of standing stones itself necessarily implying the presence of the particular site type known as *tazunu*. He notes the presence of standing stones in various cultural contexts in a number of different areas of Cameroon.

A number of village sites associated with these megalithic burial sites are now known as well. The ceramics discovered in association with the *tazunu* do not resemble modern ceramics from the area; however, in the course of surveying for *tazunu* sites, DAVID & VIDAL (1977) located and excavated sections of an Iron Age village site, Nana-Modé (about 100 km south of the point where the pipeline right-of-way crosses the Chad – Cameroon frontier), which yielded dates of *ca* AD cal 700 and ceramics very similar to that used by modern Gbaya communities. It is possible that these *tazunu* sites are associated with the early differentiation of Adamawa-Ubangian-speaking populations noted above.

Beyond the *tazunu* sites (which have attracted a good deal of attention, given their striking appearance and implications for social patterning), other archaeological surveys in adjacent areas of Cameroon and the Central African Republic have yielded limited data on prehistoric occupations in these regions. Survey work in the Ouham Préfecture in northwestern Central African Republic (GOTILOGUE & LANFRANCHI 1997) has led to the discovery of a large number of iron-working sites, relevant to the interpretation of similar sites in southwestern Chad (see *Chapters 7* and *9*). The area around Bocaranga, in the extreme northwest of CAR, has yielded surface finds of a polished stone axe, similar to those located by Courtin in Chad, and some perforated granitic disks known as *kwés* of unknown function and age (DE BAYLE DES HERMENS 1975: 196, 243). South of Bocaranga, the site of Gbi Gboyo, unfortunately undated, contained a level with quartz flakes (VIDAL 1987), which the excavator believes to be more than two millennia old. Research along the eastern edge of the Adamawa Plateau in Cameroon (MARLIAC 1987) at the sites of Djohong and Senabou indicates the presence of Late Stone Age surface scatters, dating to various periods of the Holocene. Unfortunately, this area of the eastern Adamawa Plateau has been relatively little studied, at least in comparison with the regions around Ngaoundéré.

No original written sources, either European or African, deal directly with this part of the survey area before the end of the 19th century. However, available oral sources indicate that the region was one of the areas subject to repeated raids for slaves from both the north (Baghirmi, Hausa and Kanuri) and west (Fulani) through the 19th century at least (Brown 1983, 1996: 26–27). In addition, it appears that the area around Komé may have been subject to raids from Dar al-Kuti in the east (Cordell 1985) through the same time period, so that some slaves may have been traded back to the Dar al-Kuti capital at Ndelé, now a major (and almost unknown) archaeological site on the Chad – CAR border.

Previous archaeological research in eastern Cameroon

For the most part, the previous research relevant to Project archaeological work in southwestern Chad is equally relevant to eastern Cameroon. As noted, research along the eastern edge of the Adamawa Plateau in Cameroon (Marliac 1987) indicated that *tazunu* were located at Djohong, close to the pipeline right-of-way, while surface scatters of stone tools, with tabular bipolar cores, burins and bladelets, were found at Djohong and Senabou. Marliac describes the latter as Late Stone Age in character, dating to between 10,000 and 2000 years ago. However, it should be noted that these sites were not dated radiometrically or stratigraphically, but rather through the typological affiliations of the stone tools discovered. Given the rather general characteristics of the assemblages from these sites and the lack of detailed lithic typologies from eastern Cameroon, this dating of the Djohong and Senabou materials should thus be regarded as tentative. However, most such lithics-dominated assemblages found in the course of Project research had to be dated through typological comparisons as well.

There has been relatively little archaeology undertaken in eastern Cameroon, and the work done so far has to this point not been extensively published. In the Boumbe II river valley, on the frontier between Cameroon and the Central African Republic near Batouri, Loumpet (1998) discovered a number of sites yielding probable bifacial stone tools and production debris. The material is found in alluvial deposits, and it is somewhat unclear whether these sites constitute a primary context of deposition.

Considerably further to the west, and at the same time that Project research was taking place, a parallel CHM project was being undertaken in conjunction with road maintenance between Bertoua and Garoua-Boulaï (Mbida, Asombang & Delneuf 2001; Delneuf, Asombang & Mbida 2003). In the course of that project, 119 surface scatters and 28 buried sites were located, of which 23 were artificially constructed pit sites and 5 were iron-working sites. Most of the sites were found in the survey zone closest to Bertoua, and of these, most were dated to the Iron Age. These site types are comparable to those discovered in the course of the CEP cultural heritage management work (see *Chapter 8*).

This area has also seen some palaeoanthropological and palaeontological research by groups led by Michel Brunet and David Pilbeam, in the rift zones along the Mbéré River valley and the edge of the Adamawa Plateau (Flynn *et al.* 1987). The materials discovered by those researchers included some Tertiary mammals, but no hominid skeletal or artifactual material was located. Nevertheless, it should be noted that such material might be encountered in the course of future archaeological or construction work, especially along the Mbéré River valley.

No original written sources, either European or African, deal with the survey area before the end of the 19th century, although there are limited ethnohistorical sources that treat the area as part of the southeastern border of the Adamawa sultanate. The political instability of the late pre-colonial and early colonial period (Burnham *et al.* 1986; Burnham 1996) may have led to important degrees of settlement dispersal and mobility, which could help to explain the relatively low archaeological visibility of recent habitation sites in this region. We do not, at this point, know when this state of affairs began in this part of Africa.

Previous archaeological research in central and coastal Cameroon

A relatively greater amount of archaeological research has been undertaken in regions adjacent to the pipeline right-of-way in southcentral and coastal Cameroon than in southwestern Chad and eastern Cameroon. Along the southwestern extension of the right-of-way, we are thus working in areas where an existing — albeit tentative — culture-historical framework is in place. This research is quite restricted in time and space. It has been associated with two factors: (a) the proximity of sites to urban areas and especially to Yaoundé, the capital of Cameroon and the seat of the only Cameroonian university with an archaeology program, and (b) research interests in the 'Bantu Expansion' phenomenon. By far the most archaeological research has taken place in the area around Yaoundé, with somewhat less work conducted along the coastal plain and much less done to the east of Yaoundé. Considerably the greatest amount of attention has been paid to the phenomenon of 'pit sites', the most visible site type in the region. Before the work associated with this project, little was known about the prehistory of other areas and other time periods in this part of southern Cameroon.

The earliest archaeological investigations in this region of relevance to the present Project were probably those of J.B. JAUZE (1944), who conducted limited excavations at the Obobogo site, on the outskirts of Yaoundé, recovering significant amounts of pottery. This was the earliest of the Cameroonian pit sites to be excavated, and it lent its name to the designation of this cultural tradition in that country (DE MARET 1992). Limited research on similar sites in the Yaoundé area in the late 1960s and early 1970s (*e.g.* MVENG 1971) was succeeded by an appreciably greater intensity from the late 1970s onwards, as Cameroonian and Belgian archaeologists recognized their importance, and especially their implications on significant populations occupying the area over the last 3000 years (DE MARET 1980, 1992; DE MARET *et al.* 1983; ESSOMBA 1992a, 1992b; MBIDA 1996, 1998). This work has continued and diversified over the last two decades, and at this point there are half a dozen significant sites known from the area immediately around Yaoundé. Research by German and Cameroonian archaeologists along the Sanaga River close to the Atlantic coast (EGGERT 2002) uncovered more pit sites, significantly expanding the area within which this archaeological phenomenon is found — although the cultural relationships between populations producing such sites in different parts of southern Cameroon may be complicated. The importance of these sites is considered below.

In the initial research undertaken in southern Cameroon by Belgian and Cameroonian archaeologists in the late 1970s, fieldwork extended into the Grassfields area of Bamenda. A number of important sites were discovered in this area and subsequently investigated further, including Abeke, Mbi Crater and especially Shum Laka, where a unique Pleistocene and Holocene cultural sequence was exposed (DE MARET *et al.* 1987; ASOMBANG 1988; LAVACHERY 1998, 2001; LAVACHERY & CORNELISSEN 2001; CORNELISSEN 2003). The location of these sites is quite significant in a regional context, for two reasons. In the first place, their more open savanna and montane/gallery forest landscapes provide an environmental contrast to the sites in the area around Yaoundé, located in denser tropical and mixed forest — at least for past environmental conditions that approximate those of today. It is likely that the contrast between higher-altitude, more northern sites and those lower and situated further to the south would be maintained even through some degree of regional change in ancient environments. In the second place, on linguistic grounds, the Grassfields are very close to the area of origin of the Bantu languages, and thus the 'Bantu Expansion' (see *Chapter 3*). These sites therefore have the potential to provide insight into the condi-

tions of life for proto-Bantu-speaking populations over the period of initial expansion and differentiation of these languages.

More limited excavations have taken place at a number of sites in the Cross River region of southeastern Nigeria, an area with a culture-historical record again comparable to that of the Grassfields of Cameroon (see for example HARTLE 1980; CHIKWENDU 1998). In the lowland environments of southwestern Cameroon in and around the Banyang Mbo Wildlife Sanctuary, surveys and excavations over the last decade have uncovered a number of surface, open and rock shelter sites dating to different periods between the Middle Stone Age and the historical period (MERCADER & MARTI 1999; OSLISLY, MBIDA & WHITE 2000; MERCADER *et al.* 2006). This material displays a variety of similarities and differences with both the higher-elevation sites in the Grassfields and the lowland sites around Yaoundé.

At the end of the 1970s, limited collections of ceramics and lithics were also being made in the coastal area of Cameroon, between Kribi and Campo, as well as near Yaoundé, in the context of a larger project studying the geomorphology of these regions (OMI 1977; KADOMURA 1984). However, the cultural affiliations and ages of these collections remain uncertain, and their usefulness in interpreting prehistoric data in these regions is limited. Much more significant in this region has been the research by French and Cameroonian archaeologists, led by Richard Oslisly, in the coastal area between Kribi and Campo (OSLISLY *et al.* 2006). It led to the discovery of a variety of pit sites in that region, again significantly extending the area in which this archaeological phenomenon was noted, as well as to the formulation of an initial chronology for the human occupation of the area.

Typological questions

There are significant typological issues involved in the definition of cultural transitions in this area, perhaps best exemplified in the debates over terms like 'Late Stone Age', 'Iron Age' or especially 'Neolithic'. In francophone archaeological terminologies, the presence of polished stone tools and/or pottery in an archaeological assemblage has been considered sufficient evidence to qualify it as 'Neolithic' (SINCLAIR *et al.* 1993; STAHL 1994). However, in anglophone terminologies 'Neolithic' designates the economic transformations associated with the appearance of agriculture and animal husbandry (CHILDE 1951), with ceramics and polished stone tools considered a by-product of the economic 'revolution' involved in farming. In sub-Saharan Africa, however, where direct evidence for food production is hard to come by because of poor preservation of organic material, even the contemporaneity of the two phenomena is in some cases (and especially in West and Central Africa) not established. Moreover, in many cases, the use of stone tools has continued among iron-using groups, who should presumably be identified as 'Iron Age', while pottery is nearly ubiquitous among iron-using populations. Iron itself is rarely preserved in the archaeological record in sub-Saharan Africa and, if not produced in large amounts locally, is often invisible in the archaeological record. Hence, the beginnings of the 'Iron Age' can be as difficult to pinpoint as the start of the 'Neolithic', and the wider effects of that technological innovation just as hard to identify.

These have been issues of debate in African archaeology for some decades (see for example CLARK *et al.* 1966; KLEINDIENST 2006). In some cases, researchers avoid some of these problems by using alternative techno-chronological appellations such as 'Ceramic Late Stone Age' or 'Stone to Metal Age' (SINCLAIR *et al.* 1993; DE MARET 1994; LAVACHERY 2001) (although such individualized terminologies may not be widely understood beyond the regions where they were originally introduced), or by using terms borrowed from ethnography like 'foragers' and 'farmers', depending on the focus of the research. In this text, we will continue to use the traditional technological/economic designations — Middle and Late Stone Age, Neolithic and Iron Age — in large part because of the necessity to use such very general (and admittedly imprecise) terminologies when describing materials encountered on sites where no absolute dating is possible (surface sites, for example), and in regions where no detailed archaeological chronologies exist (see *Chapters 7* and *8*).

Summary of archaeological sequences

The Pleistocene

Relatively little is known of the human occupation during the Pleistocene in this part of Africa. LOUMPET (1998) describes the lithic material found near Batouri on the Cameroon — Central African Republic border as being related to the Acheulean, although from published illustrations it seems possible that it might date to the Middle Stone Age and thus is comparable to some of the material found in the course of Project work along the right-of-way in the Mbéré River Valley area in particular (see Chapter 8). Data from Shum Laka and Mbi Crater indicate that that region has been inhabited for the last 32,000 years at least, and that hunter-gatherers at those sites had already mastered microlithic technologies (ASOMBANG

1988; LAVACHERY 1998, 2001; LAVACHERY & CORNELISSEN 2001; CORNELISSEN 2003). In northern Gabon, where palaeoenvironmental research indicates the persistence of tropical forest through the Holocene and probably through the late Pleistocene as well, there is limited evidence of occupation by populations using Lupemban-Tshitolian toolkits, with bifacial tools and projectile points, since *ca* 40,000 bp (ASSOKO NDONG 2002; CORNELISSEN 2002; CLIST 2005, 2006b). Middle Stone Age material from the lowest levels at the Njuinye site outside the Banyang Mbo Wildlife Sanctuary in the lowland forests of southwestern Cameroon appears on typological grounds to date to the late Pleistocene as well (MERCADER & MARTI 1999). Interestingly, it seems to resemble the Gabonese material more closely than that from Shum Laka.

The Holocene is much better known, and it is during this period that African populations switched from foraging to farming as a primary economic pursuit. Data on that transition are accumulating in this area of Africa, especially with more sophisticated approaches to data recovery and analysis. However, data pertaining to the socioeconomic organization of ancient populations are less often preserved than is evidence relating to material culture (stone tools, pottery, metallurgy) and its evolution. So the technological transitions (the appearance of ceramics, the transition from the 'Neolithic' to the 'Iron Age', and so on) are often still better understood. Such shifts are actually part of complex technological, economic and social processes. Those processes, resulting from interactions between human groups of different cultures in very dissimilar environmental conditions, did not take place simultaneously in every region of Africa. While some populations were using 'Neolithic' technologies in certain areas, their neighbours might still have been making use of 'Late Stone Age' technologies, or on the other hand could have advanced to the 'Iron Age'. In addition, these technological changes were not always necessarily paralleled by transformations in economies, so that one might find, for example, foragers who made ceramics or used iron tools.

We should also note that, in Central Africa as in other parts of the continent, only the most visible sites, located closest to modern population centers, are usually discovered: rock shelters in the Grassfields area of Cameroon, mounds in the Sudanic and Sahelian zones to the north, and pit features along roads near Yaoundé, N'Djamena, Libreville or Kinshasa. It is thus dangerous to assume that these patterns of site discovery reflect genuine prehistoric land use strategies rather than the development of archaeological research — whether that research be academic in nature or, as in the present case, part of a cultural heritage management impact mitigation program.

Microlithic technologies: Late Stone Age foragers

The Late Stone Age, more or less comparable in timing to the European Upper Palaeolithic and Mesolithic, is primarily a technological term. It refers to a period when African prehistoric populations used primarily (but not exclusively) microlithic stone tool technologies. In Central Africa, this technology appears during the Late Pleistocene (VAN NOTEN 1977, 1982; CAHEN 1978a; CLIST 1993; MERCADER & BROOKS 2001; ASSOKO NDONG 2002). The oldest dates associated with microliths are clustered between 45,000 and 30,000 bp. This is in fact the lower limit of the radiocarbon dating technique, and so the appearance of these technologies in Central Africa might even be earlier. In the early Holocene, the technology was still thriving, and microlithic stone industries dated to between 10,000 and 7000 bp have been identified in Gabon (see for example CAHEN 1978b, 1982; CLIST 1989) and Cameroon, as at Shum Laka rock shelter in the Grassfields (LAVACHERY 2001; CORNELISSEN 2003). At the rare sites in Central Africa where animal remains were recovered, as for example at Matupi rock shelter and Ishango in northeast Democratic Republic of Congo, Ntadi Yomba rock shelter in southern Congo-Brazzaville and Shum Laka in Cameroon, the species identified are wild animals (VAN NOTEN 1977; BROOKS & SMITH 1987; LAVACHERY 2001; CORNELISSEN 2003). Any evidence for food production and/or long-term settlement is also absent; late Pleistocene and early Holocene (Late Stone Age) populations were almost certainly mobile foragers.

The end of the Late Stone Age and the beginning of the Neolithic: from foraging to farming

Between 7000 and 5000 bp, two significant new technologies made their appearance in the area around the Gulf of Guinea: ceramics and macrolithic stone tool production techniques (SHAW 1978; MACDONALD & ALLSWORTH-JONES 1994; LAVACHERY et al. 1996). In these assemblages, pottery and/or heavy-duty ground stone tools remain quite rare, and most of the industry consists of a typical microlithic Late Stone Age tradition. These two new technologies might have originated further to the north. In the southern Sahara, comb-decorated pottery and polished stone axes appear as early as 9500 bp at sites such as Tagalagal, Temet and Adrar Bous (ROSET 1987; MUZZOLINI 1993). Until about 5000 bp they are associated with stone industries known as the Saharo-Sudanese Neolithic, characterized by a large number of bifacial arrowheads. By approximately 9500 bp, pottery is also known at Ounjougou in Mali (HUYSECOM et al. 2002). By ca 6300 bp it is known in the Lake Chad plain, at the site of Konduga in Nigeria,

and around 5200 bp at Kourounkorokalé rock shelter in Mali (BREUNIG et al. 1996, MACDONALD 1997). All of these assemblages show clear stylistic ties with Saharan ceramics; simple- or rocking-comb or stick impressions are the most common decoration techniques. A direct link between the emergence of industries with polished stone tools and pottery in the Sahara and those of the Sahelian zone north of the Gulf of Guinea seems likely, especially given the abundant north-south linkages provided by the Niger and Benue river systems and the Lake Chad Basin. It is probable that the development of these technologies in Central Africa was related to their earlier appearance further to the north.

While we know that ovicaprids were domesticated as early as 7500 bp in the Sahara, with management of Barbary sheep occurring one to two millennia before that (GAUTIER 1987; GARCEA 2004), the subsistence strategies of pottery-making populations of the Gulf of Guinea are still largely unknown. The only site that provides us with some information close to the research area is Shum Laka rock shelter (LAVACHERY et al. 1996; LAVACHERY 2001) in the Grassfields of northwestern Cameroon. At this site, during the period 7000–5000 bp, archaeological data reveal that hunting in the forest was still very important but that exploitation of the incense tree (*Canarium schweinfurthii*) was already evident. The simultaneous appearance of pottery, of heavy-duty stone axes and of the practice of arboriculture indicates significantly more intensive use of local environments, and thus probably the beginning of a transition to food production and the first steps towards the 'Neolithic'. In the forest zone further to the south, mid-Holocene foraging populations were still producing microlithic stone industries and were not using pottery. Late Stone Age assemblages have been dated (albeit not with a high level of confidence: see DE MARET 1992) to 6000 bp at Obobogo, near Yaoundé in Cameroon, and to between 7500 and 4000 bp in Gabon (Lélédi 10, Owendo, Ikengué, Grotte Pahouin, Okala) (OSLISLY 1993; CLIST 2005).

Neolithic farmers

Around 5000 bp, while microlithic Late Stone Age industries still characterized the rest of West Africa, heavy-duty tools (primarily bifacial axes, sometimes polished) came to dominate the assemblages of southeastern Nigeria and northwestern Cameroon (LAVACHERY 1998). Pottery, frequently decorated with incision, comb- and stick-stamping or grooving, also became much more frequent. This phenomenon is found in rock shelters like Abeke (in the Cameroonian Grassfields) by 5600 bp, at Shum Laka (Grassfields) between 5000 and 4000 bp, at Ezi-Ukwu Ukpa (Cross River, Nigeria) after approximately 4900 bp and at Mbi Crater (Grassfields) by *ca* 4200 bp (Hartle 1980; de Maret *et al.* 1987; Asombang 1988).

Identical stone implements were still in use on Bioko (Equatorial Guinea) at the beginning of the 20th century as axes to fell trees when preparing new fields (Tessmann 1923). The development of these tools from 5000 bp onwards in the Grassfields is probably evidence of an increasingly intensive environmental exploitation, probably involving a large population and deforestation. Related assemblages are, however, not restricted to the Grassfields. Farther to the east, in the Central African Republic, the assemblages associated with the *tazunu* megalithic funerary/ritual monuments, dated to at least 3000 bp, include stick-decorated pottery and a stone industry with polished axes (Zangato 1999).

Botanical studies can shed some light on the nature of the intensification processes underway during this period, at least in the Grassfields. At Shum Laka and Mbi Crater, remains of burnt endocarps of *Canarium schweinfurthii* became progressively more frequent through the mid-/late-Holocene (Asombang 1988; Lavachery 2001). This implies that the intensification processes first visible in the early Holocene were continuing, with more pottery, more heavy-duty axes and concomitantly more exploitation of culturally useful trees. It is very likely that full-scale farming systems appeared in this area between about 5000 and 3000 bp.

Village sites

After 3000 bp, pottery became considerably more abundant in this part of West and Central Africa, and also began to appear in areas where it was previously unknown. This is the case, for example, in the Lake Chad Basin of Nigeria and Cameroon. Early occupation phases of the mounds of Gajiganna, Bama (Bornu 38), Kursakata (Bornu 24), Doulo Igzawa 1, Ghwa Khiva and Sou Blamé, dating to the period 3000 – 2500 bp, yield rich comb- and incision-decorated pottery assemblages, associated with polished axes but only rarely with other stone tools (Connah 1976, 1981; Rapp 1980; Breunig *et al.* 1996, 2001; MacEachern 1996; Gronenborn 1998). Iron and slag made their appearance on a number of these sites just before 2500 bp, albeit not in great quantities. In the Cross River region of southeastern Nigeria, a comb-decorated pottery collection with a poor stone industry is dated to the same period in Ugwuagu rock shelter (Chikwendu 1998).

Pottery is found in Central Africa at this time. In the area of Yaoundé, just north of the forest in southern Cameroon, a number of sites with numerous pit features (such as Obobogo, Okolo, Nkang, Ndindan and Nkometou) are dated between 3000 and 2000 bp (de Maret 1985, 1992; Atangana 1992; Essomba 1992a; Mbida 1992, 1998; Eggert 2002). Such pits can appear in large numbers at particular sites; more than 120 at Nkometou and approximately 30 at Nkang, for example (Essomba 1992a; Mbida 1992). Although we should not exaggerate site size, such concentrations of pits on a single site that may not have been contemporaneous do appear to represent the remains of substantial, permanent villages in this area between about 2800 and 1500 bp. These sites are often grouped together as the 'Obobogo Group or Tradition' (de Maret 1992). Recently, other 'pit sites' were discovered elsewhere in southern Cameroon, such as near the coast between Edea and Kribi (Eggert 2002; Oslisly *et al.* 2006), in the Tikar Plains (Delneuf, Otto & Thinon 2003) and in eastern Cameroon, near Bertoua (Delneuf, Asombang & Mbida 2003). Very similar Neolithic sites, with generally comparable ceramics, were also identified in northern Gabon as the 'Okala Tradition' (Clist 1995).

The pits at these sites, sometime several meters deep, were probably initially dug to be used as silos, latrines or water wells, but were transformed into refuse pits later in their uselife. They usually contain large amounts of artifactual and organic debris, including ceramics, rare lithics, iron and slag in some cases and faunal remains (including ovicaprids). Large amounts of charred *Canarium schweinfurthii* endocarps and oil palm (*Elaeis guineensis*) nuts have been found in a number of these pits, suggesting some manner of arboriculture. The discovery of *Pennisetum* millet at Obobogo and at the Balimbé site in Central African Republic (Zangato 2000) suggests both the initial adoption of plant domestication and contacts to the Sahelian and Sudanian zones to the north where that cereal crop was probably initially domesticated. Similar innovations are indicated by the identification of ovicaprid remains at Nkang (Obobogo Group) and Toubé 1 (Yindo Tradition), as well as by phytoliths of banana in Nkang (Mbida *et al.* 2000; Mbida, Doutrelepont *et al.* 2001; Assoko Ndong 2002). It is quite likely that these populations already had been sedentary farmers from 2600 bp onwards. This parallels the cultural trajectory of the Lake Chad Basin, where settlements become more sedentary after 3500 bp and where we see the progressive adoption of millet agriculture, as opposed to the gathering of wild grains, after about 3200 bp.

The appearance of iron production

It seems likely that iron working was adopted by Obob-ogo Group farmers, although the dates at which this would have happened remain debatable (Lavachery *et al.* 1996; de Maret 2002; Killick 2004; Clist 2005). Previous estimates for the first documented adoption of iron in the region have ranged from about 3500 – 2400 bp, although there is no unequivocal evidence for iron technologies before the middle of the third millennium bp. The absence of iron-smelting furnaces or significant slag heaps dated to the period of the appearance of the first villages, both in the Yaoundé area and the Lake Chad region, suggests either that iron was not produced locally at that time, or that the context of use was very different from later periods.

Stone tool industries seem to survive both in West and Central Africa after 3000 bp, but are found most often in rock shelters: this is the case in the upper layers of Rop and Dutsen Kongba rock shelters in Central Nigeria where typical Late Stone Age quartz industries gave dates younger than 2800 bp (York 1978; David 1993). In western Cameroon, at Shum Laka, Mbi Crater and Fiye Nkwi rock shelters, 'Grassfields Neolithic' industries are dated between 3000 and 800 bp (Asombang 1988; Lavachery & Cornelissen 2001). A number of hypotheses have been put forward to explain the apparent survival of stone industries in rock shelters (York 1978; Clist 1990, 2006a; David 1993; Lavachery 1996; Lavachery & Cornelissen 2001): (1) some microlithic assemblages could have been produced by nomad foragers who still lived in the forests and utilized rock shelters, (2) stone tools could have survived the introduction of iron in areas where metal was rare and expensive and (3) the often disturbed stratigraphic contexts of rock shelters could have caused the mixing of initially distinct assemblages. These explanations are not, of course, mutually exclusive.

Iron-using farmers

The early socioeconomic role of metallurgy in West and Central African societies is still poorly understood. The origins of the technology are unclear, and there has been a significant debate over the last decades about whether the ultimate origins of African iron working lie within the continent itself or should be ascribed to contacts ultimately with the Mediterranean world (see for example Descoeudres *et al.* 2001; Bocoum 2002; Killick 2004; Alpern 2005). At this point, our understanding of the chronologies of iron working is such that neither local origins nor foreign importation of that technology into sub-Saharan Africa can be excluded. It is also important that we keep in mind the varying contexts and meaning of 'iron working'. There

is a significant difference between the discovery of artifacts that prove that iron tools were used in a particular community, those indicating that smithing was carried out in a community (small quantities of slag or smithing furnaces found, for example) and those suggesting that smelting was mastered by that particular community (large smelting furnaces, slag heaps). It is quite possible that particular groups could have obtained iron objects while not mastering iron working themselves, and indeed while otherwise maintaining 'Late Stone Age' or 'Neolithic' cultural adaptations. Similarly, 'Iron Age' groups could have obtained iron blooms from other 'Iron Age' communities, and could thus potentially have mastered smithing without smelting iron themselves.

As noted above, the generally accepted oldest evidence for iron working found in West/Central Africa is dated to approximately 2700 – 2500 bp. It appears in two areas: in the Senegal valley, where iron artifacts dated to between 800 – 500 cal BC were discovered at the Walalde site (Deme 2004), and in a region comprising Nigeria, Cameroon, CAR and Gabon, where evidence for iron smelting has been found on a number of sites. The relatively restricted time period for the appearance of iron technology may imply a widespread introduction of that technology into local societies, or it may be related to problems of calibration of radiocarbon dates in the middle of the third millennium bp (Killick 2004). In northern Cameroon, the Doulo Igzawa 1 and Ghwa Kiva sites yielded slag and artifacts associated with dates of *ca* 2500 bp and later (MacEachern 1996). At Taruga in central Nigeria, furnaces are dated to *ca* 2500 bp (Fagg 1969; Calvocoressi & David 1979), while in the south of the country, the Opi Hills furnace site has yielded somewhat younger dates of about 2300 – 2000 bp (Okafor 1993). The Oliga site in Yaoundé yielded dates ranging from 2800 to 1900 bp but clustering around 2400 – 2200 bp on furnace remains and other debris (Essomba 1992b; Clist 2005). Oliga can be geographically associated with the neighbouring Obobogo sites, but the difficulty lies in associating the charcoal samples with the furnace remains (Clist 2005), and the furnace remains with the village sites. In southeastern Gabon, evidence for iron working at the Moanda 1 and 2 sites is dated to between 2350 and 2100 bp (Clist 2005). In western Central African Republic, the first evidence for metallurgy associated with the *tazunu* sites is dated to 2600 bp (Zangato 1999). Given the data available, it seems as if populations in this part of Central Africa, after adopting agriculture at around 3000 bp, came to master iron working at some time within the following five centuries and certainly by 2500 bp. As has already been noted, however, it is quite possible that evidence for iron metallurgy at or before 3000 bp will emerge in the future.

Pottery decoration underwent a significant transformation through this period as well. Ceramics associated with the Taruga furnaces are decorated with a new technique: roulette impressions (FAGG 1972). They are the oldest examples of carved wooden roulette, twisted string roulette and knotted strip roulette in the region. Iron Age pottery in nearby Rop rock shelter displays the same types of decoration. In the Grassfields region of Cameroon, contemporary ceramics from the Mbi Crater and Shum Laka rock shelters are also primarily roulette decorated (ASOMBANG 1988; LAVACHERY 1998, 2001). The same phenomenon is documented in the Lake Chad Basin, where roulette-decorated pottery gradually became dominant at sites such as Daima (Bornu 29), Bama (Bornu 38), Kursakata (Bornu 24), Ghwa Khiva, Gréa Manaouatchi and Doulo Igzawa 1 (CONNAH 1981; MACEACHERN 1996; GRONENBORN 1998). Along with metallurgy, roulette decoration seems to have originated from the Saharo-Sahelian region: the oldest pottery displaying such patterns was dated to the first half of the fourth millennium bp at Karkarichinkat in Mali, at Dhar Titchitt in southern Mauritania and at the Ndondi Tossokel sites in the Malian Méma, with many similarities to Dhar Tichitt (MUNSON 1968; SMITH 1974; MACDONALD 1996).

Further to the south, in the Yaoundé area, Obobogo Group pottery decoration does not show such significant change through this period. Ceramics of a different style but using the same comb-decoration techniques were discovered in the Tikar area, north of Yaoundé, and dated to 2500 – 2200 bp (DELNEUF, OTTO & THINON 2003). Pottery associated with iron tools found in pits along the coast, at sites like Mouanko and Bwambé, continued to be decorated with comb-grooving and -stamping between 2200 – 1700 bp (EGGERT 2002; CLIST 2005; OSLISLY *et al.* 2006). In eastern Cameroon, north of Bertoua, pit sites such as Wélé Maroua, dated to 2000 – 1800 bp, yield a comb-decorated pottery, associated with slag (MBIDA, ASOMBANG & DELNEUF 2001; DELNEUF, ASOMBANG & MBIDA 2003). In northern Gabon, Okala Group sites feature comb-decorated pottery found in pit features and comparable to the Cameroonian material from the Obobogo sites — but not associated with iron working (CLIST 2005). Comb- and stick-grooving and -stamping are still the only decorative techniques known at the end of the second millennium bp. In the forest zone around Yaoundé and in northern Gabon, Obobogo and Okanda Group sites are evident until around 1600 bp, when these two forest traditions suddenly disappear, leaving a long gap in the archaeological record thereafter.

Complex societies

The second half of the Iron Age, with its beginning dated to around 1000 bp, corresponds to the emergence of sociopolitically complex societies in this region (WARNIER 1984; VANSINA 1990; SHAW *et al.* 1993). These are characterized by three main elements when compared to the earlier Iron Age cultures: the development of significant degrees of social/political hierarchy, concentrations of population and eventually urbanization, and inter-continental trade. At the same time, of course, many communities retained localized, relatively egalitarian modes of authority, and forager populations persisted at least along the southwestern part of the Project research area. As suggested by local oral traditions and the writings of the first Arab and European explorers, these communities are often seen as the direct ancestors of the modern local populations.

Later Iron Age sites are, unfortunately, only rarely excavated in West and Central Africa, and this period is generally poorly known when compared to the earlier Iron Age. This is less true for the Lake Chad Basin, where the period between 1200 and 500 bp corresponds to a spectacular development of earlier traditions (at sites such as Houlouf in northern Cameroon, Yau and Birni Ngazargamo in Nigeria and Mdaga in Chad) and entirely new cultural developments in social complexity (LEBEUF *et al.* 1980; MARLIAC 1991; GRONENBORN 2000, 2001; HOLL 2001; DAVID 2004). Most of the communities on the plains south of Lake Chad developed from an early Iron Age cultural substratum, and there are considerable cultural continuities — for example in ceramics — from earlier Iron Age precursors. In the middle of the first millennium bp, there is a significant rupture in occupation through much of this region, with the abandonment of many mound sites. This rupture is probably associated with the growing importance of predatory states and slave raiding in the area.

Only a few sites from this period are known in the Cameroon Grassfields. Sites in the Fundong area demonstrate that high levels of iron production existed in the area between 1400 and 400 bp (WARNIER 1984; ROWLANDS & WARNIER 1993). At Shum Laka, ceramic decorative techniques ancestral to those used on modern 'Grassfields' pottery appeared by the end of the second millennium bp (with unfortunately a hiatus in the occupation through the middle of the first millennium AD), while iron artifacts (a ring and a bracelet fragment) probably date to 900 bp or earlier (LAVACHERY 1998, 2001). In the Banyang Mbo area a few kilometers to the south, some 19 sites were identified in a 30x40 km zone (OSLISLY, MBIDA & WHITE 2000): pit features, pottery horizons and smelting furnaces were dated to between 1000 and 300 bp. The ceramics collected from these sites, and those from the neighbouring sites of Njuinye and Ale Mekudian, show significant similarities with contemporary Ibo and especially Yoruba ceramics from southern Nigeria, but less evidence of relations with

Cameroonian groups in the Grassfields and the southern part of the country (MERCADER *et al.* 2006). This is claimed to indicate the positioning of the communities producing this pottery on the margins of a larger-scale Ibo-Yoruba cultural sphere. In nearby southeastern Nigeria, the Igbo-Ukwu site reveals a spectacular command of copper, bronze and iron metallurgy dated to approximately 1100 bp, associated with ceramics that appear to be related to later Igbo traditions, decorated with roulette impressions and applied zoomorphic figurines (SHAW 1970, 1993; CRADDOCK *et al.* 1997).

Discussion: archaeology, climatology and linguistics

After many millennia of use of microlithic technologies, the Late Stone Age foragers who lived in the Cross River and Grassfields areas started, *ca* 7000 bp, a long cultural transition to the Neolithic. This was signaled in their material culture by the first appearance of pottery and heavy-duty polished stone axes, and in their subsistence strategy by a more intensive exploitation of local food resources and, eventually, food production. This parallels the historical linguistic evidence, which indicates that proto-Benue-Congo speaking populations, occupying the Niger-Benue confluence at about that period, cultivated yams and a variety of other plants, bred goats/sheep and knew how to make pottery (BLENCH 1993a, 1994–1995; WILLIAMSON 1993). Archaeological and linguistic data indicate that populations of the Saharan and Sudanic zones to the north had by that time already been engaged in similar adaptations for some millennia (EHRET 1993; MUZZOLINI 1993). It is likely that increasing levels of contact between these two areas took place in the early-/mid-Holocene, in a context of deteriorating Saharan environments and population movements (R.J. MCINTOSH 1993, 2000; CLAUSSEN *et al.* 1999; FOLEY *et al.* 2003). This may well have led to the adoption of some food production techniques earlier associated with southern Saharan groups — including sheep/goat herding — by proto-Benue-Congo populations in the mid-Holocene. According to linguists, these proto-Benue-Congo groups probably settled in the Gulf of Guinea area between 7000 and 5000 bp; this population movement was associated with further linguistic diversification, giving birth to the proto-West Benue-Congo (southwestern Nigeria) and proto-East Benue-Congo (southeastern Nigeria) language groups (WILLIAMSON & BLENCH 2000).

Around 5000 bp, heavy-duty stone tools appeared in the Cross River/Grassfields region. This development in the lithic toolkit was paralleled by the intensive exploitation of *Canarium schweinfurthii* as a probable precursor to modern arboricultural systems, and prob-

ably — as indicated by historical linguistics — by yam exploitation. It is tempting to credit these developments to proto-Cross-Bantoid speakers, who may have been settled in the area at about the same period. Historical linguistics suggest that proto-Bantu speaking populations inhabited the Grassfields area between 5000 and 3000 bp and that they had terms in their vocabulary for 'field', 'cultivation' and 'to plant' (EHRET 1984; VANSINA 1985; WILLIAMSON 1993; BLENCH 1994–1995). Words for a number of tree species, including oil palm (*Elaeis guineensis*) and *Canarium schweinfurthii*, testify to their economic importance. Terms for 'axe' and 'digging stick' yield further insight into regional arboricultural systems. Proto-Bantu speakers also herded domestic animals, as they had a word for 'sheep/goat' and even for 'cattle'. By approximately 5000 bp, village sites like Balimbé and Batumé appeared in the western part of the Central African Republic (ZANGATO 1999, 2000), with similar lithic and ceramic technologies, and also with evidence for the use of oil palm and *Canarium* and (*ca* 3000 bp) domesticated *Pennisetum* millet. The proto-Adamawa-Ubangian languages, of which the cradle is probably somewhere in the Benue River Basin in Cameroon, are likely to have split from the main Niger-Congo phylum during the mid-Holocene (SAXON 1982). This corresponds to a period of significant climatic changes in the area. The appearance of the *tazunu* monuments in this region at about 3000 bp probably signals some form of socioeconomic differentiation in these village communities. Iron metallurgy had appeared in the region by 2600 bp at least, but there appears to have been a significant amount of cultural continuity (in ceramic decorative techniques and *tazunu* construction, for example) into the second millennium AD.

Just before 3000 bp, we see in southern Cameroon the sudden appearance of pottery assemblages, found in large pit features that are probably the remnants of long-term settlements. Well before 2500 bp, these populations had settled a significant part of southeastern Cameroon and Gabon. This spread of farming (and, by 2600 bp at least, metallurgy) into Central Africa can probably be related to the spread of Bantu languages (and presumably of Bantu-speaking populations) from the Grassfields area into the forest to the south and east (DAVID 1980; DE MARET 1994; VANSINA 1995). As acknowledged by their own oral traditions (VANSINA 1986; KLIEMAN 2003a, 2003b), these Bantu farmers met indigenous foragers in the forest, who Westerners have called Pygmies. These people did not produce pottery and iron, nor did they cultivate plants or herd animals. Specialist hunter-gatherers of the rainforest, they acted as 'guides' for the first Bantu settlers. It is quite possible that the ancestors of the present-day Pygmies were actually the producers of the Late Stone Age assemblages of Central Africa.

Maps

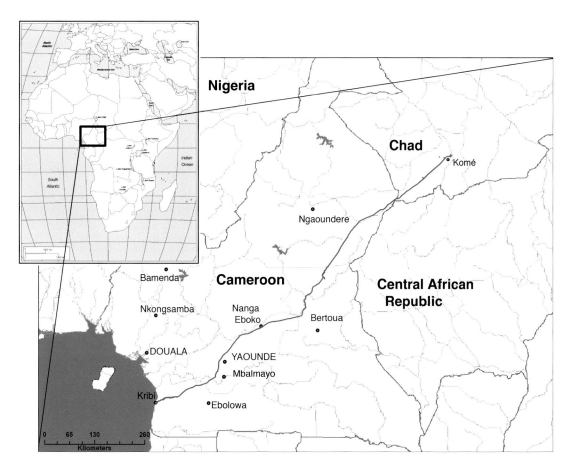

Map 1. Pipeline extents in Chad and Cameroon.

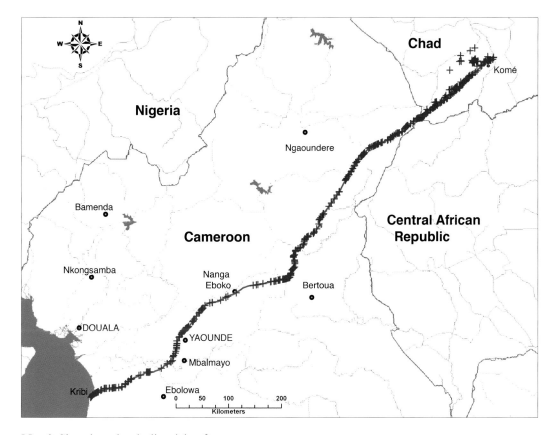

Map 2. Sites along the pipeline right-of-way.

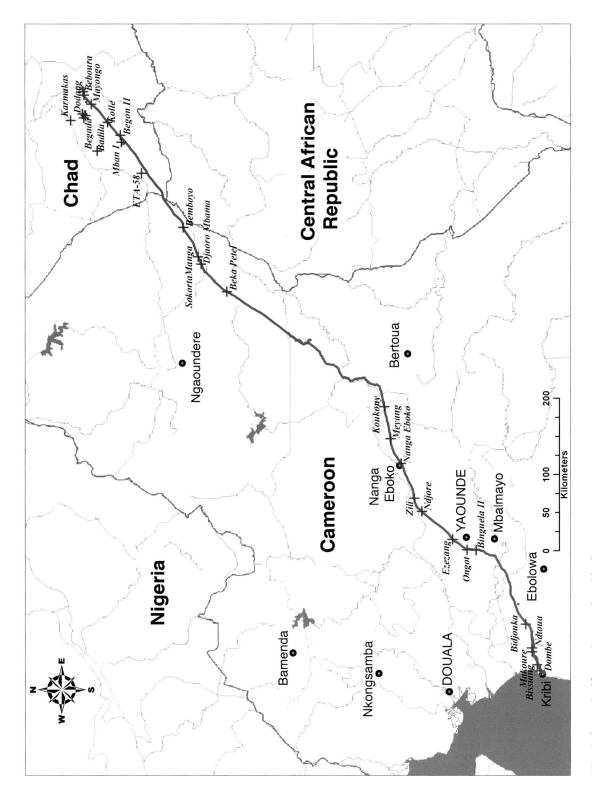

Map 3. Some significant sites mentioned in the text.

36

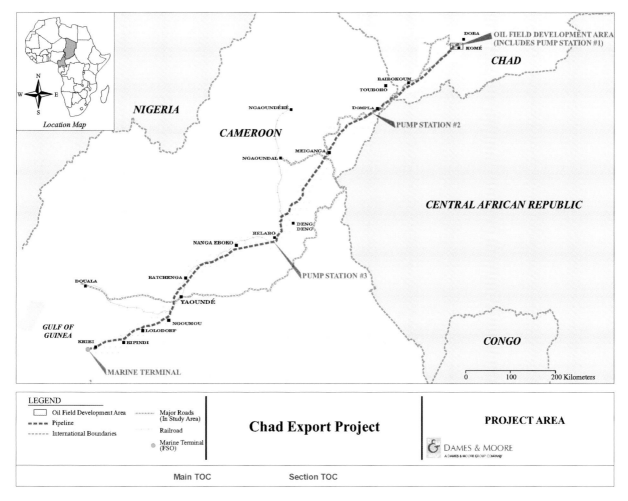

Map 4. Chad Export Project area.

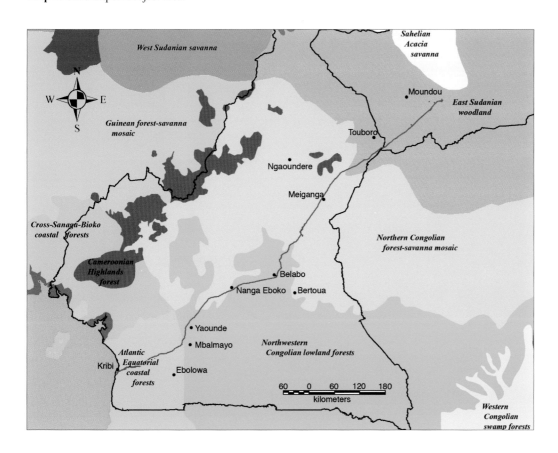

Map 5. Eco-zones in the Project area.

37

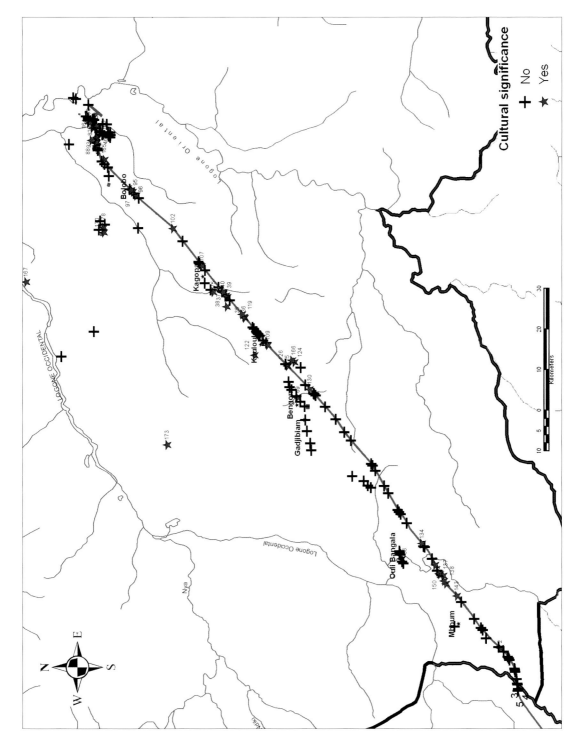

Map 6. Chad site distribution and significance.

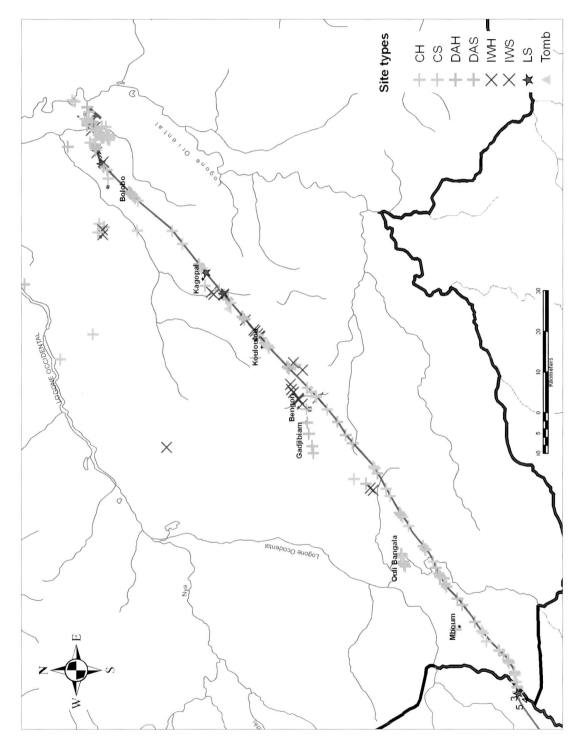

Map 7. Chad site types (CH= Ceramic horizon, CS= ceramic scatter, DAH= Diverse artifact horizon, DAS: Diverse artifact scatter; IWH: Iron working horizon, IWS: Iron working scatter, LS: Lithic scatter).

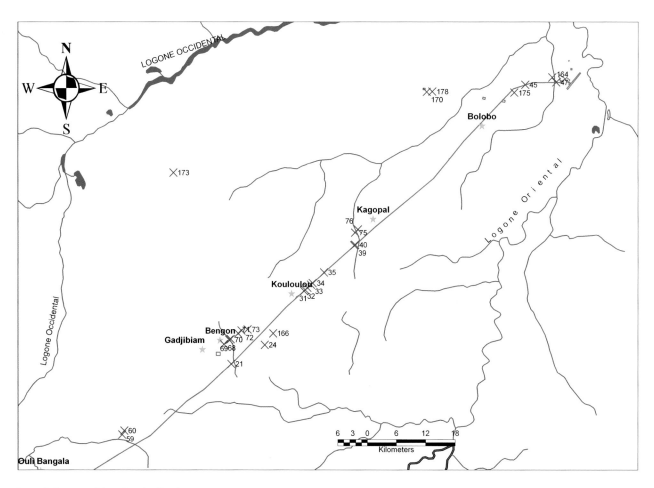

Map 8. Iron-working sites in Chad.

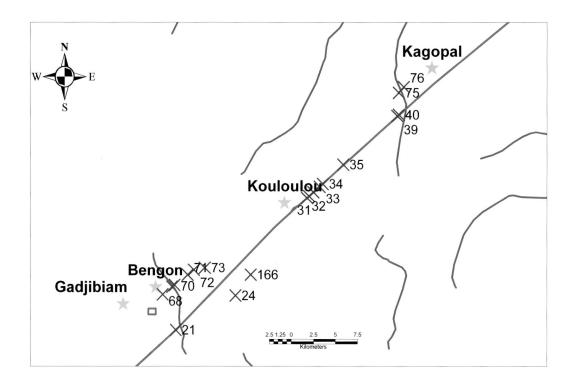

Map 9. Iron-working sites in Chad — Gadjibian to Kagopal.

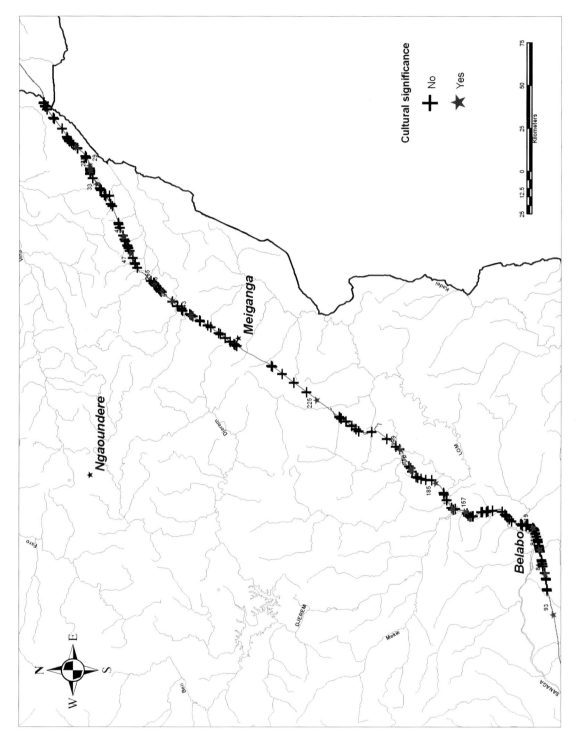

Map 10. Cameroon North site distribution and significance.

41

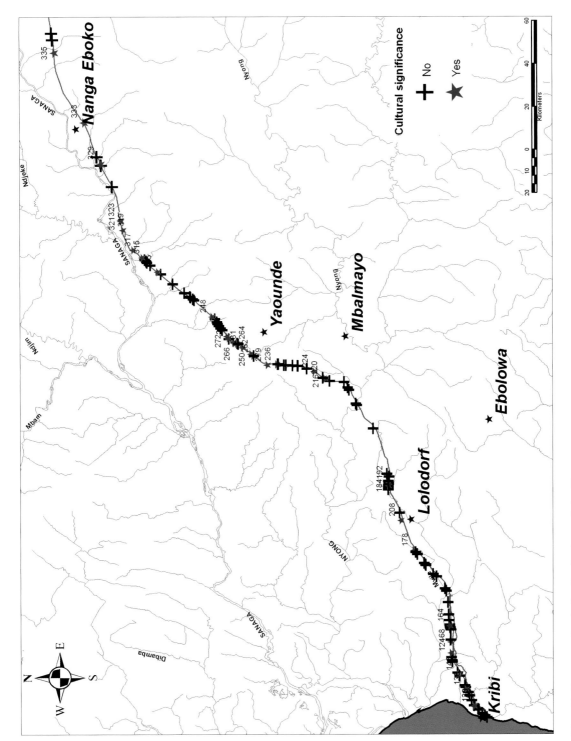

Map 11. Cameroon South site distribution and significance.

42

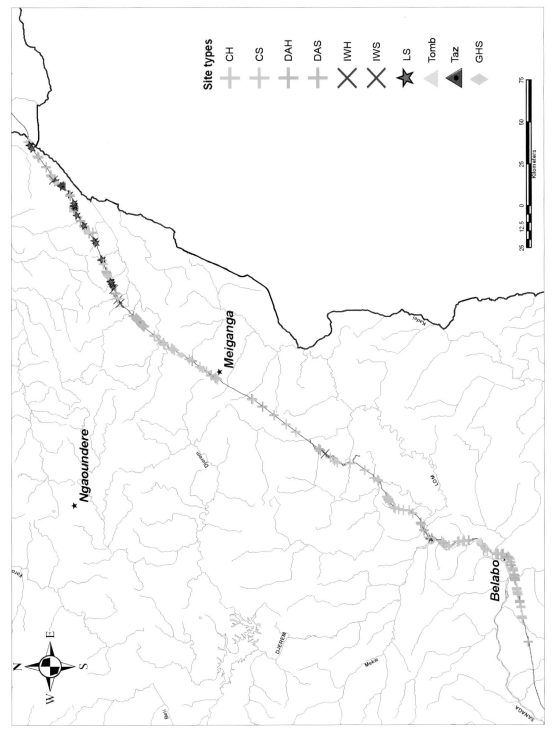

Map 12. Cameroon North site types (CH= Ceramic horizon, CS= ceramic scatter, DAH= Diverse artifact horizon, DAS: Diverse artifact scatter, IWH: Iron working horizon, IWS: Iron working scatter, LS: Lithic scatter, Taz: Tazunu, GHS: Grinding stone/hollows).

43

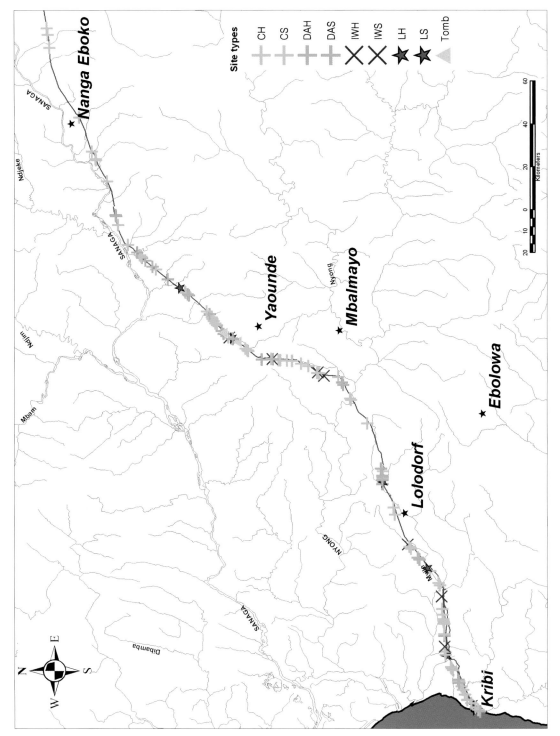

Map 13. Cameroon South site types (CH= Ceramic horizon, CS= ceramic scatter, DAH= Diverse artifact horizon, DAS: Diverse artifact scatter, IWH: Iron working horizon, IWS: Iron working scatter, LH: Lithic horizon; LS: Lithic scatter).

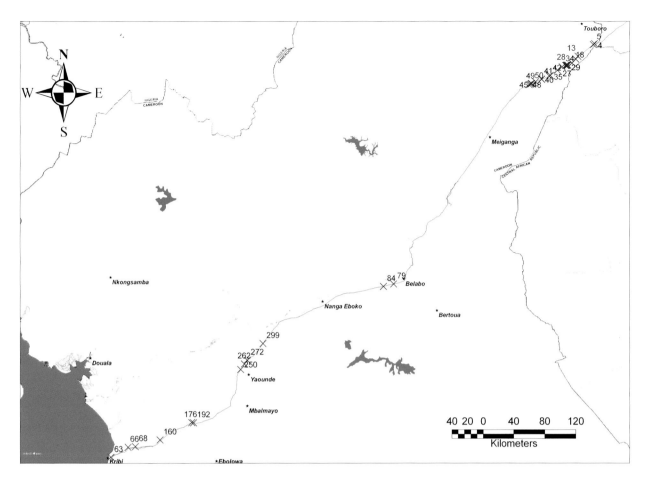

Map 14. Sites with MSA and LSA components – Cameroon.

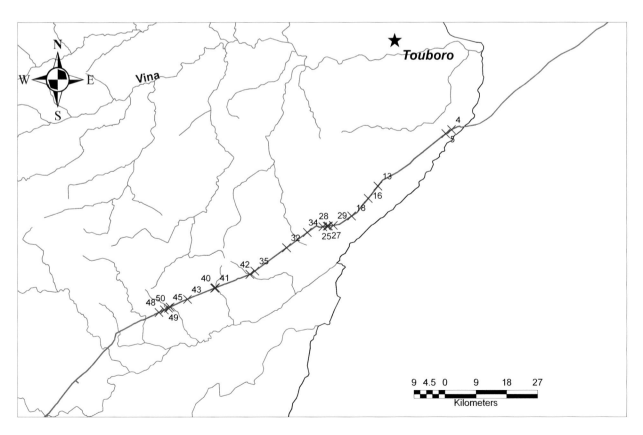

Map 15. Sites with MSA and LSA components – Belel to Mbéré (Cameroon).

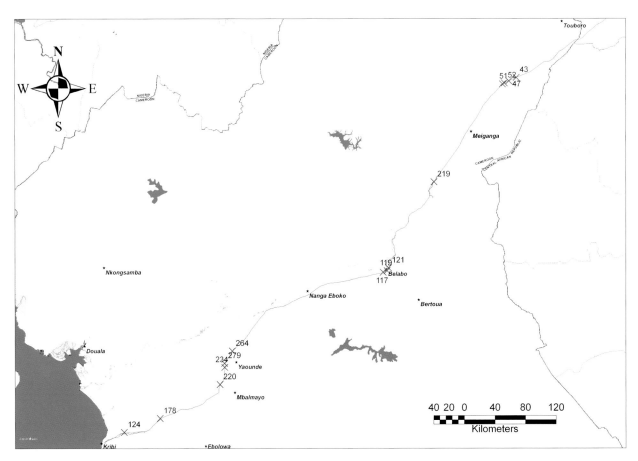

Map 16. Furnace sites in Cameroon.

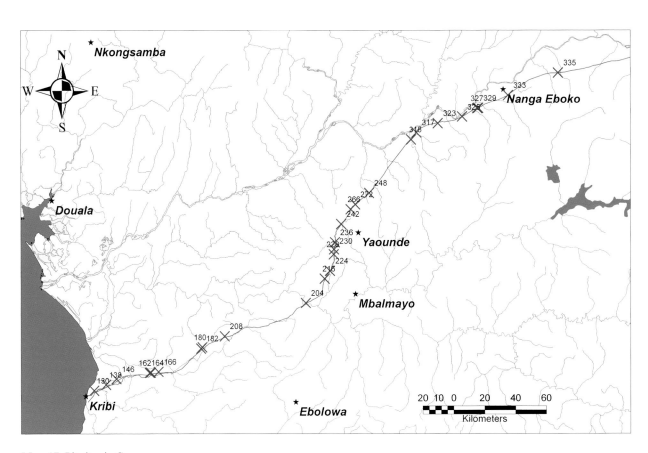

Map 17. Pit sites in Cameroon.

5 – ARCHAEOLOGICAL IMPACT MITIGATION PROCEDURES

Cultural heritage management in Cameroon and Chad

Procedures for the mitigation of the Chad Export Project construction impacts upon cultural resources were developed in accordance with accepted cultural heritage management procedures, and pursuant to the goals of the Project CHM program. The latter included: the protection of the cultural patrimony of Cameroon and Chad, the development of our understanding of Central African prehistory and history, and the training of archaeological personnel and support for archaeological institutions in both host countries. In the context of a relatively unknown archaeological record and significant weaknesses in the CRM/archaeological infrastructure in these two countries, the importance of a holistic consideration of all of these goals was deemed to be extremely important (for further discussion of these issues in an African context, see for example GOODLAND & WEBB 1987; S.K. McINTOSH 1993; MABULLA 2000; MITCHELL 2000; MacEACHERN 2001a). In all of these cases, the authors emphasize the need for an approach to CHM that takes a variety of institutional factors into account, on a continent where archaeological resources are underdeveloped.

In far too many cases, archaeological research on the African continent is still carried out by Europeans and North Americans, with relatively little input or control from the citizens of the countries where such research is carried out. This situation can be traced in large part back to a lack of resources available for the training of students of archaeology, for the control of national cultural heritage and for local programs of archaeological research and analysis carried out in Africa by Africans. These problems are compounded in regions where relatively little is known of the archaeological record in general, because that lack of background information makes it very difficult to both kindle the interest of local and international authorities and deploy available financial and archaeological resources.

Under those circumstances, a conventional North American CHM strategy, with avoidance of all sites as the primary goal of the project, did not appear appropriate to the case at hand. The archaeological survey along the length of the pipeline right-of-way in Cameroon and Chad combined elements of what in North America would be considered Phase I and Phase II, cultural resource identification and evaluation. This combined approach resulted largely from the lack of available data for the construction of predictive models

for site location, and also from difficulties of access to areas of the right-of-way. Sites encountered during the survey were assigned priorities, according to the criteria noted below. As is generally the case during CHM procedures, decisions concerning strategies for dealing with these sites were made based upon a variety of criteria. In the case of the Project CHM program, relevant factors included site priorities/characteristics, Project guidelines (see *Chapter 2*) and the expressed wish of the national governments of Cameroon and Chad for involvement and training of national archaeologists. The Project archaeological program was designed to provide training in CHM procedures and to make possible research in regions unreachable without Project logistical and technical support.

Personnel, organization and logistics

Cameroon

There were significant challenges involved in arriving at an organizational structure that included personnel with expertise in both cultural heritage management and Central African archaeology. The final structure involved Project archaeological staff who worked for the Environmental Management Plan Departments, both in Cameroon (COTCO) and in Chad (EEPCI). The archaeological staff in Cameroon comprised 13 to 17 people at the peak of construction, including the following personnel: (1) one Senior Archaeologist; (2) three experienced Junior Archaeologists; (3) four Assistant Archaeologists; (4) three drivers; and (5) two to six local laborers. All but the Senior Archaeologist (Lavachery) were Cameroonian nationals. The Senior Archaeologist and the three Junior Archaeologists were COTCO contractors, while the Assistant Archaeologists as well as the drivers and the local laborers were sub-contracted workers.

Given the extension of the pipeline right-of-way in Cameroon over almost 900 kilometers, archaeological work was organized around the two main work areas of the pipeline: (1) Spread 1 in the north, from KP 189 (the Chad border at the Mbéré Bridge) to KP 647 (Ewankang); and (2) Spread 2 in the south, from KP 647 (Ewankang) to KP 1069 (the coast at Ebomé). The archaeological staff was divided in three teams: two teams were devoted to surveying and monitoring Spreads 1 and 2 respectively, with the third team being in charge of excavating important sites. An experienced Junior Archaeologist headed each of these teams. Laborers were hired locally to help with the basic earthwork in the field. The Project's EMP Monitoring Supervisor oversaw the CHM program both in the field and in COTCO headquarters in Douala.

Chad

The Project's archaeological staff in Chad comprised seven to nine people at the peak of construction, including the following personnel: (1) one Senior Archaeologist (Tchago); (2) three experienced Junior Archaeologists; (3) one driver; and (4) two to four university students, working part-time. In addition, two expatriate senior archaeologists worked in part-time collaboration with the Chadian team. MacEachern directed the survey program in 1999 and 2000, and acted as an advisor between 2001 and 2005. The COTCO senior archaeologist (Lavachery) oversaw the program in Chad from February to December 2003, and was assigned in Chad from January to July 2004 to manage the archaeology program along with Dr. Tchago. The Senior Archaeologist and the two Junior Archaeologists were EEPCI contractors. The students, as well as the driver and the local laborers, were sub-contracted workers.

Site prioritization and Site Treatment Plans

Site prioritization

The system of site prioritization used by the archaeologists engaged in fieldwork in Chad and Cameroon for the Project was developed in response to two primary considerations: (1) the requirements of the *Environmental Management Plans* for Chad and Cameroon (see *Chapter 2*); and (2) the relatively small amount of background information on archaeological resources available in the region. The prioritization system was thus developed as a planning tool, to allow Project archaeologists (1) to efficiently manage a large and complex sample of different site types, in diverse environments and dating to various periods of prehistory, and (2) to use this information to develop Site Treatment Plans for each site. Central to this planning was the concept of site significance. For the purposes of this CHM project, a significant site is one that yields a quantity and diversity of data in a sufficiently well-preserved context, such that Project construction activities on that site could lead to a substantial negative impact upon the cultural heritage of Chad or Cameroon. CHM efforts were thus directed to mitigating the impact of Project activities upon these significant sites.

For planning purposes, sites located during CHM survey and monitoring activities were categorized as having high, medium or low priorities for future work. High priority sites were defined as archaeologically important sites where mitigation of construction impacts (a) was mandated under existing CEP agreements and procedures and/or (b) would allow for significant data about the cultural heritage of Central Africa to be obtained prior to Project-related disturbances. Thus, for example, pre-existing agreements and other sections of the *Environmental Management Plan* already required protection of modern cultural properties, for example burial sites and modern sacred sites, while the Management Plan mandated four site types (burials, megalithic sites, Early Stone Age and palaeontological sites) as especially significant and of high priority. Further mitigation procedures for high priority sites were warranted and developed according to the Site Treatment Plan that was produced for each site discovered in the course of Project CHM work. A variety of possible mitigation procedures existed for these sites, including site avoidance, site burial, hand clearance, and data recovery through surface collection, excavation and analysis.

Medium priority sites were defined as having the same general characteristics as non-mandated high priority sites, but with less cultural material preserved and/or available for research identified at the time of discovery, thus requiring further assessment. Further monitoring during construction, to ascertain the final site priority/importance, was undertaken for all medium priority sites. Low priority sites — the great majority of sites located during Project CHM research — were defined as sites that did not meet Project criteria for significance, the destruction of which would not constitute a significant loss of data on Central African prehistory. No further treatment was mandated for low priority sites according to the relevant Site Treatment Plans. The prioritization of a site is not a definitive and permanent measure of its scientific importance, but rather a temporary classification regarding potential and further treatment requirements. In this regard, some high priority sites might well be re-evaluated as non-important after further study, while medium and low priority sites could be re-evaluated as important.

The criteria used to define the significance of archaeological sites are both diverse and complex. However, some of the relevant criteria used to decide site significance can be summarized as follows:

(1) *Age of the located materials.* This is a self-explanatory criterion: all other things being equal, the older a site is, the more important it is. Older sites tend to be more rare, and finding one is an opportunity to understand the distant past of a particular region. This is especially the case in an area where the prehistory is not well known, and where early human occupations are not well understood. In this area, Pleistocene-era sites (those of the Early or Middle Stone Age) are often found during major construction projects, because

they tend to be buried or in erosional environments where contextual information is limited.

(2) *Density and/or variety of the finds.* To be considered significant, a site will probably also present a high density and/or variety of artifacts. Isolated finds are very difficult to interpret, since a representative sample of the material is needed in order to be able to understand the activities carried out at the site by prehistoric peoples.

(3) *Context of the finds.* For archaeological materials to be most informative from a scientific viewpoint, they should be as close as possible to a primary context — that is, as the ancient people who produced those materials left them. If natural or cultural processes (erosion, animal burrowing, agricultural disturbance, excavation of borrow pits) have disturbed a site too heavily, the original association and position of artifacts cannot be easily reconstructed. Sites are very frequently discovered as they are unearthed by erosion or digging; archaeological interventions will therefore often focus on the parts of the site that are still relatively undisturbed.

(4) *Social significance of the finds.* Certain kinds of sites (for example, recent tombs or ritual structures) can be of great social and/or ideological significance to local populations. In that case, they will be judged to be significant, and (for the purposes of the Project CHM effort) should not be damaged either by archaeologists or by construction activities unless agreement and proper compensation are negotiated. As noted above, burials were always classified as high priority sites.

(5) *Precursory archaeological knowledge of the area.* Prior archaeological knowledge of the area where a site is found may also be an important criterion in establishing site significance. Medium priority sites could, for example, eventually be re-classified as high priority sites, if no high priority sites are discovered in a region that was previously unexplored.

Site Treatment Plans

Upon the discovery of an archaeological site in the course of Project activities, and depending on its classification as low, medium or high priority, a Site Treatment Plan was prepared and transmitted to the COTCO and EEPCI EMP Departments and to the construction contractors. Site Treatment Plans typically stipulated one of five possible archaeological intervention approaches: (1) no treatment; (2) continued monitoring during construction (grading or trenching operations); (3) avoidance; (4) intentional backfill (of the trench, in sites exposed during trenching operations); and/or (5) data recovery. ***Table 2***

shows the frequencies of this intervention approaches by country and site priority. All Site Treatment Plans for low priority sites (those having no scientific and/or cultural significance) gave clearance for construction to proceed at the location without requiring any further archaeological treatment. All Site Treatment Plans for medium or high priority sites known to extend mostly out of the right-of-way recommended *monitoring during construction*. This required the presence of an archaeologist during or immediately after grading or trenching operations, depending on the construction phase during which the site was first identified.

Avoidance of an archaeological site was usually achieved by narrowing the right-of-way at the specific location. Such an approach was adopted when (1) a site identified during the pre-construction survey and classified as requiring additional investigation (*i.e.*, a high priority site) could not be excavated before pipeline construction needed to commence, or (2) the portion of a high priority site in the right-of-way identified during construction monitoring (especially grading operations) was considered important and therefore needed to be protected. High priority sites identified during trenching operations sometimes were protected from further construction-related impacts by *intentionally back-filling the trench* as soon as possible after the pipeline was installed.

Data recovery involved a controlled excavation at a site. A site's Site Treatment Plan required excavation when (1) the site was accorded high (or in some cases medium) priority for further archaeological work; (2) the site would be severely impacted by pipeline construction activities, with impact on more than 10 % of the site surface; and (3) relocating the construction footprint (on the pipeline right-of-way, access road or well pad, for example) was not possible. The purpose of excavating a site is to collect archaeological data in such a way that further interpretation of the nature of the site is possible after the site has been impacted by construction activities.

Organization of research

A complex CHM program of the sort carried out by the Chad Export Project includes multiple elements, including field components and laboratory analyses. These different activities frequently went on at the same time, with the involvement of different personnel on the archaeological research staff (and, in this case, simultaneously by the different staffs in Cameroon and in Chad). Since such various activities play different roles within a project as a whole, any comprehension of the structure of the overall project requires that they be understood in relationship to one another.

A pre-construction survey was undertaken over the whole area to be impacted by Project construction activities. The goals of this survey included: (1) the discovery of surface and sub-surface sites in the area; (2) the development of predictive models of site distribution in that area; and (3) the prioritization of the sites located. The pre-construction survey involved both surface survey and sub-surface testing. The surface survey consisted of a systematic walkover and inspection of the ground surface of the Project footprint (in 30 m wide transects) by two to six trained archaeologists. Sub-surface testing was done by an auguring program involving two 1–2 m deep cores taken every 200 meters (along the 30 m wide survey transects) with additional testing in areas with significant geographical features (see below). There was no systematic collection of artifacts during the pre-construction survey. However, rare objects were occasionally picked up and recorded for fear of their subsequent disappearance. Otherwise, to the extent feasible, potentially important cultural resources were left in place at significant sites until they could be further evaluated.

The surface survey was carried out along the entire Project footprint in Cameroon and in Chad. However, this technique is not adequate to identify sites when soil surface visibility is low because of vegetation cover or very recent sedimentation. Sub-surface testing is therefore the only practical approach to ameliorate these unfavorable field conditions. The efficiency of sub-surface testing depends to a large extent on the geomorphological conditions in place in particular areas. The parameters influencing the decision to execute additional sub-surface testing are thus (modern) vegetation cover and geomorphology. It should be noted, of course, that environmental conditions have almost certainly changed significantly throughout the history of the region, and thus that modern environmental conditions are not necessarily informative of conditions in the past, especially for sites more than 3000 years old — a period that marks the last major climatic change in this part of Central Africa.

Vegetation cover

Four different vegetational zones were encountered in the OFDA and along the pipeline right-of-way (see *Chapter 3*), and different survey strategies were adopted for each. They included first, *wooded savanna*, where surface visibility for archaeological purposes is optimal after seasonal burning. Since erosion is also prominent, the use of the surface survey approach was considered to be adequate in that zone. In *semi-deciduous forest* and in *mixed forest*, sub-surface testing was necessary in forest and savanna areas during the rainy season.

In the *Atlantic Littoral Forest*, the right-of-way was almost impenetrable in many areas, except along certain tracks, and sub-surface testing was therefore required for the whole zone.

Geomorphology

Within these vegetation zones, specific geomorphological features important to prehistoric peoples and/or to archaeologists are recognized: (1) erosion zones; (2) sedimentation zones; (3) natural resources locations; and (4) natural shelters. Of these, *erosion zones* (for example, rifts, riverbanks, gullies, hillsides, hilltops) often reveal archaeological sites as they are naturally uncovered by rain and wind. Eroded areas were more numerous in the savanna zones, due to a lack of vegetation cover to protect the soil, and were particularly extensive in the Adamawa Plateau. No sub-surface testing was necessary in erosion zones. *Zones of thick and/or recent sedimentation* (for example, alluvial plains, the bottoms of hill slopes, marshes) presenting no erosion processes and/or hospitable landscape features for past populations, were localized along the pipeline right-of-way and were treated as low potential areas for archaeological sites of value. Zones subject to inundation and sedimentation were numerous in southern Cameroon. Sub-surface testing in recent sedimentation zones was of little value, because non-recent archaeological sites are buried too deep below surface to be impacted by grading operations.

Natural resources locations are typically landscapes that allowed easy access to one or several valued resources (for example, wild game, fisheries, fertile soils, grazing areas, valued raw materials) for prehistoric populations. Such locations include rifts, forest/savanna ecotones, permanent watercourses and workable stone outcrops. These specific geomorphologic features may well have been considered hospitable by prehistoric peoples, and thus offer a higher chance to yield archaeological materials. Natural resources locations were investigated with the greatest care and sub-surface testing was increased in such locations. *Natural shelters* are primarily hilltops and rock shelters, which were favored by prehistoric populations for protection from bad weather, for defense against wild animals, for refuge from human enemies, and so on. As stable elements of the landscape, natural shelters attracted prehistoric inhabitants of a given region through time and generally offer high likelihoods of yielding archaeological sites. Rock shelters, presenting a limited protected space, also offer better preservation conditions for artifacts, as well as the opportunity to yield continuous stratigraphic sequences. Natural shelter sites were investigated with the greatest care and sub-surface testing was increased in such locations.

Construction monitoring

Given the frequently difficult field conditions encountered in the Project footprint (*i.e.*, dense vegetation, steep topography and lack of access roads), the pre-construction survey could not be 100 % effective at locating sites. Therefore, construction monitoring was a key component of the Project's CHM program in Cameroon and in Chad. Construction monitoring involved a systematic inspection of earthmoving activities to identify and locate important sites that could not be found during the pre-construction survey and to monitor high and medium priority sites identified during the pre-construction survey. The earthmoving operations watched as part of the construction monitoring effort involved either grading or trenching.

Generally, *grading* operations resulted in the removal of 20 to 50 cm of topsoil. This exposed large surfaces of bare ground ideal for the detection of archaeological sites and artifacts. As a result, buried sites (several hundred to several thousand years old) not revealed by natural erosion were discovered on the graded surfaces or in profiles at the edges of the graded sectors. Archaeological sites were typically left for the Project's archaeologists to study without interference by pipeline construction activities for several weeks.

The pipelines *trenches* were dug to a depth of 2 to 3 m below the graded surface, with a width of 1.5 to 3 m. The same remarks made above for grading operations apply to trenching activities except that the excavation of the trench resulted in a double profile ideal for the detection of archaeological sites (living floors, structures, pits) in the stratigraphy. Moreover, sites buried even deeper in the ground (that is, potentially much older) could be discovered during trenching operations. Since the trench was narrow, impact to exposed sites was minimal. Pipeline construction workers were asked by Project archaeologists to either backfill the trench carefully, so as not to damage a newly discovered site, or to leave the trench open so that the site could be studied.

Excavation methods

Data collection associated with site excavation usually consisted of: (1) auger surveys to determine the vertical and horizontal extent of cultural deposits; (2) the opening of a sufficient number of test pits (depending on the size of the site) to distinguish occupation layers; (3) appropriate excavation of features, including pits, furnaces and tombs; (4) collection of all significant artifacts and soil samples in the excavated area; and (5) completion and curation of field notes, photographs, maps, profiles and so on. Excavation of identified high priority sites that would be impacted by construction activities took place either before, during or after construction, depending on the work phase during which specific sites were discovered (pre-construction survey or construction monitoring) and the urgency of treatment with regard to the construction schedule. Four site types were excavated: (1) pit features; (2) iron-smelting sites; (3) one rock shelter; and (4) open-air sites.

Pit features were among the most frequent types of archaeological features excavated during the Project. They were always excavated as homogeneous stratigraphic units, as it was concluded that, when discarded, the pits were backfilled in a very short time and that all the artifacts contained within are more or less contemporaneous (see *Chapter 8* for further information on this assumption). All the pit features excavated were visible in the trench profile or in the profile of the graded area. The procedures for excavation of pit features were as follows. First, a general map of the site was drawn at a scale of 1:20. The profile of the trench where a pit appeared was cleaned, and the top of the pit was unearthed by opening a unit of 2–4 m² on top of the structure. At that point, horizontal and vertical plans of the feature were drawn at a 1:10 scale. Excavation proceeded in artificial horizontal levels of 20 cm, with all sediments sieved through a 0.5 cm mesh screen. During the course of the excavation, all artifacts, including potsherds, flaked stone and slag, were collected for processing; when present, bone, shell, charcoal and other organic materials were also collected. Soil samples (2–4 kg each) were collected for later flotation, and sediment colors were taken with a Munsell Soil Color Chart. All collected artifacts and samples were labeled according to their location (site, square, depth) and the circumstances of collection.

The excavation of *iron-smelting furnaces* had two primary goals: (1) the dating of the feature(s) by stratigraphy and/or radiocarbon dating; and (2) the arrival at an understanding of how these complex technological features were built and how they functioned. Procedures for the excavation of furnaces were as follows. First, a general map of the site was drawn at a scale of 1:20. The furnaces were then excavated by halves, in order to assess the relation of the feature to the stratigraphy. Excavation proceeded in artificial horizontal levels of 10 cm, with all parts of the furnace (walls, tuyères, slag, and so on) left in place to be photographed and drawn at a scale of 1:10. All sediments were sieved through a 0.5 cm mesh screen, with all artifacts, including potsherds, flaked stone and slag collected for processing. If present, bone, shell, charcoal (for ^{14}C dating), and other organic materials were also collected. Soil samples (2–4 kg each) were collected for later flotation, and sediment colors were taken with a Munsell Soil Color Chart. All collected artifacts and samples were labeled according to their location (site, square, depth) and the circumstances of collection.

Only one *rock shelter* was excavated (see *Chapter 8*). Generally, these sites, being often limited in space and re-occupied through time, can be disturbed horizontally, and thus rock shelter excavation usually focuses on stratigraphy. A general map of the site was drawn at a scale of 1:20, and several 1x1 m squares were selected for excavation to assess the extent of the cultural deposits both vertically and horizontally. Excavation proceeded in artificial horizontal levels of 10 cm until the bedrock was reached, with all sediments sieved through a 0.5 cm mesh screen. All significant features were mapped and photographed. During the course of the excavation, all artifacts, including potsherds, flaked stone and fired rock, were collected for processing, as was bone, shell, charcoal and other organic materials when present. Soil samples (2–4 kg each) were collected for later flotation, and sediment colors were recorded using a Munsell Soil Color Chart. All collected artifacts and samples were labeled according to their location (site, square, depth) and the circumstances of collection.

Contrary to rock shelters, *open-air sites* are most often excavated with a greater emphasis on horizontal exposures. In this regard, the excavations focused on the understanding of ancient patterns of human behavior on the sites, and the objective, beyond dating, was to identify the different features present and the activities carried out by past inhabitants. The procedures used were generally similar to those on the other classes of sites. A general map of the site (1:20 scale) was drawn, and an appropriate percentage of the total surface of the site impacted was chosen for excavation. Excavation proceeded in artificial horizontal levels of 10 cm, and all the sediments were sieved through a 0.5 cm mesh screen. In the course of the excavation, all artifacts, including potsherds, flaked stone and fired rock, were collected for processing. Large artifacts or features were left in place as long as possible (to be drawn and photographed). If present, bone, shell, carbon (for ^{14}C dating), and other organic materials were also collected. Soil samples (2–4 kg each) were collected for later flotation, and sediment colors were recorded using a Munsell Soil Color Chart. All collected artifacts and samples were labeled according to their location (site, square, depth) and the circumstances of collection.

Data analysis

COTCO and EEPCI built fully equipped archaeological laboratories in both Cameroon and Chad. These laboratories were progressively made available to the archaeological communities in Chad and Cameroon as the Project CHM effort was completed. The laboratories comprised: (1) a 'clean' laboratory and office for computer work, mapping, drawing, writing and so on; (2) a 'dirty' laboratory for cleaning, measuring and refitting of artifacts and similar activities; and (3) a temporary storage room for the curation of both unstudied and studied materials.

The analysis of the collected data (both artifacts and related field data) had two objectives: (1) to establish a complete descriptive catalogue of the material collected; and (2) to allow a preliminary interpretation of the data. Analysis thus focused on the description of the artifacts collected (potsherds, lithics, soil and organic samples, and so on) and the interpretation of the sites (stratigraphy, formation processes, behavioral patterning). Artifact processing procedures were as follows. All artifacts collected were labeled with site number, square and feature number, depth (below surface or datum) and an inventory number. Ceramics were washed, labeled, refitted, described and catalogued. Potsherds were washed with clean water and soft brushes, so as not to damage the decoration or remove possible organic or other deposits. All sediments removed from artifacts in the course of washing were kept for flotation. Potsherds were refitted, when possible, with the objective of a better understanding of the shape and decoration of the original ceramics and of the site formation processes that led to the vertical and horizontal distribution of recovered sherds. For all potsherds or a sample of potsherds (depending upon the number collected), the following information was collected when possible: (1) external and internal decoration; (2) morphology; (3) traces of manufacture techniques; (4) vessel dimensions; and (5) organic deposits, where present.

The recording system was designed to be compatible with local ceramic analyses, and cataloguing was done according to established regional standards (BALFET *et al.* 1983; SOPER 1985; RICE 1987; MBIDA 1996; GOSSELAIN 2002). The types of ceramic decoration located in the course of Project research were consistent with previous discoveries in the region for generally similar time periods. These included various combinations of stick-impression and grooving, comb-impression and grooving, appliqué and different forms of rouletting (for some illustrative examples, see *Figures 1–6*). In the Project research area, roulette types commonly encountered included carved wooden roulette, twisted string roulette, knotted strip roulette and wrapped string roulette. The latter includes a flexible core, around which a cord is wrapped, and is either impressed into or rolled across the pot surface.

Data were entered in a numeric format in a standardized database in Microsoft Excel format and will be made available for future analysis. Each potsherd was entered individually in the catalogue, with entries including information on: (1) site number; (2) site name (nearest village); (3) unit from which the material was excavated (square, feature); (4) depth below surface; (5) level (artificial and/or natural); (6) date of discovery; (7) dimensions of the sherd; (8) thickness; (9) part of vessel profile represented; (10) decoration (tool used, technique applied, position on the sherd and vessel); and (11) inventory number.

Lithic artifacts were cleaned with clean water and soft brushes so as not to damage artifact features, including fine retouch, organic deposits and so on. All sediments removed from the artifacts were kept for flotation. Artifacts collected were labeled with the following information: (1) site number; (2) unit from which the material was excavated (square, feature); (3) depth below surface; and (4) inventory number. The following information was collected on all flaked stone artifacts: (1) raw material; (2) artifact type (flake, core, tool, and so on); (3) presence/absence of cortex; (4) type of retouch (for formed tools); and (5) type of debitage (for cores). The artifacts were processed and stored so that a more detailed analysis (*e.g.,* refitting, microwear analysis or identification of starch residues) may be completed on a sample of materials at a later date.

All flaked stone artifacts were sorted, catalogued, and basic qualitative and quantitative analyses were completed, including a description of all formed tools and chipped stone debris. While stone tool typology cannot be overlooked, the emphasis was put on flaking techniques, considered more culturally significant (BORDES 1961; CRABTREE 1975; AMICK & MAULDIN 1989; INIZAN *et al.* 1995; AMBROSE 2002). The stone artifact terminology used was based on both English and French speaking literature (BREZILLON 1968; BRADLEY 1975; LAVACHERY 2001). Cataloguing was done in a system compatible with local archaeological analyses (LAVACHERY 2001). Data were recorded in Excel format in a standardized database system, and will later be made available for further analysis. Each stone artifact, whether tool, core, flake or chunk, was entered individually in the catalogue. Each entry comprised information on: (1) site number; (2) site name (nearest village); (3) unit from which the material was excavated (square, feature); (4) depth below surface; (5) level (artificial and/or natural); (6) date of discovery; (7) artifact category (tool, flake, core, fragment); (8) tool category; (9) core category; (10) flake category; (11) dorsal pattern on flakes; (12) dimensions; (13) raw material; and (14) inventory number.

All charcoal and other samples were catalogued and conserved, in preparation for radiocarbon dating and other forms of analysis. If more than 50 g of charcoal was collected and the occupational context preserved, the

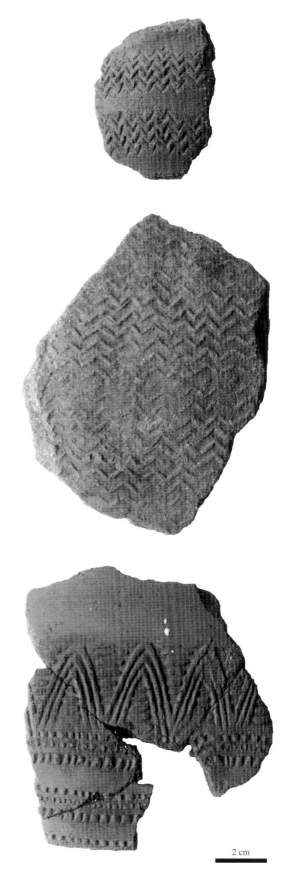

Fig. 1. Examples of carved wooden roulettes, from (top) ECA-199 and (middle and bottom) ECA-243.

Fig. 2. Examples of twisted string roulette, from (left) ETA-97 and (right) ECA-130.

Fig. 3. Examples of knotted strip roulette, from (top and left) ECA-243, and (right) ECA-93.

2 cm

Fig. 4. Example of wrapped string roulette, from ECA-329.

2 cm

Fig. 5. Examples of comb impression, from (left) ECA-199 and (right) ECA-228.

sample was catalogued and conserved for macrobotanical analysis. Flotation was undertaken on each catalogued soil sample or, if a large number were collected, upon a sample of the total collected. The resulting material was dried and conserved for palaeoenvironmental analyses, if warranted, for example, by the age of the site. Slag, iron and furnace material was cleaned (dry), catalogued, weighed, described and conserved. Metallurgical analysis can be completed later in specialized laboratories abroad. Animal (and a very limited amount of human) bone was cleaned, catalogued, described, conserved and, if necessary, radiocarbon dated. Analyses can later be completed by experts in the analysis of bone, such as a physical anthropologist.

2 cm

Fig. 6. Examples of comb-grooving, from (top) ECA-335 and (bottom) ECA-250. The latter also displays stick impression and incision.

6 – Site patterning and site treatment in the Chad Export Project research area

Site designation

A total of 472 archaeological sites were discovered along the pipeline right-of-way in Cameroon and Chad, and in the Oil Field Development Area in Chad, between the beginning of Project CHM work in 1999 and its end in December 2003 (*Maps 2* and *3*). Of these sites, 302 were found in Cameroon and 170 were found in Chad. Given their very different characteristics and contexts of preservation, not all of these sites were deemed to be of equal priority for Project conservation and data recovery efforts. As explained in the last Chapter (in the section 'Site prioritization and Site Treatment Plans'), for the purposes of the Project, a significant site is one that yields a quantity and diversity of data in a sufficiently well-preserved context, such that Project construction activities on that site could lead to a substantial negative impact upon the cultural heritage of Chad or Cameroon. Sites were thus classified during the process of site discovery and appraisal in one of three priority categories, according to both their scientific/cultural value and the degree of potential impact from Project construction activities. This prioritization ultimately led to a determination of site significance for each site, and to the application of mitigation measures on significant sites, as detailed in the Site Treatment Plans. *Table 1* summarizes the number of sites and their prioritization and significance for both Cameroon and Chad.

Approximately two-thirds of the sites identified were classified as low priority for further work (67 % in Cameroon and 58 % in Chad) and, while some of these sites were later upgraded to high priority during the construction monitoring phase, none were eventually to be designated as significant sites. Medium priority sites amounted to about a fifth of the total site number (16 % in Cameroon and 25 % in Chad) and a substantial number of them were ultimately designated as significant sites (26 % in Cameroon and 62 % in Chad). High priority sites represented 17 % of the total number of sites in Cameroon and in Chad. In both countries, the great majority of high priority sites (88 % in Cameroon and 97 % in Chad) were declared of significant cultural value. All sites given medium and high priority for further work were accorded some post-discovery archaeological treatment.

Sites eventually declared significant (after determination of their significance during construction monitoring and/or data recovery) represent 19 % of the total number of sites in Cameroon and 29 % in Chad, showing a substantial difference. The main reason for this difference in significant sites in Cameroon and in Chad can be traced back to the greater proportion of Chadian sites classified as medium priority for further treatment and ultimately designated as significant: 55 % in Chad versus 26 % in Cameroon. This is mainly a reflection of different approaches to classification and/or fieldwork conditions, and primarily a consequence of the two parallel programs being run independently from 1999 to 2003.

Post-discovery site treatments

The 172 medium and high priority sites (36 % of the total number of sites) necessitated 178 post-discovery treatments, such as monitoring during construction, avoidance, intentional backfill of the trench, or data recovery (some sites were given several treatments, for example construction monitoring followed by data recovery, explaining why the total number of site treatments does not equal the total number of sites). A significant number of sites were monitored twice, during both grading and trenching activities, but these treatments were grouped under the generic term *construction monitoring*. *Avoidance* includes narrowing of the right-of-way, as well as rerouting or cancelation of construction work.

Table 2 summarizes site treatments on medium and high priority sites in both Cameroon and Chad. Almost two-thirds of all treatments on medium priority sites were construction monitoring (74 % in Cameroon and 43 % in Chad), while 22 % were excavated (43 % in Chad and only 4 % in Cameroon) or avoided (12 % only in Cameroon). The majority of high priority sites were excavated (data recovery) (55 % in Cameroon and 74 % in Chad) or avoided (21 % in Cameroon and 13 % in Chad). Data recovery was thus the preferred treatment option for high priority sites both in Cameroon and in Chad, with avoidance the most frequent alternative to excavation.

Site types

The 472 archaeological sites identified were grouped into two categories, buried and surface sites, according to the stratigraphic context(s) in which the data were found. The definitions of these site types are fairly obvious: at surface sites, all artifacts and features detected were encountered on the ground surface, while in buried sites at least a part of the inventory of artifacts and features discovered were found beneath the ground surface. These categories were then divided into 11 types, according to the artifacts and/or features present.

Priority	Cameroon				Chad				Total	
	#	%	Sig. #	% Sig.	#	%	Sig. #	% Sig.	#	%
Low	201	67	0	0	99	58	0	0	300	64
Medium	50	16	13	26	42	25	26	62	92	19
High	51	17	41	80	29	17	28	97	80	17
Total	302	100	54	18	170	100	54	32	472	100

Table 1. Site prioritization and significance in Cameroon and Chad (Sig. = significant).

Priority	Treatment	Cameroon		Chad		Total	
		#	%	#	%	#	%
Medium	Data Recovery	2	4	18	43	20	22
	Construction Monitoring	38	74	18	43	56	60
	Trench Backfill	5	10	6	14	11	12
	Avoidance	6	12	0	0	6	7
	Total	51	100	42	100	93	100
High	Data Recovery	31	55	23	74	54	62
	Construction Monitoring	7	13	3	10	10	12
	Trench Backfill	6	11	1	3	7	8
	Avoidance	12	21	4	13	16	18
	Total	56	100	31	300	87	100

Table 2. Site prioritization and treatments in Cameroon and Chad.

SURFACE SITES					BURIED SITES				
	Cameroon		Chad			Cameroon		Chad	
Site type	#	%	#	%	Site type	#	%	#	%
Ceramic scatter	97	50	65	50	Ceramic horizon	56	51	10	26
Diverse scatter	50	26	43	32	Diverse horizon	46	42	18	46
Lithic scatter	24	12	5	4	Lithic horizon	2	2		
Grinding stone/hollow	10	5							
Iron-working scatter	7	4	17	13	Iron-working horizon	5	5	11	28
Modern tomb	3	2	1	1					
Megalith	(2)	1							
Total	**193**	**100**	**131**	**100**	**Total**	**109**	**100**	**39**	**100**

Table 3. Site types in Cameroon and Chad.

They included for surface sites: (1) ceramic scatters (potsherds and, rarely, whole pots); (2) lithic scatters (with items of worked stone and/or production debris); (3) iron-working scatters (containing furnace fragments, tuyères and/or slag); (4) diverse scatters (with multiple artifact classes encountered — potsherds, stone tools, slag and/or other materials); (5) grinding stones and hollows; (6) megaliths (*tazunu* and related sites — see *Chapter 4*); and (7) modern tombs. Buried site types included: (1) ceramic horizons (potsherds); (2) lithic horizons (with items of worked stone and/or production debris); (3) iron-working horizons (containing furnace fragments, tuyères and/or slag); (4) diverse horizons (with multiple artifact classes encountered — potsherds, stone tools, slag and/or other materials).

Table 3 shows the breakdown of all sites in Cameroon and Chad into these site categories and types. Most of the sites discovered in the course of the work in both countries are surface sites (64 % in Cameroon and 77 % in Chad). Among surface sites, the majority are ceramic scatters (50 %) on both sides of the border, followed by diverse artifact scatters (26 % in Cameroon and 32 % in Chad). Buried sites (36 % in Cameroon and 23 % in Chad) exhibit primarily ceramic horizons in Cameroon (51 %), while diverse artifact horizons dominate the category in Chad (46 %). Potsherds are thus by far the most common artifacts found in the Project area. However, iron-working scatters (13 %) and horizons (28 %) are very frequent in Chad, while lithic scatters are more characteristic of the sites located in Cameroon (12 %).

Age distribution of sites

Since no charcoal samples were collected at sites that did not necessitate data recovery (non-significant sites, avoided sites, and so on), the great majority of all sites identified (90 % in Cameroon and Chad) were not subject to absolute dating. Any examination of the distribution of site ages for sites discovered in the process of Project CHM research was thus a somewhat tentative endeavor, especially given the lack of a well-developed regional chronological sequence. The approximate age of the discovered sites can be evaluated by typological comparison of the archaeological material found with materials from sites of known age in Cameroon and neighboring countries, with some corrective furnished by absolute dating on the minority of sites where such techniques were used. Of course, this raises a set of questions very well known in African archaeology, concerning the relationship between artifact typologies, chronological periodization and cultural evolution, and between broadly anglophone and francophone approaches to such periodization (see *Chapter 4*, and see also HOLL 1993; SINCLAIR *et al.* 1993; STAHL 2005). While recognizing the importance of these issues and the necessity of avoiding simplistic categorization, we are of the opinion that the use of the traditional technological/economic age categorizations best allows us to make use of pre-existing research for site evaluation.

Consequently, four broad age categories are used in this report: (1) the Middle and Late Stone Age (with flaked stone tools and production debris the primary archaeological materials recovered from sites); (2) the Neolithic (with polished stone tools and pottery the primary archaeological materials recovered from sites); (3) the Iron Age (with pottery, iron and iron-working products the primary archaeological materials recovered from sites); and (4) the Recent Period (the historical/ colonial period where European goods had appeared on archaeological sites). These categories are technological in nature, given the characteristics of data recovered during Project research activities; they are observations about tool use only and do not necessarily imply the existence of particular economic or social systems in the past. We must also keep in mind the distinction between the use of any finished product (the tools) and the actual mastering of the production techniques (the process by which the tools are made).

Most of the sites discovered in the course of this project were not excavated, and we do not have any certainty about the homogeneity of the assemblages observed on those sites. Moreover, the lack of developed ceramic typologies in these archaeologically mostly unknown regions makes it difficult to determine the age and/or cultural affiliation of any given assemblage on initial examination. There is obviously no clear-cut dividing line between the Iron Age and the historical period, and some of the Iron Age sites are almost certainly less than a century old. A significant number of sites are tentatively dated to the Neolithic/Iron Age period (*ca* 5000 – 1000 bp), usually through a combination of ceramic typology, the presence of lithics (especially ground stone tools), and/or the absence of smithing/smelting debris. Not all Iron Age sites can be expected to yield evidence of iron working, and such sites can be difficult to distinguish from Neolithic ones, especially when a stone industry is present. For this reason, Neolithic and what appear to be early Iron Age period sites are thus grouped together, as are sites from the late Iron Age and the Recent period.

The age distribution of sites discovered in the course of Project CHM work in Chad and Cameroon is given in **Table 4**. Middle/Late Stone Age, Neolithic, Iron Age and Recent occurrences are all represented among the sites discovered by the Project along the pipeline right-of-way in Cameroon, with the expected ratio of ancient and recent sites based on data extrapolated from other regions. However, only Iron Age and Recent occurrences are unquestionably represented among the sites discovered by the Project in Chad. Middle/Late Stone Age or Neolithic sites may be present in the southern part of the pipeline easement in Chad, near the Lim River, but as noted in *Chapter 3*, this is a zone of significant sediment accumulation, and earlier sites may well be buried below the depth of Project construction impacts. It is thus unlikely that any sites discovered in Chad would be more than 3500 years old, even if the local Neolithic and Iron Age is of comparable antiquity to that found in neighboring regions (*cf.* DAVID & VIDAL 1977; DE MARET 1994; MACEACHERN 1996; ZANGATO 1999). Most of the sites discovered during Project CHM activities are probably much more recent, dating to within the last few centuries, if their stratigraphic context is to be taken into account.

	Cameroon		Chad		Total
	#	%	#	%	#
Stone Age	33	11	2	1	35
Neolithic/Iron Age	103	34	26	15	129
Iron Age/Recent	156	52	139	82	295
Indeterminate	10	3	3	2	13
Total	**302**	**100**	**170**	**100**	**472**

Table 4. Assemblage of age distributions in Cameroon and Chad.

These data also suggest that the regions crossed by the pipeline in Cameroon have been inhabited more or less continuously since the Stone Age. The fact that even small and very ancient prehistoric sites have been identified in different areas is also an indication that the methodology implemented for the pre-construction survey and construction monitoring allowed for the discovery of a fairly representative sample of archaeological sites in the areas traversed by the pipeline. The archaeological records of the Chadian segments of the right-of-way and in the OFDA are much more recent, but the results in Cameroon suggest that the difference is genuine and related to local geomorphology, and not a consequence of sampling error or different methodologies.

Geographical distribution of sites

Table 5 indicates the patterning in geographical distributions, excluding sites discovered in the OFDA and along the roads. Archaeological sites were located in almost all areas along the pipeline right-of-way, albeit with substantial differences in site density (see *Chapters 7* and *8*). In general, site densities are highest in the Sudano-Guinean wooded savanna zone found along the northern part of the pipeline right-of-way, in Chad and in northern Cameroon. We can see that site density is about 20 % higher in these wooded savanna zones than in the coastal Atlantic littoral forest, with the site density in the semi-deciduous forest-savanna mosaic and mixed forest zones lying almost exactly between the two. This difference is statistically significant, at the p = 0.05 level. This could be due in large part to the greater visibility of sites in the more open vegetation of the Sudano-Guinean savanna area, especially during the dry season, when compared to the progressively denser vegetation of the semi-deciduous forest-savanna mosaic, mixed forests and Atlantic littoral evergreen forest regions to the south. However, given the generally higher population densities today in the savanna zones

Environment	Right-of-way KM	Site number	Site density (sites/km)
Wooded savanna	495	203	0.41
Semi-deciduous/mixed forest	380	139	0.37
Atlantic littoral forest	194	64	0.33
Total	1069	406	0.38

Table 5. Environmental distribution of sites along the right-of-way in Cameroon and Chad.

(Adamawa [8.8 inhabitants/km²] and North Provinces in Cameroon [13.8 inhabitants/km²], Logone Oriental [16.9 inhabitants/km²] in Chad) compared to the less densely settled forest zones (East [5.3 inhabitants/km³] and South [9.1 inhabitants/km²] provinces in Cameroon) (CHAD EXPORT PROJECT 1999a, 1999b), it is also possible that this site distribution in part reflects past population distributions and land use patterns.

Also notable are a number of regions where site densities are considerably reduced, as for example east of Nanga-Eboko, along the Lom River (KP 666 to 719) and in the Ngoumou–Lolodorf area (KP 904 to 941) in Cameroon. These areas are to be found in Atlantic littoral forest ecozones, but environment types and human population densities do not appear to be consistently different from those found in neighboring areas with considerably higher site densities. Along the pipeline right-of-way in Chad, site density also appears lower than average in the Bebe–Kagopal region (KP 45 to 67). Reasons for this variability are at present unknown, but may well be different for each area: land use preferences (with specific areas considered unsuitable perhaps for agriculture, and thus sparsely inhabited) and/or specific geomorphological contexts (with erosion or sedimentation destroying or burying sites, for example) could explain the lack of archaeological remains in such areas. We will return to these questions in *Chapters 7* and *8*.

7 – Archaeological sites in Chad

Introduction

A total of 170 archaeological sites were discovered in the course of Project CHM fieldwork in southwestern Chad, between 1999 and the end of major Project CHM activities in that country in December 2003. The complete list of sites discovered in Chad over this period, and their basic characteristics, is shown in *Appendix A*, with site treatments in *Appendix B*. Their distribution is shown in *Map 6*, with a distinction made between significant and non-significant sites. These sites were discovered along the 169 km length of the pipeline right-of-way in that country, as well as in the Oil Field Development Area and along local roads on which Project construction activities took place in 2000. Of the 170 sites, 55 were designated as significant, indicating that they contained a quantity and diversity of archaeological materials and data in a sufficiently well-preserved context, such that Project construction activities on that site could lead to a substantial negative impact upon the cultural heritage of Chad (see *Chapter 5*). Most of the remaining sites were ceramic surface scatters, frequently small, almost always undatable and generally uninformative about the country's past. Accordingly, it does not seem useful to describe each site individually. This chapter thus contains two sections: (1) a description of the entire body of archaeological sites discovered in Chad, with emphasis on spatial and chronological distributions and diversity in site characteristics; and (2) more extended descriptions of a number of the sites designated as significant. A consideration of what these sites tell us about the culture history of this part of Central Africa can be found in *Chapter 9*.

Overall distribution of sites in Chad

Unlike Cameroon, where almost all sites were discovered within the Project pipeline right-of-way, sites in Chad were discovered in three spatially distinct localities: (1) within the pipeline right-of-way, during pre-construction survey and construction monitoring; (2) along the roads paralleling the right-of-way, during pre-construction survey before imminent road upgrading in 2000 (MacEachern 2001b); and (3) in the Oil Field Development Area, during pre-construction survey and construction monitoring. Research in the right-of-way and road surveys were quite similar, in that both involved work along extensive linear transects through the same regions of southern Chad. These transects were separated by relatively minor distances, from less than a kilometer to approximately eight kilometers at most. Survey and monitoring procedures in the OFDA

were somewhat different, as these involved (1) pre-construction survey using randomly oriented transects across spatially extensive regions (the three oil field areas — Bolobo, Miandoum and Komé) and (2) periodic construction monitoring over extended periods of time. Indeed, this was the only component of the Project CHM effort still active as of late 2006, as periodic well pad construction monitoring continues to take place.

The spatial patterning of archaeological sites discovered in the Project area, already referred to in Chapter Six, is perhaps the most obvious form of archaeological variability in the region. An examination of *Map 6* indicates that significant variability in site locations along the pipeline right-of-way exists. Thus, for example, there are relatively high linear site densities on both sides of the Lim River, between Kouloulou and Kagopal and between Komé Base Camp and Begada (*ca* 0.90–1.0 sites/km of easement). The concentration of sites along the Lim is reproduced in the pipeline right-of-way and road surveys. There are, in contrast, significantly lower site densities in the area between the Lim River and Gadjibian and between Kagopal and Bolobo (approximately 0.32 and only 0.10 sites/km of easement respectively). These variations may correlate in some cases to environmental differences. Thus, the Lim River sites are all within five kilometers of a rare permanent water source in the area and correspondingly close to relatively rich overbank soils, whereas the zone between Kagopal and Bolobo includes large areas of (a) blackfly-infested open woodland on relatively poor lateritic soils and (b) seasonally inundated swampland. The low densities of modern occupation in this latter area probably testify to its lack of attraction for Iron Age populations.

More generally, when sites are found in the Project area in Chad, they tend to be found in strong local concentrations, even within zones of higher or lower site densities. Therefore there are clusters near the modern communities of Begada, Bolobo, Kagopal, Kouloulou, Begon, Ouli Bangala and Bitoi II, for example. These clusters probably relate to concentrations of human activity, around habitation areas and/or production facilities for example (see below). It is unlikely, given the mobility of pre-colonial settlement in this region (see *Chapter 3*) and the radiocarbon dates derived from a number of these sites, that these prehistoric activities relate directly to the antecedents of the nearby modern communities. However, some habitation sites were occupied within the last few centuries, and their placement may be at least related to environmental and economic potentials very similar to those of today.

There has been a tendency for linear areas on the pipeline right-of-way where few sites were located during the initial pre-construction survey to be somewhat 'filled in' with sites during later construction monitoring and data recovery work (no monitoring was done during road amelioration work after the road survey in 2000). Thus, for example, the initial pre-construction survey and the subsequent road survey (MacEachern 1999, 2001b) located relatively few sites along the pipeline right-of-way between the Cameroonian frontier on the Mbéré River and the Lim River, approximately 40 kilometers away, nor were many sites located in the Oil Field Development Area. Subsequent work has indicated that there are in fact moderate site densities between the Mbéré and the Lim (approximately 0.60 sites/km of easement) as well as in the OFDA. Such increases in the densities of sites detected are to be expected, given continuing work. However, it is to be noted that in no cases these latter increases in site densities do approach the densities in the Kouloulou-Kagopal area.

Spatial and chronological distribution of different site types

Ceramic and diverse artifact scatters and horizons

Sites in the Project area in Chad are distributed unevenly across the landscape, with considerable clusters in some areas and much lower site densities in others. Beyond that overall unevenness in distribution, however, there are very important differences in the characteristics of sites found in this region, and significant patterning in the ways in which sites with particular characteristics are encountered in the landscape and existed through time. The site types encountered in Chad, and the numbers and percentages of sites of each type, are briefly described in *Chapter 6* (*Tab. 3*). Just over three-quarters (131) of the sites in Chad were surface sites, while the rest (39) were buried sites. The great majority of the surface sites (108 sites, 82 %) were scatters, where the artifact samples recovered were either exclusively or primarily potsherds; other materials found on these sites included grindstones and grindstone fragments, iron artifacts and/or iron-working debris, artifacts of colonial or recent European manufacture, and so on. The same pattern is reflected in the buried sites (28 sites, 72 %), where the cultural horizons located yielded either exclusively or predominantly ceramic artifacts. Ninety nine of the 108 surface sites with potsherds (all 65 of the ceramic scatters and 34 of the 43 diverse artifact scatters) were ultimately judged not to be culturally significant: these were almost all small, low-density artifact scatters, most of them less than 10 m². It is likely that most of these sites are the result of human use of landscapes away from habitation sites, through for example pot breakage *en route* to/from or

in the vicinity of water sources or periodic occupation of the temporary shelters that are still a feature of field systems in this area. These scatters were encountered at fairly high frequencies throughout the entire length of the pipeline in Chad, although it is to be noted that clusters exist near the Lim River water crossings, on the right-of-way and at Oulibangala, and in areas near the Cameroon border where the right-of-way crosses active field systems. These small surface sites are very difficult to date with any accuracy, especially given the lack of material for radiocarbon dating and of an established ceramic chronology for the region. The presence of artifacts of European manufacture allows to identify eleven of these sites as recent in date. Many more of them are probably recent as well.

The nine diverse artifact scatters judged to be culturally significant were quite different in character. These sites, consisting of the cluster of Diba I sites (ETA-4/136, ETA-6/135, ETA-138, -139, -140/141), Beboura (ETA-46), Begada (ETA-185) and Woum (ETA-142) were of variable size (from 20x20 m to 1500 linear meters along the right-of-way at Beboura), but were all characterized by (1) a greater variety of artifact classes encountered at the site, including ceramics, grindstones and grindstone fragments, slag and artifacts of European manufacture; and (2) generally higher densities of ceramics than on the ceramic and diverse artifact scatters of lower significance. In general, larger sites were associated with a greater diversity of artifact types encountered. About half (four out of nine) of these sites were encountered during the pre-construction survey, while the other five were found during construction monitoring. Prioritization was accorded to a number of these sites because (1) of surface artifact density and variety, and (2) it was expected that buried cultural materials might be located. Indeed, during data recovery excavations at three of these sites (Beboura [ETA-46] and two of the Diba I sites [ETA-4/136 and ETA-6/135]), substantial cultural deposits, including living floors, were uncovered. This indicates, of course, that the distinction between artifact scatters and artifact horizons may in some cases be a matter of the mode of site evaluation. Radiocarbon dates from two of these sites (Beboura [ETA-46] and Diba I [ETA-6/135]) yielded recent/modern dates (*App. C* and *Fig. 7*). It is likely that these sites represent relatively recent, small-to-medium size habitation sites, as indicated by the artifacts (relatively high ceramic densities and a more diverse artifact suite than on most of the other ceramic/diverse artifact scatters) and the evidence for living floors at the excavated sites.

The 10 ceramic horizons and 18 diverse artifact horizons display enough similarities that they should probably be considered together. The difference is almost certainly one of sampling. Ceramics are the overwhelming artifact

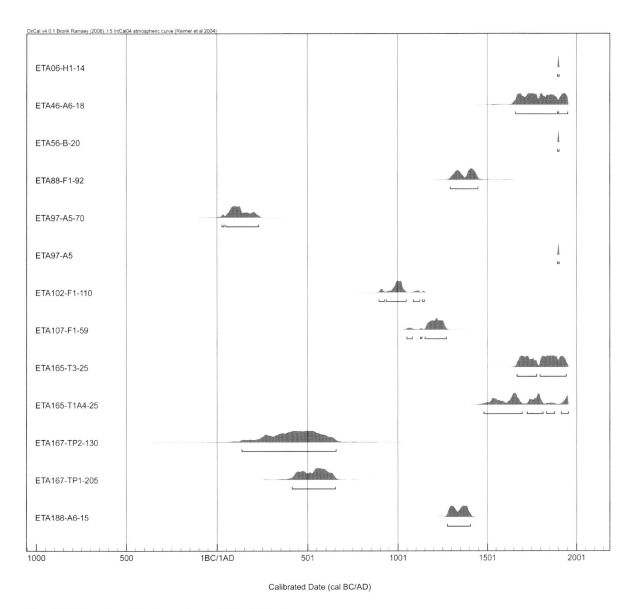

OxCal v4.0.1 Bronk Ramsey (2006); r:5 IntCal04 atmospheric curve (Reimer et al 2004)

Calibrated Date (cal BC/AD)

Fig. 7. Radiocarbon dates for settlement sites in Chad.

category recovered at all of these sites, so the designation of a diverse artifact horizon only depends upon the discovery of other artifact categories besides ceramics. These other artifact categories include grindstones and grindstone fragments (strongly indicating a domestic occupation), other lithics, animal bones and shell (in almost all cases quite fragmented), and slag, furnace wall fragments and other iron-working debris. All of these sites were determined to be culturally significant, and mitigation procedures were undertaken at all of them: for the great majority of sites (26 out of 28), this involved data recovery excavations, while two sites were buried for site protection. Unlike the scatters, most of these sites (19 out of 28) were discovered in the course of construction monitoring. This is not unexpected, as in areas of significant sedimentation and in many cases quite low artifact densities (see below), it is more likely that buried sites will be located during grading

or trenching operations than during surface survey, even with an auger program.

These sites are again quite variable in size. All of those designated as ceramic horizons were rather small, with an average size of approximately 20x20 meters, and most of the diverse artifact horizons were of similar size. The latter category also included, however, six sites (Begon II [ETA-25/128, -127], Mayongo [ETA-97], Ngon Mbang [ETA-165], Karmankass [ETA-167] and Dodang [ETA-188]) where cultural remains extended for several hundreds of meters — for approximately 1000 meters along the pipeline right-of-way at Ngon Mbang, for example. Data recovery at these sites also varied. In some cases, small excavations (2–4 m²) yielded very low artifact densities and shallow stratigraphies, indicating that further data recovery was unnecessary. At Oulibangala (ETA-56), excavations over 450 m² revealed deposits that probably include at least two different occupations, one in the Neolithic and one in Iron Age/recent times, but unfortunately it seems that the material from these occupations was probably subject to significant admixture. Considering all sites, cultural deposits were of highly variable depth, from less than 0.2 m to more than 2 m. The remains of living floors and pits were commonly encountered at these sites. The former were indicated by areas of compacted earth, by artifact concentrations and by rare exposure of features that might be hearths, the latter by changes in color and texture during excavation and through exposure during trenching and grading operations.

These ceramic and diverse artifact scatters and horizons appear to be the remains of low-density habitation sites, probably produced by shifting and/or repeated occupation using a primarily organic architecture in a delimited area, rather than by simultaneous occupation of the whole site area by large communities: the low artifact densities argue against the latter. This interpretation of shifting occupation is also congruent with ethnohistorical data on Sara populations from the late pre-colonial and colonial periods (see *Chapter 3*). The presence of iron-working debris intermixed with habitation remains on these sites has a number of implications. It is quite likely that some forging and repairing of iron tools took place in domestic contexts during the Iron Age in this area. However, furnace wall and tuyère fragments point to the presence of smelting activities, whereas ethnographic and ethnohistorical data indicate that smelting did not often take place in domestic areas in this region, nor indeed in many other areas of Africa (HERBERT 1993; BROWN 1996). Given that occupation on these sites was probably discontinuous in both space and time, it is more likely that these artifacts are the result of iron-smelting activities taking place away from contemporaneous habitation sites, but in areas that would at other times be occupied by such sites.

The depths of cultural deposits on some of these sites indicate continuous or repeated occupation of the same locales over extended periods of time. Radiocarbon dates were obtained for a number of these sites (*App. C* and *Fig. 7*), although most are represented by a single date only. In the two cases where two prehistoric dates were obtained from a single site, Karmankass (ETA-167) and Ngon Mbang (ETA-165), it is interesting to note that the dates substantially overlap. The spread of radiocarbon dates for these ceramic and diverse artifact horizons is quite broad, with the oldest, Mayongo (ETA-97), dated to the first few centuries AD, and the most recent, Ngon Mbang (ETA-165), dating to the late pre-colonial period. Oulibangala (ETA-56) yielded a modern date, but as noted above, this site has probably been subjected to extensive disturbance of deposits. A number of the sites (including Beto [ETA-102], Kaba [ETA-107] and Begon II [ETA-25/127-128]) yielded dates in the period cal AD 950 – 1250, dates corresponding to the period of greatest florescence of iron working in the area (see below), with the Begon II site closely associated with a number of known iron-working sites in the same area.

Iron-working horizons and scatters

The 11 iron-working horizons and 17 iron-working scatters located in Chad display even more patterning, both spatially and chronologically and in terms of their lay-outs, than do the ceramic and diverse artifact horizons and scatters (*Maps 8* and *9*). All iron-working sites found in Chad were discovered during pre-construction survey. All of the iron-working horizons were designated as culturally significant, while none of the iron-working scatters received such a designation. This differentiation is closely related to the presence or absence of coherent iron-smelting furnace remains on the site (see below).

The internal characteristics of these iron-working sites will be discussed first, because of the relevance of these features in deciding site function and patterning. The most common and distinctive of these sites consist of the collapsed/eroded remains of iron-smelting furnaces, with each furnace associated with a distribution of discarded slag (sometimes in heaps) from smelting activities, and in some cases with other artifacts (*Figs. 10, 11, 12, 19*). Seventeen such sites were found, with furnace preservation ranging from very good to very poor. In the best case, half a meter of vertical furnace wall remained standing, while in other cases the furnace walls could be detected only as circles of burned daub associated with slag and charcoal concentrations. Between 1 and 48 such furnaces were found at each site, with the greatest number at the Begon II 'Chef du Village' site (ETA-166). All of the iron-working sites designated as culturally significant yielded fairly coherent furnace remains, and indeed this was the primary factor used to distinguish significant furnace meriting excavation from sites where only scattered fragments of furnace walls, without coherent structures, were found. The latter were not designated as culturally significant, although it is quite possible that sub-surface furnace remains might be found at these sites through excavation.

The 11 slag scatters found ranged from low-density surface scatters to substantial heaps of slag, without any visible furnace remains. It is quite possible that these slag scatters were actually associated with furnace remains destroyed or completely buried, or located off the right-of-way in areas not examined. The slag found on these sites is massive, black and quite dense; it varies in size from small pieces of 1–2 cm in diameter to substantial fragments with the longest axis measuring over 20 cm. Few other artifacts were associated with the iron-working sites, although pottery is occasionally located on these sites (see below on proximity to other sites). The collapsed furnaces that we did locate appear to have been quite substantial; some are over two meters in diameter. Tuyère fragments associated with some of these furnaces suggest that they were forced-draught furnaces (see *Chapter 8*, and also TCHAGO 1994), but the possibility of some tall, natural-draught furnaces cannot be entirely excluded.

Most of these sites are found in a small number of spatially delimited clusters, especially between the villages of Gadjibian and Mbann, between Kouloulou and Kagopal and in the Komé Base Camp – Doba area near the Komé Field. This area covers only about 35 kilometers of the 178 kilometer length of the pipeline right-of-way in Chad, and proportionate distances in the approximately 101 kilometer road survey. The most important exceptions to this concentration of sites along the right-of-way are the two iron-working horizon sites of Maikery (ETA-170) and Miandoum (ETA-178), both deemed significant and discovered within a kilometer of each other during pre-construction survey work in the Oil Field Development Area and thus at a distance of about 10 kilometers from the pipeline right-of-way itself. However, the proximity of those two sites, and of the two non-significant iron-working surface scatters (ETA-59 and -60) located during survey near Bessao (again less than a kilometer apart), reinforces the main point that iron-working sites in Chad tend to be found in proximity to one another. This tendency is far more marked than is the clustering tendency for ceramic and diverse artifact sites noted above. Slag is found more widely at sites, but even slag does not appear along the southern part of the right-of-way, between Mbaisseye and the Cameroonian border on the Mbéré River.

It is difficult to determine the relationships between these iron-working sites and habitation sites, partly because only a small proportion of these sites have been dated. In this context, it is important to differentiate between iron smelting, the production of iron blooms from ore, and smithing, which involves the production of iron tools from the resulting bloom and the maintenance of those tools. These activities are often separated in African societies (see for example HERBERT 1993). Smelting activities will usually be associated with larger production facilities (which might involve larger and/or more numerous furnaces) and larger amounts of by-products, especially slag (see below). The iron-working

sites discovered northeast of Gadjibian (including ETA-68–73) and near Kagopal (ETA-75 and -76) in the course of the road survey in 2000 were relatively isolated from habitation sites, while those found between Kouloulou and Bedia, and in the OFDA, are closer to such habitation sites. All of the furnaces and slag distributions on these iron-working sites appear to be associated with smelting activities. It is not clear that any of these habitation sites are in fact contemporaneous with iron smelting in the same area, especially given the likelihood that local settlements were quite mobile. There is no unequivocal evidence for iron smelting closely associated with settlements. Much more scattered and smaller amounts of slag were found at a number of the ceramic/diverse artifact horizon sites, including Bedia (ETA-36, -121, -119/120), Begon II (ETA-25/128, -126, -127), Dodang (ETA-188), Beboura (ETA-46), and Diba I (ETA-4/136). Five small furnaces were actually found at the Beboura (ETA-46) site in the course of excavations there. It is very likely, however, that these discoveries are the remains of smithing activities rather than smelting.

Further patterning exists. Of the 28 sites, 18 (including ETA-21, -24, -33, -35, -38, -39, -40, -45, -60, -71, -72, and -75) were located in close proximity to the seasonal watercourses that cut the pipeline right-of-way in this area, and most were found on the immediate banks of such watercourses. This was especially characteristic of the sites found in the Gadjibian – Kagopal area. Twelve of these were found on the western side of these watercourses, and in many cases the remains of iron-working activities appear to be distributed along the edges of such seasonal watercourses for considerable distances (often some hundreds of meters) beyond the pipeline right-of-way. Many are quite substantial sites. Their location to the west of seasonal watercourses may be related to the prevalence of West winds through the dry-season smelting period, since these winds would somewhat increase the efficiency of furnace draughts, while trees useful for charcoal production may be more common in the comparatively well-watered area near such watercourses. The areas where these site concentrations are found offer ample supplies of lateritic ore and charcoal for iron processing, but it is unclear whether such resources are more prevalent in these areas than they are elsewhere along the right-of-way.

This geographical patterning in iron-production sites strongly suggests that some community-based specialization for iron working existed in this region, with iron (in the form of smelted blooms or finished tools) being circulated to communities beyond the area of immediate production. If iron was being produced more generally, we would expect to find furnace sites and slag heaps more widely distributed along the pipeline right-of-way and on the roads, especially in the same areas where concentrations of habitation sites were encountered. This would include, for example, some areas between the Mbéré River and Bessao. The few sites found between Bessao and Mbaisseye — for example, small, low-density slag scatters like ETA-59 and -60 — do not constitute any evidence for iron production; they are more likely the results of smithing activities rather than smelting. As noted, further to the south there are no signs of iron working at all. The mechanisms by which iron would have been circulated between communities during the pre-colonial period are at present unknown. In recent times, there do seem to have been certain communities recognized for their iron production, and iron from those localities was sometimes traded over distances of 50–100 kilometers at least, sometimes in the form of standardized ingots designated by some authors as 'money' (RIVALLAIN 1988a, 1988b; TCHAGO 1994: 206–214).

Whether we can use these ethnographic data to interpret exchange mechanisms in the area almost a thousand years ago remains to be seen (see below). However, observations on these iron-working sites in the course of the archaeological survey are compatible to some degree with data derived from ethnohistorical research by Brown and MacEachern during the 1999 survey work (MACEACHERN 1999), and subsequently by Tchago and students. Informants interviewed during that research agreed that such iron-working sites would be located at some distance from settlements and that particular areas would be repeatedly chosen for iron-working activities if conveniently located to settlements and necessary resources. In a gendered division of labor common in sub-Saharan Africa, women had no role in the construction of the furnace (and the tuyères, usually the only ceramic artifacts made by men in these societies) or in the operation of the smelt. The internal patterning of these sites agrees with the memories of informants that furnace remains were paired with very large slag heaps where waste from smelting episodes was discarded. The furnaces themselves are described as *ca* 1.25–1.5 m high, with a single bellows and tuyère assembly forcing air in at the base, an open exhaust at the top and a slag-tapping hole opposite the tuyère assembly. This is generally in agreement with the results of the survey and excavations (see below). Probable tuyère fragments were found on a number of the iron-processing sites. Smelts are said to have lasted a day, with the charcoal – ore mixture being lit early in the morning and the iron bloom extracted late in the afternoon.

Informants gave conflicting information on two significant aspects. Some informants claimed that no special selection for watercourse-margin site locations existed, while others recognized that iron smelting would preferentially take place in such areas. In addition,

some informants said that these furnaces were of single use, broken open at the end of the smelt to recover the iron bloom, while others claim that they were used for multiple smelts within a single season. The substantial nature of these furnaces, and the evidence for layering in furnace walls, may make the latter explanation more plausible. The slag heaps also seem in many cases far too large to derive from single smelting episodes, although they might of course be receiving slag from other furnaces not preserved. It is unclear whether these data conflicts result from changes in iron-working practices between pre-colonial and recent times (especially given the age of some of these sites — see below), from diversity in those practices in the area, from loss of knowledge about the craft after fifty years, or from the paucity of archaeological data on these sites.

The geographical patterning of iron-working sites located in this area is at least matched by their chronological patterning (*App. C* and *Fig. 8*). A total of 17 radiocarbon dates were obtained from furnace features on eight of the iron-working sites in the area. In four cases, multiple dates came from a single site: in two cases (Kolle [ETA-40] and Badila [ETA-173]), this consisted of single dates on two different furnaces at the same site; in one case (Begon II Chef du Village [ETA-166]) two dates on each of the two furnaces excavated were taken; and at one site (Mban I [ETA-69]), three dates were obtained from one furnace, while a single date was gained from another. On the latter site, this was done in order to test an anomalously early (mid-second millennium cal BC) date first obtained from a smelting furnace. This date may be erroneous. Two further samples on the same furnace provided dates in the cal AD 950 – 1200 range, which agrees with the results from a number of other sites.

The concentration of radiocarbon results is quite striking: of the 16 results (*i.e.*, ignoring the anomalously early date from Mban I [ETA-69] Furnace 1) obtained from iron-smelting furnaces on the Chadian sites, 12 yield calibrated dates between AD 900 – 1200, of which 10 fall substantially between cal AD 1000 and cal AD 1200 (*Fig. 8*). Of the other dates, one (from Missi Madji [ETA-164]) falls in the period cal AD 650 – 900, two (from Kolle [ETA-40] and Kagopal [ETA-75]) between cal AD 1200 – 1400, and one (from Furnace 2 at Mban I [ETA-69]) between cal AD 1450 and cal AD 1650. To some degree, this may reflect the relatively large number of dates (seven in total) taken from ETA-69 and ETA-166, but the pattern is reflected at other sites as well. Most of these dates are from the sites found between Gadjibian and Kagopal, but the Bekia site (ETA-175) near Komé Base Camp and Badila (ETA-173) also yielded dates broadly in the cal AD 1000 – 1200 range. The closest dated iron-working site in Cameroon, Djaoro Mbama (ECA-47), belongs to an

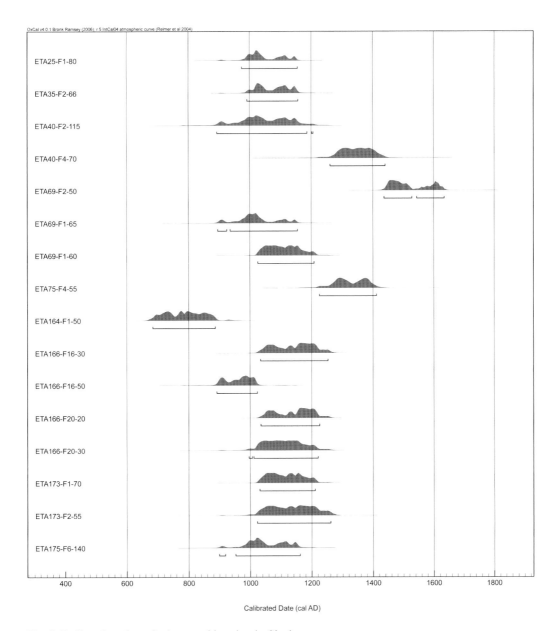

Fig. 8. Radiocarbon dates for iron-working sites in Chad.

entirely different period: five samples from that site cluster closely around the late first millennium BC/beginning of the first millennium AD (see *Chapter 8*).

Of the cases where multiple dates were run on single furnaces, the Mban I (ETA-69) Furnace 1 case has already been mentioned: two of three dates overlap in the cal AD 900 – 1200 period, while the third date was taken from the very base of the furnace. Furnace 2 at the same site dates to cal AD 1430 – 1640, which may be an anomaly or imply multiple uses of the same site. The two furnaces dated at Kolle (ETA-40) give similar results, with Furnace 4 yielding a date which is 100 – 200 years later than that of Furnace 2. There is in principle no reason why a favored site should not be reused in this fashion. Two furnaces from Begon II Chef de Village (ETA-166) were

each dated twice. The Furnace 20 dates were substantially identical in the cal AD 1000 – 1200 period, while the two Furnace 16 date ranges do not overlap — although they do adjoin — at the 2-sigma confidence level. The latter might possibly imply the use of the same furnace over many years, or the introduction of extraneous charcoal into the furnace — hardly a surprising occurrence in an area where iron smelting is taking place.

These radiocarbon results, if broadly representative of the furnace sites discovered during Project activities, imply that a definite peak in iron production activities occurred in this area between 800 and 1000 years ago, with much less activity before that and less iron production again after cal AD 1200. It is to be noted that only one date, from Mban I (ETA-69), could possibly have been derived from iron production after cal AD 1600, given that more recent smelting sites should be more visible if they existed. This restricted period of peak iron production is matched by the restricted geographical patterning of iron-working sites encountered in the course of the survey in Chad (see above). The reasons behind an increase in iron production over this period remain unknown. It is interesting to note, however, that the end of the period of intense production at *ca* cal AD 1200 correlates closely with a dramatic fall in water levels in Lake Chad, from levels considerably higher than those of the present (MALEY 1981; BRUNK & GRONENBORN 2004). Lake Chad is fed in large part by the Chari-Logone river system, and thus reflects hydrographic conditions in this part of the Project area. One possibility, then, is that climate change and attendant loss of wood for charcoal led to a reduction in iron-smelting activities in the area at about cal AD 1200. Undoubtedly, other possible explanations exist.

Lithic scatters

Five small, low-density lithic scatters were found along the pipeline right-of-way in Chad during monitoring activities. None of these sites was greater than 30 m^2 in area, and none was designated as culturally significant. The raw material involved was primarily quartzite, and no diagnostic tools were located. These sites cannot be reliably dated, and are quite uninformative concerning the prehistory of the region. Excavations at Oulibangala (ETA-56) yielded some stone artifacts (TCHAGO 2000), including a number of biface fragments and flakes on quartz and quartzite, along with examples of the grinding tools that make up the dominant lithic category on Iron Age and recent sites. The site yielded a single, modern radiocarbon date. The Oulibangala site appears to contain a genuine pre-Iron Age component, albeit one mixed with later material in the areas excavated. There has not been enough material located to date that assemblage on typological grounds.

Tombs

One modern cemetery with multiple tombs was located near the village of Bedia in the course of the road survey in 2000. It was designated as an archaeological site (ETA-74), because it was not immediately associated with a modern village and because such modern tombs were designated as high priority locations in the Management Plans for Cultural Properties in both Chad and Cameroon (see *Chapter 2*). No CRM activities took place on this site: the position of the tombs was reported, and further negotiation over their location and any possible construction impacts was handled by the Project socioeconomic team.

Description of particular sites

ETA-004/136 — Diba I

ETA-004/136 was discovered during the pre-construction survey of the pipeline right-of-way on April 19, 1999. It is located in a hilly region, some 12 km south of Mbaibokoum and north of the Lim River. It appeared at the time of discovery as a small scatter of potsherds and slag (5x5 m) and was accorded only medium priority for further treatment, but subsequent construction monitoring and excavations in November 2002 revealed a larger site (50x30 m).

The site was test-excavated by Tchago in May 2002; 29 m^2 were opened. The foundations of two houses were excavated: they consisted of two circles of stones of about 3.5 meters in diameter. A collection of pottery, grinding stones and slag was unearthed. In November 2002, during monitoring of the trenching operations, a pit feature was excavated as well. The pottery at this site is decorated with carved wooden roulette -impressions and stick grooving. Some of the vessels were decorated with black and red slips. Local Mbum oral tradition attributes the site to one family that left the village of Diban (the present seat of the canton) in 1929 to found the village of Bimi II at this location. This seems to be confirmed by the excavation, as ETA-04 is a rather large settlement that was inhabited in recent times. The presence of pit features (implying substantial labor investment) suggests long-term settlement, as does the presence of smithing slag.

ETA-006/135 — Diba I

The site was discovered during the pre-construction survey of the pipeline right-of-way on April 19, 1999. Located some 600 meters north of the Lim River, it consists of four house foundations associated with a 50x50 m scatter of potsherds, grinding stones and some tin ware as well. It was accorded medium priority for further treatment. It was excavated by Tchago in May 2002; 25 m^2 were opened. Each foundation had a diameter of about 3 meters; only House 3 was excavated. A sample of charcoal, collected 14 cm below surface in House 3, was radiocarbon dated, giving a modern age (***App. C***).

The artifacts collected in ETA-06 consisted of 34 potsherds, a few granite and gneiss grinding stones, glass beads, one iron spearhead, one piece of traditional iron money (*soula*) and some tin ware. The pottery is decorated with carved wooden roulette, mat impressions and black and red slip. Local Mbum oral tradition attributes the site to one family that left the village of Diban (present seat of the canton) in 1929 to found the village of Bimi

I (the local name of the site). Given the modern age of the dated charcoal sample and the presence of tin ware, ETA-06 does appear to be a sub-recent village. It is also possible that this assemblage and its date result from a disturbance that caused the mixing of the deposits.

ETA-25/128 — Begon II

The site was discovered on April 25, 1999 during pre-construction survey of the pipeline easement. Pottery and slag were found scattered along the right-of-way over a distance of 750 meters, but the site extends laterally over more than 500 meters. The total site surface was evaluated as being approximately 375,000 m². Construction-related impact affected only less than 5 % of the site, which was accorded high priority for further treatment. The site was tested between May 6 and May 15, 2002. In total, 20 m² were excavated. Test excavation I (4x2 m) was installed on the foundation of a circular house. Potsherds, animal bones and shells were unearthed. A charcoal sample collected from the living floor of this house was dated to approximately 1000 bp, or a calibrated age between AD 970 and 1150. For test excavation II (4x2 m) a blacksmith furnace was chosen. Tuyère and furnace wall fragments as well as potsherds were unearthed. During monitoring of the trenching operations, pit features were discovered and excavated on October 26, 2002.

The base of a circular structure of 3 meters in diameter was excavated in Unit 1. The wall was made of mud bricks. The blacksmith furnace is only 40 cm in diameter and 17 cm high. On the surface, 420 potsherds were collected as well as some slag and a grinding stone fragment. The excavation yielded 84 potsherds, shells, fragments of furnaces and slag on the living floor. The pit feature yielded 78 potsherds and shells. Pottery decoration is characterized by stick grooving (42 %) and carved wooden roulette impressions (43 %). Wrapped string roulette (11 %), twisted string roulette (3 %) and cob roulette (1 %) are also present, and one example of a dragged-comb impression was also located. A few potsherds (9 %) were also partially covered with slip.

Oral tradition collected in the neighboring Begon II village attributes the foundation of the settlement to a Laka chief five generations (about 100 – 125 years) ago. However, the archaeological site is obviously much older than that. ETA-25 was an important Iron Age settlement that was inhabited some 900 to 1000 years ago, in the 10th or 11th century AD. The refuse pits as well as the blacksmith furnaces indicate long-term settlement. The presence of shell in the pits is evidence that rivers and lakes were exploited for their wild food resources.

It should be noted that this habitation site was occupied at the same time that iron smelting was taking place in the furnaces of the Begon II Chef de Village (ETA-166) site, located 1.7 kilometers to the south. It is very likely that this is the settlement site associated with that iron-working locality. One version of the local Laka oral tradition says that iron smelting used to take place near ETA-166, on the banks of the Kou-Bendir River. This suggests either that local informants might be correct in identifying the smelting site but are mistaken on its age, or that Laka blacksmiths used the same sites for smelting as their predecessors. This could be confirmed by another version of the oral tradition, which attributes the origins of metallurgy in the region to a mythic "Mbéré" population (although no iron-smelting furnace site was discovered in the Mbéré area).

ETA-35 — Bedia

The site was discovered on April 28, 1999 during pre-construction survey of the pipeline right-of-way. It consists of two iron-smelting furnaces and adjacent slag heaps, distributed over an area of 80x100 m, and is bordered in the east by a small seasonal river called Mann-Liya (*Fig. 9*). Only the base of the furnace walls is preserved (*Figs. 10* and *11*). Other furnaces were spotted outside of the right-of-way, so that the exact size of the site was not known at the time of discovery. Tchago excavated the two furnace features and slag heaps located in the right-of-way from April 28 to May 5, 2002. Further excavations were completed from March 20 to 29, 2003 with the objective of understanding the technology used and the history of the site. The furnaces were excavated to determine how they were built, how they functioned and how old they were. The slag heap was excavated to understand the history of the site, since such mounds may preserve traces of several use episodes and yield other refuse material such as pottery, necessary to understand links with nearby settlements.

A charcoal sample collected at 15 cm below surface in Furnace 2 yielded a calibrated date of AD 980 – 1170 (*App. C*). The substructures of the furnaces were well preserved, since they were buried under the surface. The features all have the characteristics of low-shaft bloomery furnaces. A shallow hole of about 1.5 m in diameter was dug in the ground to a depth of about 0.4 m and then mud walls were mounted to form a chimney around it. Only the lower part of these walls is still present (*Fig. 11*). At the base of the furnace walls a single tuyère, probably activated by bellows, was inserted to provide ventilation. The iron bloom, which formed on top of the slag, was probably recovered at the end of the process by destroying the walls of the furnaces. All the furnace walls

Fig. 9. General view of Bedia (ETA-35).

Fig. 10. Furnace remains at Bedia (ETA-35).

Fig. 11. Furnace 2 at Bedia (ETA-35).

display three to five layers of clay, each of them apparently burned on the inside. This is perhaps an indication that the furnaces were used several times — broken open to retrieve the bloom and then refurbished for another smelting. The large amount of slag next to each furnace also suggests multiple smelting sessions. Altogether, 100 potsherds, as well as slag and tuyère fragments, were also collected in the excavations of Bedia. Pottery decoration was mostly carved wooden roulette impressions (73 %), with some stick impressions (9 %) and grooves (18 %). One potsherd displayed black and red slip.

ETA-35 seems to have been a rather large iron-smelting site that was probably used over the course of several years, sometime during the 11th and 12th centuries AD. The fact that a significant amount of pottery was found on the smelting site suggests that habitation areas were located not far away, perhaps at ETA-36.

ETA-36 — Bedia

The site was discovered during pre-construction survey of the pipeline easement on April 28, 1999. A small surface scatter of slag, potsherds and possible furnace fragments, was spread over a surface area of 4x4 m. It was initially accorded low priority for further work, but was upgraded to high priority during monitoring of the trenching operations in October 2002, when a pit feature was identified in the ditch. Tchago and his team of the Université de N'Djamena excavated the pit feature on October 25, 2002. ETA-36 is a small settlement site. It is located a mere 375 meters northeast of site ETA-35 (above). It is possible that the two sites were part of a single contemporaneous ensemble, dating to the 11th – 12th centuries AD.

ETA-38 (110) — Ouao

The site was identified during pre-construction survey of the pipeline easement on April 28, 1999. It was recorded as an iron-smelting site, as furnace remains and slag were found over a distance of 60 m along the right-of-way. The site was accorded high priority for further work. During the monitoring of the trenching activities on October 21, 2002, a pit feature was identified in the ditch (initially catalogued as ETA-110). Tchago and his team from the Université de N'Djamena excavated the pit feature on October 21, 2002. Pottery and slag were collected in the pit feature.

ETA-38 is apparently an Iron Age village. Pits, furnaces and slag point to long-term settlement. The fact that artifacts indicative of everyday life (pits, pottery) are mixed with artifacts of metallurgy, as well as the absence of slag heaps, suggests that these were the by-products of blacksmith activities and not smelting. ETA-38 is only 500 meters northeast of ETA-37, where other pit features were identified. The two sites could actually be a single, very large village.

ETA-39 — Kolle

The site was discovered during pre-construction survey of the pipeline easement on April 28, 1999. It consisted of the remains of two iron-smelting furnaces, large slag heaps and a few potsherds, scattered over an area of 80x30 m. These features were located along the course of a small seasonal river, the Mann-Deub. The site was accorded high priority for further work, and was excavated for data recovery before impact by construction. Tchago opened 29 m² and unearthed two iron-smelting furnaces. These furnaces are 1.4 m and 1.2 m in external diameter respectively. Two slag heaps of 7.6 m and 6.1 m in diameter were situated close by. Rouletted ceramic was found on the site at its discovery but none was collected during the excavations. ETA-39 is an iron-smelting site of unknown antiquity. The scarcity of potsherds suggests that the site was not located close to a habitation area.

ETA-40 — Kolle

The site was discovered on April 29, 1999 during pre-construction survey of the pipeline right-of-way. Furnace remains and slag were found scattered over a 30x30 m area, along the Mann-Deub seasonal river. The site was accorded high priority for further treatment and was excavated from April 15 to 19, 2002 by Tchago and his team from the Université de N'Djamena. Six iron-smelting furnaces were excavated. The furnaces had diameters of between 1.07 m and 1.83 m, while slag heaps had an average diameter of about 7 m. A few potsherds were collected on the surface, close to the furnaces.

Two charcoal samples from Furnaces 2 and 4 have been radiocarbon dated to 1000 and 620 bp, respectively, which, calibrated at 2 sigma, approximate the period cal AD 890 – 1220 and cal AD 1260 – 1440. The disparity between the two dates can be explained either by a collection error or contamination of either one of the charcoal samples or by an occupation of the site at two different times, whether continuous or periodic. ETA-40 is very similar to ETA-39: it is an iron-smelting site consisting of a battery of furnaces (and associated slag heaps) located close to the banks of a seasonal river. On both sites, very few potsherds were found, suggesting that iron smelting took place at

some distance from any settlement. Located only 216 meters apart along the same river, ETA-40 and -39 could actually be considered as a single large site.

ETA-46 — Beboura

The site was discovered on May 3, 1999 during pre-construction survey of the pipeline easement, 1 km northwest of the village of Beboura. It consists of a very large surface scatter of diverse artifacts such as potsherds and slag, spread along 1500 m of the right-of-way. The site was accorded high priority for further treatment. Tchago and his team of the Université de N'Djamena excavated ETA-46 between April 5 and April 14, 2002. Three test pits were opened on two furnaces (Pits I and II) and one potter's workshop (Pit III), for a total of 68 m². Pit I yielded 145 potsherds as well as a few fragments of tuyères and slag. Five small blacksmith furnaces were unearthed. Pit II yielded 328 potsherds and some slag. Pit III yielded 57 potsherds, a few tuyère fragments and slag. A single blacksmithing furnace was found nearby. The pottery is decorated with stick grooving (44 %), carved wooden roulette impressions (22 %), twisted string roulette (22 %) and wrapped string roulette impressions (11 %). Some vessels display a black and red slip.

A single charcoal sample was dated and a result of 150 bp obtained. This gives a calibrated age of AD 1650 – 1950. ETA-46 appears to be a sub-recent village, probably inhabited sometime between the 17th and 20th centuries AD.

ETA-56 — Oulibangala

The site was identified on June 16, 2000 during pre-construction survey of the Komé–Mbéré road, and lies some 400 m southwest of the Lim River and 600 m east of Oulibangala village. It consists of a scatter of a mix of apparently flaked stone items, pottery, slag and bottle glass. The site also includes a large mound of 90x60 m, some 32 m high, split in the middle by the road. A stone line is visible in the bank that was cut out from the mound by the road. The site was accorded medium priority for further work. Tchago and his assistants conducted a test excavation on the site from October 25 to 30, 2000 (TCHAGO 2000). Tchago established two grids east and west of the N-S oriented road (A and B), respectively of 30x10 m and 15x10 m. Only surface collection of artifacts was undertaken in Area A (300 m²), but excavation took place in Area B (150 m²).

A total of 215 artifacts was collected on the surface in Areas A and B: 141 stone items, 69 potsherds, 2 glass beads, 2 glass bottles and 1 iron barbed harpoon. In Trench B, 378 artifacts were collected: 237 stone items, 139 potsherds, 1 glass bead and 1 piece of traditional iron money. It appears that pottery decoration techniques from the surface collection are quite different from those encountered in the excavation. While pottery collected on the surface displays roulette impression decoration, pottery unearthed in Trench B is mostly decorated with comb stamping. The lithic material collected on the surface and in Trench B appears as a mix of natural rocks and some genuine flaked stone items. A single charcoal sample collected in Trench B was radiocarbon dated, but a modern age (younger than cal AD 1950) was obtained (*App. C*). This is probably the consequence of a mixing of materials from different occupation periods.

ETA-56 was occupied on three distinct occasions: the first may date to the LSA and/or Neolithic (stone tools and comb-decorated pottery in the stratigraphy), the second seems to date to the Iron Age (roulette-decorated pottery on the surface) and the last is recent (glass bottles and pearls on the surface and in the stratigraphy). Unfortunately, this material was mixed subsequent to deposition. It is probable that further excavations would clarify the stratigraphy and chronology of the site.

ETA-69 — Mban I

The site was discovered on June 19, 2000 during pre-construction survey of the Komé–Mbéré road (*Map 8*). It is located between the villages of Mban I (2600 m) and Mban II (600 m), and consists of a group of 5 iron-smelting furnaces on the bank of a seasonal river, the Ko-Kué. The site was accorded medium priority for further study, and was excavated in order to collect material for dating, as well as for the understanding of furnace construction and smelting procedures. Tchago and his assistants of the Université de N'Djamena opened a 2x2 m test pit on each of the furnaces (a total of 20 m²), between October 31 and November 4, 2000.

Furnaces 1–4 had external diameters of approximately 1.5 m. The furnace walls (10–15 cm thick) were constructed around a shallow pit of about 30–40 cm deep. Furnace 5 was much smaller, with an external diameter of 0.75 m, and may have been used by the smelters for the consolidation of the iron bloom. Tuyère fragments indicate that all the furnaces were mechanically ventilated. Each furnace was associated with a slag heap, 6 to 8 m in diameter and from 0.6 to 1.1 m high for smelting Furnaces 1–4 and smaller for Furnace 5. A few potsherds were collected both on the surface and in the stratigraphy.

Four charcoal samples were dated (*App. C, Fig. 8*). Initially an age of 1610 – 1250 cal BC was obtained from Furnace 1, and an age of cal AD 1430 – 1640 was obtained from Furnace 2. Given this discrepancy, and the lack of other evidence for second-millennium BC iron metallurgy in the region, two other samples were taken from Furnace 1 and dated. These yielded calibrated dates of AD 1020 – 1220 and AD 890 – 1160. However, some disagreement concerning the interpretation of these three dates for Furnace 1 remains. Some of the co-authors believe that the earlier date was probably erroneous, given the close agreement of the two subsequent dates and the consistency of the latter with other dates from iron-working sites in the Project area (see above). Other co-authors note that in the past, early dates for iron working have been mistakenly rejected in Africa and that the archaeological context does not allow us to deny the possibility that there was a more ancient occupation of the site by iron workers.

It is not clear whether the discrepancy between the later dates from Furnace 1 and those from Furnace 2 indicate a use of the site at two different time periods, or whether one of the samples (presumably that from Furnace 2) was contaminated. However, the similar situation at Kolle (ETA-40) indicates that the first explanation may be correct. ETA-69 thus appears to be an iron-smelting site that was possibly in use in the second millennium BC and certainly in use in the 11th – 12th and the 15th – 17th centuries AD. Both smelting and the refining of the iron bloom apparently took place on the site, probably using low-shaft bloomery furnaces.

ETA-75 — Kagopal

The site was identified on June 20, 2000 during the pre-construction survey of the Komé–Mbéré road. Four iron-smelting furnaces were discovered on the bank of a small seasonal watercourse, the Man-Kagpal. The site is crossed in the middle by the Kolle–Kagopal road. Only the bases of the furnaces were preserved. The site was accorded high priority for further study and was excavated by Tchago and his team of the Université de N'Djamena between November 5 and 11, 2002 in order to collect dating material as well as data for the understanding of furnace construction and smelting procedures. A 2x2 m test pit was opened on each of the furnaces, with a total of 16 m².

The furnaces had external diameters varying between 1.05 and 1.63 m. Their walls (10–15 cm thick) were constructed around a shallow pit, 30–40 cm deep. Fragments of tuyères indicate that the furnaces were mechanically ventilated. Two slag heaps associated with Furnaces 3 and 4 were identified; they had a diameter of 5 and 8 m respectively and were about 0.6 m high. A total of 21 potsherds was collected both on the surface and in the stratigraphy. Decoration is quite variable: twisted string roulette (29 %) and carved wooden roulette impressions (24 %) are dominant, but stick (19 %) and comb (14 %) grooving as well as wrapped string roulette impressions (14 %) are also present. A charcoal sample collected from Furnace 4 was dated to cal AD 1270 – 1400. ETA-75 is an iron-smelting site with low-shaft bloomery furnace technology, apparently in use in the late 13th or 14th century AD. The presence of wrapped string roulette on pottery is noteworthy.

ETA-85 — Begada

The site was discovered on October 2, 2002 during monitoring of grading operations. It appeared as a layer of pottery, slag, shell and bones, visible in the profiles of the pipeline trench. At the time of discovery, the artifacts were spread over a 25x10 m area. The site was accorded high priority for further work, and a 2x2 m test pit was excavated on October 3 and 4, 2002 by Tchago and his team. Approximately 0.85 kg of pottery was collected.

ETA-85 initially appeared as a rather small Iron Age settlement site, probably quite recent, given the good preservation of bone. Subsequent GIS analysis of site distribution revealed that ETA-85, -87 (Komé Base), -88 (Komé Base), -94 (Komé Base) and -165 (Ngon Mbang), all situated within a distance of 250 meters along the pipeline right-of-way, were probably part of a single large recent settlement complex. Indeed no clear boundary separates these sites. It is not clear, however, whether the site consists of a single long-term settlement or is a palimpsest of several smaller distinct occupations over the last few centuries.

ETA-86 — Komé Base

The site was discovered on October 3, 2002 during monitoring of the grading activities on the pipeline easement. It consists of a buried horizon of potsherds and rocks (35x28 m), and was accorded high priority for further work. A 2x2 m test pit was dug on October 3–4, 2002 by Tchago and his team from the Université de N'Djamena.

ETA-86 is a settlement area, unearthed by grading and trenching operations. Features of stones placed in an orderly manner were interpreted as wedging stones for house pillars. Situated only 585 meters west of ETA-88, it is possible that this site is actually part of the larger ETA-85/-87/-88/-94/-165 settlement complex.

ETA-88 (-94) — Komé Base

The site was discovered on October 3, 2002 during monitoring of the grading activities on the pipeline right-of-way (*Map 6*). It consisted of a small scatter of pottery and stone fragments over a 5x8 m area on the graded surface. The site was accorded high priority for further treatment. The ETA-88 Site Treatment Plan required monitoring of trenching operations. On October 8, 2002, while monitoring was taking place, a pit feature was identified in the ditch (numbered ETA-94 at the time). Immediate rescue excavations were decided upon, and a 2x2 m test pit was opened on October 8–9, 2002 to recover *in situ* data and artifacts.

The pit feature had a depth of 0.94 m and was 1.2 m wide. Most of the vertical extent of the feature had probably already been destroyed by grading operations. Approximately 6.5 kg of pottery was collected in the pit. A single charcoal sample collected at 0.92 m below surface was dated to cal AD 1300 – 1450. ETA-88/-94 is an Iron Age settlement, inhabited during the 14th – 15th centuries AD. Since the site is located only 250 m east of ETA-85, it is likely that the two sites are actually part of a single larger site, along with ETA-165 (only 150 m to the north). It is not clear, however, whether this represents a single settlement or a multi-component site with several occupations.

ETA-97 — Mayongo

The site was discovered on October 11, 2002 during monitoring of the trenching operations, between the towns of Komé and Bebe. Potsherds were noted on the surface in a 580x500 m area, and a living floor yielded pottery and slag at 0.5–0.7 m below surface. The site was accorded high priority for further treatment. About 4.3 % of the site was to be impacted by construction, and data recovery was recommended in the impacted zone. A small rescue excavation took place on October 11 and 12, 2002. Another small excavation (a 4 m² test pit, Trench V) was carried out from March 5 to 19, 2003 under the leadership of Pierre Kinyock (COTCO). Tchago undertook further excavations from October 15 to 25, 2003. In total, four 2x4 m test pits (I, II, III and IV) were opened, following the results of a large auger test program. A very rich occupation layer was identified between 0.2 m and 0.7 m below surface, depending on the location of the test pit.

About 54 kg (2854 sherds) of pottery were collected in the four test pits (*Fig. 12*). Pottery decoration was mainly made by rolled wrapped string roulette (63 %); comb grooving (13 %) and -impressions (9 %). Stick impressions (9 %) and -grooving (6 %) are also present. The importance of wrapped string roulette and

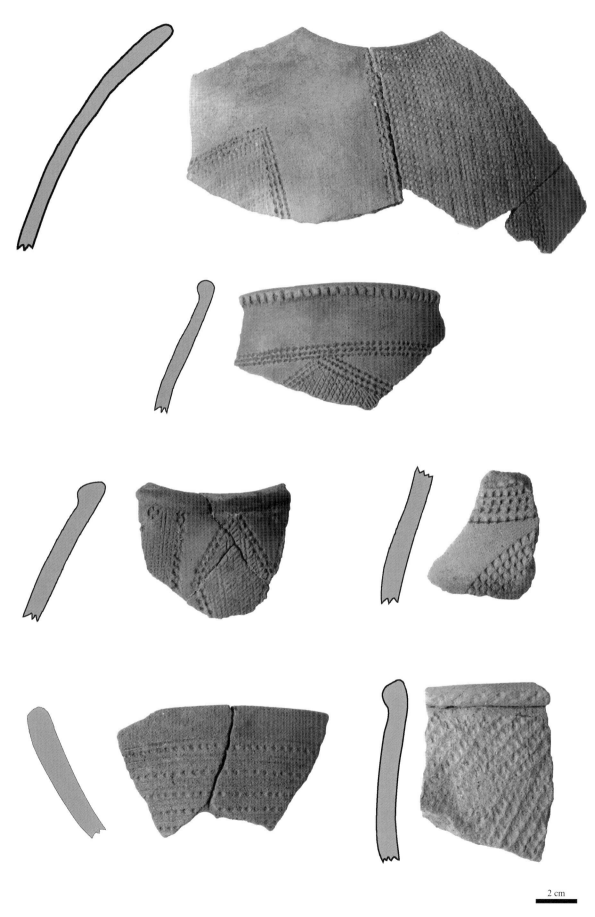

Fig. 12. Ceramics from Mayongo (ETA-97).

2 cm

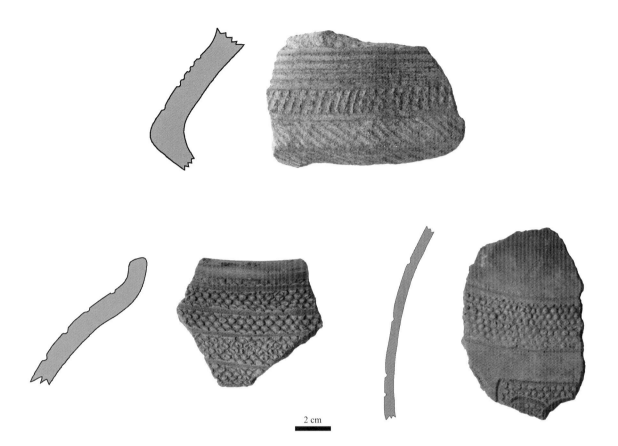

2 cm

Fig. 13. Ceramics from Kaba (ETA-107).

the absence of carved wooden roulette and mat impressions are particularly noteworthy. A single charcoal sample collected in Trench V at 0.7 m below surface, at the base of the occupation layer, yielded a calibrated radiocarbon age of AD 50 – 230. ETA-97 was a large Iron Age settlement inhabited in the early first millennium AD. The sheer amount of pottery recovered from the site suggests a long-term settlement and/or a large population. The presence of a small quantity of slag is evidence of blacksmithing activities.

ETA-102 — Beto

ETA-102 was discovered on October 13, 2002 during monitoring of the trenching activities in the pipeline right-of-way between the towns of Komé and Bebe. Potsherds were noted on a 25x12 m surface on the graded area, and a single pit feature was identified in the trench. The site was classified as high priority for further treatment, and was excavated on the day of its discovery. A 3x2 m test pit was opened and excavated to a depth of 1.3 m in the pit feature. Pottery was collected. A charcoal sample collected in the pit feature, at 1.1 m below surface, was dated to cal AD 960 – 1040.

ETA-102 appears to be a small Iron Age settlement, although a survey of the area outside of the pipeline right-of-way might reveal a much larger site. The site was inhabited in the late 10th or early 11th century AD. The potsherd scatter on the surface of the graded area probably came from the living floor nearby or from the top of the pit cut off by construction.

ETA-107 — Kaba

The site was identified on October 18, 2002 during monitoring of the ditching operations on the pipeline easement, between Bebe and Kagopal. A single pit feature was discovered in the trench profile, and potsherds were scattered on the graded surface over a 7x35 m area. The site was accorded high priority for further treatment, and immediate rescue excavations were conducted on October 20, 2002 under the direction of Tchago. A 2x2 m test pit was opened to excavate the pit feature.

Only potsherds were preserved in the pit feature. Approximately 0.85 kg of pottery (59 potsherds) was collected (***Fig. 13***). Decoration is mostly made by rolled carved wooden roulette impressions (64 %) and stick grooving (22 %). Rolled impressions with wrapped string roulette (7 %) and simple impressions with stick (2 %), comb (2 %) and wrapped string roulette (2 %) are present as well. A charcoal sample collected in the pit feature was dated to cal AD 1160 – 1270. ETA-107 appears to be a small Iron Age settlement, although a study of the area not restricted to the pipeline right-of-way might reveal a larger site. The village was inhabited in the 12th to 13th centuries AD. The potsherd scatter on the surface of the graded area probably came from the living floor nearby or from the top of the pit cut off by construction.

ETA-119/120 — Bedia

The site was discovered on October 21, 2002 during monitoring of the trenching operations in the pipeline right-of-way in the vicinity of the town of Bedia. The site consists of a 27x29 m ceramic horizon exposed on the graded surface, and two pit features observed in the pipeline trench. ETA-119 was accorded high priority for further treatment, and the pit features were excavated by Tchago and his team from the Université de N'Djamena beginning on October 24, 2002. Two 2x2 m test pits were opened. Pottery, slag and grinding stones were unearthed in the pit. The two pit features of ETA-119 are remnants of an Iron Age village of unknown age. The presence of pits (storage and/or discard) and slag (specialized activity), however, suggest substantial settlement and some spatial organization.

ETA-126 — Begon II

This site was discovered on October 25, 2002 during monitoring of the trenching operations in the pipeline easement between the towns of Kouloulou and Gadjibian. The site consists of a small (11x8.5 m) archaeological horizon unearthed by the grading operations, and a pit feature visible in the ditch profile. Potsherds, slag, grinding stones and charcoal were identified. ETA-126 was accorded medium priority for further treatment. The pit feature was excavated on October 26, 2002 with a 2x2 m test pit. Potsherds, slag and grinding stone fragments were collected in the pit feature.

ETA-126 appears to be a small Iron Age habitation of unknown age. However, the presence of the pit feature suggests some long-term settlement. The site is located only 400 meters northeast of ETA-25, where similar pit features and pottery were identified at a distance of 750 m along the pipeline right-of-way. ETA-25 was dated to the 10th or 11th century cal AD. It is highly probable that the two sites are actually part of a single large Iron Age settlement.

ETA-164 — Missi Madji

The site was discovered on December 5, 2002 during pre-construction survey in the OFDA. The site includes three iron-smelting furnaces and two slag mounds, distributed over a 75x25 m area, and was accorded high priority for further work. The Site Treatment Plan recommended that two furnaces be tested to collect dating material, while Furnace 1 and its slag heap were excavated with the objective of understanding the functioning of the furnaces and the history of the site. The excavations lasted from February 27 to March 4, 2002.

The external diameter of the furnace is about 1.55 m, built on a 0.4 m deep pit (***Fig. 14***). The walls are 12 cm thick at the base and include three layers of clay, apparently fired in succession (***Fig. 15***). The wall was opened at ground level to allow the insertion of a tuyère. The slag heap is 5 m wide and 0.45 m deep, showing at least two distinct layers of slag and furnace fragments deposits. Only a few undecorated potsherds were collected at the site. A charcoal sample collected at 0.55 m below surface in Furnace 1 was dated cal AD 685 – 890.

ETA-164 is an iron-smelting site that was probably in use between the late 7th and the late 9th centuries AD, with at least two or three use episodes. The technology in use was a low-shaft bloomery furnace. The scarcity of pottery on the site indicates smelting took place at some distance from any contemporaneous settlement.

ETA-165 — Ngon Mbang

ETA-165 was identified on November 30, 2002 during the pre-construction survey of the pipeline right-of-way. This very large settlement site has features (ceramic scatters, pottery horizons, iron-working furnaces, pit features) spread on a 1000x700 m area. Although likely not very old, the site was accorded high priority for further treatment because of its size and the diversity of archaeological features preserved. Since the site was to be impacted both by the pipeline and the high-tension cable rights-of-way (5 % of its total surface), the Site Treatment Plan recommended data recovery excavations in selected areas.

ETA-165 was excavated from May 15 to 28, 2003 and from February 3 to 12, 2004, under the direction of Tchago. A total of 52 m² was excavated in three selected areas: (1) Trench I: a blacksmithing area; (2) Trench II: a pottery production area; and (3) Trench III: a buried living floor. Artifacts (potsherds, slag, bones, iron objects) were unearthed from the surface to a depth of 0.6 m below surface. The excavation of Trench I yielded the foundation of a square mud-brick house and a small

Fig. 14. Furnace remains at Missi Madji (ETA-164).

Fig. 15. Furnace wall detail at Missi Madji (ETA-164).

blacksmithing furnace (***Fig. 16***). Wall fragments, some slag and three tuyère fragments were collected for metallurgical analyses. Approximately 64 kg of pottery (4260 potsherds) were collected in Trenches I, II and III, as were three iron objects, a single grinding stone and a single glass bead. Approximately 40 kg of sediment samples were collected for laboratory analyses (flotation, plant species identification), while 1.15 kg of charcoal samples were taken for radiocarbon dating and plant species identification, as well as 0.3 kg of animal bones.

Fig. 16. Excavation at forge area at Ngon Mbang (ETA-165).

Two charcoal samples yielded calibrated radiocarbon dates of AD 1660 – 1950 and AD 1500 – 1950 respectively. The village was thus inhabited sometime between the 15th century AD and the present. The site is too recent for the radiocarbon dates to be of much use, but they do confirm local oral tradition which indicated that the site was abandoned some 100 – 150 years ago, in the late 19th or early 20th century. ETA-165 is thus a very large sub-recent village. It was apparently occupied for quite a long time, as the presence of a very rich and varied pottery assemblage, diverse archaeological features (houses, pits, furnaces) and a fairly deep stratigraphy indicate. Taking into account the oral tradition as well as the archaeological data, ETA-165 could have been inhabited between the 17th and the 19th centuries by the ancestors of modern Mbay Doba/Sara populations.

We should note, however, that ETA-165 is situated only 150 m north of ETA-88. In fact, no clear-cut boundary separates the two sites and, on the grounds of distributions of features and artifacts, ETA-88 and -165 have to be considered as a single large site. ETA-88 was, however, dated to the 14th – 15th centuries, 200 – 300 years earlier than the probable age of ETA-165. This indicates that the very large and diffuse artifact scatters typical of the area belong in fact to multi-component sites. These can probably be interpreted as several succeeding villages installed in the same area over the centuries. Establishing a detailed chronology and plan of such huge sites would take very large and time-consuming excavations.

ETA-166 — Begon II (Chef du village)

ETA-166 was discovered during the excavation of ETA-25 at Begon II village (May 6–15, 2002), using information from local informants. The site, located some 1.7 km south of ETA-25, consists of 48 iron-smelting furnaces with bases still intact and spread along the right bank of the river Kou-Begon, over a distance of approximately 1000 m. Other furnaces have been identified on the other bank of the river, but are not considered here. The site was accorded high priority for further work. The Site Treatment Plan recommended that several furnaces should be excavated (with 6 m² opened for each feature) as well as slag mounds (with 2 m² opened for each), with the objective of understanding the functioning of the furnaces and the history of the site (*Fig. 17*).

The excavations, under the direction of Tchago, took place from May 5 to 13, 2003. Two furnaces (F 16 and F20) and a single slag heap were excavated. Seven tuyères were collected for metallurgical analyses. Some pottery was also discovered: 151 potsherds were collected (1.5 kg). Some 20 kilos of sediment samples were collected for flotation analyses. Four charcoal samples from Furnaces 16 and 20 were radiocarbon dated. The dates obtained all cluster between cal AD 950 and 1260. Whereas the two dates for Furnace 20 fall into the same time period, the dates for Furnace 16 do not overlap. This may imply that (1) the oldest sample could be from just under the furnace base, thus dating an older occupation, (2) the furnace could have

Fig. 17. Slag mass at Begon II (ETA-166).

Fig. 18. Gravel pits at Karmankass (ETA-167).

been reused on different occasions, or (3) it could be the consequence of contamination of one of the samples or of the imprecision of the dating method.

ETA-166 is a very large iron-smelting site. It was used, perhaps on several occasions, between the 10th and 13th centuries cal AD. The smelting technology is the low-shaft bloomery furnace. As noted above, this site is contemporaneous with the settlement of site ETA-25, located some 1.7 km to the north. Laka oral tradition also specifies that their ancestors occupied the two sites. While it is improbable that oral tradition accurately reflects events

more than two or three centuries old, it is possible that Laka smelters re-occupied their predecessors living and smelting sites, thus symbolically appropriating the power of the fabled 'Mbéré' metallurgists. More extensive excavations of the sites are necessary to verify this hypothesis.

ETA-167 — Karmankass

The site was discovered during pre-construction survey of a gravel borrow pit area on February 5, 2003 (***Fig. 18***). It is situated close to the Banoundji River, a tributary of the

Fig. 19. Stratigraphy at Karmankass (ETA-167).

to 2.5 m and unearthing archaeological material (*Fig. 18*). The site was therefore significantly disturbed before Project archaeologists arrived.

The importance of the site necessitated three treatments in the Site Treatment Plan: partial site avoidance, data recovery and monitoring. Before any other intervention, two areas were delimited for protection. Those two areas correspond to zones where the local population stockpiled the gravel heaps they intended to sell to the Project. As such, these areas were not used for quarrying, and archaeological remains are probably still preserved. This is why Project archaeologists marked off these zones for protection. Two activities, quarrying on the site and screening of materials at the Komé 5 camp, were also monitored. Monitoring of gravel quarrying on site by the Project sub-contractor allowed the archaeologists to delimit the extent of the site and to stop work if exceptional features were discovered. Occasional monitoring of gravel screening at Komé 5 (dry screening through a 2.5 cm mesh) allowed for the recovery of the largest artifacts lost during quarrying.

Logone River, in a valley stretching between the villages of Bemboura and Beladjia. It consists of several archaeological layers yielding potsherds and stone tools, buried in sands and gravel that form a low hill (approximately 200x300 m in extent). The hill is the result of the Logone and its tributaries depositing gravel in a meander, probably during the transition between wet and dry climatic phases during which the level of Lake Chad changed. There have been four such major transgressions since the late Pleistocene, of which the first began at approximately 50,000 bp. Successive deposition of gravel and sand led to the creation of this mound at the time Lake Chad was low again and the river receded. The archaeological material, being very fragile and only slightly eroded, cannot have the same origin as the gravel. Large cobbles of workable raw material are rare in the region, and thus this gravel mound would have been exploited by prehistoric populations through time as a quarry and/or workshop, from temporary settlements close by. People from nearby modern settlements (Bemboura, Beladjia, Dandili I and II, Karmankass) have exploited the site for gravel for several years, digging dozens of pits to a depth of 1.8

Three 2x2 m test pits were excavated under the direction of Lavachery and Tchago from April 16 to 29, 2003. Excavations took place to a depth of 2.5–3 meters, depending on the location of the archaeological horizons and safety considerations, with the aim of understanding the context and the spatial organization of the archaeological artifacts in relation to site formation processes. The larger gravel being deposited upriver to the west, it was expected that artifact density might vary horizontally as well as vertically throughout the site.

The stratigraphy of the three test pits is approximately the same from top to bottom: (1) a level of clay (0 to 0.2 m deep); (2) a level of sands interstratified with fine gravel layers (approximately 0.2 m to 1–2 m deep); and (3) a level of gravel (approximately 1–2 to 2.5–3 m). Generally speaking, the gravel layer is the thickest and closest to the surface in test pits II and III (closer to the river). This can be explained by the specific site formation processes. The river branch to the northwest deposits gravel first, then sand, and finally clay, with the lighter material being deposited later than heavier material (*Figs. 19* and *20*).

Fig. 20. Excavation at Karmankass (ETA-167).

Gravel exploitation was stopped by the Project EMP Department until representatives of the Ministry of Culture visited the site to take the necessary steps to officially declare the site part of the cultural patrimony of Chad, and protect it. According to the Site Treatment Plan, two delimited zones of approximately 20,000 m² and 10,000 m² were designated for protection. On April 25–26, 2003, Dr. Tchago Bouimon and the Director of National Heritage (Ministry of Culture) decided to abandon Protected Zone 1 (which was almost sterile) but to extend Protected Zone 2. Between April 3 and May 5, 2003, mechanical trenches in disturbed zones at the edges of the mound, as well as monitoring of sediment screening in Komé 5, allowed the discovery of more potsherds and stone artifacts. This sample, however, was collected without controlled archaeological context.

The only archaeological materials unearthed in ETA-167 are potsherds and flaked chert artifacts. It is important to note that, while the natural gravel present in the stratigraphy is completely rounded by erosion, the artifacts are not. Potsherds are only moderately rounded, with decorations still identifiable (*Fig. 21*), while stone tools, flakes and cores are clearly much less eroded than the gravel on which they are flaked.

Only 5.7 kg (380 potsherds) of pottery were collected in the three test pits excavated. The density of potsherds is not very high, which is not surprising for an open-air site. This density, however, varies both horizontally and vertically. While pottery density is rather low (635 grams) and uniformly spread vertically from 0.4 to 2.2 m below surface in Test Pit I (southeast, farthest from the river), it is richer (850 grams) and clustered between 1 m and 1.4 m below surface in Test Pit II (middle). Test Pit III (northwest, closest to the river) yielded a very rich collection of pottery (4.2 kg), most of it (88 %) clustered between 1.2 and 1.8 m below surface. Only 1.7 kg of lithic material was unearthed: 952 grams in Test Pit I, 336 grams in Test Pit II, and 439 grams in Test Pit III. Lithic artifacts display more or less the same vertical distribution as the pottery. Slight variations in the horizontal distribution can be explained by the paucity of the lithic items. 77 kilos of sediment samples were also collected for flotation.

This allows two remarks to be made: (1) the richest archaeological layer by far is located between 1 m and 1.6 m below surface in Test Pits II and III, and to a lesser extent this is confirmed in Test Pit I; and (2) the archaeological material is much richer to the

Fig. 21. Ceramics from Karmankass (ETA-167).

northeast of the mound, closer to the river (Test Pit III) than to the southwest (Test pit I), further from the river. Pottery decoration is quite varied: the dominant technique is rolled impression with wrapped string roulette (27 %), but grooves made with comb (20 %) or sticks (20 %) are also frequent. Carved wooden roulette (13 %) and twisted string roulette (13 %) impressions are present as well. Comb is also used for simple impressions (7 %).

Two charcoal samples were dated. One was collected in Test Pit II at 1.3 m below surface, and yielded a calibrated date of AD 130 – 670 — not at all a precise date. The second sample, collected at 2.05 m below surface in Test Pit I, gave a calibrated age of AD 410 – 660. The question whether the artifacts are in primary context or not is fundamental. Is the site a settlement or a quarrying site, or is it simply a natural accumulation of gravel and cultural artifacts eroded out from the banks upstream? The fact that artifacts are much less eroded than the gravel, and that the gravel was used as raw material for the stone tools, implies that the distribution of archaeological material is due to human intervention, and one may assume that it is in a primary context or that it only moved short distances. This suggests that the charcoal dates probably reflect the actual date of habitation/exploitation of the site. The spatial distribution of the potsherds and stone tools suggests (1) that the site was visited on several occasions during the first half of the first millennium AD, but that its main period of use was probably between the 4th – 6th centuries, (2) that the site was occupied for gravel exploitation but people also lived on the mound for undetermined periods, and (3) that the settlement area was situated to the northwest, on the richest gravel zone and closest to the river.

ETA-170 — Maikery

The site was identified on February 14, 2003 during pre-construction survey in the OFDA, and comprises two iron-smelting furnaces and two slag heaps in a 25x15 m area. The site was accorded medium priority for further work, and the Site Treatment Plan recommended limited excavations to allow further assessment of site importance. One furnace and one slag heap were excavated under the direction of Lavachery and Tchago from February 23 to 27, 2003. The furnaces in ETA-170 were completely destroyed through natural processes, and no precise data on their dimensions and shape could be recovered. No pottery was discovered on the site. ETA-170 is an iron-smelting site of unknown age. No trace of habitation was identified on the site.

ETA-173 — Badila

ETA-173 was discovered on October 9, 2001 during pre-construction survey of the pipeline easement. It consists of a single iron-smelting furnace, located some 6 km south of Badila village, and was accorded high priority for further work. The site was excavated from October 9 to 16, 2001 by a team from the Université de N'Djamena, led by Tchago.

The furnace had an external diameter of 1.2 m. A slag heap (2.8 m in diameter) was situated less than 2 m south of the furnace. No pottery was identified. While local Ngambaye oral tradition attributes an age of a few centuries to the site, two charcoal samples collected in the furnace yielded calibrated dates of AD 1030 – 1230 and AD 1010 – 1270. ETA-175 was thus an iron-smelting site, exploited in the 11th – 13th centuries AD. It was apparently situated at some distance from any settlement.

ETA-175 — Bekia

ETA-175 was identified on April 6, 2003 during pre-construction survey of the OFDA, near Komé. The site comprises a group of ten iron-smelting furnaces (F1 to F10) and two slag heaps, dispersed over a 450x80 m area. It is located some 30 m southeast of a seasonal branch of the Nya River and 800 m south of the village of Bekia. The site was accorded high priority for further treatment.

Two furnaces (F5 and F6) that were located on the right-of-way of the flow-line to be constructed were excavated between June 14 and 21, 2003 under the direction of Tchago. The other furnaces were listed in the Chadian Cultural Heritage Register for protection. Besides the iron-smelting features (furnaces and slag), a small amount (0.15 kg) of pottery was collected. A charcoal sample collected in Furnace F6 was radiocarbon dated, yielding a calibrated date of AD 970 – 1160. ETA-75 is thus a rather large iron-smelting site, in use between the late 10th and the first half of the 12th century AD. Smelting took place at some distance from any contemporaneous habitation site.

ETA-178 — Miandoum

The site was discovered on June 21, 2003 during pre-construction survey of the OFDA, and is a large (250x500 m) iron-working area where smelting furnaces remains and slag were identified. Only one furnace

Fig. 22. Furnace 1 at Miandoum (ETA-178).

stood in the area to be impacted by construction. The site was accorded high priority for further work. The iron-smelting furnace, the only archaeological feature in the right-of-way, was excavated on July 24, 2003 (***Fig. 22***). It presented the usual technical characteristics of a low-shaft bloomery furnace: the base of a wall built around a shallow pit, tuyère fragments, and an associated slag heap. ETA-178 is an iron-smelting site of unknown age.

ETA-188 — Dodang

ETA-188 was discovered on July 27, 2003 during pre-construction survey of the OFDA. Pottery and slag were identified scattered over a large (500x300 m) area on the north bank of the Loule River. Buried artifacts were observed in erosion gullies, suggesting some antiquity for the site. Local informants confirmed that the village was abandoned some 30 years ago but that buried potsherds were there before they settled the place. Dodang is the name of the founder of the latest village.

The site was accorded high priority for further work. Since no avoidance was possible, excavations for data recovery took place between August 5 and 13, 2003 under the direction of Tchago. Three test pits, with a total area of 14 m², were opened on the flow-line right-of-way. Their location was determined after a systematic auger testing program that covered the entire right-of-way of the flow-line. Test Pits I (2x1 m), II (2x2 m) and III (2x4 m) were excavated to a depth of 0.4 m below surface. The pottery horizon laid between 0.1 m and 0.3 m below ground level. Only pottery was collected: (1) Test Pit I yielded 168 potsherds (plus 21 potsherds on the surface); (2) Test Pit II yielded 375 potsherds; and (3) Test Pit III was sterile (plus 42 potsherds on the surface). Decoration techniques are very rich and varied (***Figs. 23*** and ***24***): the most frequent technique is comb grooving (28 %), followed by carved wooden roulette (18 %) and twisted string roulette (15 %) impressions. Stick grooving is also common (15 %), as are simple impressions made with wrapped string roulette (12.5 %) and comb (7.5 %). Some rare rocking-comb impressions (2.5 %) and appliqué (2.5 %) are also present.

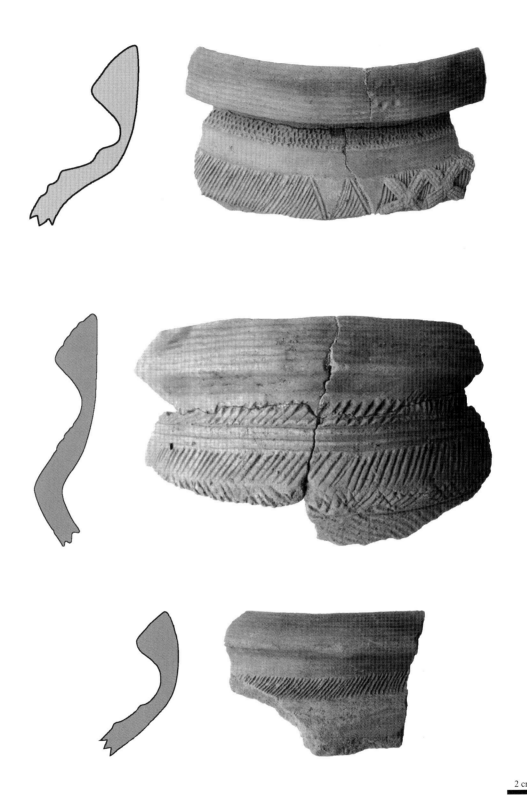

Fig. 23. Ceramics from Dodang (ETA-188).

A single charcoal sample, collected at 15 cm below surface in Test Pit II, was radiocarbon dated, and a calibrated age of AD 1280 – 1420 was obtained.

ETA-188 appears to have been a large Iron Age settlement, inhabited sometime between the 13th and 15th centuries AD.

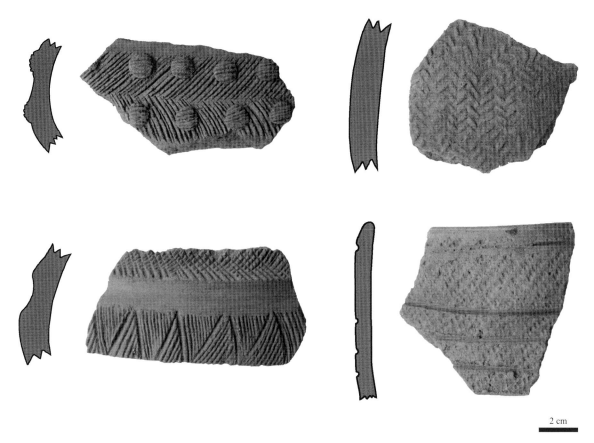

2 cm

Fig. 24. Ceramics from Dodang (ETA-188).

Culture history — Chad

MSA/LSA/Neolithic

As noted above, there is very little evidence for human occupation along the right-of-way in Chad during the Middle Stone Age, Late Stone Age or Neolithic periods. What evidence does exist — five small surface scatters and one disturbed multi-component site (Oulibangala [ETA-56]) — is rather uninformative. It is likely that the prevalence of sediment accumulation through most of this zone has resulted in the burial of most pre-Iron Age cultural occurrences. However, the limited data available do indicate that the region was occupied at least sporadically during the late Pleistocene and early-/ mid-Holocene. It remains for archaeologists to locate undisturbed sites that will yield more information about those occupations.

Iron Age

The data on Iron Age occupations in this region are primarily data on iron-working activities. This is natural, given the rather striking nature of the iron-working

remains, but it does mean that we have rather less information on the characteristics of contemporaneous habitation sites. This renders the recognition of cultural phases within the Iron Age of southwestern Chad more difficult, and also makes comparison with surrounding areas somewhat more challenging. This issue is complicated by the difficulties of accurately dating large, diffuse habitation areas, possibly the scenes of multiple settlement episodes, with just one or two radiocarbon dates.

These challenges can be appreciated when we look at the ceramic variability along the right-of-way. The within-site diversity in ceramic decoration techniques — stick grooving, comb dragging and impression, use of carved wooden and various kinds of fiber roulettes, mat impression — is substantial across this sample, as is the continuity in the use of these techniques. The most significant change in decoration techniques through time is visible in mat impressions, which are not found on the earliest sites in the sample (Mayongo [ETA-97] and Karmankass [ETA-167]), while carved wooden roulettes were used through most of the settlement sequence except at the earliest site, Mayongo. Spatially, some interesting patterns do exist (see below), although further work will be required to comprehensively examine the extent and nature of changes in ceramic decorations and morphologies through space and time.

The earliest substantial evidence for occupation along the right-of-way in Chad dates to the early part of the first millennium AD, at Mayongo and Karmankass. These appear to be large settlement sites, probably occupied by sedentary farmers. The depositional context at Karmankass, with potsherds and lithics found along a gravel meander near the Banoundji River, is somewhat different from that at other sites in the region, but the artifacts do not appear to have been extensively reworked or moved and are probably in or close to primary context. There is evidence for iron working (but not smelting) at Mayongo, but not at Karmankass; conversely, unstandardized stone tools are found at the latter site but not at the former.

The first direct evidence for iron smelting in the region dates from the late first millennium AD, at the Missi Madji (ETA-164) site, where a shaft furnace with a single tuyère was used to produce the bloom mass. It is not clear whether the furnace used a force draft (with bellows) or induced draft (with a chimney). No decorated pottery was recovered from the excavation, and the cultural affiliation of the iron workers remains unclear. There was a significant increase in metallurgical activity in this region one or two centuries after the Missi Madji furnace was in use. Twelve dates from iron-working furnace sites (ETA -25, -35, -40, -69, -166, -173, -175) are grouped in the period between cal AD 900 and cal AD 1200, as are two dates from settlement sites, Beto (ETA-102) and Kaba (ETA-107). These furnaces seem to be of identical technical tradition as that found at the earlier site of Missi Madji.

Iron production seems to be demarcated spatially as well as temporally, with smelting sites concentrated in a small number of clusters, especially between the villages of Gadjibian and Mbann, between Kouloulou and Kagopal and in the Komé Base Camp – Doba area. In other areas — for example along the southern extremity of the right-of-way in Chad, between Mbaisseye and the Mbéré River — there is no substantial evidence for iron working at all. This and the size of iron-production sites in the clusters indicate the existence of exchange networks, by which producer villages provided iron (in the form of ingots or finished tools) to non-producer communities, in exchange for goods or services at present unknown. As noted above, there are also common elements in ceramic decoration through much of this area, with carved

wooden rouletting, comb-impression and -dragging found along most of the linear length of the right-of-way. However, the wrapped string roulette technique is only found between Komé and Gadjibian, which generally corresponds to the area where iron smelting took place. Mat impression is somewhat more widespread but, like the evidence for iron production and slag, is not found in the southern extremity of the right-of-way, between Mbaissaye and the Cameroon border. The patterns were found on both the settlement and the iron-working sites, suggesting that they belong to the same cultural grouping, which was particularly dynamic in the 10th – 13th centuries AD.

A succeeding phase of occupation is illustrated by four dates, falling between cal AD 1200 and cal AD 1400. Those are associated two settlement (Komé [ETA-88] and Dodang [ETA-188]) and two iron-working sites (Kolle [ETA-40] and Kagopal [ETA-75]). Kagopal ceramics show the same decorative techniques as were in use in the preceding period. However, decoration on pottery from the contemporaneous Dodang site seems somewhat different, with comb tracing as the dominant technique and mat impression unknown. These differences could be due to the relatively small samples of pottery taken from sites like Kagopal, or they might indicate the presence of two distinct social groupings in the region. Blacksmithing seems to have taken place fairly widely along the right-of-way, but the iron-smelting furnaces were found in the Kolle–Kagopal area, indicating that these sites might be a development of the vibrant iron-working tradition of the 9th – 12th centuries AD.

Three dates falling within the last 400 years are derived from recent sites: Ngon Mbang (ETA-165) and Beboura (ETA-46). These sites appear in local Sara oral tradition, and they seem to be related to the modern local occupations. Ceramics from these sites are decorated with carved wooden and wrapped cord rouletting, mat impression and the use of black and red slips, again indicating continuity from earlier times. Sara oral traditions also confirm that iron smelting continued to take place through this period. The 15th – 17th century AD date from Mban I (ETA-69) Furnace 2 is the most recent dated episode of iron smelting in the Project research zone, but of course this took place at a site where iron working was already practiced 800 – 1000 years ago. This demonstrates how such workshops were used on different occasions through time, and also reinforces the view that there has been a significant degree of cultural continuity in the area over the last millennium at least.

8 – Archaeological sites in Cameroon

Introduction

A total of 302 archaeological sites were discovered in the course of Project CHM fieldwork in Cameroon, between 2000 and the end of major Project CHM field activities in that country in late 2003. The complete list of the sites discovered in Cameroon over this period, and their basic characteristics, is shown in *Appendix D* and site treatments in *Appendix E*. Site distributions are shown in *Maps 10* and *11*, with a distinction made between sites determined to be culturally significant and those not so determined. Site types are indicated in *Maps 12* and *13*. All of these sites were discovered along the 894-kilometer length of the pipeline right-of-way in Cameroon. No road survey was done in the country, and no sites were discovered in the course of research by the authors in other areas of Project construction. However, cultural remains on a number of sites were located in the course of preliminary survey work undertaken in 2000 (Oslisly, Tueche *et al.* 2000). Those sites, ECA-409 to ECA-413, are included in this listing and analysis. Of the 302 sites, 54 (19 %) were ultimately designated as being culturally significant, indicating that they contained a quantity and diversity of archaeological materials and data in a sufficiently well-preserved context, such that Project construction activities on those sites could lead to a substantial negative impact upon the cultural heritage of Cameroon (see *Chapter 5*). As in Chad, most of the remaining sites found were small surface scatters, dominated by ceramics but in many cases also yielding other materials like slag, and generally in any single case relatively uninformative about the country's past. This chapter will thus be divided in the same way as *Chapter 7*, with some changes given the length of the pipeline right-of-way in Cameroon. It contains two primary sections: (1) a description of the entire body of archaeological sites discovered in Cameroon, but divided to cover the northern and southern extents of the right-of-way (with the division at KP 647 — Ewankang [ECA-93]) and further cultural sub-divisions examined in the south; and (2) more extended descriptions of a number of the sites designated as significant in each area.

Distribution of sites in Cameroon — North

A total of 184 sites was found in the northern part of the survey area in Cameroon, which extends from the Chad border to Ewankang (ECA-93) over a distance of 469 km. This yields a linear site density of 0.39 sites/kilometer. As in Chad, the spatial patterning of archaeological sites discovered in the Project area, already referred to in

Chapter 6, is the most obvious form of archaeological variability in the region (*Map 10*). There are relatively high linear site densities between the Chadian border and the Belel construction camp approximately 118 kilometers to the west along the right-of-way (0.47 sites/kilometer), as well as on the other extremity of the region, to the east and west of Belabo (and COTCO's Pump Station 3) and near the confluence of the Sanaga and Lom Rivers (0.49 sites/kilometer). Most of the latter site concentration is made up of small surface sites, dominated by ceramics but with some occurrences of lithics and slag, and for the most part designated as not culturally significant. Some exceptions do exist in this area, including for example the Lom II (ECA-157) and Koukony (ECA-84) sites, both with significant deposits of buried ceramics and other materials.

The site concentration between the Chad border and Belel is quite different. It includes a greater diversity of site types, with the highest concentration of both lithic scatters and iron-working sites in the Project area in Cameroon (see below), and also contains a relatively high proportion of sites judged to be significant. This high density of sites can probably be traced to two different factors: (1) high rates of erosion on the sides of valleys cutting into the edge of the escarpment marking the southeastern edge of the Adamawa Plateau, directly north of the Mbéré River valley, which exposed large amounts of MSA and LSA lithic material; and (2) intensive occupation of this area during the Iron Age and (probably) Neolithic, including iron smelting during the Iron Age, especially on the heights at the edge of the Adamawa Plateau. The area between Belel and Meiganga exhibits slightly lower site densities (0.44 sites/kilometer), with significant sites including Beka Patel (ECA-243), a habitation site dating from the early second millennium AD. Many of the sites in this area lie in a single cluster east of the hamlet of Gasol (see below).

There are, in contrast, significantly lower site densities in the area between Meiganga and the Lom River, where with a right-of-way length of 158 kilometers, only 29 sites were found (0.18 sites/kilometer). In a 68 kilometer zone directly southwest of Meiganga, only six sites were found (0.09 sites/kilometer). The area east of Nanga Eboko also displays low site densities, although most of this area lies in the southern zone and thus will be considered below. In all of these areas, modern environments and population densities do not seem to be notably different from neighboring areas where much higher archaeological site densities are found. The reasons for this variability in site density are at present unknown, but they may in fact be quite different for each area. Thus, for example, site density differences may be due to: (1) preferences in the utilization of territory (with some specific zones considered generally unsuitable for social or ideological reasons, and thus not densely populated); (2) historical contexts (as certain areas may have been subjected to demographic catastrophes, for example through epidemics or slave raids); (3) specific geomorphological factors (when erosion or sedimentation processes destroy or hide archaeological sites); and/or (4) some combination of all of these factors.

As in Chad, sites in the northern part of the Project area in Cameroon are often found in local concentrations, and this is markedly so within zones of generally lower site densities. Thus, there is a significant cluster of sites on the right-of-way near the hamlet of Gasol southeast of Belel, with 12 sites in 9.5 linear kilometers in a zone where the overall site density is approximately 0.5 sites/kilometer. These sites (ECA-54/265, -55, -58/261, -255, -257, -259, -263) include a number of ceramic and diverse artifact scatters and horizons, with relatively high numbers of grinding stones and grinding stone fragments as well as some other lithics. It is likely that this represents a habitation zone at some point during the Iron Age, with limited evidence of an earlier Neolithic occupation. Unfortunately, none of these sites have been dated to this point. A similar cluster of sites was encountered around Dang-Patou (ECA-209, -211, -213, -215, -217, -219, -221, -223), 75 kilometers southwest of Meiganga. This material appears to be Iron Age/Recent in date, and includes ceramics and, on some sites, grinding stone fragments. ECA-219 is an iron-smelting site, with furnace remains and slag uncovered. Again, this cluster probably indicates a settlement during the late Iron Age, albeit one perhaps somewhat isolated from neighboring communities.

Spatial and chronological distribution of different site types — Cameroon North

Ceramic and diverse artifact scatters and horizons

As in Chad, most of the sites found in the northern zone in Cameroon (146 of 184, or approximately 79 %) are surface sites, while the remaining 38 sites were buried. Of the surface sites, 75 (51 %) were ceramic scatters, with the artifacts recovered almost exclusively limited to potsherds. Only two of these sites, Pangar (ECA-171) and Lom 1 (ECA-185), were judged to be culturally significant because they provided good ceramic samples from areas previously unknown archaeologically and because (in the case of ECA-171) the ceramic distribution extended for 600 m along the right-of-way.

Another 33 (22 %) of the surface sites were diverse artifact scatters, again with mostly ceramics dominating. Other materials found on these sites included grindstones and grindstone fragments, lithics, iron-working debris, artifacts of European manufacture. Again, only two of these 33 diverse artifact scatters were judged to be culturally significant. One site in the Pangar area (ECA-173) was again so designated because of its size (500 m along the right-of-way), its location in a previously unknown area, and because of the possibility of a buried horizon at the site (none was eventually located). The other site, Belabo SOCOPAO (ECA-119), was also designated because of its size (600 m along the right-of-way) and because it was thought that a buried cultural horizon likely existed at the site. The right-of-way was narrowed in that area, so that damage to such a horizon was avoided. Thus, only four (ca 4 %) of 108 ceramic and diverse artifact surface scatters were ultimately judged to be culturally significant. As in Chad, the remaining sites were almost all small, low-density artifact scatters, and many were probably the result of human landscape use away from habitation sites. There was little evidence of the large surface sites with increased artifact diversities, judged to be culturally significant in southwestern Chad (see *Chapter 7*). This may relate to differences in pre-colonial settlement patterns in these regions, such as higher settlement mobility and/or less repeated use of particular localities along the northern extent of the right-of-way in Cameroon than in Chad. It is noteworthy that some reasonably large diverse artifact sites (*ca* 200 m linear length on the right-of-way), with grindstone fragments and some other lithics as well as pottery, were found close to the border with Chad. These sites comprise ECA-6, -8 -9, -36 and -37, and they may be the closest Cameroonian analogues to the large Chadian surface sites.

The situation was considerably different for the buried sites. Again, the ceramic and diverse artifact horizons display enough similarities to be considered together. The only real distinction between the two is the degree to which ceramics dominate the other artifact assemblages. As in Chad, other artifact categories encountered on these sites include grindstones and grindstone fragments (strongly indicating a domestic occupation), other lithics, artifacts of European manufacture, as well as slag, furnace wall fragments and other iron-working debris. As in Chad, most of these sites (30 of 37) were discovered in the course of construction monitoring, with seven others found during pre-construction survey. Of the 15 ceramic horizon and 22 diverse artifact horizon sites located in the course of research in this area, 12 (32 %) were judged to be culturally significant. This is a very different situation compared to Chad, where all such sites were judged to be culturally significant. This difference can be ascribed to two factors: (1) real differences in site patterning in the two areas, with relatively fewer large settlement sites found in eastern Cameroon than in Chad, and (2) stricter criteria for initial site prioritization applied in Cameroon than was the case in Chad. In Chad, all of these sites were initially assigned medium or high priority for further examination (50 % each), while in eastern Cameroon 12 sites (32 %) were designated low priority, 14 sites (38 %) medium priority and only 11 sites (30 %) high priority at the time of initial discovery.

Mitigation procedures were undertaken on all of the sites designated as culturally significant. In two cases, Mbinang (ECA-81) and Seka (ECA-255), this involved avoidance of the site area through narrowing of the right-of-way. The site of Koukony (ECA-84) was intentionally buried. At Pangar (ECA-199) and Ewankang (ECA-93), avoidance was combined with limited excavation. In all other cases, data recovery excavations were conducted, in areas varying between 2 – 12 m².

These sites are again quite variable in size. Almost all of the ceramic horizon sites extended for 50 m or less along the pipeline right-of-way, and many were smaller than 10x10 m. Diverse artifact horizon sites were on average larger, suggesting as in Chad that the distinction between these site types is primarily one of sampling insofar as larger sites tend to yield a greater diversity of artifacts. Smaller sites were for the most part not judged to be culturally significant. The most striking exception is Sokorta Manga (ECA-43), located on the escarpment north of the Mbéré River Valley (see below), of which an area of about 50x30 m was to be affected by the right-of-way. The diversity and density of artifacts and features at that site led to it being given a high priority, and very productive excavations were later undertaken there. Other such sites were considerably larger. Deposits at Koukony (ECA-84) extended for *ca* 650 m along the right-of-way, with high artifact densities in parts of this area and evidence for occupation at different time periods. Ewankang (ECA-93) similarly yielded high densities of artifacts over 300 m along the right-of-way and Seka (ECA-255) over 500 m, while at Beka Petel-Gamboro (ECA-243), similar densities were found in a 200x200 m area. Other sites, such as Lom I (ECA-181), are similarly large (700 m linear extent), but have very low artifact densities in that area: such sites were subject to monitoring but not designated as culturally significant. Cultural deposits were of highly variable depth, from less than 0.1 m to approximately 1.4 m. Cultural horizons probably associated with living floors were encountered on a number of sites, but pits were significantly fewer in this area than either in Chad or (especially) in southern Cameroon (see below).

The derivation of dates of occupation for these sites as always has been difficult. Radiocarbon dates were obtained for a number of sites (*App. F* and *Fig. 25*). Two dates from Iron Age deposits at Beka Petel – Gamboro (ECA-243) overlapped for the period cal AD 1100 – 1300; two dates from Sokorta Manga (ECA-43), while not overlapping, suggest occupation approximately 1000 years ago. Pangar (ECA-199) yielded a single date from the same period. It is interesting to note that these dates correspond to the period of intensive iron working and substantial occupation in southwestern Chad. Two dates from Bemboyo (ECA-24), the major site closest to that border, indicate only late pre-colonial to recent occupation. The spread in single dates from other sites is again quite broad, with the earliest, Koukony (ECA-84), dated to the early-/mid-first millennium AD, while more recent sites like Lom I (ECA-163) again date to the late pre-colonial period.

However, it is noteworthy that more lithic material (including flaked and ground/polished stone artifacts) was recovered from diverse artifact surface and buried sites in Cameroon than was the case across the border in Chad (see *Chapter 7*, and below), probably indicating multiple occupations of the same locality. Thus, for example, at Sokorta Manga (ECA-43) a cultural horizon yielding large quartzite flakes and cores was found below the Iron Age horizon. In addition, the cultural affinities of some of the pottery recovered might be interpreted, in other regions of southern Cameroon, as indicating a Neolithic time period. On seven sites, ceramics were found either associated with lithics in the absence of any evidence for metallurgy (ECA-44, -73, -255, -259) or and/or with ground and polished stone tools (ECA-42, -54, -177), again probably indicating Neolithic cultural affiliations. In general, these data point to substantial habitation along the northern section of the pipeline right-of-way in Cameroon over the last 2000 years. They also suggest that the region has probably been occupied since the Middle Stone Age at least — a conclusion supported by the discovery of a substantial number of lithic scatters as well (see below). Further discrimination of the timing and modes of those earlier occupations will require substantially more fieldwork in the region.

Iron-working horizons and scatters

Less evidence for iron working was found along the right-of-way in northern Cameroon than in Chad — again indicating the regional nature of iron production in the latter area. Only one important iron-working site was found and designated as culturally significant. This is the site of Djaoro Mbama (ECA-47), where excavations in a 12 m² area uncovered *in situ* furnaces and other iron-production features. In addition, four surface scatters (ECA-12, -51, -52, -219) with evidence for iron working in the form of slag and tuyère and furnace fragments were also found in this area, but were not determined to be culturally significant (***Map 16***). Four diverse artifact sites (ECA-43, -117, -119, -121) also yielded smaller amounts of slag and tuyère fragments. As in Chad, it is possible that these remains at the latter sites indicate the production or repair of iron tools in a habitation site and/or the multiple use of the same locality at different times, for iron production and settlement. This is in contrast to the 11 iron-working horizons and 17 iron-working scatters found in southern Chad, along with 11 diverse artifact scatters/horizons with some evidence for iron working (see *Chapter 7*). Few inferences about spatial patterning can be made from the relatively small number of iron-working sites along the northern part of the right-of-way in Cameroon. However, there do appear to be at least two distinct clusters of sites associated with iron working in this region, one east of Belel (ECA-43, -47, -51, -52) and a second near Belabo (ECA-117, -119, -121).Two sites (ECA-12, -219) appear to be isolated. More research in these areas would be needed to determine whether spatial clusters of iron-working activity similar to those in Chad existed in the region.

Djaoro Mbama (ECA-47) yielded a very useful series of five radiocarbon dates, taken from cultural horizons, furnaces, pits and other features on the site (***App. F*** and ***Fig. 25***). Excavations on two *in situ* furnace structures indicated the use of low-shaft bloomery furnaces with 2–4 tuyères, similar to those found in Chad. All of these dates indicate the use of this site for iron smelting during the end of the first millennium BC and early in the first millennium AD. This is, of course, approximately a thousand years before the peak period of iron production along the right-of-way in southwestern Chad (with closely comparable furnace morphologies), although the single date from the Missi Madji site (ETA-164) in Chad falls between the two periods. The dates from ECA-47 are somewhat later than the single date from Makouré (ECA-124) in southern Cameroon (see below), but they are comparable to early dates for iron working from a number of neighboring areas of Central Africa. It is unclear whether the two dates of *ca* 1000 years ago from Sokorta Manga (ECA-43) also indicate the period of exploitation of the iron-working remains found on that site.

Lithic scatters

In contrast to the situation for iron-working sites, we see much more evidence for ancient stone tool production and usage in eastern Cameroon than in southwest-

ern Chad, and indeed more than in southern Cameroon (***Map 14***). This is almost entirely due to the existence of a concentration of 22 lithic scatters between the Chad border and the right-of-way southeast of Belel, along the escarpment north of the Mbéré River Valley (***Map 15***). In addition, bifacial and flaked stone tools and lithic debitage are more common in diverse artifact scatters in this same area than is the case in other parts of Cameroon and Chad. This increased frequency of sites yielding stone tools is almost certainly due to the geomorphology of the region, with processes of erosion dominating on the slopes at the southeastern edge of the Adamawa escarpment and exposing artifact-bearing strata that in both southwestern Chad and in most areas of southern Cameroon are buried under more recent sediments (see *Chapter 3*). In parts of this zone, the pipeline right-of-way runs transversely east-west across the extremely abrupt topography created by watercourses draining off the Adamawa Plateau south into the Mbéré River. On the steep slopes associated with these watercourses, lithic scatters were almost the only archaeological occurrences noted on erosional surfaces. One additional lithic scatter, ECA-177, is situated on the Lom River northeast of Belabo.

Unfortunately, the characteristics of these sites — with artifacts very frequently in secondary contexts and a lack of datable materials — make it extremely difficult to assign them to precise cultural periods in the past. In the absence of any but technological data, those sites yielding only stone tools are considered to belong to the Middle or Late Stone Age, while those sites where lithics and ceramics are found may date to the Neolithic. One complicating factor is that a site yielding both ceramics and stone tools may also be a multi-component (MSA/LSA and Iron Age) site without any explicit evidence for iron working. Examination of the characteristics of both artifact classes — the stratigraphy of multi-component assemblages, ceramic decoration techniques, the presence or absence of polished stone tools (strongly indicating Neolithic cultural affiliations), the typological affiliations of other lithic artifacts — may be useful in distinguishing those cases.

Sites (or levels within sites) ECA -4, -5, -13, -16, -18, -25, -27 to -29, -32, -34, -35, -40 to -43, -45, -48 to -50, -79 and -84 only yielded lithic artifacts. Unfortunately, most of these sites consist of extensive, low-density distributions of flaked stone and debitage found in erosive contexts on hillsides, often among much larger amounts of non-cultural lithic material. Most of them did not yield the minimal criteria necessary to be designated as culturally significant. Thus most have not been further examined after their discovery, and consequently we do not have excavation

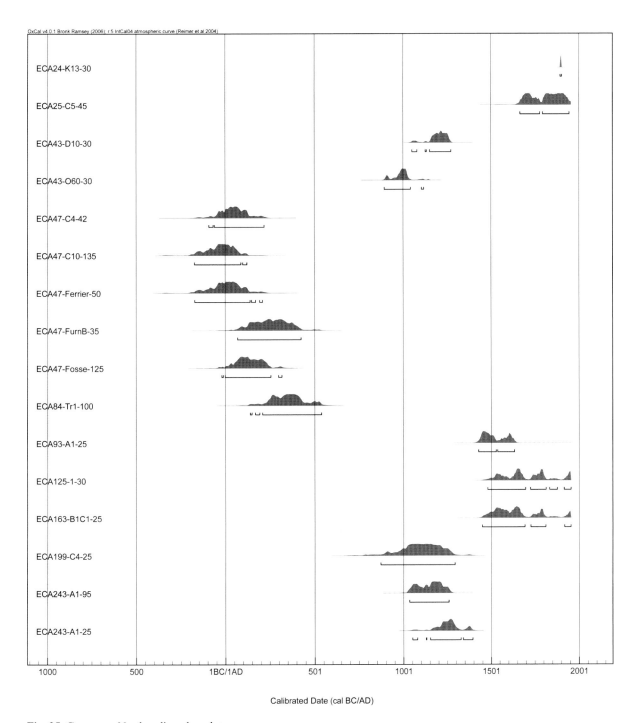

Fig. 25. Cameroon North radiocarbon dates.

data and dates allowing us to define the characteristics of pre-Iron Age occupation of this region. These sites have been attributed to the Middle Stone Age or Late Stone Age according to the presence or absence of specific technological and typological attributes. Most of the collections from these sites consist of debitage, large flakes, cores on quartzite and formed tools, the latter including especially bifaces and large scrapers. Most of the cores are irregular, with one or two striking platforms, but some *Levallois* cores have also been identified. No microlithic component

has yet been identified in these lithic assemblages, but it would be extremely difficult to detect such artifacts in these conditions and the possibility cannot be eliminated. As it stands, comparison with assemblages in neighbouring countries, including Congo – Brazzaville and Gabon, suggests that most of these assemblages date from a period of the MSA between 50,000 and 10,000 bp.

At Sokorta Manga (ECA-43), lithic materials were discovered in the stratigraphy, in a level between

0.4 and 0.6 m below surface and below the Iron Age level dated to approximately one thousand years ago (see below). In that level, large quartzite flakes and cores were located at mid-slope of the hillside that marks the site. This material can probably be associated with the bifacial tools (including a foliate point) on quartzite recovered from the surface at the top of that hill. Further excavations would be necessary to confirm this hypothesis. On seven sites between the Chad border and Ewankang (ECA-93), ceramics were found associated with a lithic industry (ECA-44, -73, -255, -259) and/or with polished stone tools (ECA-43, -54, -177). In the absence of evidence for iron working, this suggests in technological terms that these assemblages may date to the Neolithic — if they are in fact homogeneous assemblages. However, only four of these sites (ECA -43, -54, -255, -259) yielded stratified cultural deposits, and only one (Sokorta Manga [ECA-43]) has been excavated and dated. The dates from that site refer to Iron Age levels. It is thus impossible to evaluate the homogeneity of these assemblages, and a mix of Iron Age pottery and MSA/LSA lithic materials cannot be excluded. Thus the existence of Neolithic assemblages in the northern zone of the pipeline right-of-way is likely, but not proven.

Grinding stones and grinding hollows

Ten sites in the northern zone in Cameroon were identified as grinding stones or grinding hollows. The former term is fairly obvious: it reflects the discovery of grindstones or grindstone fragments without other artifacts. The latter term may require more explanation: 'grinding hollow' in this case refers to single or (usually) multiple artificial hollows ground into natural rock outcrops, usually granitic boulders and whalebacks in this area. Such sites are quite common throughout sub-Saharan Africa, but relatively little archaeological attention has been paid to them, perhaps because they do not usually yield much information, even about the age of formation, to the archaeologist (but see DAVID 1998). These sites are often somewhat difficult to distinguish from naturally occurring hollows in rock, but their regularity and existence in clusters is usually a guide to their human manufacture. They often occur close to habitation sites, and it is generally assumed that they were used in food preparation, as a precursor or adjunct to the grindstones now commonly found in this area. Other possible uses include grinding of pigments or other non-food items, preparation of iron ore for smelting or reduction of iron blooms after smelting and/or sharpening of the edges of stone or metal tools. One of the difficulties with these occurrences is that the time of their formation is usually impossible to establish, as they include nothing that can be dated. DAVID's (1998) article

concludes that some in northeastern Nigeria may date to the Neolithic or early Iron Age, although these were more eroded than those found during Project fieldwork. On the other hand, the discovery of wooden grinding equipment still *in situ* on one such site (ECA-14) both suggests that these grinding hollows were in use less than two decades ago and gives some indication of their use in this case at least. The wooden 'hammer' found near the cupules on that site was recognized by Cameroonian crew members as a tool for pounding manioc.

Of these ten sites, four (ECA-01, -14, -22, -38) were grinding hollow sites, while the other six (ECA-11, -46, -221, -401, -402, -405) were isolated finds of grindstones and/or grindstone fragments. As might be expected, the latter are found in various areas along the right-of-way, but the grinding hollows are found primarily in the open country between the Chad border and Belel, where relevant granite outcrops exist and where site visibility is fairly high.

Tazunu

As noted in *Chapter 4*, a distribution of megalithic sites, clusters of standing and horizontal stones arranged on low earth mounds and called *tazunu* in local languages, have been found around Bouar in the Central African Republic, with a possible extension into the Djohong area of Cameroon, close to the pipeline right-of-way. Two possible *tazunu* sites (ECA-15, -17) were located during the survey, both on the plains between the Mbéré River and the Adamawa Plateau and near the village of Dompta. *Tazunu* were designated as important cultural heritage sites according to the Treatment Plan for the Management of Cultural Resources in Cameroon, and so were automatically accorded high priority for further analysis. Upon further analysis, it was determined that both of these sites were natural occurrences of vertical standing stones and not *tazunu*. No further work was undertaken, but both site numbers remain on the site list, as an indication of the process undertaken for determining their status.

Tomb

One modern tomb was located near the hamlet of Bambo in the course of Project work in the northern zone in Cameroon. It was given an archaeological site number (ECA-127) and accorded high priority, as mandated in the Management Plans for Cultural Properties in both Chad and Cameroon (see *Chapter 2*). The right-of-way was narrowed in the area around the site to avoid any disturbance of the tomb.

Description of particular sites — Cameroon North

ECA-24 — Bemboyo

The site was discovered on June 27, 2001 during pre-construction survey and classified as high priority for further work. The site (about 30x250 m in the right-of-way) is situated on top of a hill. The total surface area of the site is evaluated at 250x300 m. Pottery as well as stone flakes and slag were identified in erosion gullies on the hillsides. Several pits of approximately 2x1 m, covered with small stones and gravel and interpreted as tombs, were discovered. Only one of these pits was located in the right-of-way. As 10 % of the site was to be impacted by construction, the site treatment plan recommended partial data recovery. An area of 24 m² was excavated. Twenty square meters were opened on top of the hill and yielded, at an average depth of 0.15–0.2 m below surface, an assemblage of pottery, a considerable quantity of worked stone flakes, debitage, and some small pieces of slag. One hearth feature, situated on the other side of the hill, was excavated, as was one of the pit features; the latter revealed no archaeological materials.

No charcoal was found in the levels associated with the artifact assemblage, but radiocarbon dating was attempted on two charcoal samples, one coming from the hearth feature, the other from the pit feature. Both samples yielded recent dates (*App. F* and *Fig. 25*) incompatible with the archaeological material recovered in the major excavation. It is likely that both of these features are more recent disturbances. There is no evidence of disturbance in the stratigraphy of the main excavation. Considering the presence of both stone tools and slag, which indicate that iron was modified on site but was not abundant enough to replace stone tools, the village may have been occupied during the early Iron Age. Comparison with similar sites in the region points to an age between 2000 and 700 years ago. Such an assemblage of artifacts, with large quantities of pottery and stone tools, suggests a long-term Iron Age settlement where varied domestic activities took place. The fact that only a small amount of slag fragments was identified suggests that iron smithing, and not smelting, was carried out on the site.

ECA-43 — Sokorta Manga

Site ECA-43 was discovered during pre-construction survey on July 7, 2001 and accorded high priority for further work. Pottery, polished stone tools and evidence for blacksmithing activities (a small amount of slag and tuyère fragments — *Fig. 26*) were discovered on the slopes of a small valley in a wooded savanna environment. The artifacts were scattered in the pipeline easement on a surface of 50x30 m. Most of the site, with a

Fig. 26. Slag and tuyère fragments from Sokorta Manga (ECA-43).

2 cm

Fig. 27. Ceramic from Sokorta Manga (ECA-43).

total area of 150x200 m, lies outside of the right-of-way, higher up the hillside where more pottery, stone tools and grinding stones were discovered. Stone Age tools, such as bifacial points, were also found on the surface.

Only 5 % of the site was to be impacted by pipeline construction. However, given the rarity of the polished stone tools, the Site Treatment Plan recommended data recovery. The site was excavated between December 10 and 15, 2001. Eight square meters were opened to a depth varying from 0.3 to 1 m. The eight squares yielded a layer of occupation between 0.2 and 0.4 m below surface, at the base of the topsoil, from which pottery, stone tools and charcoal were collected. This archaeological layer corresponds to the material found during pre-construction survey. One square also yielded quartzite artifacts at a depth of 0.6 to 0.8 m below surface. These were the by-products of the manufacture of large stone tools (one of these was a beautiful bifacial point, found on the surface on top of the hill). Overall, the site yielded a low density of archaeological material. Most of the materials collected both on the surface and in the test pits were potsherds. Potsherds unearthed in the 8 m² excavated amounts to only 3.8 kg, or 267 sherds. They all belong to the same Iron Age assemblage. Vessels were decorated mostly with carved wooden roulette (67 % of total decorated sherds), but comb stamping, either simple or rocking comb, was used as well (33 %) (*Fig. 27*).

Approximately 4.6 kg of stone artifacts were recovered, including grinding stones, stone tools, flakes and

cores. While the grinding stones are made of granite, the raw material for flaked stone tools and their manu-factured by-products is quartzite. Two distinct assem-blages are present: the older consists of large cores and flakes, unearthed between 0.6 and 0.8 m below surface in one test pit. No standardized tools were found in the stratigraphy, but a number of bifacial points of the same material were collected on the surface and probably belong to the same assemblage. The more recent tool-kit was found associated with the pottery and consists of grinding stones, *ad hoc* stone flakes and cores. The only polished stone adze was found on the surface and is probably part of the Iron Age assemblage. Some slag and tuyère fragments were also identified in the upper occupation layer, albeit in small quantities.

Two charcoal samples collected in the 0.2–0.4 m occupation layer were dated with the radiocarbon technique (*App. F* and *Fig. 25*), placing the occupa-tion between cal AD 960 and 1275. The 0.6–0.8 m occupation layer did not yield any charcoal for dating, but the lithic industry shows technological and typo-logical affiliations with the Middle Stone Age, and an approximate age range of between 10,000 and more than 50,000 years ago is possible.

ECA-43 was inhabited on two occasions: during the Middle Stone Age (in the late Pleistocene) and the Iron Age (somewhere between the 10th and 14th centuries AD). The presence of finished quartzite tools on this site suggests that the hill was a temporary camp during the MSA. The presence of pottery, polished stone tools and slag is evidence that a variety of specialized activities, such as blacksmithing, were carried out during the Iron Age. The existence of iron was not sufficient, however, to make stone tools obsolete.

ECA-47 — Djaoro Mbama

Djaoro Mbama was discovered during pre-construction survey between Dompta and Belel, on July 4, 2001. The site, an iron-producing area of 60x20 m, yielded a large amount of slag, tuyères and furnace wall fragments scat-tered on an erosion surface in a small and steep valley in the wooded savanna zone. Most of the site lies outside of the right-of-way, lower down the hill toward the river.

ECA-47 was accorded high priority for further work, and the Site Treatment Plan recommended data recovery in the impacted zone of the site. Twelve square meters were excavated between January 28 and March 12, 2002 (*Fig. 28*). Two well-preserved iron-smelting furnaces (Features A and B) were discovered at a depth of about one meter below surface (*Fig. 29*). Other furnace features

Fig. 28. Tuyère and furnace wall fragments at Djaoro Mbama (ECA-47).

Fig. 29. Furnace remains at Djaoro Mbama (ECA-47).

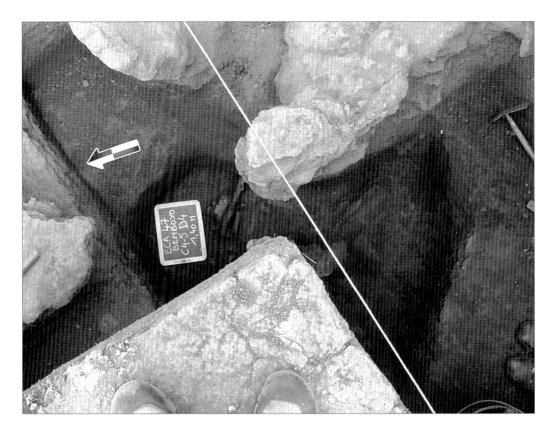

Fig. 30. Pit below furnaces A and B at Djaoro Mbama (ECA-47).

were identified *in situ* underneath the cultural layers, extending down to 1.4 m below surface. In particular, a pit (Feature C) filled with iron-working debris including slag, tuyères and furnace fragments, was discovered under Feature A (*Fig. 30*). A substantial layer of slag (about 1 meter thick) was discovered a few meters to the west of the furnaces and is interpreted as the slag heap associated with their functioning. As noted above, radiocarbon dates were obtained from five charcoal samples collected between 0.4 and 1.45 m below surface (*App. F* and *Fig. 25*). The ages obtained all cluster tightly and place the occupation at Djaoro Mbama between 2000 and 1800 bp. However, once calibrated, the period of utilization of the site falls between 170 BC and AD 430.

The structure of the furnaces is very well preserved. Features A and B show many of the features characteristic of low-shaft bloomery furnaces. A shallow pit approximately 1.5 meters in diameter was dug to a depth of about 0.3 m, and mud walls were then built around this pit to form a chimney. Only the lower sections of these walls are preserved. At the base of the walls, two to four tuyères were inserted to provide ventilation for the furnace. The base of the furnace that makes up Feature A was also equipped with a vent leading to a small reservoir dug into the earth just outside

the structure, which probably allowed the removal of the fused slag (*Fig. 31*). The bloomery mass was apparently extracted by fully or partially destroying the furnace walls.

Most of the artifacts collected from ECA-47 were furnace and tuyère fragments (15 kg) and slag (13 kg). In addition, 76 potsherds were recovered from the excavations, dispersed in the furnace features and in the slag heap. Relatively little of the pottery was decorated, but simple comb impression (38 %) and dragged-comb (37 %) decoration dominate. There was also some use of rocking-comb impressions and stick grooving (25 %). No stone artifacts were recovered from the site.

ECA-47 was an iron-smelting site that probably functioned over a long period between the second century BC and the fifth century AD. The site was obviously used repeatedly for iron smelting, as is indicated by the presence of several furnaces features on top of one another, the sheer amount of slag produced and the depth of the stratigraphy. The technology used is that of iron smelting by bloomery technique with low-shaft furnaces, comparable to examples described in western Cameroon (WARNIER 1992). On the other hand, the small amount of pottery is evidence that the site was never inhabited as such.

Fig. 31. Slag vent at Djaoro Mbama (ECA-47).

ECA-84 — Koukony

ECA-84, discovered during grading operations on November 6, 2001, is situated near Koukony village in the vicinity of Belabo. On top of a hill, a very rich and diversified archaeological assemblage, consisting of pottery, stone tools and slag, was found scattered on about 650 meters over the pipeline easement. The mix of pottery, stone tools and slag was surprising, and the site appeared as an accumulation of heterogeneous assemblages on an erosion surface that was disturbed by grading operations. As about 5 % of the site surface was already impacted by construction at the time of its discovery, it was classified as high priority for post-discovery treatment in order to avoid further impact and to assess its real importance.

Site treatment required further monitoring during trenching operations to verify whether *in situ* archaeo-logical material could be identified. This took place on January 10, 2002 and revealed that part of the archaeological material effectively came from a layer much deeper than the graded surface. A well-delimited horizon of pottery was identified at about 0.5 m below the graded surface in the trench. It also appeared that most of the stone tools identified on the graded surface came from an even older horizon, as no comparable stone artifacts were present in the potsherd layer.

Some typical *in situ* potsherds and a few charcoal samples were collected before backfilling of the trench. No data recovery excavation took place on the site. Approximately 0.7 kg of stone artifacts were collected from the surface of the site including large cores and bi-facial tools on quartzite, typical of the late Middle Stone Age or the early Late Stone Age. Approximately 0.35 kg of pottery (19 potsherds) were collected during trenching. Most of the pottery is decorated with comb impression or with dragged-comb grooving (85 %), but twisted string roulette (8 %) and grooving with a comb-gouge (a two-toothed instrument used at an oblique angle) (7 %) are present as well. One charcoal sample collected in the pottery and slag layer in the trench was dated and gave a calibrated age of AD 210 – 540. The Stone Age artifacts remain undated but their typology would point to a late MSA/early LSA affiliation (from more than 50,000 bp to 8000 bp).

ECA-84 was occupied on several occasions: first in the MSA and/or LSA, probably before 8000 bp, and again in the Iron Age around 1700 bp (between the third and sixth centuries AD). The total surface area of the site (approximately 400,000 m²) indicates that this was a large settlement, and/or that it is a palimpsest of remains from multiple occupations of the same locality. Given the density of the archaeological material identified, it is likely that the site was inhabited for a long time. Blacksmithing appears to have been carried out in the village.

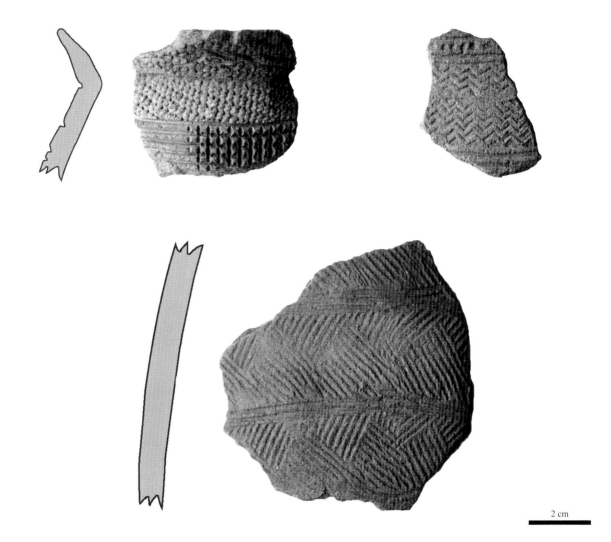

2 cm

Fig. 32. Ceramics from Ewankang (ECA-93).

ECA-93 — Ewankang

ECA-93 was found during monitoring of the grading operations on November 24, 2001. On the surface exposed by grading, this site yielded pottery, as well as a few stone tools and slag, over a distance of more than 300 meters. Its total surface probably approximates 90,000 m². Most of the site lies outside of the right-of-way and construction related impact was evaluated at 8.3 % of the total area. Because of its size and the density and diversity of the archaeological material, ECA-93 was classified as high priority for further treatment. The Site Treatment Plan required non-impacted areas of the site to be avoided by narrowing of the right-of-way. A 1 m² test pit was excavated on December 18, 2001 in order to assess the homogeneity of the assemblage and collect some datable samples. The archaeological material was clustered in the topsoil. The sediments became sterile at 0.3 m below surface.

About 2 kg of pottery (119 potsherds) and 150 grams of stone artifacts were collected. Pottery decoration is varied: 56 % of decorated sherds display impressions made with a fiber or (more rarely) carved wooden roulette, although comb dragging (37 %) is also significant (*Fig. 32*). A few unstandardized quartzite tools, flakes and cores are also present in the assemblage. A single charcoal sample, taken from the cultural level between 0.2 m and 0.3 m below surface, yielded a calibrated radiocarbon date of AD 1425 – 1635.

ECA-93 appears to be a late Iron Age settlement, inhabited sometime between the 15th and the 17th centuries AD. The quantity of pottery, the extent of the site and the slag indicate that it was a large settlement, and/or that it is a palimpsest of remains from multiple occupations of the same locality. The community seems to have housed several specialized artisans (potters, blacksmiths) with stone tools still in use to some degree. Pottery similar to that found at Ewankang is very common in the region east of Nanga Eboko and west of Belabo (sites ECA-90, -91, -92, -94). This pottery is sometimes associated with clay smoking pipes, which would be normal at this period given contacts with the transoceanic European trade.

ECA-119 — Belabo SOCOPAO

The site was discovered on December 13, 2001 during monitoring of grading activities. It is situated in Belabo, near the SOCOPAO offices in the semi-deciduous forest zone. Archaeological material is scattered over a distance of about 600 meters along the pipeline right-of-way, on the hillside of a small valley. Potsherds, slag and blowpipe fragments were identified in the right-of-way. It was accorded medium priority for further treatment. The Site Treatment Plan advised avoidance of the non-impacted parts of the site by narrowing of the right-of-way and monitoring of the trenching operations. One kilogram of pottery was collected on the surface, as well as a sample of 1.3 kg of slag. Most of the collected pottery is decorated with carved wooden roulette. The SOCOPAO site is a pre-colonial settlement site. Given the stratigraphic context of the archaeological material close to the surface and the roulette decoration of the pottery, it is probable that the site is relatively recent.

ECA-163 — Lom I

ECA-163 was discovered on February 13, 2002 during monitoring of construction activities, immediately after the clearing operations. The site is situated on top of a steep hill, in a very hilly but open environment in the semi-deciduous forest zone. Furnace fragments, slag and a few potsherds were found scattered in a 20x20 m area. Two small iron-working furnaces, as well as potsherds and slag, were identified beyond the right-of-way as well, and ECA-163 appeared to be a large and diffuse surface site, about 60,000 m² in total. It was accorded high priority for further work because of the presence of the iron-working features. Three 1 m² test pits were excavated on February 15 and 16, 2002 to assess the importance of the buried material in the right-of-way. More furnace fragments, some small pieces of slag and three potsherds were unearthed between 0 and 0.15 m below surface. Fifteen potsherds, decorated with knotted strip roulette, and a few slag pieces were collected on the surface and in the test pits.

Based on the material recovered, the site was tentatively identified as a recent surface site (less than 200

years old) and downgraded to low importance. To verify that hypothesis, a charcoal sample was collected below the main archaeological layer, between 0.2 and 0.3 m below surface, and dated. It yielded a calibrated age of AD 1470 – 1950. The calibration curve indicates that the most probable age of the sample should be situated between the 17th and the 19th centuries AD. The main occupation phase of the village probably postdates the 17th century. ECA-163 thus appears to be a late Iron Age settlement site, installed on top of a steep hill. Artifact density is low and artifacts are mostly found on the surface. The presence of two small iron-working furnaces on the surface outside the pipeline easement and slag scattered all over the hill indicates that some blacksmithing activity took place in the village. ECA-163 may well be a pre-colonial Gbaya village.

ECA-171 — Pangar

ECA-171was found during pre-construction survey on March 8, 2002. The site is a very large, low-density surface ceramic scatter, located on a hilltop in the wooded savanna zone. Potsherds decorated with roulette impressions were dispersed over 600 meters along the pipeline easement, which is 25 meters wide. Potsherds were also visible outside the right-of-way over several hundred meters. The total surface area of the site is approximately 350,000 m², and clearing impacted less than 5 % of the site. Given its extent and the fact that the region is very poorly known archaeologically, the site was accorded medium priority for further treatment. The Site Treatment Plan called for avoidance of the non-impacted parts of the site on the pipeline easement. No further earthmoving was permitted on the edges of the graded area in the site's perimeter. ECA-171 was a large Iron Age village site.

ECA-177 — Lom I

ECA-177 was discovered on March 11, 2002 during monitoring of trenching activity. It is located in the vicinity of Lom I village, on the north bank of the Lom River, in the semi-deciduous forest zone between the towns of Belabo and Mararaba. A single polished stone axe was found on the surface next to the trench, on a flat plateau (altitude 740 m). Although ECA-177 is technically an isolated find, it could indicate the presence of an important site not far from the right-of-way. Polished stone tools are very rare in the Project area and, as such, the location was accorded high priority for further treatment. The ground stone tool was collected. A very careful surface survey in the area (including the graded surface of the right-of-way, the trench and the immediate area around the right-of-way limits) and a systematic auguring program could not identify other associated artifacts. No significant information can be extracted from an isolated find except the age of the artifact: polished stone tools are usually dated to the Neolithic or the early Iron Age (between *ca* 5000 and 1000 years ago) in Central Africa (ZANGATO 1999; LAVACHERY 2001; ASSOKO NDONG 2002).

ECA 199 — Pangar

ECA-199 is a buried archaeological horizon, spread over 200 m on the right-of-way, discovered during construction monitoring on April 4, 2002. The site is located near the town of Pangar, in the wooded savanna zone. The assemblage, identified in a well-defined archaeological layer situated between 0.5 and 0.6 m below initial surface (before grading operations), consists of decorated pottery, stone flakes and clusters of charcoal. The site was accorded high priority for further treatment. The Site Treatment Plan recommended narrowing of the right-of-way, with avoidance of the non-impacted part of the site, and limited data recovery. Two 1 m² test pits were opened, to a depth of 0.8 m; sterile soil was reached at 0.6 m below surface.

Some 4 kg (222 potsherds) of pottery were recovered from the test pit. The pottery is for the most part decorated with simple or walking-comb impressions (55 %), but carved wooden and fiber roulettes are also frequent (42 %). The stone industry consists of large unretouched quartzite flakes and cores. A single charcoal sample was radiocarbon dated; with a significant standard error, the 2-sigma age range of the sample is rather imprecise, at cal AD 885 – 1295. The site was thus an Iron Age settlement site that was inhabited sometime between the 9th and the 13th centuries AD. The association of stone tools and rouletted pottery in such a recent site is apparently not uncommon in the region north of the Lom River (see Sokorta Manga [ECA-43]).

ECA-243 — Beka Petel-Gamboro

ECA-243 was discovered on April 4, 2002 during pre-construction survey. The site is located on a large plateau in the wooded savanna zone. At the time interpreted as a low-density surface scatter of pottery, it was classified as low priority for further work. On June 6, 2002, during the monitoring of the grading operations, it was discovered that the site actually included an important buried component. The site is located just 100 m west of Gamboro village, in a flat wooded savanna environment; Beka Petel is the closest village on the main road.

The site includes two thick archaeological levels, with very dark organic soil and rich pottery assemblages that appear to be part of a deposit spread over a 200x200 m area. About 12.5 % of the site had been uncovered by the bulldozers, and cultural material was then clearly visible in the embankment of the graded area. ECA-243 was upgraded to high priority for further treatment.

The Site Treatment Plan called for avoidance of the unimpacted parts of the site (in the portions of the right-of-way that were not yet graded) and data recovery. A 2x1 m test pit was opened and excavated to a depth of 1.2 m below ground level between July 8–9 and 15–18, 2002. Two distinct cultural horizons were clearly visible: the upper one between 0.1 m and 0.3 m below surface (Horizon I), and the lower between 0.5 m and 1.2 m deep (Horizon II). A substantial artifact assemblage was collected through surface collections and excavation. It included 3.5 kg of pottery in Horizon I and 14 kg of pottery in Horizon II. Some slag was collected as well. A glass bead was found on the surface. In both levels, the most common pottery decoration technique was comb impression (51 and 52 %), with carved wooden and fiber roulette also frequent (44 and 49 %). The only significant difference was the absence of walking comb impression in the lower level.

Two charcoal samples collected in Unit A1 at 0.2–0.3 m and 0.9–1.0 m below surface were sent for radiocarbon dating (*App. F* and *Fig. 25*). The more recent horizon was dated to cal AD 1170 – 1315, while the older one was dated to cal AD 1025 – 1275. The two horizons seem to be distinct from both a stratigraphic and chronological standpoint. The two calibrated dates overlap in the AD 1170 – 1275 period, making it possible that the refuse dump was created over a relatively short period. The area excavated thus appears as a refuse area, used between the 11th and 15th centuries AD. The sheer amount and density of pottery unearthed in approximately 2 m³ and the size of the site indicate that ECA-243 was a large Iron Age settlement, possibly inhabited over a long time and/or by a fairly large population.

Culture history — Cameroon North

The evidence for MSA/LSA occupation in this area has been discussed in the section on lithic sites above. For the Iron Age, 15 useful dates have been obtained from nine sites between the Chad border on the Mbéré River and Ewankang (*App. F* and *Fig. 25*). These dates can be provisionally divided into two chronological phases: (1) an earlier phase between *ca* 100 cal BC and cal AD 600 and (2) a later phase between cal AD 900 and the present. The earlier phase is represented by dates from only two sites, Djaoro Mbama (ECA-47) and Koukony (ECA-84). After that, there appears to be a chronological hiatus; no site is dated between cal AD 600 and cal AD 900. The second phase is known from six sites: Pangar (ECA-199), Sokorta Manga (ECA-43), Beka Petel (ECA-243), Ewankang (ECA-93), Lom I (ECA-163) and Bemboyo (ECA-24). There exists, within this latter phase, a small chronological hiatus at approximately 500 years ago, but this may well be due to the dating method. Nevertheless, the hiatus will be used to divide Phase IIa from Phase IIb. It should finally be added that the date of Bemboyo (ECA-24) seems too young for the type of material discovered (see above) and that it probably refers to a recent reoccupation of the site.

Iron Age Phase I

The characteristics of the Djaoro Mbama (ECA-47) and Koukony (ECA-84) sites have already been discussed. These two sites provide significant evidence for both local iron production and settlement during this period. Unfortunately, relatively little pottery was collected from these sites, which limits the detailed cultural comparisons that can be made. In both cases, decorative techniques are dominated by comb impression and dragged-comb grooving, techniques also in use in contemporaneous sites in the Nanga region along the right-of-way to the south (see below). The presence of roulette impressions at Koukony should nevertheless be noted.

Iron Age Phase II

The succeeding phase begins after a hiatus of at least 300 years and ranges between cal AD 900 and the present. The early part of this phase, IIa, is represented by three large Iron Age settlement sites, Sokorta Manga (ECA-43), Pangar (ECA-199) and Beka Petel (ECA-243). These are hilltop sites, which yielded artifact assemblages including roulette-decorated pottery, stone tools (sometimes including polished tools) and debitage, slag and grinding stones. Furnace fragments (primarily pieces of tuyères) were identified on several sites. The ubiquity of slag at Sokorta Manga and Beka Petel shows that metallurgy was widespread, although iron could not have been produced in every village. Other undated sites, including Bemboyo (ECA-24), Lesouaka (ECA-54) and Mbinang (ECA-81), where similar assemblages were found, probably date to the same phase of occupation, although the absence of absolute dating makes it impossible to be certain of this.

The pottery of this phase displays decorative techniques similar to those used at Koukony (ECA-84) several centuries earlier. The principal difference is the appearance of roulette decoration on certain sites. In Sokorta Manga (ECA-43), the pottery is still decorated mainly with simple comb impressions (88 %), but carved wooden roulettes are also present (12 %). At Pangar (ECA-199), the pottery is similarly still decorated with simple- or rocking-comb (55 %) impressions, but carved wooden or fiber roulettes are much more frequent (42 %). Beka Petel (ECA-243) similarly displays 51 % and 52 % comb impressions (depending on the level), and 44 % and 49 % carved wooden or fiber roulettes impressions. The only notable difference between the two levels is the absence of the rocking-comb technique in the oldest ceramics at Beka Petel. Lastly, pottery from these three sites displays decorative motifs in undulating or festooned bands, which is in certain aspects characteristic of modern Gbaya ceramics (GOSSELAIN 1995).

It is very probable that stone tools were still being produced during this period. At Sokorta Manga and Pangar, pottery was found in association with coarse debitage and cores. Even if at least a part of this debitage is actually older, the presence of ground and polished stone tools suggests a technology later than the MSA/LSA. Indeed, at Sokorta Manga a flaked adze with a polished edge was discovered on the surface. This tool is, technologically and typologically, completely different from the bifacial tools already mentioned, and must certainly be associated with the Iron Age assemblage. The polished stone axe discovered close to Lom I (ECA-177) was probably also produced during this period. It shows striking similarities to the adze from Sokorta Manga. Other similar, but undated sites from the area, such as Bemboyo (ECA-24) and Lesouaka (ECA-54), display an assemblage that also includes pottery, slag and lithic debitage (including fragments of polished stone tools at Lesouaka).

Phase IIb of the Iron Age in this area seems somewhat impoverished when compared to Phase IIa. It corresponds to the creation of villages such as Ewankang (ECA-93), Lom I (ECA-163) and Yébi (ECA-125) during the last four centuries. They yield assemblages comprising pottery and slag, very similar to those of Phase IIa. Traces of lithic industries are, however, fewer during this later period. Only at Ewankang did archaeologists recover some large unretouched quartzite flakes and cores. Several undated sites, interpreted as settlements and yielding artifacts of European manufacture, such as tin or glass artifacts, can probably be associated with this period. It should be stressed that, except for Ewankang, the sites of this period seem both smaller and materially impoverished compared to sites of Phase IIa. Earlier trends in ceramic decoration continued. At Ewankang, in the extreme south of the zone, roulette decoration (56 % — primarily string roulettes but also some carved wooden roulettes) and comb grooving (37 %) dominate during this period. At Yébi (ECA-125), roulettes (56 %) and stick grooving (33 %) dominate, whereas comb grooving is rare. At Lom I (ECA-163), the use of fiber roulettes is common through the assemblage.

The sites of Yébi and Lom I are probably related to settlements in the area of the modern Mbum and Gbaya populations. However, the lack of ceramic material studied to this point does not allow us to make a direct comparison with modern pottery production. Pottery from Ewankang, for example, seems very different from modern ceramics. One finds similar ceramics on a series of undated sites in an area ranging between Nanga Eboko and Belabo (ECA-81, -90, -91, -92, -94), sometimes associated with clay tobacco pipes.

Northern Cameroon: discussion

Northern Cameroon has probably been populated since the MSA, given the presence of typical lithic assemblages from this period on several sites. Metallurgy made its appearance approximately 2000 years ago at the latest. The Iron Age can be divided into two phases, possibly with two sub-phases in the later phase. Between *ca* 100 cal BC and cal AD 600, inhabitants of the area already lived in large settlements and produced pottery that was predominantly comb decorated, but the first roulettes were already in use at that time. Between cal AD 900 and cal AD 1400, large settlement sites proliferated. Roulette decoration became increasingly prevalent on ceramics during this period, at the expense of comb decoration. Stone tool usage still survived even in an iron-using context, as the presence of ground and polished stone tools attests. Lastly, between approximately 500 years ago and the present, large villages seem to disappear; known sites from this period are impoverished except in the extreme southwest of the zone, on the forest margins.

Distribution of sites in Cameroon — South

One hundred and eighteen sites were found in the southern part of the survey area in Cameroon, which extends over 421 km between Ewankang (ECA-93) and the Atlantic coast at Ebomé, near Kribi. The resulting linear site density of 0.28 sites/kilometer is the lowest in the entire survey area and a statistically significant decrease in site density from the northern zone. Since the boundary between these zones generally corresponds to

the boundary between wooded savanna and mixed forest zones, it is likely that this distinction can be ascribed to the same factors as discussed in Chapter Six: (1) the greater visibility of sites in more open environments and (2) somewhat higher average prehistoric population densities in those zones, as is in fact the case at present.

As in other parts of the Project research area, significant differences in overall site density also exist within this zone. Therefore, site densities are high in the area immediately west of Yaoundé, with 42 sites in a linear right-of-way length of 111 km (0.38 sites/km) and in the forest zone immediately east of the Atlantic coast, with 40 sites in 92 km (0.44 sites/km). On the other hand, densities are extremely low — the lowest in the entire Project research area — in the area around and to the east of Nanga Eboko (8 sites in 110 km, or 0.07 sites/km) and only somewhat higher in the Ngoumou – Lolodorf area closer to the coast (17 sites in 94 km, or 0.18 sites/km).

The reasons for this variability in site density are at present unknown but, as in Chad and northern Cameroon, they may in fact have various reasons in different areas including: (1) cultural preferences; (2) the effects of specific historical events; (3) geomorphological factors; and/or (4) some combination of all of these factors. There seems to be somewhat less clustering of sites on a more local level than in northern Cameroon. Both in areas of relatively high site density and low site density, sites appear to be distributed on the right-of-way fairly evenly. There is however a cluster of sites around the Minkan – Bikoue locality about 18 km east of Lolodorf, including ECA-170, -172, -174, -186, -188, -192, -194, -198 and -200. Of these, ECA-186, -192 and -200 were determined to be culturally significant. Most of the sites in this cluster appear to date to the Late Iron Age, although one lithic scatter (ECA-176) and one lithic horizon (ECA-192) were also discovered in the area.

Spatial and chronological distribution of different site types — Cameroon South

Ceramic and diverse artifact scatters

In contrast to the situation in both Chad and the northern zone in Cameroon, well under half of the sites found in the southern zone in Cameroon (49 out of 118, or approximately 42 %) were found on the surface, while the other 69 sites were buried. This much higher proportion of buried sites in southern Cameroon is probably due to the significantly lower surface visibility (and high levels of vegetational debris left even in cleared areas) in the forest zone. Of the total of 118 sites, only 27 (23 %) were surface ceramic scatters, while another 13 (11 %) were diverse artifact scatters. Ceramics again dominated in all cases in the latter category. Other materials found on these sites included grindstones and grindstone fragments, lithics, iron-working debris and artifacts of European manufacture. None of these sites were determined to be culturally significant — obviously a very different situation than in other parts of the Project research area. These determinations were based on the fact that these sites are for the most part small and low-density surface features.

Ceramic and diverse artifact horizons

The characteristics, complexity and importance of the ceramic and diverse artifact horizon sites in southern Cameroon warrant these to be considered separately. Of the 118 sites found in this area, 63 (54 %) belong to these two categories, including 40 ceramic horizons and 23 diverse artifact horizons. To an even greater degree than in other areas, the distinction between these two site types reflects the variation in sampling during survey, monitoring and data recovery excavations rather than any cultural differentiation or variation in site types. This is because, for this sample of 63 sites, two characteristics can be recognized: (1) the most obvious features on many of these buried sites are single or multiple pits (*Map 17*), filled with a variety of cultural material (including ceramics, lithics, slag, and plant and animal remains), and characteristic of Neolithic and early Iron Age occupation of southwestern Cameroon and neighboring areas (see *Chapter 4*); and (2) there is substantial spatial and cultural variability within this site sample, a potential indication of the presence of different cultural groups living along the right-of-way in prehistoric times. This variability, along with the dating of these sites, will be considered at the end of this chapter. It should be noted that these numbers include two very significant rock shelter sites, Ndtoua (ECA-68) and Bikoué II (ECA-192), and that excavations on the former site have yielded an extremely important cultural sequence covering the second half of the Holocene.

Only 15 (24 %) of these 63 sites were discovered during pre-construction survey, while 48 were discovered in the course of construction monitoring. This is not surprising, given a reduced surface visibility and a concomitant reliance on auger testing in the forest zone. A total of 27 (43 %) of the sites has been designated as culturally significant, a higher proportion than in other parts of the right-of-way. This probably reflects the relatively higher proportion of these sites as a percentage of the total site numbers in this region. Twenty eight sites have also yielded pit features. The overlap between the two categories is important but not total: an amount of

21 ceramic/diverse artifact horizon sites both have pit features and were designated as culturally significant. Of these, 18 (ECA-130, -138, -146, -216, -224, -236, -242, -248, -250, -266, -272, -279, -315, -317, -323, -329, -333, -335) were subjected to data recovery excavations, while three (ECA-164, -182, -208) were protected through intentional burial. Of the other sites (without pits but culturally significant) in this category, one (Ndtoua Rock shelter [ECA-68]) was subjected to data recovery excavations, two (Bikoué-Si [ECA-186] and Bikoué II Rock shelter [ECA-192] were avoided through narrowing of the right-of-way, and three (Minkan [ECA-200], Nkoayos [ECA-305], and Bikoto [ECA-321]) were protected by intentional burial.

It is noteworthy that these sites are, on average, smaller than sites determined to be culturally significant in the northern zone in Cameroon and in Chad. Most of the pit sites so designated measure less than 30x30 m, with sites like ECA-182 (200 linear meters on the right-of-way), ECA-208 (150 linear meters), ECA-272 (300 linear meters), ECA-315 (200 linear meters) and ECA-333 (350 linear meters) being the exceptions. Culturally significant non-pit sites tend to be larger on average than pit sites. This is not surprising: pit sites in this area yield a large amount of cultural material in a restricted area, and the linear extent of such sites tends to be determined by the number of pits encountered. Small sites, with single pits, are probably in most cases representative of much larger concentrations of pits.

Iron-working horizons and scatters

Three iron-working surface scatters (Bifoum [ECA-154], Nkoelon [ECA-202] and ECA-234) and four buried iron-working horizons (Makouré [ECA-124], Mvile [ECA-178], Ngoumou [ECA-220] and Yegue Assi [ECA-264]) were located in the course of the Project CHM activities. All but ECA-202 were discovered in the course of construction monitoring. In addition, slag and/or iron was found on nine pit sites (ECA-266, -268, -270, -272, -279, -323, -327, -329, -335) between Yaoundé and the area east of Nanga Eboko. It is likely that most of these occurrences indicate production or repair of iron tools in a habitation site. This is a somewhat larger number of sites than were found in the northern zone in Cameroon, but significantly fewer than in southwestern Chad.

Of the iron-working sites, only the four iron-working horizons were determined to be culturally significant: the scatters were small surface distributions of slag and/or furnace fragments and other cultural materials. These sites are scattered between Yaoundé

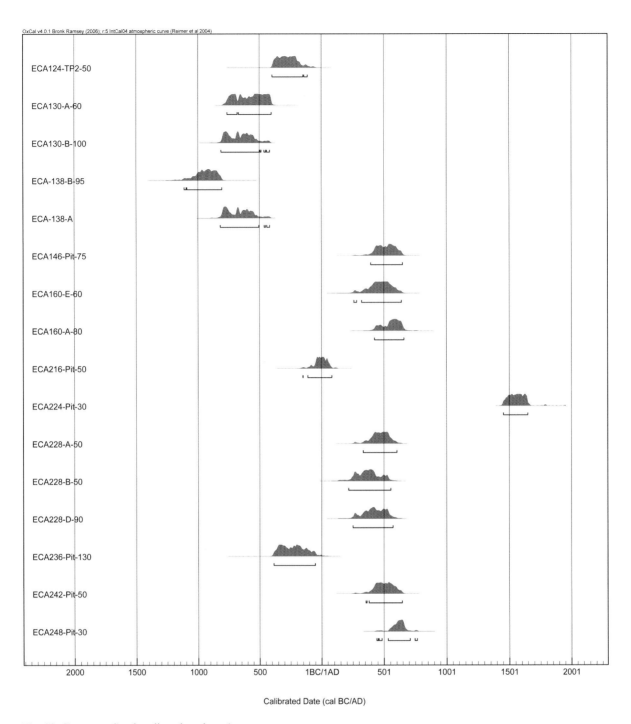

OxCal v4.0.1 Bronk Ramsey (2006); r:5 IntCal04 atmospheric curve (Reimer et al 2004)

Calibrated Date (cal BC/AD)

Fig. 33. Cameroon South radiocarbon dates 1.

and the Atlantic coast, and few inferences about spatial patterning can be made given their relatively small number. It is noteworthy that none were found in the area around Nanga Eboko, even if site densities in that area are generally low. Of the four iron-working horizons, one (ECA-124) was subject to data recovery excavations and site avoidance through narrowing of the right-of-way, two (ECA-178, -220) were avoided through narrowing of the right-of-way and one (ECA-264) was protected by intentional burial.

Excavations at Makouré (ECA-124) yielded data on the first iron-smelting site to be discovered in the forest zone of southern Cameroon (see below). Unfortunately, and in contrast to Djaoro Mbama (ECA-47), no furnace remains were recovered *in situ*. It appears that either the furnaces were almost completely destroyed in the course of recovery of the iron bloom, or that excavations took place in a slag discard area. The technology appears to be that of a low-shaft bloomery furnace. A charcoal sample from the site (*App. F* and *Fig. 33*) yielded a calibrated

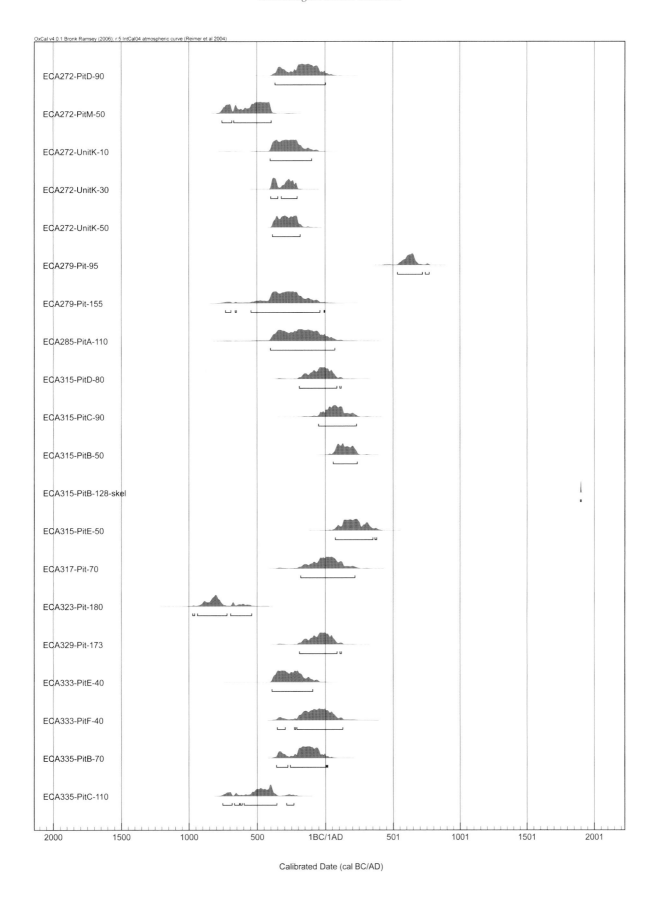

Calibrated Date (cal BC/AD)

Fig. 34. Cameroon South radiocarbon dates 2.

radiocarbon date of 395 – 100 BC, indicating iron working in southern Cameroon at a date slightly earlier than at Djaoro Mbama or at any of the sites in southern Chad. Confirmation and refinement of that chronology will, of course, have to await further work.

Lithic scatters and horizons

Four lithic surface scatters (ECA-63/108, -66, -160 and -262 [Ebot]) and two buried lithic horizons (Bikoué-Si [ECA-176] and Mvomdoumba [ECA-299]) were discovered in the course of Project fieldwork in southern Cameroon. Three of these sites were discovered during pre-construction survey, and the other three during construction monitoring. Only one, ECA-262, was determined to be culturally significant, and was protected by intentional burial.

In addition, and perhaps more importantly, substantial amounts of lithic materials were recovered on the surface or from the stratigraphy of a number of diverse artifact sites: Ndtoua Rock shelter (ECA-68), Bikoué II Rock shelter (ECA-192), Minkan I (ECA-200), Leboudi (ECA-250) and Ezezang (ECA-272). Two of these latter sites (ECA-68 and ECA-272) were subject to data recovery excavations. ECA-68 yielded a radiocarbon date of *ca* 5500 bp, or 4460 – 4225 cal BC, associated with a LSA microlithic industry (***App. F*** and ***Fig. 33***). The relatively small number of these sites makes it difficult to detect any significant spatial patterning, although three of them (ECA-250, -262 and -272) are within 14 km of one another in the vicinity of Yaoundé, while ECA-176 and -192 are only 2 km apart, east of Lolodorf.

The lithic assemblages from these sites are quite variable. Excavations at Ezezang (ECA-272) yielded lithic materials from 0.4–0.8 m below surface. Most of the artifacts were made on quartzite, and include large bifacial tools, often unfinished, on block cores and backed flakes, of which some were of microlithic proportions. The methods of flaking and tool production were generally unspecialized, and seem to have been organized with the goal of producing large flakes and tools on blocks. Similar assemblages were found at Leboudi (ECA-250) and at Ebot (ECA-262). From a typological and technological point of view, these assemblages are typical of the late MSA/early LSA. The location of all three sites near Yaoundé (see above) is interesting. At this stage of analysis, it is not possible to establish whether this geographical distribution is due to the spatial patterning of a prehistoric technological system or to geomorphological conditions (erosion, vegetation cover, topography) that permit the discovery of these sites.

Excavations at Ndtoua (ECA-68) yielded very different lithic assemblages, described in more detail below, but in general dominated by microlithic tools and debitage on quartz, with a significant macrolithic component in the lowest level. This parallels the lithic assemblages recovered from Bikoué-Si (ECA-176) and Bikoué II (ECA-192), situated in close proximity east of Lolodorf. These assemblages probably date to the LSA, as indicated by the earliest date at Ndtoua (ECA-68), although they could also be Neolithic in cultural affiliation.

Tombs

Two modern tombs were located near Yaoundé in the course of Project work in the southern zone in Cameroon. They are approximately eight kilometers apart. Both were given archaeological site numbers (Ngoya [ECA-281] and Mvog Dzigui [ECA-291]) and accorded high priority, as mandated in the Management Plans for Cultural Properties in both Chad and Cameroon (see *Chapter 2*). The right-of-way was narrowed around the sites to avoid any disturbance of the tombs, their positions were reported, and further negotiation over their locations and any possible construction impacts was handled by the Project socioeconomic team.

Description of particular sites — Cameroon South

ECA-68 — Ndtoua Rock shelter

ECA-68 was discovered on September 12, 2001 near Ndtoua village, in the Atlantic littoral forest zone and approximately 36 km from the Atlantic coast. It is a small rock shelter beneath a large block of granite discovered in the right-of-way (***Fig. 35***). The surface under the overhang is about 12x4 m (48 m²). Two archaeological layers were discovered in the course of auger testing: the more recent one (0.2 m below surface) included potsherds and a few quartz flakes; the older one (0.4 m below surface) consisted of quartz flakes reminiscent of a microlithic stone industry. As ECA-68 is one of the first rock shelters discovered in the southern forest of Cameroon, the site was classified as high priority for further treatment. Avoidance was not possible and the Site Treatment Plan recommended data recovery. Excavations took place between October 9 and 24, 2001 and on November 15 and 16, 2001. A grid was laid and a systematic program of auger testing was implemented to delimit the extent of the cultural levels. Most of the area beneath the overhang yielded very little sediment to excavate, with large rocks present just below the soil surface. Three 1 m² test pits were opened — units C6,

Fig. 35. General view of Ndtoua (ECA-68).

Fig. 36. Excavations in progress at Ndtoua (ECA-68).

Fig. 37. Quartz shatter and flakes from Level III at Ndtoua (ECA-68).

E7 and E8 on the grid (*Fig. 36*). Only pit C6 was dug to any significant depth, reaching bedrock at 1.8 m below surface.

Four archaeological levels were identified. The most recent, Level IV, situated between the surface and 0.3 m below surface contained a few potsherds, a few stone flakes and one iron tool. The next level, Level III, between 0.4 and 0.8–0.9 m below surface, yielded a rich stone industry and rare pieces of pottery. The stone artifacts were clustered in a well-defined area and can be interpreted as the *in situ* by-products of stone tool manufacture (*Fig. 37*). The next cultural level, Level II, found between 0.8 and 1.3 m below surface, consisted of a rather poor stone industry, with very small quartz and rock crystal flakes. No ceramics were found in this unit. Level I, between 1.3 and 1.8 m below surface, consisted of an assemblage of much larger flakes and tools on quartz. The last 0.3 m of sediments at the bottom appear to be an accumulation layer where archaeological artifacts, sand, river pebble and degraded rock are mixed at the contact with bedrock.

Level IV yielded 0.3 kg of quartz artifacts, 0.2 kg of pottery (11 potsherds) and one single iron tool (a fragment of a blade). The quartz industry comprises of 93 % lithic shatter, 4 % flakes and 3 % cores. No standardized tools were identified. Three potsherds were decorated with stick grooving.

Level III yielded 1.2 kg of quartz artifacts and 0.25 kg of pottery (14 potsherds). The quartz industry

consists of 89 % shatter, 5 % flakes, 4 % unspecialized cores and 2 % tools. The toolkit is composed of small scrapers and backed flakes. Four potsherds were decorated with comb and stick grooves.

Only 0.45 kg of quartz lithics were collected in Level II. The quartz industry comprises of 91 % shatter, 5 % flakes, 3 % cores and 1 % tools. The latter include scrapers and backed flakes.

Approximately 8.5 kg of quartz tools, cores, flakes and fragments were recovered in Level I. The quartz industry consists of 79 % shatter, 12 % flakes, 5 % unspecialized cores and 4 % tools. The toolkit is composed of scrapers and backed flakes.

Four charcoal samples, associated with three archaeological layers, were dated (*App. F* and *Fig. 38*). The most recent cultural level, Level IV (0.2–0.3 m below surface) was dated to approximately 700 bp, calibrated at AD 1225 – 1400. Two samples from Level III (located at 0.4–0.5 m and 0.8–0.9 m below surface [the latter at the base of the level]) yielded dates very close to 1900 bp, calibrated to 50 BC – AD 245. The lowest cultural level, Level I (1.7–1.8 m), was dated to 5490 ± 70 bp, or 4460 – 4225 cal BC. Level II, which is not dated, thus has a probable age somewhere in the interval between 1900 bp and 5500 bp. The stratigraphy of the site spans the whole second half of the Holocene. Ndtoua rock shelter was therefore first occupied during the 5th millennium BC, with a subsequent occupation dating between the first century BC and the third century AD. The most recent cultural level is dated to the 13th – 14th centuries AD.

ECA-68 is a small rock shelter probably used by humans for short-duration stays during hunting parties. This is suggested by the scarcity of pottery in the Iron Age layers. It appears that artifacts were trapped between large blocks of granite as seen in Pit C6. Where artifacts accumulated, the stratigraphy is almost two meters thick. Four cultural layers are present from bedrock to surface, spanning the last six millennia of the Holocene. The oldest occupation, Level I, is actually an accumulation of artifacts and natural debris on top of the bedrock. The assemblage is composed of a Late Stone Age industry on quartz, dated to the late fifth millennium BC. It is not known whether the presence of large cores and flakes is the result of a natural process or is a cultural phenomenon. The

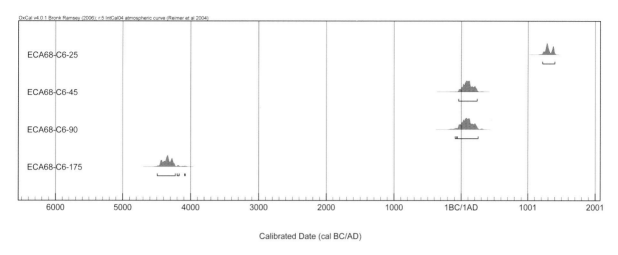

Fig. 38. Radiocarbon dates for Ndtoua (ECA-68).

Fig. 39. Initial
site examination
at Makouré
(ECA-124).

overlying Level II is a somewhat poor Late Stone Age microlithic quartz industry, probably dating somewhere between the fourth and first millennium BC. Level III, dated to the beginning of the first millennium AD, sees the appearance of pottery in Ndtoua, associated with a rich microlithic quartz industry. The last occupation, Level IV, is dated to approximately 700 years ago and consists of a poor assemblage of *ad hoc* quartz artifacts, pottery and a single iron blade.

Ndtoua rock shelter, albeit very limited in space, presents an exceptional cultural stratigraphy that spans the transition from the Late Stone Age to the Iron Age in a previously unexplored part of the Cameroonian tropi-

cal forest. The discovery of an assemblage associating a LSA technology and pottery, and dating to the Iron Age, is especially noteworthy.

ECA-124 — Makouré

ECA-124, Makouré, is an iron-working site, discovered on December 29, 2001, when iron-smelting furnace fragments and slag were identified in the embankment created by the grading operations at the edges of the pipeline easement (*Fig. 39*). The site is spread over an area of 100x20 m at least. The features are buried some 0.5 m below surface and were exposed

Fig. 40. Tuyère fragments at Makouré (ECA-124).

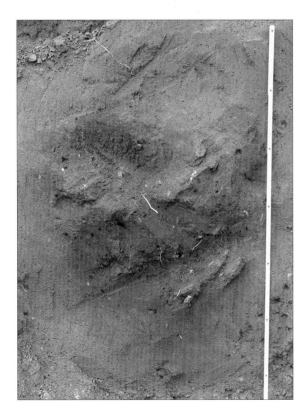

Fig. 41. Profile of Pit A at Dombè (ECA-130).

threatened with destruction during further construction activity, ECA-124 was classified as high priority for further work.

The Site Treatment Plan recommended that the features exposed by grading operations be excavated for data recovery. This was done between January 5 and 9, 2002. Four 1 m² test pits were opened and dug to a depth of 0.7 m below surface to reach sterile levels. The excavations yielded mostly fragments of tuyères, parts of furnace walls and slag (***Fig. 40***). No *in situ* feature was identified as the furnace(s) had apparently been entirely destroyed after the smelting operations. It is also possible that the area excavated was located in the refuse part of the site. One charcoal sample was dated and gave a calibrated radiocarbon date of 395 – 100 BC (***App. F*** and ***Fig. 33***). Makouré is an iron-smelting site that was used sometime between the 4th and the 2nd centuries BC. Although no intact furnace was found, it seems that the technology used was a traditional bloomery furnace. The absence of pottery or other domestic materials suggests that the site never functioned as a settlement.

ECA-130 — Dombè

ECA-130 was discovered on January 9, 2002 during monitoring of trenching activities. The site is located in the suburbs of Kribi, in the Littoral Atlantic forest zone, and consists of two prehistoric pit features, cut

by the earthmoving operations. Makouré is one of the earliest iron-working sites found in the forests of southern Cameroon. Because of the remarkable nature of the site, and due to the fact that the features were

2 cm

Fig. 42. Ceramics from Pit A Dombè (ECA-130).

in half by the ditching operations. Potsherds were identified in the profile. The site was accorded high priority for further work, as it is one of the first of this type found in the area. The two pit features, A and B, were excavated for data recovery on January 10, 11 and 12, 2002, and all artifacts contained in the pits were collected.

The pit features at ECA-130 consist of deep and narrow shafts, with straight and vertical walls, approximately 1.5 meters in diameter and 2.5 meters in depth (*Fig. 41*). The dark color of the pit fills contrasts with the natural reddish-ochre soil, probably a result of the decay of organic material. Pit A yielded approximately 5 kg of pottery (292 potsherds) and 3 kg of lithic material, while 6.6 kg of pottery were unearthed in Pit B. Morphologically,

this pottery most frequently exhibits globular bodies, with beveled (35 %) or rounded (31 %) external rims. Angular (17 %), grooved (10 %) or flat (7 %) lips are less common. The necks of the vessels are mostly concave (74 %) or straight (20 %), with only a few convex necks (that is, closed bowls). Pottery decoration is quite diverse (*Figs. 42* and *43*): simple comb stamping is the most frequent technique (31 %), followed by stick- (24 %) and comb grooving (15 %). Rocking-comb (11 %) and rocking-blade impression (10 %) techniques are also frequent. Stick impressions (8 %) and -punctations (2 %) are less common. Decoration is very common, but is particularly frequent on the neck of the vessels, with 69 % of neck sherds decorated, or on the upper part of the vessel body (67 %). Rims are sometimes decorated (28 %), while the bottoms of the vessels never are.

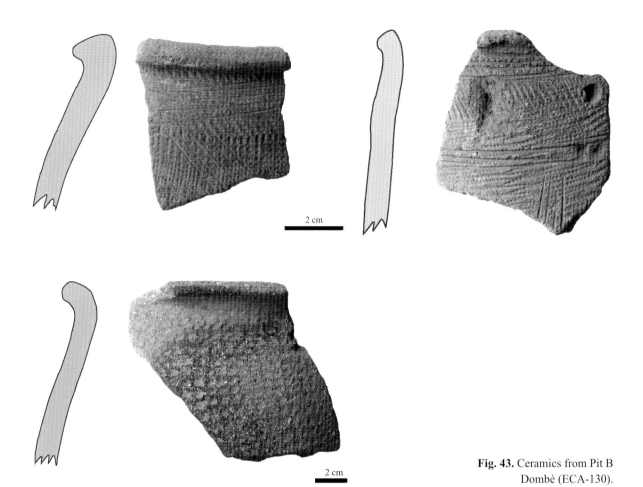

2 cm

2 cm

Fig. 43. Ceramics from Pit B
Dombè (ECA-130).

Fig. 44. Drawing of Pit A at Bissiang (ECA-138).

Fig. 45. Section of Pit A at Bissiang (ECA-138).

Lithic artifacts consist of only a few grinding stones and hammerstone fragments. The absence of any significant amount of stone flakes and tools is noteworthy. Radiocarbon dating of two charcoal samples collected in the pit features yielded virtually identical dates, between about 800 – 400 cal BC (*App. F* and *Fig. 33*).

The construction of large pit features is probably evidence of long-term settlement, given the energy investment needed to excavate them. Ethnographic comparisons suggest that these pits were used as water wells, clay mines, silos or latrines. When their primary use was completed, they were used as refuse pits and it is as such that archaeologists usually find them. Thus, ECA-130 was probably a prehistoric village, inhabited by sedentary farmers. The fact that it was occupied during the first half of the last millennium BC indicates that

it was one of the first villages of the region (see *Chapter 4*). The absence of any stone artifacts other than grinding stones raises the possibility that the inhabitants of this site were already using iron. Confirmation of this possibility will require the identification and dating of tools and/or smelting or smithing remains from the period. Iron tools would probably have been rare and expensive at this time, not to be thrown away but rather recycled when worn out or broken.

ECA-138 — Bissiang

ECA-138 was discovered in the trench during monitoring of trenching activities on January 19, 2002 (***Figs. 44*** and ***45***). The site, located in the Atlantic Littoral forest zone, consists of three prehistoric pit features cut in half

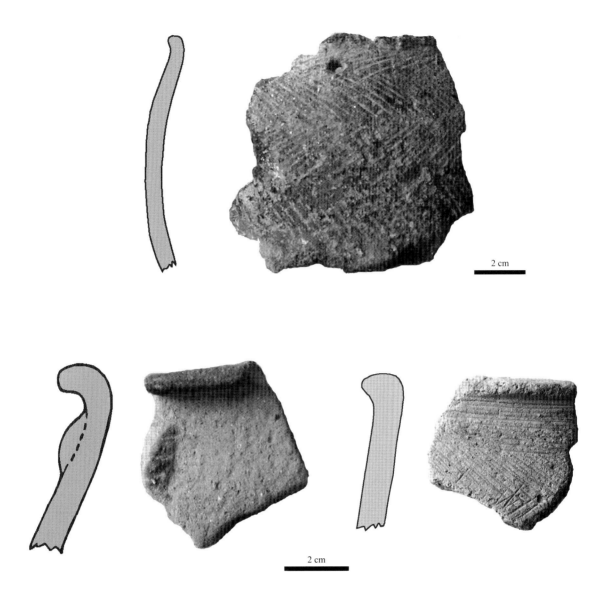

Fig. 46. Ceramics from Bissiang (ECA-138).

by the ditching operations. The site was classified as high priority for further work, as it is one of the first of this type found in the area. The three pits (A, B and C) were excavated from January 21 to 25, 2002. All the artifacts contained in the pits were collected. Pit A (with a diameter of 1.5 m and a depth of 2 m) yielded 6.3 kg of pottery (350 potsherds), and Pit B (diameter 1.1 m, depth 1.8 m) contained 8.9 kg of pottery (493 potsherds). A grinding stone was also located in pit B. Pit C, of which only the bottom was left (diameter 1.1 m, depth 0.8 m) yielded only 0.3 kg of pottery (18 potsherds).

Bissiang ceramics usually have rounded (32 %) or flat (24 %) rims, but grooved (19 %), externally beveled (14 %) and angular rims (14 %) are also quite common (***Fig. 46***). The necks are primarily concave (66 %) but convex necks (*i.e.*, closed bowls) are also frequent (25 %). Straight necks are rare (9 %). All the identified bases are flat, and some handles were excavated. Pottery decoration is dominated by rocking impression technique, either with a blade (33 %) or with a comb (12 %). Comb- (19 %) and stick (16 %) grooving is also frequent. Simple stamping with a stick (9 %) or comb (5 %) are present but uncommon, as are appliqué on handles (4 %) and punctations (2 %). A large part of the vessel body is decorated, especially on the neck (72 % of shoulder sherds are decorated) and on the upper part of the vessel body (68 % of sherds are decorated). Rims are rarely (19 %) decorated, and pot bottoms are always smoothed and undecorated.

Two charcoal samples were radiocarbon dated, with Pit A yielding a calibrated radiocarbon date of 820 – 425 BC, while Pit B dated to 1105 – 805 BC (*App. F* and *Fig. 33*). Two hypotheses can be put forward to explain this: (1) the two pit features are not contemporaneous, meaning that the site was occupied over an extended period of time or on two separate occasions, or (2) the discrepancy derives from the statistical uncertainty inherent in the dating method and the most probable age of the site is approximately 800 cal BC. The latter seems less likely. In any event, ECA-138 appears to have been occupied during the first half of the last millennium BC. A date at the end of the 2nd millennium BC is improbable but not impossible.

As at ECA-130, the construction of large pit features is probably evidence of a fairly long-term settlement, given the energy investment needed to excavate them. In many other features, including the broad characteristics of the ceramics and the age of the site, Bissiang substantially resembles Dombè.

ECA-186 — Bikoué-Si

ECA-186 was discovered on March 23, 2003 during monitoring of grading operations on the pipeline right-of-way. The site is situated near Bikoué-Si village, near Lolodorf in the Atlantic Littoral forest zone. It consists of a low-density horizon of ceramics and possible flaked stone artifacts, spread over about 50 m along the graded surface of the pipeline easement, with a total observed area of approximately 1500 m². Because of the rarity of flaked stone artifacts on the right-of-way, the site was accorded high priority for further treatment. The non-impacted part of the site was avoided by narrowing of the right-of-way from 30 m to 25 m.

ECA-186 appears to have been a Neolithic or Iron Age campsite. The association between pottery and stone tools, which would normally indicate a Neolithic site, is however not established. Further study would be necessary to ascertain that (1) there is indeed a genuine stone industry and (2) that the stone industry and the pottery are part of the same assemblage and not the result of accidental mixing.

ECA-192 — Bikoué II

ECA-192 was identified on April 10, 2002 during pre-construction survey. The site is a rock shelter, located near Lolodorf, in the Atlantic Littoral forest zone. Auger tests revealed two occupation levels, the upper one with pottery and the lower one with flaked stone. Due to the scarcity of multi-component sites in the Lolodorf area, it was accorded high priority for further work. The Site Treatment Plan recommended avoidance. The site was marked off for protection during construction and the right-of-way was narrowed so that the blasting of the overhanging rock could be cancelled. ECA-192 was probably occupied on at least two occasions, during the Late Stone Age and the Iron Age. Further study might reveal other archaeological horizons buried more deeply in the stratigraphy.

ECA-224 — Oboukoé

ECA-224 was discovered during construction monitoring on July 13, 2002. Situated in an unexplored region of the right-of-way in the Atlantic Littoral forest zone, the site was classified as high priority for further work. It consisted of a single refuse pit, partly destroyed by bulldozers in the embankment of the graded area. The structure contained an impressive amount of wood charcoal — a unique opportunity for ^{14}C dating and wood species determination — as well as fragments of pottery. The site was excavated between July 18 and 20, 2002.

Two overlapping pit features were located in the excavation. While the older pit feature was dug to a depth of 1.3 m and had a diameter of 1.4 m, with a roughly rounded profile, the more recent pit was only 0.6 m deep but much larger (about 2.1 m) and had a square profile. Only 0.75 kg of potsherds was collected. Pottery decoration techniques were restricted to comb- and stick grooving. A charcoal sample, collected in the older pit, was dated to cal AD 1445 – 1660 (*App. F* and *Fig. 33*).

ECA-224 appears to be a late Iron Age settlement site that was inhabited sometime between the 15th and 17th centuries AD. At least two phases of pit construction took place at the site, and the later of these may have involved the modern village of Oboukoé. It is not uncommon to find that prehistoric pit features are used by modern populations to facilitate the digging of new pits, as they are filled with much softer sediments than the natural lateritic soil.

ECA-228 — Binguela II

ECA-228 was discovered on August 5, 2002 during construction monitoring (trenching operations). The site consists of four pit features identified in the trench (Pits A, B, C and D), located in the mixed forest zone, and was classified as high priority for further work. The Site Treatment Plan recommended data recovery, and the four pit features were excavated. The excavations took place between August 6 and 8, 2002.

117

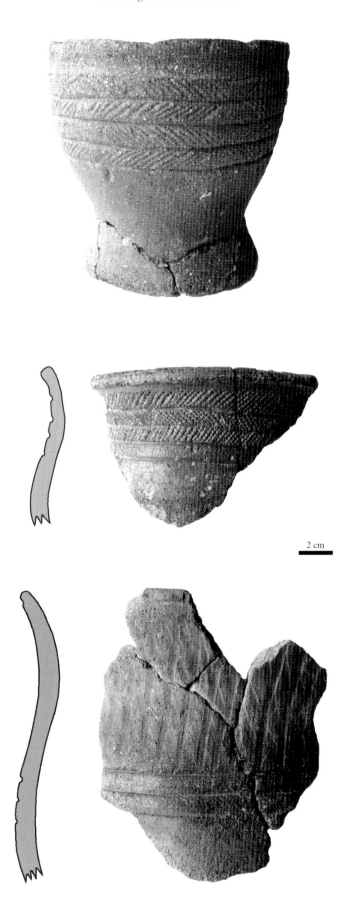

2 cm

Fig. 47. Ceramics from Binguela II (ECA-228).

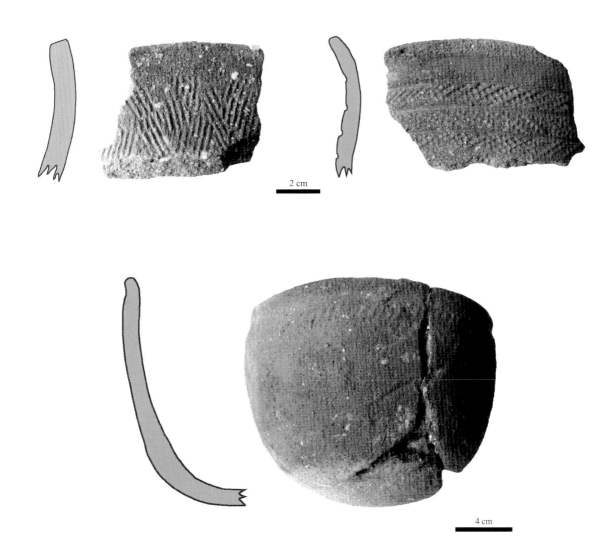

2 cm

4 cm

Fig. 48. Ceramics from Binguela II (ECA-228).

Pit A (1.8 m in diameter, 0.6 m deep) yielded 4.1 kg of pottery; Pit B (1.25 m in diameter, 0.8 m deep) yielded 5.1 kg of pottery; only 0.15 kg of pottery were collected in Pit C (2 m in diameter, 0.85 m deep) and 0.65 kg in Pit D (0.65 m in diameter, 1.2 m deep). Pottery decoration techniques (samples from Pits A and B) consisted mostly of grooving with a comb-gouge (32 to 39 % depending on the pit), dragged-comb (14 to 45 %) and dragged-stick (13 to 36 %) techniques (*Figs. 47* and *48*). Simple- and walking-comb impression is present but rare (less than 10 %). Burnt nuts of *Elaeis guineensis* and *Canarium schweinfurthii* were collected in Pit A. Three charcoal samples, collected in Pits A, B and C, were radiocarbon dated; the three dates, in very close agreement, indicate that the site was occupied between cal AD 230 – 610 (*App. F* and *Fig. 33*).

ECA-228 is an Iron Age settlement site that was inhabited sometime in the 3rd to early 7th centuries AD. As four pit features were discovered in the ditch, it is highly probable that more pits are present in the area but were not unearthed by grading operations, which implies a relatively large settlement.

ECA-236 — *Zoatoupsi*

ECA-236 is a refuse pit site discovered in the pipeline trench near the village of Zoatoupsi on August 16, 2002 during construction monitoring. The site is located on a plateau, in the mixed forest zone, and was accorded high priority for further treatment. The single pit feature was excavated between August 17 and 20, 2002.

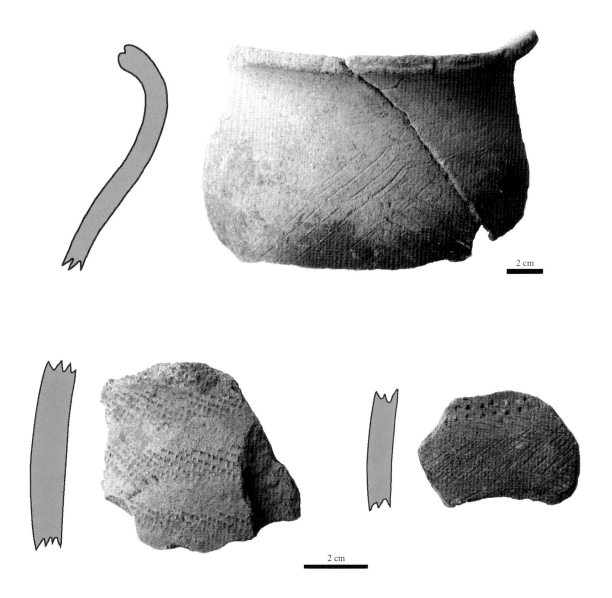

2 cm

2 cm

Fig. 49. Ceramics from Zoatoupsi (ECA-235).

Pottery, some stone tools and charcoal were collected. The excavation reached down to 3.4 m below the graded surface.

The Zoatoupsi pit is quite large with 2 m in diameter and almost 4 m deep. Its sides are vertical. Approximately 11.5 kg of pottery (642 potsherds) was collected in the pit feature. Pottery decoration techniques are dominated by comb grooving (42 %) and rocking blade impressions (31 %), while stick grooving (21 %) and simple comb impression (6 %) are less frequent (***Fig. 49***). Burnt nuts of *Elaeis guineensis* and *Canarium schweinfurthii* were collected in the pit feature. A single charcoal sample was radiocarbon dated, yielding a calibrated age between 390 – 40 BC (***App. F*** and ***Fig. 33***).

ECA-236 is a small Iron Age site occupied during the late first millennium BC. The depth of the pit feature is exceptional, suggesting that it could have been used as a well. This is evidence for long-term settlement, certainly by sedentary farming populations. The amount of *Elaeis* and *Canarium* nuts identified in the pit argues in favor of such a hypothesis. Although these trees were never domesticated as such, they were protected and sometimes even planted. Such behavior (protection and intensive gathering) is interpreted as a first step towards full-scale food production; at this point, we do not know the point along this trajectory that had been reached by the inhabitants of Zoatoupsi. The time period and the absence of stone tools imply that these farmers were probably already using iron.

ECA-242 — Ozom

ECA-242, situated near Ozom village, was identified on August 29, 2002 during construction monitoring. The site is located in the mixed forest zone. A group of four refuse pits was partly unearthed by trenching activities. Very little archaeological material was visible but, given the number of pits, the site was accorded high priority for further work. Only one pit was excavated between September 2 and 4, 2002. The excavation reached down to a depth of 1 m below the graded surface (1.3 m below surface). The feature yielded pottery as well as wood charcoal, clustered between 0.4 m below surface and the bottom of the pit at 0.8 m below surface.

Only three potsherds were discovered in the pit. A charcoal sample collected between 0.4 and 0.6 m below surface was radiocarbon dated, yielding a date of cal AD 385–645 (*App. F* and *Fig. 33*). ECA-242 seems to have been an Iron Age settlement site inhabited sometime between the 4th and the 7th centuries AD. The pit was apparently filled primarily with organic material that disappeared with time, hence the paucity of the artifacts collected.

ECA-250 — Leboudi

ECA-250, situated near Leboudi village in the mixed forest zone, was discovered during construction monitoring on August 5, 2002. Iron Age pottery and lithics were located on the graded surface, obviously mixed by construction activity. It was first catalogued as ECA-285 and classified as medium priority for further work. As such, monitoring of the trenching activities was scheduled to determine whether material in primary context was to be found in depth. On this occasion, three pit features (Pits A, B and C) were discovered and it was decided that excavations were necessary. The site was then re-classified as high priority for further work. Excavations took place from September 9 to 11, 2002. Excavation of Pit A continued to a depth of 1.5 m below the graded surface. Only the bottoms of Pits B and C were preserved, and only a few potsherds were found. Stone artifacts scattered on the graded surface were systematically collected as well.

The flaked stone tools and cores collected on the graded surface present the technological and typological characteristics of the Middle Stone Age or early Late Stone Age: several bifacial core axes were identified. A grinding stone and an iron arrowhead were also found on the surface. Only Pit A was sufficiently well preserved to be of interest and yielded a significant amount of prehistoric material. This pit, with a diameter at the top of 1.5 m, was only 0.9 m deep (0.6 to 1.5 m

below surface). The archaeological material was clustered between 0.6 and 1.2 m below surface, and the last 0.3 m at the bottom of the pit were sterile. A total of 186 potsherds was collected (3.3 kg), as well as grinding stone fragments and slag. The pit also yielded a large amount of burnt nuts of *Elaeis guineensis*.

Pottery decoration techniques consisted primarily of comb grooving (42 %) and -stamping (6 %), rocking blade (31 %) impressions and stick grooving (18 %). The stone tools could not be dated but, given their typological characteristics, an age between 50,000 and 10,000 bp is estimated. A single charcoal sample, collected at 1.2 m below surface in Pit A, gave a radiocarbon age of 400 cal BC – cal AD 80 (*App. F* [ECA-250] and *Fig. 34* [ECA-285]).

ECA-250 seems to have been occupied on two different occasions: during the Middle Stone Age (in the late Pleistocene) and during the early Iron Age (between the 3rd century BC and the 1st century AD). The stone tools were found on the graded surface and were probably already in secondary context at the time of construction. The Iron Age material, on the other hand, was found *in situ*. The pit features are probably the remnants of a long-term forest settlement by farmers. The amount of *Elaeis* nuts identified in the pit argues in favor of such a hypothesis. As at other sites of this period and area, it is likely that the inhabitants of this community were already farmers.

ECA-264 — Yegue Assi

ECA-264 was identified on September 14, 2002 during the monitoring of the trenching operations. The site, located in the mixed forest zone in the Yaoundé area, consists of a small, 2 m long, buried distribution of furnace fragments and slag. It was accorded high priority for further treatment. The Site Treatment Plan recommended intentional backfill of the trench without further earthmoving. Since the pipe was already laid in the ditch, backfilling took place the same day. ECA-264 is a small iron-smelting site of unknown age. It is possible that this site is related to ECA-266 (see below), located only 650 meters to the south.

ECA-266 — Yegue Assi

This site, situated near Yegue Assi village in the mixed forest zone, was discovered on August 12, 2002 during construction monitoring, and was first catalogued as ECA-289. Some pottery, slag and one hammerstone were found on the graded surface of a hillside, and the

Fig. 50. Pit profile from Ezezang (ECA-272).

site was estimated to be of low priority for further work. During monitoring of trenching activities on September 14, 2002, two prehistoric refuse pits (A and B) were identified in the ditch and the site was re-classified as high priority for further work. Excavations started immediately and lasted until September 19, 2002. Pit A was excavated to a depth of 0.6 m below the graded surface (about 1 m below natural ground surface). Only the bottom of the feature was preserved. Pottery, slag and a hammerstone were collected. The pottery was decorated with comb- and stick grooving.

ECA-266 is a small Iron Age settlement of unknown age. The absence of roulette decoration suggests an age of more than 500 years. It is not impossible that ECA-266 could be linked with ECA-264 (see above), which is located only 650 meters to the north.

ECA 272 — Ezezang

ECA-272, situated near Ezezang village, was discovered during construction monitoring on August 22, 2002. Situated on top of a hill (altitude 750 m) in a savanna area of the mixed forest zone, the site is about 300x300 m in size. The right-of-way crossed the site on the hillside, and artifacts were identified over more than 300 linear meters on the right-of-way, over an area of 9000 m². It was

estimated that construction would impact about 10 % of the total surface area. Several periods of occupation were recognized on the day of discovery. The oldest archaeological layer consisted of a small assemblage of flaked stone artifacts, identified in the trench. The most recent human occupation comprised a large group of prehistoric refuse pits and a 'living floor' yielding abundant pottery. Ten pit features were identified in the right-of-way, in the trench and on the graded surface. All these features were already partly impacted by construction, with parts of the features removed by earthmoving operations.

The site was classified as high priority for further work, and the Site Treatment Plan recommended data recovery. Operations started on September 15, 2002 and proceeded through the month of October. A controlled collection of surface artifacts was undertaken first: pottery and stone tools were identified. Found on the surface of the graded area of the right-of-way, these came either from the overlying topsoil removed by the bulldozers, from the pottery horizon or from the top of the pit features. This collection is hereafter named the GS assemblage. Two pits were excavated in the trench (Pit D and M) and one test pit (Unit K) was dug on the side of the trench to reach the pottery horizon and the stone industry layer below.

The two pits had been transected longitudinally by the ditch and grading had removed their tops (*Fig. 50*).

Pit D was excavated down to 1.5 m and Pit M down to 1.3 m below grading surface. Considered sealed features, with all artifacts contained within to be contemporaneous, the stratigraphic context of the pits was first analyzed and then the features were emptied completely, with all sediments collected as a single stratigraphic unit. They yielded mostly pottery and a few stone artifacts, hereafter called the D and M assemblages.

Pit D is 1.6 m in diameter and 1.6 m deep and is actually a combination of two pits, a later pit having been dug inside the earlier one. Pottery (4.25 kg), a significant amount of lithic material (a hammerstone, a quartzite core and flakes), slag and burnt nuts of *Canarium schweinfurthii* and *Elaeis guineensis* were collected. Pit M is 1.4 m in diameter and 1.2 m deep. It yielded pottery (5.85 kg), stone implements (hammerstones, a large complete lower grinding stone, a few quartzite cores and flakes), slag and burnt nuts of *Canarium schweinfurthii* and *Elaeis guineensis*. The excavations of Unit K proceeded to a depth of 1 m before reaching sterile soil. The stratigraphy of this unit revealed two distinct occupation phases: in the 0–0.2 m below surface level, only potsherds were unearthed, while from 0.4 to 1 m below surface the majority of artifacts are quartzite tools and the by-products of their manufacture. Test pit K yielded pottery (0.55 kg in the first 0.2 m below surface) and a very rich quartzite industry (16.35 kg).

All of these artifacts present a remarkable technical and typological unity independent of their find spot: Pit D, Pit M, Unit K or the graded surface. The pottery assemblage appears to be a homogeneous industry. Some 656 potsherds and 648 stone artifacts were collected in the pits and in the stratigraphy (*Fig. 51*). Given the size of the area that was excavated, this is an impressive density of finds. The whole site probably contains thousands of potsherds and stone fragments and several dozen of pit features.

Most of the stone industry was found in Unit K and is made of quartzite. The toolkit is composed mainly of large bifacial core tools (often unfinished) on blocks, and some backed flake tools with a microlithic component. Flaking methods are largely unspecialized and appear to be organized towards the production of large flakes for trimming and core tools. From a technological and typological standpoint, this industry is typical of the late Middle Stone Age or early Late Stone Age.

The pottery from the pit features and the upper level in Unit K is characterized by rounded (43 %) or angular (24 %) rims, although fluted (16 %) and flat (11 %) rims also appear. Lips with internal (3 %) or external (3 %) bevels are rare. Just beneath the rim, simple (27 %) or double (13 %) flanges are common. One example with a triple flange was also identified. Necks are most often concave (67 %) or straight (26 %), but convex necks (7 %) are also present. All vessel bodies are globular, with flat (77 %) or concave (23 %) bases. Vessels are decorated primarily on the neck (88 % of neck sherds are decorated), on the upper part of the body (54 %) and on the rim (46 %). Handles are rare and are added to the neck or body of the pots. Decoration frequencies are distributed as follow: comb grooving (26 %) and -stamping (19 %) are most common, while rocking comb (15 %) and -blade (13 %) impressions are also found. Stick grooving is present (11 %), as is appliqué for handles (9 %), while stick stamping (2 %) is rare. Carved wooden roulette impression (6 %) is present only in mixed and/or surface assemblages, suggesting that the technique belongs to a recent pottery tradition.

No radiocarbon dates were obtained from the Stone Age contexts, but on technological ground the approximate age of the industry could be bracketed between more than 50,000 and 8000 years bp. Of course, the culture-historical sequence of the region is almost unknown, and it is therefore difficult to make any precise comparison with similar dated assemblages. Pits D and M, as well as three contexts between 0 and 0.6 m below surface in Unit K, were dated with five radiocarbon dates (*App. F* and *Fig. 34*). All of these dates fall in the same bracket. Ezezang was occupied between 775 – 80 cal BC, although we cannot definitively say whether that occupation was continuous.

The non-contemporaneity of the pottery assemblage and the quartzite industry is open to question, since potsherds and stone tools are mixed in all the features excavated. However, proportions between the two vary from place to place. Stone tools are rare in the pit features and pottery is concentrated in the top layers (0–0.2 m below surface) of the stratigraphy in Unit K, while stone tools cluster at lower levels (0.4–0.6 m below surface). There is thus a stratigraphic distinction between the pottery assemblage and the stone industry, although this is not reflected in the radiocarbon dating. Ezezang appears to have been occupied on two occasions at least: during the late Middle Stone Age/early Late Stone Age and during the Iron Age, in the late first millennium BC.

While the Stone Age horizon might have been a small open-air campsite or workshop, the Iron Age horizon was more likely the remnant of a substantial village. Its size, the number of pit features and the large quantity of pottery recovered are evidence of long-term settlement by farmers. The amount of *Canarium* and *Elaeis* nuts identified in the pit also argues in favor of such a hypothesis.

Fig. 51. Ceramics and lithics from Ezezang (ECA-272).

ECA-279 — Ongot

ECA-279 was discovered on July 24, 2002 during construction monitoring (trenching operations). The site is located on a hilltop, in the mixed forest zone. A single pit feature was identified in the ditch, and the site was accorded high priority for further treatment. The pit feature was excavated between August 26 and 28, 2002. The test pit (0.5x2 m) was dug to a depth of 2.45 m below graded surface.

The artifacts were not homogeneously distributed in the unit. Three distinct archaeological horizons were encountered: (1) Horizon I, on top of the pit feature (0–0.65 m below surface); (2) Horizon II, the upper part of the pit feature (0.85–1.05 m below graded surface); and (3) Horizon III, the bottom of the pit feature (1.25–2.25 m below graded surface). Sterile levels separate the three horizons, at 0.65–0.85 m and 1.05–1.25 m below graded surface. The pit feature is narrow and not very deep. Its narrowness is due to the fact that only the edge of the pit was left in the ditch profile. The total diameter of the feature, when it was complete, is estimated to have been 1.5–1.8 m, with a total depth of about 2.6 m. The main characteristic of the pit is that its walls are straight and vertical from top to bottom.

Relatively few artifacts were collected from the excavation. Horizon I yielded 0.3 kg of pottery (17 potsherds) and slag; Horizon II contained only 0.05 kg of pottery (3 potsherds) but was very rich in charcoal (mainly *Coula edulis*); and Horizon III consisted of a 0.4 kg pottery assemblage (22 potsherds) and very little charcoal. While the pottery assemblage of Horizon I appears recent, with roulette decoration present, the assemblages collected in the pit feature (in both the upper and lower horizons) are only decorated with stick- and comb grooving. Two charcoal samples collected in the pit feature were radiocarbon dated. The first, associated with Horizon II material (0.85–1.05 m) was dated to cal AD 545 – 700, while the second, collected in Horizon III (1.45–1.65 m), was dated to 515 – 45 cal BC (*App. F* and *Fig. 34*).

ECA-279 was an Iron Age settlement occupied on three different occasions: (1) in the last half of the first millennium BC (Horizon III); (2) in the 6th – 7th centuries AD (Horizon II); and (3) in the last two to three centuries before the colonial period (Horizon I). Pits were dug during the first occupation period and were reused (or contaminated) at the time the second settlement was installed.

ECA-315 — Ndjoré

ECA-315, located near Mbandjock, was discovered on October 31, 2002 during construction monitoring (trenching operations). The site, not far from the village of Ndjoré, is located on a 600 m high plateau, in the semi-deciduous forest/savanna zone. It consists of several archaeological features discovered in the pipeline trench. They include six pits (A, C, E, F, G and H) and one tomb (B), spread over 300 meters along the right-of-way. In the pits and on the graded surface, pottery, slag, furnace remains (tuyère fragments) and stone implements (flakes, hammerstones and grinding stones) were identified. Part of a human skull, buried at the bottom of a pit feature, was visible in the profile of the trench. The absence of a tombstone and the

archaeological context of the grave were considered evidence that the burial was ancient. Local populations did not know of any of their relatives buried in the zone. Because archaeological burial sites are very rare in Central Africa, the site was classified as high priority for further work.

The Site Treatment Plan recommended rescue excavations for data recovery. The archaeological features were marked off and the construction crew was notified immediately that an important site had been discovered and that, while they could proceed with the laying of the pipes, they should not backfill the trench. The senior EMP monitor at Nanga Eboko was notified and measures were taken so that the site was protected while under study. Excavation of the tomb (Feature B) was conducted on November 1 and 2, 2002. Project archaeologists unearthed the skeleton but, as the bones appeared to be very brittle and threatened to crumble, it was decided not to remove them in the absence of the senior archaeologist. The bones were then covered with plastic sheets and wooden planks for protection.

Excavations of the other pit features proceeded, on November 6 for Pit E and November 13 and 15 for Pit C (*Figs. 52* and *53*). The pits yielded decorated pottery, with some vessels unbroken, slag, stone tools (some quartz flakes, grinding stones, hammerstones), clay pipes and charcoal. On November 16, 2002, Project archaeologists eventually collected the bones from Feature B. They were wrapped in paper and packed in boxes to be transported to Douala, where they were stored in the EMP laboratory at COTCO on November 18, 2002.

Feature B is an oblong funeral pit (1.8x0.7 m) dug to about 1.35 m below ground surface. It is perfectly oriented on a north-south axis. No traces of a wooden coffin were identified, but while the soil that filled the grave had a dark reddish-brown (Munsell Soil Color Chart 5YR3/3) color, the edges of the grave were of a much lighter yellowish-brown (10YR5/8). The deceased appears to be an adult of medium stature (about 1.6–1.7 m). Only the remains of the skull, two femurs, two tibias and two fibulas were preserved as well as small, unidentified bone fragments. The skeleton, buried at 1.35 m below surface, was lying on its back, almost fully extended and oriented on a north-south axis. No grave goods were found in the tomb, but 22 potsherds (0.4 kg) were collected in the first 0.6 m below surface.

Pit features C, D and E are of diverse shapes and depths, perhaps implying different uses. Pit C is a large, 2 m deep bottle-shaped pit that was much larger at the bottom (1.7 m) than at the top (1.1 m).

Fig. 52. Profile of Pit C at Ndjoré (ECA-315).

This characteristic is often due to the presence of water at the bottom of the pit at the time it was still in use, causing lateral erosion and cave-ins. It yielded 9.9 kg of pottery (550 potsherds) and grinding stone and hammerstone fragments, as well as slag. Most of the pottery (86 %) was buried at the bottom of the pit (1.2–1.8 m deep).

Pit D was smaller: approximately 1.1 m deep and only 0.8 m in diameter. It yielded 6 kg of pottery (333 potsherds), as well as some stone artifacts (a hammerstone and grinding stone fragments). Pit E is even smaller, but only the bottom of the pit is preserved: it is wider (2.1 m) than it is deep (1.2 m). Approximately 6.6 kg of pottery (367 potsherds) was collected, as were grinding stone fragments.

Morphologically, Ndjoré pottery most frequently displays rounded rims (76 %), although flat (12 %) and angular (12 %) rims are also present. Necks are for the most part concave (86 %), or more rarely straight (14 %). All base sherds display convex, rounded bases. Pottery decoration techniques are mostly comb grooving (46 %) and -stamping (30 %). Stick grooving (11 %) and -stamping (3 %) are also present, as well as stamping with a rocking comb (3 %). The formation of appliqué

handles from simple clay bosses is rather common (11 %), while perforations are rare (3 %).

Four charcoal samples (from Feature B, and Pits C, D and E) and one human bone sample (from Feature B) were radiocarbon dated (*App. F* and *Fig. 34*). The dates obtained for the charcoal samples are distributed between 180 cal BC – cal AD 385, with some degree of overlap. It is surprising that, while a charcoal sample collected at 0.4–0.6 m below surface in Feature B was dated to cal AD 45 – 230, the skeleton buried lower in the same pit (at 1.2–1.35 m below surface) gave a modern age: the ^{14}C percentage is higher than the 1950 reference standard.

ECA-315 is a large Iron Age settlement site, occupied sometime between the 2nd century BC and the 4th century AD. It seems most likely that Ndjoré was inhabited in the 1st – 2nd century AD. The presence of a very rich pottery assemblage and grinding stones, as well as slag, confirmed that daily occupations like food processing (cooking) took place. More specialized crafts like blacksmithing were also carried out. The numerous pits dug suggest long-term settlement. At the time, the inhabitants of the site were probably already using iron, as implied by the absence of stone tools.

Fig. 53. Skeletal remains from Ndjoré (ECA-315).

that the grave was dug partly into an Iron Age refuse pit or through an Iron Age occupation layer.

ECA-323 — Zili

Zili was discovered on November 11, 2002 during the monitoring of trenching operations. The site is located on a plateau, in the semi-deciduous forest zone. A single pit was identified in the ditch, and the site was accorded high priority for further work. The pit feature was excavated on December 3 and 4, 2002. A 2x2 m test pit was dug to a depth of 2.4 m before reaching sterile soil. The pit feature is 1.5 m in diameter and 2.1 m deep. About 10 kg of pottery (550 potsherds) were collected in the pit feature, as well as a quartz hammerstone and slag. Burnt nuts of *Canarium schweinfurthii* were also identified.

The pottery is abundantly decorated, with more than a third of the sherds bearing some decoration (***Fig. 54***). Pottery decoration techniques are dominated by comb- (58 %) and stick grooving (24 %),

The presence of a human skeleton is quite exceptional because usually, in acid tropical soils, buried bones are not preserved for more than 20 to 50 years. Indeed, its radiocarbon age appears to be modern. The question of the contemporaneity of the archaeological pits and the tomb thus remains open. The Babute populations of the nearby village of Ndjoré did not, however, claim ownership of the tomb, so we are left with two possible explanations: (1) the tomb is indeed modern, but belongs to a neighboring Beti group that moved away less than 50 years ago or (2) the tomb is actually contemporaneous with the Iron Age village but the sample was somehow contaminated. While the radiocarbon date seems to be in favor of the first hypothesis, the absence of a tombstone, coffin and any other modern artifact in the grave and in its vicinity suggests that the burial is at least pre-colonial. If the bone sample is indeed post-1950, we have to assume

while simple comb- or stick impressions (9 %) are rare, as are walking comb and -blade impression (9 %). The morphology of ceramic vessels at ECA-323 includes for the most part rounded (73 %) or flattened rims, with a few angular rims. Beveled interior (3 %) and exterior (2 %) rims are quite rare. A majority (56 %) of the rims is decorated with a single flange; there is one example of a double flange in the collection. Necks are primarily straight (80 %) or convex (14 %), indicating the importance of open vessels. Vessel bases are most often convex (75 %), although flat bases (25 %) also exist.

A single radiocarbon date was run on a charcoal sample collected at 1.9 m below surface in the pit feature, and a calibrated age of 910 – 560 BC was obtained (***App. F*** and ***Fig. 34***). Given the slag found in the pit, ECA-323 thus appears to be a very early

Fig. 54. Ceramics from Zili (ECA-323).

Iron Age settlement, inhabited in the first half of the first millennium BC. While only one pit feature was identified, the amount of pottery found suggests a larger site. The presence of such pit features is evidence of fairly long-term settlement, given issues of space management and work input. Ethnographic comparisons suggest that these pits were used as water wells, clay mines, silos or latrines. When their original use had ended, they were used as refuse pits, and it is as such that archaeologists usually find them.

Zili is thus likely to be one of the very first sedentary settlements in southern Cameroon, probably occupied by populations practicing intensive arboriculture or farming. The number of *Canarium* nuts identified in the pit argues in favor of such a hypothesis. Although this tree was never domesticated as such, it was protected and sometimes even planted. The absence of any stone tool assemblage indicates that the inhabitants of Zili were already using iron tools by the 6th century BC, and possibly some centuries earlier.

ECA-329 — Doumba

ECA-329, situated near Doumba village not far west of Nanga Eboko, was discovered during construction monitoring on November 26, 2002. The site, a single refuse pit identified in the ditch in the semi-deciduous forest zone, was accorded high priority for further work. The pit feature was excavated from December 10–11, 2002. A 2x1 m test pit was dug to a depth of 2.1 m before reaching sterile soil. The pit feature was cut in half by the ditch and its top had probably been removed by the grading operations. The pit was 2 m in diameter and in depth; its walls were straight and vertical.

Approximately 3.7 kg of pottery (208 potsherds) and slag were collected in the pit. The pottery primarily displays rounded (47 %) or flat (37 %) rims, with a few angular rims (16 %). Necks are most frequently concave (69 %), with straight (19 %) and convex (12 %) examples less frequent. Bases are flat (50 %) or concave (50 %). Pottery decoration techniques are mainly comb grooving (62 %); comb stamping (13 %) and rocking-comb stamping (13 %) are present, while stick stamping (6 %) and -grooving (6 %) are rare. Decoration is primarily placed on the neck of the vessel, with 59 % of neck sherds decorated. This reduces to 9 % for the vessel body, while rims or bases were not decorated.

A single radiocarbon date was run on a charcoal sample collected between 1.63 and 1.83 m below surface in the pit feature, and a calibrated age of 180 BC – AD 95 was obtained (*App. F* and *Fig. 34*). ECA-329 thus appears to be a small Iron Age settlement occupied between the 2nd century BC and 1st century AD. While only one pit feature was identified, the amount of pottery found suggests a larger site.

ECA-333 — Nanga Eboko

The site, situated on the outskirts of Nanga Eboko, was discovered on December 5, 2002 during monitoring of trenching operations. It consists of six pit features (numbered A to F) spread over 350 meters in the trench. A total area of 122,500 m² was evaluated. ECA-333 was accorded high priority for further work. Two pit features (E and F) were excavated from January 14–15 and 28–31, 2003. Two test pits of 2x1 m were opened. Test Pit E was dug to a depth of 2.1 m below surface and Test Pit F was dug to 1.8 m below surface before reaching sterile soil. Pit feature E was 2 m deep and 1.6 m in diameter; 4 kg of pottery were collected (225 potsherds). Pit feature F was 2.1 m deep and 1.45 m in diameter; it yielded approximately 4.1 kg of pottery (231 potsherds).

Since the pottery assemblages from both units are practically identical, they are described together. Nanga ceramics display rounded (48 %), angular (29 %) and flat (19 %) rims. Beveled rim exteriors are rare (5 %). Flanges under the vessel neck are also rare, both double (10 %) and single (5 %). Necks are most frequently concave (71 %) or straight (24 %), with convex (2 %) or angular (a kind of negative corrugation – 2 %) necks much more rare. Vessel bodies are all globular, and all bases are convex. Pottery decoration techniques are overwhelmingly dominated by

comb grooving (81 %). Rocking blade impression is present (8 %) but other techniques like stick grooving (5 %) and -stamping (3 %) are seldom seen. Appliqué handles are also rare (3 %). Decoration is almost exclusively found on the necks: 76 % of neck sherds are decorated, while the percentages fall to 5 % for rims and 4 % for vessel bodies. Bases were not decorated.

Two charcoal samples were radiocarbon dated: the calibrated age of the sample from Pit E was 390 – 60 BC and that from Pit F was 350 BC – AD 120 (*App. F* and *Fig. 34*). There is thus a substantial overlap in the dates in the late first millennium BC. ECA-333 is an Iron Age settlement site probably inhabited during that time. The absence of stone tools in the pits suggests that iron had replaced such tools in the village, although no trace of metallurgy was identified.

ECA-335 — Meyang

The site, located between Nanga Eboko and Belabo, was discovered during construction monitoring on January 21, 2002. It consisted of three pit features partly unearthed by the pipeline trench, and spread over 22 meters along the ditch. The site was accorded high priority for further treatment. Pits B and C were excavated from January 17–27 and February 1–8, 2003. Pit B was dug to a depth of 1.8 m below surface, with archaeological material clustering between 0.4 and 0.6 m below the graded surface (*Fig. 55*); Pit C reached down to a depth of 2 m below the level of the graded surface, with artifacts clustering from 0.8–1.6 m below surface.

Pit B, whose top section had been removed by a bulldozer, was 1.8 m in diameter and 1.6 m deep. It yielded 8.65 kg of pottery (481 potsherds), as well as burnt nuts of *Elaeis guineensis*. Pit C was 2 m in diameter and 1.8 m deep. More than 18 kg of pottery were collected (1019 potsherds), as well as charred *Elaeis guineensis* nuts. In both pits, the lower layers were almost sterile.

Pottery decoration techniques are identical in both units and consist almost exclusively of comb grooving (91 %). Stick grooving (7 %) and -stamping (2 %) are present but rare. The position of decoration is also similar in the two pits: most of the neck sherds are decorated in the collection from Pits B (59 %) and C (70 %), while neither body sherds (19 % and 17 %) nor rim sherds (7 % and 12 %) are often decorated. The morphologies of the vessels from the two pits seem to be somewhat more different, even though the same range of forms is present in both cases. Vessels from Pit C are characterized by concave or (rarely) flat bases, primarily convex (50 %)

Fig. 55. Profile of Pit B at Meyang (ECA-335).

or straight (33 %) necks and either flat (34 %) or rounded (31 %) rims; 37 % are decorated with a simple flange below the neck. Only convex bases are found in Pit B pottery , along with primarily straight (43 %) or concave (39 %) necks. Rims are most frequently rounded (52 %) or have an interior bevel (24 %), while 29 % have a simple flange and 2 % a double flange. Angular rims, with a straight or exterior bevel, are rare in both assemblages.

Pit C was dated to 755 – 365 cal BC, while Pit B was dated 360 cal BC – cal AD 20, with charcoal samples collected in the richest layers of both features (*App. F* and *Fig. 34*). Pit C thus appears to be a few centuries older than Pit B: the two dates do not overlap. The similarity of the pottery assemblages discarded in the two pits suggests either that they are actually contemporaneous and that the discrepancy in age is due to a dating inaccuracy, or that little change in ceramic assemblages occurred over the course of some centuries. ECA-335 is thus an Iron Age settlement that was inhabited sometime between the 8th century BC and the 1st century AD. The very large quantity of pottery found in Pit C is evidence of a long-term occupation, as is the presence of the pits themselves.

Culture history — Cameroon South

MSA/LSA

Only five sites are exclusively attributed to the MSA/LSA between Ewankang and the Atlantic coast. These are Ndtoua Rock shelter (ECA-68), Bikoué II Rock shelter (ECA-192), Leboudi (ECA-250), Ebot (ECA-262) and Ezezang (ECA-272). Ndtoua (ECA-68) and Ezezang (ECA-272) have been excavated, but only Ndtoua yielded a mid-Holocene radiocarbon date associated with an LSA microlithic industry. Similar assemblages were recovered at Bikoué-Si (ECA-176), Bikoué II (ECA-192) and possibly at Ebot (ECA-262). At Ezezang, the stone tool assemblage is made up primarily of large bifacial tools and backed flakes, some of which were of microlithic proportions. Similar materials were found at Leboudi (ECA-250) and at Ebot (ECA-262). As noted above, these assemblages are typical of the late MSA/early LSA, and the proximity of all three sites is of interest.

Even though these data are inadequate for a complete analysis of forager prehistory in southern Cameroon, they nevertheless establish that the forest zone was occupied before the Iron Age. The rarity of MSA/LSA assemblages (0.02 sites/km) seems, as in the zone between Belel and Ewankang to the north (see above), to be due to geomorphological contexts. In southern Cameroon, the vegetation cover renders erosive processes far less significant, and thus pre-Holocene and early Holocene cultural remains were relatively invisible, even after grading operations. Low site densities are probably also related to the relatively low densities of prehistoric forager populations in this region.

Neolithic

The situation of the Neolithic is more complex. As in the northern zone in Cameroon and in Chad, no pre-Iron Age assemblages with ceramics and lithics were definitively identified in this zone. Thus, the existence of a Neolithic presence (using the definition put forward in Chapter Four) remains unproven. Ceramics were found in association with lithics at Bikoué II Rock shelter (ECA-176) and at Minkan I (ECA-200). At the latter site, ceramics typical of the early first millennium AD were associated on the surface with a lithic assemblage, although at that period stone tools had long disappeared from habitation sites, while at ECA-176 pottery and quartz flakes and a core were discovered in an area where earth removal had taken place. In both cases, the association between ceramics and lithics is far from proven. It is impossible to confirm that (1) these assemblages are homogeneous and (2) they date to pre-Iron Age times. At this point, it appears more likely that these associations are due to mixing of assemblages through natural or cultural processes.

Iron Age — Nanga Eboko region

This region comprises the area along the right-of-way between the communities of Nkol Ebenga (KP 655) and Ndjoré (KP 772). Six pit sites have been dated in this region, with 11 dates between 900 cal BC and cal AD 400 (*Fig. 33* and *34*). There does not appear to be a chronological hiatus in this period, although two dates (from Zili [ECA-323] and from Pit C at Meyang [ECA-335]) are substantially older than the others. While the context and associated ceramic typology for the Zili date seem secure, this is not the case for the Meyang date. Pit C at Meyang has yielded a date of 755 – 365 cal BC, while Pit B is dated to 360 cal BC – cal AD 20; there is thus no overlap between the dates. This would indicate that either the date from Pit C is contaminated, or Meyang was occupied or reoccupied during most of the first millennium BC. The ceramic analysis (see below)

supports the first assumption. It appears that there are two chronological phases in the Nanga Eboko region.

Nanga Eboko region: Iron Age Phase I
(*ca* 1000 – 500 cal BC)

The Zili (ECA-323) site is obviously much older than the majority of the other sites of the area. It dates to the first half of the first millennium BC, whereas the rest of the dated pits (except for Meyang Pit C) are all more recent than 300 cal BC. The first phase of the Iron Age of this area, dated to the early first millennium BC, thus involves a sedentary population, living in permanent villages where some form of iron working (presumably forging) was taking place. They produced a rich pottery assemblage, decorated with comb grooving and rocking blade impressions, with the most striking morphological characteristics being straight necks and rims decorated with flanges. The characteristic archaeological structure is the refuse pit in permanent villages. The presence of *Canarium* is especially noteworthy (see below).

Nanga Eboko region: Iron Age Phase II
(300 cal BC – cal AD 500)

The second phase of the Iron Age in the Nanga Eboko region is represented by six dated sites: Meyang (ECA-335), Nanga Eboko (ECA-333), Ndjoré (ECA-315), Ndokoa (ECA-317) and Doumba (ECA-329). Nine of the ten dates associated with these sites lay between 300 cal BC and cal AD 500. These sites, like Zili, are generally located on hilltops or plateaux, and are characterized by refuse pits containing significant amounts of pottery. These groups of pits are probably the remnants of permanent villages.

Meyang (ECA-335) and Nanga Eboko (ECA-333) are the oldest of these sites, located to the east of the modern city of Nanga Eboko. Three pits (including two that were excavated) were identified at Meyang and six (including two excavated ones) at Nanga. All yielded a significant amount of pottery. Carbonized nuts of *Elaeis guineensis* were also collected at Meyang. Only one pit was found at the site of Doumba (ECA-329), just to the west of Nanga Eboko, and it only yielded pottery. Ceramics at the first two sites are very similar: the decoration is characterized by the prevalence of comb grooving (between 82 % and 96 %). The only other decorative techniques used are stick grooving (between 2 % and 18 %) and, only in Nanga, simple comb stamping (1 to 2 %). Doumba pottery is almost identical, although simple (6 %) or rocking comb (6 %) impressions are also present.

The sites of Ndokoa (ECA-317) and Ndjoré (ECA-315) are slightly further to the west. Only a single pit was found at Ndokoa, in contrast to the eight pits found in the trench at Ndjoré. All pits contained ceramics. In Ndokoa, the sparse pottery was associated with fragments of grinding stones and hammerstones. In Ndjoré, seven of the pits yielded pottery associated with grinding stone fragments and hammerstones, as well as slag. The Ndjoré pottery is not dominated by comb grooving, although this technique remains important (26–32 % of the assemblage in different pits), but by walking comb stamping (34–52 %). Ndokoa ceramics, although contemporaneous and produced in similar environments, is characterized by high frequencies of comb impressions (38 %) and -grooving (38 %), although this may be a statistical error resulting from the small sample size. Morphologically, Ndjoré ceramics are strikingly similar to that of Doumba (ECA-329). In both assemblages, vessels are distinguished by high concave necks (the only part of the vessel that is decorated), a globular body and a convex base.

Nanga Eboko region: unexcavated sites
A number of other pit sites were discovered in the Nanga Eboko region: Nkoteng (ECA-325), Doumba (ECA-327), Biyanga (ECA-337) and Nkol Ebenga (ECA-339). These sites were not excavated, and so it is impossible to assign them to a particular chrono-cultural unit in the region. Pottery was found on all of these sites, sometimes with associated slag (as at Doumba ECA-327). The existence of these sites confirms the importance of the pit phenomenon in this part of southern Cameroon, and also makes it possible to delimit the geographical distribution of this phenomenon: Nkol Ebenga (ECA-339) at KP 655 is the most northern and the most eastern pit site discovered on the pipeline right-of-way in Cameroon.

Sites without pits were also identified in this area, at Avangan (ECA-331), Bikoto (ECA-321), Kondengui (ECA-319) and around Ndjoré (ECA-313, -311, -309). Further towards the west, for a distance of 30 kilometers, there are no more pit sites until Yaoundé. However, a number of sites have been identified in this area, close to Nkoayos (ECA-305, -303 and -301). None of these sites have been excavated, and thus it is impossible to unequivocaly assign them to particular chrono-cultural units in the region. However, the assemblages recovered from these sites do give some indication of cultural affiliations: pottery was found on all of these sites, sometimes with associated slag (at Bikoto and in the Ndjoré area) and in other cases with a limited lithic industry (at Nkoayos and Bikoto). The site of Bikoto (ECA-321) is particularly interesting: it yielded a somewhat sparse archaeological horizon with potsherds, some slag and tuyère fragments, apparently associated with a polished stone tool. The stratigraphic context of this assemblage was not studied in detail, but it suggests that polished stone tools could be part of a typical Iron Age toolkit in this area, as in the north (see above). No iron-working sites were discovered in this area, but the presence of slag at sites of both phases shows that forging, at least, was known in the period when these populations began to develop sedentary villages.

Iron Age — Yaoundé region

This region comprises the area along the right-of-way between the communities of Afan Esele (KP 801) and Nkolnlong (KP 904). Nine sites have been dated in this region, and the resulting 16 dates can be divided into three chronological groups. The earliest dates range between 700 cal BC and cal AD 200, including dates from the sites of Ezezang (ECA-272), Ongot (ECA-279), Leboudi (ECA-250), Zoatoupsi (ECA-236) and Ngoumou (ECA-216). The second chronological period dates between cal AD 300 and cal AD 750, and includes the sites of Binguela II (ECA-228), Ozom (ECA-242) and Ongot (ECA-279). The third episode is much more recent, and is represented only by one site, Oboukoé (ECA-224). It dates to the period cal AD 1450 – 1650.

Yaoundé region: Iron Age Phase I
(700 cal BC – cal AD 200)
Sites from the oldest phase of this area are located on hilltops (at Ezezang, Ongot and Ngoumou) or on high plateaux (Zoatoupsi, Leboudi). They are all pit sites, and are probably the remnants of permanent villages: one pit each was found at Ngoumou, Ongot and Zoatoupsi, three pits at Leboudi and ten pits at Ezezang. These pits yielded pottery, sometimes associated with fragments of grinding stones (Ezezang and Leboudi), slag (Ezezang and Leboudi), carbonized endocarps of *Elaeis guineensis* (Ezezang, Zoatoupsi and Leboudi) and of *Canarium schweinfurthii* (Ezezang and Zoatoupsi).

Pottery from the Yaoundé region is characterized by a prevalence of comb grooving (from 39 % to 55 % of the assemblages). Rocking blade and -comb impressions are always present, although in variable proportions (from 5 % to 31 %). From the morphological point of view, a very characteristic type of vessel is found on these sites: the rims are decorated with flanges (simple, double, and even triple), the neck and body are rectilinear, and the bottom is often flat. This pottery is typical of Ezezang (ECA-272). These features are also characteristic of the pottery from Zili (ECA-323) from Phase I in the Nanga Eboko region.

Yaoundé region: Iron Age Phase II
(cal AD 300 – 750)
The second phase of the Iron Age sequence in the Yaoundé region begins after a chronological hiatus of a century and is represented by the sites of Binguela II

(ECA-228), Ozom (ECA-242), Essong Missang (ECA-248) and Ongot (ECA-279, horizon II). As in Phase I, sites of this period are characterized by pit features, and are probably the traces of permanent villages. One pit was found at Ongot (the same structure as that mentioned in the preceding phase), three pits at Essong, and four pits at Binguela and Ozom. Again, these sites are found on plateaux (Binguela) or hilltops (Ongot, Essong). Pottery, slag (Ongot), and carbonized endocarps of *Elaeis guineensis*, *Canarium schweinfurthii* (Binguela) and *Coula edulis* (Ongot) were recovered from these pits.

Even if the general characteristics of the sites themselves seem not to have changed much since the preceding phase, the ceramics of Phase II of the Iron Age are quite different from those of Phase I. The best-documented assemblages come from the sites of Binguela and Essong. In these cases, the dominant decorative technique remains comb grooving (14–55 % of assemblages), but grooving with a comb-gouge appears, amounting to between 5 % and 39 % of the assemblages. The frequency of stick grooving (13 % to 36 %) is variable, and rocking comb and -blade impressions become very rare. Morphologically, we see that vessels with rectilinear profiles and flanged rims have disappeared. This one type is replaced (at Binguela and Ongot) by large vases with concave necks, also found during the contemporaneous Phase II in the Nanga Eboko region (see above). A very new type of vessel profile also makes an appearance during this period, as containers with carinated shoulders are found at Ongot.

Yaoundé region: Iron Age Phase III
(cal AD 1450 – 1650)

The only example of a site from this phase is Oboukoé (ECA-224), an isolated pit on a hilltop containing some potsherds, associated with a large amount of charcoal. The structure was dated between the 15th and 17th centuries AD, demonstrating that the tradition of pit construction lasted after the end of Phase II, even if the intensity of the phenomenon had apparently decreased.

Yaoundé region: unexcavated sites

Other sites with pits were identified in this region: Angon II (ECA-230), Afan-Essele (ECA-254), Yegue Assi (ECA-266), Nkolnlong (ECA-268) and Nkometou (ECA-270). All of these sites yielded pottery and (at Yegue Assi, Nkometou and Nkolnlong) slag. These sites were not excavated, and so it is impossible to assign them to particular chrono-cultural units in the region: the majority of them probably belongs to Phases I/II but it is possible that some are more recent.

Two iron-production sites were also discovered: Ngoumou (ECA-220, near ECA-216) and Yegue Assi (ECA-264, near ECA-266). They are characterized by a thick layer of slag, along with furnace wall and tuyère fragments, more than 0.5 m below surface and certainly indicating intense iron-smelting activity. The presence of small quantities of slag in settlement sites, along with isolated iron-smelting furnace sites, indicates that (1) metallurgy was characteristic of all phases of occupation in this area, and (2) iron smelting was carried out away from settlement sites. The latter argument implies that slag found at the pit sites is probably the residue of forging. Finally, surface sites were also identified throughout the zone: near Afan-Essele (ECA-252, -256, -258), Essong Missang (ECA-246), Nkometou (ECA-238, -240, -244, -295) and Ekabita (ECA-232). These sites yielded pottery, sometimes associated with slag (at Essong and Nkometou) and even clay pipes (Essong). This context, as well as the characteristics of the assemblages, suggests a rather recent age: these sites probably date to Phase III.

Iron Age — Littoral region

This most southern zone of the right-of-way, in the Kribi–Lolodorf region, comprises the area between the communities of Bikoka (KP 970) and the Atlantic coast (KP 1069). The eleven radiocarbon dates from this zone relate to three types of sites: (1) open-air settlement sites characterized by pits, as in the other regions of southern Cameroon, (2) an iron-smelting site and (3) a rock shelter. The early levels at Ndtoua Rock shelter (ECA-68) have been discussed above. There appear to be two chronological phases for the pit sites in this region: an earlier (Phase I) covers the first millennium BC, while the second (Phase II), after a hiatus of more than three centuries, ranges between cal AD 300 – 700. The dates for Ndtoua (ECA-68) supplement the sequence (see above); Level III at that site is dated between 50 cal BC – cal AD 245, and so exactly in the chronological hiatus between the two phases for the settlement sites. Level IV is much more recent, dating to the 13th – 14th centuries cal AD.

Littoral region: Iron Age Phase I
(*ca* 1000 – 1 cal BC)

Phase I is represented by three sites: Bissiang (ECA-138), Dombè (ECA-130) and Makouré (ECA-124). Bissiang and Dombè are pit sites, probably the remains of permanent villages. These two sites yielded pottery, associated with fragments of grinding stones and hammerstones. Ceramics of the two sites are rather similar: both assemblages are dominated by rocking impressions (more than 50 % of the decoration), but while a blade is used at Bissiang (from 36 % to 50 %

in the different pits), a comb was the tool of choice at Dombè (from 40 % to 43 % in the different pits). The frequencies of comb grooving (from 7 % to 28 %) and of simple comb impression (from 5 % to 24 %) are variable, both in the pits within a site itself and also between sites. In the current state of the study, one might hypothesize that the change from rocking blade to rocking comb impressions resulted from a change through time within the same tradition of ceramic decoration. From a morphological viewpoint, the two assemblages are very similar as well: the majority of the vessels are containers with flat or rounded rims, sometimes grooved (at Dombè), with concave necks (open vases), with globular bodies, and flat (at Bissiang and Dombè) or convex (only at Dombè) bases. Convex rims, as closed bowls, also exist in the two assemblages.

At the end of this phase, between the 4th and the 2nd centuries BC, these populations were producing iron locally, as is indicated by the Makouré iron-smelting site. The remains of several furnaces were discovered there, as indicated by the recovery of fragments of walls and tuyères, associated with a considerable amount of slag. No pottery was collected on the site, suggesting that it was not a settlement.

Littoral region: Iron Age Phase II
(cal AD 300 – 700)

The second phase of Iron Age occupation in the Littoral region is represented by only two dated sites: Bidjouka (ECA-160) and Bidou II (ECA-146). The two sites are the remains of settlement sites with pits, three in the case of Bidou, and six at Bidjouka. Both are located on hilltops, in the Atlantic Littoral forest.

Only pottery was found at these sites. The sample of ceramics of Bidjouka is more informative, since only a few potsherds were found at Bidou. This material is very different from the pottery of the preceding phase. The dominant decorative technique is now comb-gouge grooving, varying from 32 % to 46 % in the different pits. Simple- (from 11 % to 30 %) and rocking (14 % to 20 %) comb impressions remain relatively common. Morphologically, this pottery is quite varied: rims are generally flat, and concave necks (open vases), globular bodies and flat bases are also characteristic. Unusually, a rare but very characteristic vessel with a carinated shoulder is present in these assemblages.

Two other undated sites from the area have also yielded ceramics with characteristics similar to those of Bidjouka, and can probably be placed in this phase: Grand Zambi (ECA-152) and Minkan I (ECA-200). Grand Zambi is a site with one pit identified, which

yielded only pottery, whereas Minkan I displayed an archaeological horizon where potsherds were associated with lithic debitage. Whereas the Grand Zambi assemblage, collected in the pit, is certainly homogeneous, that of Minkan I seems to have been mixed by erosion or other natural processes. The pottery of Grand Zambi is to a great extent decorated with comb grooving (73 %) and the comb-gouge technique seems absent, but vessels with carinated shoulders are quite abundant. At Minkan I, on the other hand, ceramic decoration is mainly simple comb impression (47 %), the comb-gouge technique is present but rare (8 %) and carinated containers were not identified.

Littoral region: unexcavated sites

Other pit sites were discovered in the Littoral region between Lolodorf and the coast: Bikoka (ECA-208), Bikoka (ECA-182), Mbikiliki (ECA-158), Mvile (ECA-180), Grand Zambi (ECA-166) and Ndtoua (ECA-162). These sites were not excavated, and so it is impossible to assign them to a particular phase in the region. They do, however, reinforce the importance of the pit phenomenon in the Atlantic Littoral forest and near the coast. Another iron-smelting site was discovered in Mvile (ECA-178), close to the town of Lolodorf. A stratigraphic level with slag and furnace fragments was discovered at that site. Unfortunately, since it is undated we cannot evaluate its age.

Southern Cameroon: discussion

Southern Cameroon has been populated since the MSA, as the existence of a number of sites with tools and debitage typical of this period attest. This occupation probably dates to the later part of the period between 50,000 and 10,000 bp. The LSA is represented by several forest microlithic assemblages, one of which (Ndtoua Rock shelter [ECA-68]) dates to the mid-Holocene. The tradition of microlithic stone tool production survives for a millennium after the arrival of metallurgy, since a similar industry with associated pottery dates to the beginning of the first millennium AD at Ndtoua.

The first agricultural populations arrived in southern Cameroon at approximately 1000 cal BC, and pit sites characterize the earliest Iron Age of the area. These pits, sometimes several meters deep, were probably initially dug as silos, latrines or wells for settlements, but were recycled as refuse pits when their initial function had ended. These structures, the result of a significant labor investment and thus built for long-term use, are probably a useful index of sedentism. They may thus indicate the appearance of permanent village settlements in the area, although the southern Chadian case should remind us that even sedentary populations may shift their settlement locations over timescales of decades or centuries. Sedentary populations have thus probably occupied southern Cameroon for at least three millennia.

The geographical distribution of the pit sites in southern Cameroon is not uniform. The pit sites identified are grouped in three regions: around Nanga Eboko, around Yaoundé and in the Littoral region between Lolodorf and Kribi. Two chrono-cultural phases are known from the Nanga Eboko region during the Iron Age. Phase I, dating to the first half of the first millennium BC, is represented only by one site, Zili, a village where iron working had already been practised. Ceramics from this site are quite characteristic: vases with straight necks and flanges, decorated with stick- and comb grooving. In Phase II, the region presents a certain chronological and cultural unity. All these sites seem to represent sedentary communities, and most of the radiocarbon dates fall between 300 cal BC and cal AD 500. The pottery from this phase is characterized by comb grooving, but the importance of this technique appears to vary geographically. It seems to be more dominant, indeed exclusive, in the eastern part of the zone, while in the west the technique is found alongside other forms of impressions.

The Iron Age around Yaoundé is divided into three phases of occupation (with the third represented by only one site). Phase I (700 cal BC – cal AD 200) and Phase II (cal AD 300 – 750) appear to be characterized by the existence of large, probably sedentary villages where iron working and possibly a form of arboriculture (intensive exploitation of oil palm and incense tree [*Canarium schweinfurthii*]) were prac-

tised. Pottery developed slowly from one phase to the next, both from a decorative and a morphological point of view. During Phase I, pottery is characterized by rims with flanges, with rectilinear profiles and flat bottoms, decorated particularly with comb grooving and rocking blade- and comb impressions. In Phase II, two types of vessels characterize the ceramic sample: large containers with high concave necks, globular bodies and convex bottoms, and small containers with carinated shoulders and flat bottoms. The characteristic decoration during this period is comb-gouge grooving.

The Littoral region exhibits two distinct chronological phases: Phase I covering the first millennium BC and Phase II dating between cal AD 300 – 700. Settlement sites with pits are characteristic of both phases, but the pottery shows a significant evolution from one phase to another. Whereas the pottery of Phase I is characterized by globular vessels decorated with rocking blade- and comb impressions, that of Phase II is characterized by carinated vessels and/or a decoration of comb grooving.

The existence of three different cultural zones in the Iron Age of southern Cameroon is remarkable, although this should be put into context. The three zones are actually separated by large areas where no pit sites have been found, but it is of course possible that future research will fill in these empty intervals. There exist substantial typological differences in the pottery of the three regions, but there do not appear to be massive or sudden changes across the 'borders' of these three geographical regions. We observe instead a regular progression of decorative techniques and morphologies along the Project pipeline transect.

Introduction

The last three chapters have described some of the results of the Chad Export Project's cultural heritage management program over the period 1999 – 2003. The total amount of data generated by this program has been formidable. If all of that material were to be included, this text would be many times its present length. At the same time, a CHM program of this kind must be seen as a preliminary attempt to understand prehistoric trajectories of cultural change in the area under investigation, not as a definitive work on the topic. Such an understanding is, of course, only one among a number of priorities for a program of this sort, along with protection of the cultural heritage, support for archaeological institutions and training of archaeological personnel in both countries. In addition, we believe that one of the strengths of this CHM program lies in the opportunity that it affords for continuous comparison of archaeological sequences, on many sites and along a linear transect covering large areas in Central Africa, where important cultural processes took place in the past — in other words, in its regional perspective, not in extremely detailed analyses of particular archaeological occurrences. We therefore hope that this work will serve as an initial set of guideposts for further investigations in the regions where Project research took place, both on sites that have been located during the present research and on issues raised in this text but not yet resolved.

An essential element of such a program is the placement of the program's results in the wider context of Central African cultural history, as it has been elucidated through archaeological, historical, linguistic and other means. This especially involves looking at (1) the chronological data, derived from comparative artifact typologies and radiocarbon dating, that are the foundation of regional cultural history, and (2) data on economies and environmental variation through time, which will help us understand how people adapted to Central African environments in the late Pleistocene and Holocene. The more than 80 radiocarbon dates that have been derived from the Project CHM program to date provide a particularly rich body of data for anchoring those regional cultural histories, especially in areas of Project activity where absolute dates have for the most part not been available (that is, southwestern Chad and northeastern Cameroon). In this chapter, we consider the implications of the Project research results in comparison to data from surrounding areas. As before, we observe the distinction between the three research zones along the right-of-way: Chad, northern Cameroon and southern Cameroon.

Regional comparison — Chad

Regional comparisons in Chad are substantially handicapped by the dearth of comparable archaeological research in the region (see *Chapter 4*), and by the geomorphological conditions in most of the Project area in that country, which have probably concealed many pre-Iron Age sites under a mantle of more recent sediments (see *Chapter 3*). Results from fieldwork along the northern extent of the right-of-way in Cameroon, from other sites in contiguous parts of northern and eastern Cameroon (Marliac 1987; Loumpet 1998) and from CAR (de Bayle des Hermens 1975), certainly indicate the presence of populations using Middle and Late Stone Age technologies in those areas, and there is no reason to believe that such populations did not occupy similar areas in southwestern Chad. The contrasting results from the Project area in Chad, and from the right-of-way along the edge of the Adamawa Plateau in eastern Cameroon, probably demonstrate the dramatic effects that different sedimentary/erosive regimes can have on site preservation and visibility.

The limited work undertaken more than forty years ago in the area by Courtin (Courtin 1962, 1963) suggests that Neolithic material may be found in localities immediately adjacent to the right-of-way but in different geomorphological contexts, especially those associated with inselbergs and inselberg edges. Along the right-of-way, sites like Oulibangala (ETA-56), situated near the Lim River, are probably most likely to yield pre-Iron Age materials. However, the results at that site indicate the potential for site disturbance in localities close to active watercourses. Material from Oulibangala can probably be compared to that from Neolithic sites like Balimbé 68 in the western Central African Republic (Zangato 2000), where lithics, including ground and polished stone axes and pottery decorated by stick grooving, were found in contexts dating to the second millennium BC. The relative lack of both Neolithic and very early Iron Age materials — indeed, of any dated contexts from before the first millennium AD — is one of the two most striking research results in this region. The other is, of course, the concentration of iron-production activities approximately one thousand years ago (see below).

This absence is especially notable when considering the abundant evidence for Neolithic/early Iron Age materials, both those pre-dating and those related to the *tazunu* sites in northwestern Central African Republic (David & Vidal 1976; David 1982b; Vidal 1992; Zangato 1999, 2000), situated not much more than 100 km from the southwestern end of the right-of-way in Chad. If, as has been suggested, the *tazunu* phenomenon is associated with Adamawa-Ubangian settlement in the region, then it is conceivable that this contrast could be traced to an ancient cultural frontier between Central Sudanic-speaking populations in southwestern Chad and particular Adamawa-Ubangian-speaking populations in northwestern CAR. On the other hand, given the significant interpenetration between these different linguistic groups in the region in more recent times and the degree of sediment accumulation along the right-of-way in Chad, it is also possible that these differences are due to contexts of site burial and preservation, as mentioned above for more ancient periods. We should note that evidence for Neolithic and very early (*i.e.*, pre-first millennium AD) Iron Age occupations along the northern zone of the right-of-way in Cameroon is slightly greater than is the case in Chad. This does not however compare to the situation in CAR. Neither *tazunu* nor related sites were found along the northern zone of the right-of-way in Cameroon, between the Chad border and the Adamawa Plateau and in the area around Meiganga. The ceramics found in this area do not appear to be similar to those found on the early *tazunu* sites. Given this lack of evidence in Cameroon, and for that matter the very restricted distribution of *tazunu* sites even in northwestern CAR, it is likely that the absence of evidence for *tazunu* sites in southwestern Chad can be ascribed to prehistoric cultural patterning and not geomorphological effects. Further research in more favorable geomorphological zones may well uncover additional evidence for Neolithic and early Iron Age occupations in the Project area in Chad, comparable to that in CAR, but those traces will probably not involve *tazunu* sites.

As in northeastern Cameroon, Project research in southwestern Chad uncovered relatively little evidence for large settlements and occupations by iron-using populations before the beginning of the first millennium AD. This stands in marked contrast to southwestern Cameroon and the Atlantic coast, where such evidence is abundant for the first millennium BC as well (see below), and also to CAR. In both northeastern Cameroon and southwestern Chad, we do however find relatively abundant evidence for settlement through most of the last 2000 years, while in southwestern Cameroon such evidence becomes distinctly more rare after about cal AD 600. This large-scale temporal patterning, with its alternation of habitation in the forest zone to the southwest and in the wooded savanna zone to the northeast, remains to be explained. There appears to be a short hiatus in the Iron Age cultural sequences in Chad and northeastern Cameroon dating to the middle of the first millennium AD, but at present it is not possible to determine whether this hiatus is due to real changes in occupation over this period or to sampling error in site locations and/or radiocarbon dating.

The earliest significant evidence of occupation in the Project research zone in Chad dates to the very end of the first millennium BC and the early first millennium AD, at Mayongo (ETA-97) and Karmankass (ETA-167). The latter site appears to be in or close to primary context, but further research would be required to fully understand the extent and function of this site, which is situated in gravel deposits near the Banoundji River. The former seems to be a substantial Iron Age settlement site. These sites postdate by some centuries CAR settlement sites like Balimbé and Gbabiri (Zangato 1999, 2000), where iron working appears in the early-/mid-first millennium BC — dates more comparable to those along the right-of-way in southern Cameroon. They are, however, probably contemporaneous with sites like Toala (Vidal & de Bayle des Hermens 1983), occupied at a time when the Iron Age was firmly established, and predate by some centuries settlement sites like Nana-Modé, located to the northwest of Bouar and in close proximity to the *tazunu* zone (David & Vidal 1977; Zangato 1999). Nana-Modé is contemporaneous with the iron-working site of Missi-Madji (ETA-164), the earliest such site located during Project work in Chad to date. There are significant similarities between the ceramics found at Nana-Modé and Toala and that found at Iron Age sites along the right-of-way in southern Chad (*cf.* Zangato 2000), especially in the use of carved wooden roulettes, present at all of the Chadian sites except the earliest, Mayongo. As at the CAR sites, the use of carved wooden roulettes dominates among decorative techniques at a number of sites like Bedia (ETA-35) and Kaba (ETA-107), dating to the late first and early second millennia AD. In general, however, it remains one of a number of decorative techniques in use in the region, and the long history of usage of this technique in CAR as well as surrounding regions (Langlois 2004) suggests that it should not be relied upon as a marker of Iron Age occupation.

It is in the late first millennium AD that we see a very significant increase in the evidence for occupation and (especially) craft activities in the Project area in southwestern Chad, with the appearance of a large number of smelting sites, and some contemporaneous habitation sites, dating to the period cal AD 900 – 1200. The concentration of iron-smelting sites along streams in this region is somewhat reminiscent of iron-smelting furnaces in similar contexts described in the area around Sabélé, in southwestern CAR and dated to the 13th – 14th century cal AD (Lanfranchi *et al.* 1998), although at a distance of 500 km such similarities are probably technological rather than cultural. Much more striking are the resemblances between the Chadian iron-working sites and the concentration of almost 200 furnace sites discovered in different parts of the Ouham Préfecture in northwestern CAR (GOTILOGUE & LANFRANCHI 1997), which is approximately 200 – 250 km from the right-of-way. A number of these localities seem to have been the sites of very large iron-working episodes, judging from the size of slag heaps associated with the furnace remains. Few of these furnace sites have been excavated, and only one radiocarbon date, of the 15th – 17th centuries cal AD, has been obtained (GOTILOGUE & LANFRANCHI 1997: 16). Judging from the results of radiocarbon dating in the Project research area, this date probably does not encompass the entire period of iron working in the Ouham Préfecture.

We do not know whether this spatial concentration of sites was accompanied by a concentration in a relatively short time period, as was the case in Chad. Further dating of the sites in the Central African Republic would allow for testing of the hypothesis that climatic change was involved in the diminution of iron-production efforts in southwestern Chad in the 13th century AD (see *Chapter 7*). If such a chronological patterning is not seen in CAR, it would reduce the likelihood that regional climatic effects were implicated in the Chadian case. In both areas, the abundant evidence for iron-working sites and relatively restricted evidence for settlement sites raise questions about: (1) the degree of effort invested in iron working, the likelihood that iron was being fed into regional exchange networks, and the characteristics of such networks; and (2) the relatively low visibility of settlement sites, possibly related to community mobility among Iron Age agricultural populations (as is attested ethnohistorically in Chad — see *Chapter 3*), and the use of dwellings constructed primarily of organic materials. It will be particularly interesting if future archaeological research locates similar geographical centers of iron-production efforts in neighboring regions of Central Africa.

In terms of the material recovered (especially the ceramics) and site characteristics, the Chadian settlement sites of 800 – 1000 years ago continue to display regional similarities to sites like Nana-Modé in CAR, and also to sites that have yielded pottery similar to Nana-Modé but dating to the second millennium AD (DAVID & VIDAL 1977; CLIST 1991). It may be significant that settlement at Nana-Modé resulted in the accumulation of artificial mounds, in contrast to southwestern Chad, where there is no significant evidence for such accumulations. This may, as noted above, imply different modes of settlement among Iron Age populations in the two areas. As in both CAR and northern Cameroon, a number of sites dating to the last millennium were also discovered in the course of Project work in Chad, and the latest of these figure in

Sara oral traditions. There are some detailed differences in frequencies of ceramic decoration at these sites of the last few centuries, but in general, the picture that we see in southwestern Chad — as in Project work in northeastern Cameroon (see below) and in research by other archaeologists in Cameroon (DELNEUF, ASOMBANG & MBIDA 2003) and in northwestern CAR (DAVID & VIDAL 1977; CLIST 1991) — is quite similar, with considerable degrees of cultural continuity over the last millennium at least. It seems likely that we can trace the roots of modern Sara occupation in southwestern Chad back at least to the early-/mid-second millennium AD, as has been hypothesized for Gbaya populations in CAR (DAVID & VIDAL 1977). At the same time, we need to recognize that similarities and differences in cultural scales exist through the region as a whole. The geographical variation in ceramic decoration on roughly contemporaneous Iron Age sites along the right-of-way implies that cultural/ethnic boundaries (probably quite permeable ones) may well have existed in this area in the past, as they do today, while on the other hand Iron Age communities in this region probably interacted in regional cultural spheres that took in large parts of eastern Cameroon, southwestern Chad and southern CAR, cultural spheres that included populations with different economies and with different linguistic, cultural and ethnic identities.

Regional comparison — northern Cameroon

Regional comparisons in northern Cameroon, just as in Chad, are made difficult because of the lack of archaeological data available in the area itself and in neighbouring areas. The role of geomorphological context in this region has already been mentioned. Whereas in Chad significant sedimentation processes probably concealed many of the more ancient sites, in the hills along the edge of the Adamawa Plateau very intense phenomena of erosion probably destroyed the majority of these sites.

In all of the northern part of the Project research area in Cameroon, MSA/LSA sites were discovered in significant quantities only along the edge of the Adamawa Plateau. Those were for the most part identified in erosional contexts on the surface, and so could neither be excavated nor dated. Only the Sokorta Manga site (ECA-43) yielded cultural materials in stratigraphic context, but not with associated datable material. Lithic assemblages generally include bifacial tools and macrolithic debitage, generally on quartzite, technologically identifiable with the MSA and probably dating from the end of the Pleistocene. This generally parallels results obtained in neighbouring areas further to the north in

Cameroon and in CAR. In northern Cameroon, surface lithic assemblages on quartzite, characterized by the presence of bifacial tools, large flakes and cores, were described (MARLIAC 1973, 1974, 1987, 1991). From a technological and typological point of view, the majority of these assemblages appear to be MSA. Others, as at the sites of Kontcha and Tongo (MARLIAC 1974), include worked pebbles and Acheulean bifaces, and would appear to belong to the ESA. In CAR, equivalent ESA (with worked pebbles, bifaces and axes) or MSA (with picks, points) assemblages have been found in alluvial contexts (DE BAYLE DES HERMENS 1975). We did not identify any industries of equivalent age in Cameroon. At this stage, it is impossible to say whether the first occupation of the southern edges of the Adamawa Plateau was really more recent than further to the north in Cameroon and in CAR, or whether this difference can be ascribed to the different geomorphological contexts encountered.

We also did not identify LSA industries in the northern project zone in Cameroon. On the other hand, earlier research on the eastern edge of the Adamawa Plateau (MARLIAC 1987) led to the recovery, at Djohong and Senabou (not far from the Project area), of lithic surface collections, including bipolar tabular cores, burins and bladelets. These industries appear technologically attributable to the LSA. Dates of approximately 6500 – 5000 cal BC were obtained for LSA assemblages recovered from levels below those associated with *tazunu*, at Beforo I and Zupaya in the CAR (DE BAYLE DES HERMENS 1975). This supports the hypothesis that an absence of a microlithic industry among the assemblages recovered by the Project is attributable to survey strategies that did not lead to the discovery of such materials rather than to a lack of LSA occupation in the research area.

Neolithic remains were also not identified with certainty in this part of the research area. Surface collections certainly yielded combined pottery and lithic assemblages, but it is impossible to determine whether these are mixtures of MSA/LSA and Iron Age materials from different occupations. When debitage and ceramics were found associated in stratigraphic context, as at Bemboyo (ECA-24), Sokorta Manga (ECA-43) or Pangar (ECA-199), they were accompanied by evidence that metallurgy was known and absolute dates too recent to indicate a Neolithic occupation. However, the area is bordered to the east and west by regions that have yielded Neolithic assemblages. This is the case in the Grassfields area of western Cameroon, where stone axes, sometimes polished, are associated with a blade industry and comb-decorated pottery, and dated between 6200 and 2000 cal BC (LAVACHERY 2001). In western CAR, Neolithic

settlement sites like Balimbé 68 (ZANGATO 2000), dating from the second millennium BC (2150 – 600 cal BC), also yielded stick-decorated pottery associated with a lithic industry similar to that of the Grassfields. These two developments are probably connected at least on the technological level. As with the LSA, it is not possible to say at present if Neolithic settlement was absent in this part of the research area, or if evidence for such settlement was not identified because of sampling error, either in the distribution of the sites or in the absolute dating of those sites. However, since this area is located between the Grassfields and CAR, the second hypothesis seems most likely.

The Iron Age along the southern Adamawa Plateau in Cameroon, hitherto almost completely unknown, is now better documented. The radiocarbon dates obtained on sites of the northern sector tally relatively well with the archaeological sequences of neighbouring areas. Further to the north in Cameroon and Nigeria, the mound sites of the Lake Chad Basin, of which Gajiganna is among the oldest while later developments are often associated with semi-legendary 'Sao' populations (CONNAH 1976, 1981; LEBEUF *et al.* 1980), seem to precede the Iron Age in Adamawa by approximately a millennium. Most of these mound occupations are dated to between 1000 cal BC and cal AD 1500. This settlement is sometimes related to the arrival of Chadic-speakers in the Lake Chad Basin (DAVID 1982a) and seems to be of a cultural origin different from that of the Adamawa Plateau.

To the southeast, the Iron Age of the western CAR, including the *tazunu* phenomenon, is dated to between 800 cal BC and cal AD 500 (CALVOCORESSI & DAVID 1979; DAVID 1982a; VIDAL *et al.* 1983; ZANGATO 1999, 2000). As on the southern Adamawa Plateau, the pottery is decorated with roulettes, and worked-stone industries seem to survive after the appearance of iron metallurgy until as late as cal AD 700. Similar results were obtained in the course of survey associated with the Bertoua – Garoua-Boulaï highway project, in eastern Cameroon (DELNEUF, ASOMBANG & MBIDA 2003). To the north of the line between Ngaoundéré and Petel, no pit sites were found and pottery, dated to cal AD 1200 – 1400 on one occasion, is decorated with roulettes. This occupation is probably related to that at the sites of Beka Petel (ECA-243) and Sokorta Manga (ECA-43) on the pipeline right-of-way. Further research might well result in the discovery of older sites, but at this moment there is no archaeological proof that the eastern Adamawa Plateau was occupied by farming populations before the end of the last millennium BC. The history of iron metallurgy on the southern Adamawa Plateau was completely unknown prior to Project research. Thanks to the discovery of the Djaoro Mbama (ECA-47) site, we now know that techniques of iron production had been mastered in the area by about two thousand years ago, approximately the same period as in CAR. A reduction furnace excavated at the Bécaré II site yielded a radiocarbon age of cal AD 55 – 390 (LANFRANCHI *et al.* 1998).

As in Chad, there is a hiatus in the chronological sequence of the Iron Age of northern Cameroon. The older phase is represented in the Project area only by the site of Djaoro Mbama (ECA-47) (see above). It is not itself a habitation site, but permanent villages almost certainly existed on the southern Adamawa Plateau by the beginning of the first millennium AD at the latest. Indeed, a site like Djaoro Mbama, where iron was produced in substantial quantities over a long period, would have been the result of labor by a substantial sedentary community. Not far from this region in CAR, very large villages with significant populations existed at the same period, as at Balimbé 68, with its dates of 850 – 200 cal BC, and Gbabiri I, dated to cal AD 50 – 400 (ZANGATO 1996, 1999, 2000). The absence of such sites in Project site inventories is almost certainly due to sampling issues, derived either from site positioning along the right-of-way or the absence of datable material. On the other hand, at the beginning of the second millennium AD, substantial villages existed along the right-of-way, at Sokorta Manga (ECA-43) and Beka Petel (ECA-243). Those parallel sites like Nana-Modé in the CAR, dated to AD 650–900 and yielding roulette-decorated pottery, iron and smelting debris (see above) (DAVID & VIDAL 1977; ZANGATO 1996).

We advance the hypothesis that recent sites like Yébi (ECA-125) and Lom I (ECA-163) are the first archaeological manifestations of settlement by Adamawa-Ubangian speakers in the area. Ceramics from these sites, dated to the last few centuries, are very similar to the ceramics produced by modern Mbum and Gbaya populations. Particularly characteristic is the decoration of undulating bands or festoons, produced by roulette impression (often of braided fibers, in knotted strip roulette), and bordered by stick-grooving. These results are corroborated by the data from the Bertoua – Garoua-Boulaï highway project (MBIDA, ASOMBANG & DELNEUF 2001), where similar interpretations were reached. In CAR as well, sites from the second half of the second millennium AD are attributed to the ancestors of the modern populations of the area (see above). There seems in fact to be a remarkable typological continuity in the ceramics of the area for even longer than that: the famous 'Gbaya' band decorations already existed on Sokorta Manga (ECA-43) and Beka Petel (ECA-243) pottery approximately a thousand years ago. It thus seems that Adamawa and northeastern Cameroon were,

at the beginning of the second millennium AD, part of a broader cultural unit, probably including areas of CAR and southern Chad. This is more or less the situation that still prevails in the area today.

Regional comparison — southern Cameroon

Few data exist concerning ESA/MSA/LSA occupations in southernmost Cameroon, but MSA sites were identified around Yaoundé, as at Ezezang (ECA-272) and Leboudi (ECA-250). Problems of archaeological context and availability of datable material have, as further to the north, prevented an exhaustive study of pre-Iron Age occupations by Project archaeologists. Again, earlier research in this region encountered similar problems of context and dating, as in northern Gabon (FARINE 1967a, 1967b). In that area, survey in the course of road construction revealed technologically very ancient lithic industries, with bifaces, but these are usually found in un-datable *stone-lines*, gravel deposits often found at the base of soil profiles in the area and usually interpreted as the results of late Pleistocene erosional episodes. During the program of monitoring along the Médoumane–Lalara road (OSLISLY & ASSOKO NDONG 2006), similar tools were identified in similar contexts, and were ascribed on typological grounds to the ESA. Comparable industries have in fact been dated in Gabon. At Okala, an archaeological level yielding lithic debitage was dated to approximately 40,000 years ago (CLIST 1997). Since this is close to the limits of radiocarbon dating, this industry even could be much older. In Equatorial Guinea, recent research has resulted in the discovery of MSA and LSA sites in the tropical forest (MERCADER & MARTI 1999). The site of Mosumu (MERCADER *et al.* 2002) is an open-air site, which, in a 2 m stratigraphic column, yielded a late Lupembien/Tshitolien industry, including very characteristic large lanceolate bifacial points. A date of approximately 30,000 bp was obtained at the base of the stratigraphy.

Datable LSA deposits were found only once in the Project area in Cameroon, at the Ndtoua Rock shelter site (ECA-68). This consists of a microlithic industry on quartz, dating to 4500 – 4200 cal BC. This agrees with the date of 5900 – 3700 cal BC for the microlithic industry at Obobogo, in the Yaoundé area (DE MARET 1992). There, an archaeological horizon yielding quartz debitage without pottery was situated below the levels in which Iron Age pits were found (see below). The site of Akoumou 1, in northern Gabon, included several levels of LSA lithic industries, dated between 8300 and 5300 cal BC (OSLISLY & ASSOKO NDONG 2006). Unlike the Cameroonian sites, the bifacial tool tradition is still present at Akoumou 1. LSA quartz debitage, undated but most probably Holocene in age, was revealed at Esamelan Rock shelter (MERCADER & MARTI 1999). The upper levels at Mosumu, which yielded a Tshitolien-type industry with abundant use of bifacial technology, were dated between 1100 cal BC and cal AD 500 (MERCADER *et al.* 2002). This implies that microlithic technologies, without ceramics, survived in forest areas at the time that the first pottery and polished macrolithic tool assemblages were appearing in the Grassfields (LAVACHERY 2001). It appears that, apart from Western Cameroon where a local Neolithic culture developed (see below), the remainder of Central Africa was still occupied by foragers producing stone tools with LSA technological affinities.

No Neolithic assemblages were identified in the Project area in southern Cameroon. However, a significant number of polished axes have been discovered in surface contexts, from the southernmost parts of Cameroon and in northern Gabon (FARINE 1967a, 1967b; DE MARET 1992). They were long regarded as Neolithic *fossiles directeurs* for Central Africa, but in the forest zone they were never discovered in excavations in non-Iron Age contexts (LAVACHERY 1996). *In situ*, these tools are always associated with assemblages where debitage is absent, and even with slag, as in many pit sites in the Yaoundé area (DE MARET 1994) and in northern Gabon (CLIST 2006b), dating to the last millennium BC. Further to the north, polished stone tools are older and appear in a distinctively Neolithic context, as in the Grassfields (see above), where the Neolithic is dated to between 6200 and 2000 cal BC (LAVACHERY 2001) and in western CAR where the Neolithic site of Balimbé 68 (ZANGATO 2000) is dated to 2150 – 600 cal BC. It appears that, south of the latitude of the Grassfields and of Bouar, polished stone tools appeared late, as part of an Iron Age toolkit. This hypothesis is supported by research along the pipeline right-of-way, where polished stone axes were discovered only in contexts associated with metallurgy (with slag and/or the absence of lithic debitage).

Before Project research, the Iron Age of southern Cameroon was only known along the route of the pipeline in the Yaoundé area and along the coast. Areas south and east of Yaoundé were *terra incognita*. We know now that iron-using farmers colonized the forest area between Belabo and Kribi during the early first millennium BC. Just as in Chad and northern Cameroon, a chronological hiatus in the occupation sequence separates two phases during the Iron Age. During Phase I, the populations lived in large, probably permanent villages, characterized by large pits, produced comb-decorated pottery and had access to iron. In fact, lithic

industries had been almost completely abandoned at the beginning of the colonization of the area. It seems that simple or walking comb/-blade impressions were gradually replaced by comb dragging during Phase I of the Iron Age, throughout the pipeline right-of-way in Cameroon (*Chapter 8*). This hypothesis is supported by comparisons with other assemblages in the area. At Shum Laka Rock shelter, pottery dated to *ca* 2500 – 2000 cal BC at the latest, the probable precursor to the forest ceramics of Phase I, shows high percentages (37 %) of vessels decorated with simple or walking comb/-blade impressions (LAVACHERY 2001).

Phase I ceramics of the Yaoundé area actually seem to belong to the Obobogo Group. This typological unit developed in the Yaoundé area over more than a millennium, between 1000 cal BC and cal AD 130 (DE MARET 1980, 1992, 1994; ATANGANA 1992; CLAES 1992; ESSOMBA 1992a, 1992b; MBIDA 2002). In the oldest pits on these sites, the lithic industry had already completely disappeared. During this millennium, ceramic decorations evolved on particular sites. The pottery found in the oldest pits at Obobogo (Pit 3, for example) is very different from the ceramics collected in the most recent pits (Pit 2, for example): whereas the Pit 3 ceramics, dating to 1050 – 400 cal BC, are particularly decorated with rocking (36 %) and simple (36 %) comb impressions, Pit 2 ceramics, dating to 180 cal BC – cal AD 140, are mainly decorated with comb dragging (45 %). The same phenomenon is observed at the nearby site of Ndindan (MBIDA 1996, 2002). While Pit 5 at Ndindan, dating to 760 – 390 cal BC, yielded ceramics very comparable to the 'Oboboguien', with high (45 %) proportions of rocking comb and low (10 %) percentages of comb dragging, vessels from recent units like Pit 20 dated to 360 cal BC – cal AD 70 yielded higher (42 %) proportions of comb dragging. The pottery from Ngoumé in the Tikar plain to the north, dated to *ca* 800 – 400 cal BC, also displays frequent walking-comb decoration, although comb dragging does not seem rare (DELNEUF, OTTO & THINON 2003; LEKA 2002). The Gba site, in the same area, yielded primarily ceramics decorated with comb dragging by 400 – 200 cal BC (LEKA 2002). Recent archaeological research along the coast also supports the hypothesis that comb dragging replaced the rocking-comb impressions of Phase I of the Iron Age. Ceramics from Bissiang (ECA-138) and Dombè (ECA-130), during Phase I in the Littoral forest zone, were mainly decorated with simple or rocking blade/-comb impressions around 1000 – 500 cal BC. Not far away at Bwambé, ceramics in a local style and decorated mainly with comb dragging are dated to between 400 and 100 cal BC, in association with rare stone axes (OSLISLY *et al.* 2006). At Mouanko, further to the north towards the mouth of the Sanaga, one finds the same ceramic style decorated with comb dragging, dated to between 370 BC and AD 390 (EGGERT 2002). Pottery in the Project area around Nanga Eboko, during the local Phase II, is decorated almost exclusively with comb dragging. A little further to the east, around Bertoua, ceramics from Wélé Maroua, dating to 160 cal BC – cal AD 90, are also primarily decorated with comb dragging (MEZOP 2002; DELNEUF, ASOMBANG & MBIDA 2003). The hypothesis that there are distinct typological ensembles along the pipeline right-of-way during the last millennium BC and that in the course of time comb dragging gradually replaced comb impressions seems to be confirmed. It is possible that the tradition of comb dragging originated in the eastern part of the area around Mbam, where it seems older than around Yaoundé and in the Littoral forest zone.

The absence of any significant lithic industry in the Phase I pits excavated between Nanga Eboko and Kribi indicates that these farmers probably used iron when they began to colonize the forest (DE MARET 1994; LAVACHERY 1996). The only dated smelting furnace previously known was that of Oliga (ESSOMBA 1992b) at Yaoundé, but serious sampling problems invalidated the dating of this furnace. Twelve calibrated dates between 1270 cal BC and cal AD 340 were obtained for this single structure, although several of the samples yielded an age around 390 cal BC – cal AD 1, possibly indicating the true age of use of this site. The furnaces found at Makouré (ECA-124) now show that local populations had mastered iron smelting by 395 – 100 cal BC. Research on iron working in Gabon suggests that smelting was known at an earlier date in the forest: a date of 760 – 390 cal BC was obtained for a furnace on the site of Otoumbi 2 (OSLISLY & PEYROT 1992). That date also places the slag discovered in a pit on the Zili (ECA-323) site, a feature dated to 910 – 560 cal BC, in perspective. This suggests to us that iron may well have been produced locally at the beginning of the Iron Age in southern Cameroon, during the first half of the first millennium BC.

We saw that the primary era of Iron Age pit sites can be divided into two distinct phases in southern Cameroon, particularly in the Yaoundé and Littoral forest areas. After a hiatus of several centuries, we see a second florescence of habitation sites with pits between cal AD 300 and 750. Ceramics from this period are characterized by profiles with high concave collars and, sometimes, carinated shoulders. The decorations, as at the end of Phase I, were primarily produced by comb dragging. There seems to be a general increase in the uniformity of ceramic assemblages in southern Cameroon at that time. These Cameroonian ceramics have not been described until now, but this facies apparently extends further to the south. Very similar ceramics were discovered in Gabon in one of the pits at the Lalara 1 site, dated to cal AD 560 – 760 (OSLISLY & ASSOKO NDONG 2006). One might suppose that this phenomenon illustrates an intensification of exchange between forest communities during the second half of the first millennium AD. After cal AD 700, it seems that the pit phenomenon becomes more difficult to discern, because it suddenly becomes much rarer in archaeological landscapes both in Cameroon and in Gabon. This period, which probably corresponds to the occupation of the area by the ancestors of modern populations, remains the least-known part of the cultural sequence in the forest.

10 – Conclusions

Reprise

The objective of the Chad Export Project was to make possible the exploitation of oil resources around Doba, in southwestern Chad, and the export of that oil through an underground pipeline connecting the oilfields to a marine terminal off the Cameroonian coast at Kribi. As such, the Project's area of impact encompassed very diverse areas of Africa, from a cultural as well as an environmental point of view: it runs from dry wooded savanna environments in the Komé area, populated by Central Sudanic-speaking populations, passes along the edges of the Adamawa Plateau, inhabited by Adamawa-Ubangian-speaking communities, and ends on the Southern Cameroonian Plateau and Coastal Plain, covered by tropical forest and inhabited by Bantu-speaking farmers and Bakola-Bagyeli/Pygmy hunter-gatherers.

The archaeological impact mitigation plan, conceived as an integral part of the Chadian Export Project, had the following objectives: (1) the reduction of construction-related impacts on the cultural heritage resources of the Republics of Chad and Cameroon; (2) the development of an understanding of Central African prehistory and history; and (3) support for archaeological institutions and training of archaeological personnel in both host countries. Many of the areas potentially impacted by the installation of the OFDA and the construction of the pipeline were almost totally unknown from an archaeological point of view. The program was planned in four phases: (1) a pre-construction survey; (2) construction monitoring; (3) impact mitigation and data recovery; and (4) analysis of the collected data.

Archaeological fieldwork started in April 1999 in Chad. In Cameroon, fieldwork began in June 2001 and was completed in February 2003. A total of 472 sites (302 in Cameroon and 170 in Chad) were discovered along the pipeline right-of-way, in the OFDA and in the course of Chadian road survey by the end of December 2003, during the pre-construction survey and construction monitoring phases. Of these, 180 sites required impact reduction measures, such as further construction monitoring, avoidance, trench backfill, and/or data recovery procedures. Seventy four sites (33 in Cameroon and 41 in Chad) required data recovery measures and were excavated. After complete evaluation, 58 sites were declared significant to the cultural heritage of Cameroon, as were 52 sites in Chad. Material from all these sites was subject to analysis in archaeological laboratories financed by the Project in each country. The analysis of these sites, 49 of which were subjected

to single or multiple radiocarbon dates, was a unique opportunity to examine chrono-cultural patterning in regions, which were largely unknown before this program took place.

As of late 2006, the fieldwork component of the Chad Export Project's CHM program was largely completed, although limited mitigation activities in Chad had to continue as the oilfields in the Komé area continue to be developed. Some analytical work remains to be done on recovered archaeological materials now stored in both Cameroon and Chad, and so our interpretations must remain open to challenge and change — through further work on these materials in the near future and/or through further fieldwork by Africanist archaeologists. This book thus stands as a particular point in the elucidation of Central African prehistory, not in any sense as the final word on the past of the Project research area.

Any summing up of a cultural heritage management program is always difficult, particularly when that program encompasses different goals, a large geographical area, many archaeological sites of diverse types and some regions where culture-historical sequences are not well understood. Much of the value of this report must lie in the basic data, in the details of site distribution, artifact variability and radiocarbon chronologies provided for areas both well known and little known. Such data are often difficult to summarize. Quite frequently, the implications for the culture history of such research only become clear after a substantial amount of time has gone by, and as the data generated are compared with new information and integrated into wider reconstructions of the past. At the same time, the Chad Export Project CHM program had a variety of goals that are not easy to encapsulate in an academic monograph of this sort, most especially involving the protection of heritage resources in the Project area and the development of cultural heritage management and archaeological infrastructure in the two countries involved. With those caveats in mind, we believe that there are a number of general observations that have been made in the preceding chapters which may be repeated here, concerning the contributions of this project to the prehistory of this area of the continent and future cultural heritage management programs in Central Africa.

Contributions to the prehistory of Central Africa

The Chad Export Project CHM program has generated a mass of archaeological data on the prehistory of Central Africa. It should be noted that these data were collected not only in some areas previously unknown archaeologically, but also in areas that would have been virtually inaccessible without Project logistical support. In southern Chad, these are among the very first archaeological data collected, and they constitute the core of archaeological knowledge on the prehistory of the Province du Logone-Oriental. In the southern- and western-most expansion area of Nilo-Saharan languages, where Central Sudanic languages are spoken, the definition of a 2000 year long chrono-cultural sequence allows for a preliminary reconstruction of the history of Sara populations and their predecessors. It has also been established that a very rich iron-working industry thrived in this area approximately 1000 years ago, and survived in an attenuated form until the colonial era. This sequence can now be compared with similar cultural chronologies for the Chadic- and Nilo-Saharan-speaking populations of the Lake Chad Basin, and for Adamawa-Ubangian-speaking communities in western CAR. It appears, at this stage of analysis, that populations in southern Chad are more closely comparable to their compatriots to the south in CAR than with populations in the Lake Chad Basin, although this may change as more archaeological research is undertaken to the north of the Project area, especially in the Mayo-Kébbi Province.

In northeastern Cameroon, research along the southeastern edge of the Adamawa Plateau yielded significant data on MSA/LSA occupations of an area hitherto little known. It also delivered the first data on a key area for our understanding of the diffusion of Adamawa-Ubangian languages, now spoken in Nigeria, Cameroon, Chad, CAR and Congo. These data allow us to establish productive comparisons with other research programs in CAR and in eastern Cameroon, and to establish an initial chronology of the settlement of the area by Iron Age farmers over the last two millennia. Excavations at Djaoro Mbama (ECA-47) also provided significant information on the technology of iron working in this area approximately 2000 years ago. In southwestern Cameroon, large areas of tropical forest, some of which were very difficult to access, have yielded archaeological data on the colonization of this part of Central Africa by sedentary farmers. Those significantly expand the zone within which such sites are known, after the pioneering work carried out in the Yaoundé area and the coastal zone, and will assist in comparisons between historical linguistic and archaeological data on Bantu prehistory.

Cultural patterning in space and time

The potential of these contributions becomes clearer as we look at more specific issues concerning the cultural diversity in the Project area. It is immediately obvious that there is a significant patterning in the distributions, ages and characteristics of sites in the OFDA and along the pipeline right-of-way in Cameroon and Chad. This observation is heartening, since from the beginning one obvious goal of the program involved examining site diversity along a continuous transect through different environments. This patterning no doubt stems from a number of interacting natural and cultural processes, involving among other things the environmental potentials of different areas to human groups with different economic orientations, taphonomic effects over time on site preservation and visibility, and the specifics of historical processes in certain places and at certain times. In some cases, one of these causes may have a disproportionate (and more easily identifiable) influence: it is likely, for example, that the prevalence of Middle/Late Stone Age sites along the southeastern edge of the Adamawa Plateau can be ascribed to the importance of erosion on steep hill slopes there, while the lack of such sites in southwestern Chad can be largely due to the high rates of sediment accumulation along the right-of-way in that area. In other cases, the causes of such patterns may be more obscure: why, for example, do we see significantly reduced site densities south of Meiganga, east of Nanga-Eboko and around Ngoumou-Lolodorf in Cameroon, in areas where environments and modern population densities do not appear to be significantly different from those found in neighboring areas where considerably higher site densities were found?

This patterning of site locations and characteristics in the Project area can best be appreciated at different geographical scales, probably relating to different levels of natural and cultural effects. At the largest geographical scale, the differences in timing of site appearance in southern Cameroon on the one hand, and in northeastern Cameroon and southwestern Chad on the other, are quite striking. Dated archaeological sites in southwestern Cameroon tend to be occupied between approximately 1000 cal BC and cal AD 600, with much less evidence for occupation – one pit site, Oboukoé (ECA-224), and some surface sites in the Yaoundé area — after the latter date. The region was not abandoned after cal AD 600, but the contrast with earlier periods is significant, and has been remarked upon by other researchers. Dated sites in southwestern Chad and northeastern Cameroon, in contrast, tend to be occupied between the end of the first millennium BC and the late pre-colonial period. There is relatively little evidence for occupation through the first millennium BC (although further excavations at sites like Oulibangala [ETA-56] might provide such data), but significant evidence for human occupation after cal AD 600. Indeed, the most striking results from this area are probably the evidence for intense iron production activities over the period cal AD 1000 – 1200.

These two patterns can also be compared to the situation in the western Central African Republic, where there seems to be significant evidence for substantial human occupation over most of the last 3000 years. The earlier appearance of large, datable sites in southern Cameroon may well be related to the introduction of new economic and technological orientations (including sedentism, arboriculture, new domesticates and [fairly quickly, if not initially] iron working) into that region just after 1000 cal BC, quite probably from the Grassfields area (see *Chapter 4* and *8*). We might well explain the delayed appearance of Iron Age sites in northeastern Cameroon and southwestern Chad as resulting from a combination of taphonomic effects and a later introduction of similar innovations into a very different environmental context, probably from the southern Lake Chad Basin. However, this does not take into account the early dates for iron working and sedentism in western CAR (comparable in all respects to dates in southwestern Cameroon, albeit in what appears to be a quite different cultural context) and also provides no explanation for the later near-disappearance of the 'pit site' phenomenon in southwestern Cameroon. It is tempting to ascribe the cultural innovations in southern Cameroon and western CAR to movements into these areas by populations speaking Bantu and Adamawa-Ubangian languages respectively, but the dynamics of such population movements require far more study.

Similar variability can be seen at smaller geographical scales as well. Indeed, one of the most important contributions of this program has been the discovery of regional patterning along the right-of-way in both space and time. This is especially notable in the Iron Age, as that is the period for which most archaeological data exist. At this point, we can tentatively delineate four cultural areas along the right-of-way during the Iron Age, which can be demarcated according to the modern communities near which their boundaries fall: (1) Komé – Gadjibian; (2) Gadjibian – Belel; (3) Belel – Ewankang; and (4) Ewankang – Ebomé. The first of these, between Komé and Gadjibian, located in a wooded savanna environment on alluvial plains, is especially characterized by its iron-production sites, with a peak in production between cal AD 1000 – 1200, and by large (but usually low-density) settlement sites yielding pottery decorated with wrapped string roulette. This tradition of pottery and metallurgy survived until the pre-colonial period.

In the Gadjibian – Belel area, centered on the Adamawa Plateau, most evidence for settlement dates to the last thousand years, albeit with very significant indications for iron production from the first centuries AD. Settlement sites are large and often located on hilltops, yielding carved wooden roulette-decorated pottery, slag and lithics, in some cases including polished stone tools. This tradition, without the stone tools, survived until the colonial era. The area between Belel and Ewankang encompasses the transition between the Adamawa Plateau and the Southern Cameroonian Plateau, and also between wooded savanna and semi-deciduous forest environments. Iron Age archaeological assemblages, dating to between cal AD 300 – 1600, differ from those found on the Adamawa Plateau by the absence of lithic industries. The reason for this is at present unknown, but may have to do with greater use of iron tools in more forested areas. Later, Gbaya populations, coming from CAR, established themselves in this region, and are probably associated with sites of the late pre-colonial period.

Communities adapted to life in tropical forest occupied the Ewankang – Ebomé area, on the Southern Cameroonian Plateau and the Coastal Plain, just after the beginning of the first millennium BC. These populations probably lived in large, relatively permanent villages characterized by the presence of pits, and produced iron and comb-decorated pottery until approximately cal AD 600, when as noted, the construction of pits in such settlement sites seems to have been abandoned. It is possible that stone tool-using populations in the region acquired ceramics from their farming neighbours approximately 2000 years ago.

At this regional scale the question then becomes: what, if any, human groups can we expect to correspond to the four different cultural areas just delineated? Comparison with an ethnolinguistic map of the area strongly suggests that no simple concordance exists between modern ethnic/linguistic identities and prehistoric material culture variation in the Project area — in fact we should not expect such concordance to exist. Parenthetically, it would be very useful indeed to examine modern variability in, for example, ceramics in communities along the pipeline right-of-way, for comparison with the archaeological record. It is quite probable that these areas correspond to regional constellations of culturally related communities in similar environments, within which ceramic styles and innovations could circulate, probably through the movement of female potters within and between neighboring social groups (especially through marriage). These communities might also have been linguistically related, although the complex modern linguistic situation in southwestern Chad and eastern Cameroon should alert us against any easy assumption that linguistic boundaries will simply be reflected in material or other cultural elements.

At an even smaller geographical scale, site patterning continues to be displayed in the Project study area. This is perhaps most strikingly the case in the Iron Age of southern Cameroon, where distinct clusters of pit sites, each exhibiting somewhat different ceramic characteristics and chronological successions, are found in the Nanga Eboko, Yaoundé and Littoral areas. It is notable that the changes in decorative techniques on ceramics are more gradual across these clusters of pit sites than between the regional zones described above, probably indicating that the degree of internal cultural differentiation (as mediated by flows of people, artifacts and ideas) is lower within these regional zones than between them. The presence of distinct clusters of iron-working sites in the Komé – Gadjibian zone and east of Belel probably indicates analogous kinds of cultural differentiation within these various zones, where certain communities, distinguished by greater access to resources and/or technological expertise, were for a time producing iron in substantial quantities and probably feeding it into regional exchange systems. Again, we cannot make direct connections between the functioning of prehistoric and modern ethnolinguistic groups, but the discovery by Project archaeologists of material diversity on multiple geographical and chronological scales across the research area leads to a picture of ancient cultural patterning at least generally similar to that found in the area today.

Recommendations and implications for African cultural heritage management

As already noted, the research described in this report is not the final word on the prehistory of the Project area. On the contrary, our conclusions constitute only a preliminary effort, based on the current state of analysis, and we hope that the mass of new data generated by this Project will open up new avenues of research. In terms of the Project CHM program itself, two main areas of effort remain open at this point: (1) further work remains to be done on the very large quantity of materials (especially ceramics, lithic materials and botanical remains), collected in the course of fieldwork, by archaeologists and students of archaeology in Chad and Cameroon; and (2) important sites located in the course of Project work need to be protected against destruction, and access for the scientific community to these sites needs to be ensured, in both cases through efforts by the Project and by the governments of Chad and Cameroon. Essentially, these sites and the data they have yielded need to be integrated into wider structures of cultural heritage in the two countries. This text is one element of such integration, but further effort will be needed to complete that process.

In a wider sense, our experience with the Chad Export Project cultural heritage management program has some implications for the future of similar programs in other parts of Africa, a continent where such programs face a number of very serious challenges, many of which involve the lack of resources available to dedicated researchers and heritage managers on the continent. In the first place, we believe that the success of this program helps to demonstrate the feasibility and utility of cultural heritage management procedures in large-scale African resource-extraction programs, especially those associated with oil extraction. Since oil extraction now constitutes one of the main areas of international economic cooperation on the continent, and especially in Central Africa, this is a significant conclusion. Historically, very few oil extraction projects in Africa have included cultural heritage management or archaeological components, because of a lack of interest and comprehension among the industrial participants and the inability of national and expatriate heritage managers and archaeologists to influence the planning and execution of such projects. It is thus to the credit of all actors involved in the Project — the directors and managers themselves, along with their colleagues in the governments of Cameroon and Chad and in the World Bank — that this important heritage management program has been supported in two countries over seven years to date.

Recognition of the significance of African cultural heritage management seems to be growing among Western oil companies working in the western part of Central Africa, although it is by no means general at this point. Such awareness needs to be generalized to other areas of the continent where it may not as yet exist, and to non-Western oil companies, increasingly important in petroleum exploration and exploitation in Africa. Cultural heritage management procedures also need to be implemented at an earlier stage in the exploration process. In many areas of the continent (southeastern Chad, for example), it would be very useful indeed if archaeologists were present during initial geophysical work. Even surface surveys along seismic lines in otherwise inaccessible areas would probably yield extremely important data on prehistoric cultural sequences.

In the second place, involvement of national heritage managers and archaeologists in these resource-extraction projects needs to take place as early in the process as is possible, and their involvement needs to be an explicitly stated element of such projects, accepted — indeed required — by resource-extraction companies, national governments and international organizations alike. In some cases this may be difficult to manage, as personnel and resources may not be easily available for long-term commitments to CHM efforts, and both national and expatriate researchers familiar with African archaeological occurrences may not be similarly familiar with heritage management norms and practices that Western oil company managers know from their experiences in North America or Europe. Cultural heritage management is a discipline with particular specialized skills, often but not always acquired by archaeologists, and its procedures may not be equally familiar to archaeologists in different parts of the world. Early involvement of archaeologists working in relevant areas of Africa allows for agreement over goals and procedures, and for the heritage management program to develop in an organized and orderly manner. Maximum involvement of national personnel and minimum involvement of expatriate personnel, consistent with the completion of project goals, must be an important objective of such heritage management programs.

The ideal situation will be one in which African archaeologists and heritage managers develop and implement cultural heritage management programs associated with resource-extraction projects in their own countries, and also collaborate regionally in projects where such collaboration is most useful, with the strong support of their own governments and of international organizations. In some parts of Africa, neither heritage management/archaeological infrastructures nor familiarity with heritage management procedures would be sufficient to allow such a situation to occur at this point. This brings us to our third point: the development of cultural heritage management and archaeological infrastructures in Africa, both nationally and regionally, must remain a primary goal for managers and archaeologists working on the continent, and this goal needs to be pursued with national governments and international organizations. The economic crises that have beset the continent since the 1980s have led to substantial deficits in heritage management and archaeological resources in many African countries. If pursued vigorously, involvement in CHM programs can potentially address some of these challenges, but some initial investment in CHM expertise and resources is needed to allow that involvement to take place. Given the role that the World Bank and the International Monetary Fund played in the imposition of austerity programs in many African countries, such investment might be a suitable activity for those international organizations.

Collaborations of the kind undertaken by the Chad Export Project require support and cooperation from many different quarters: national governments, international financial organizations, multinational corporations and archaeologists, both citizens of African countries and expatriates. Given hindsight, we can see ways in which the Project CHM program's organization could have been improved and areas where further effort might have yielded more data on the prehistory of this part of Central Africa. At the same time, we believe that this program has resulted in extremely valuable information on Cameroonian and Chadian prehistory, information that will, we hope, lead to new insights into the African past.

REFERENCES

Adelberger, J. 1995. Zum Verhältnis von Sprache, Ethnizität und Kultur in den Muri-Bergen Nordost-Nigerias. In: Fleisch, A. & Otten, D. (eds.), *Sprachkulturelle und historische Forschungen in Afrika*. Rüdiger Koppe Verlag, Köln, pp. 13–27.

Alpern, S. 2005. Did they or didn't they invent it? Iron in sub-Saharan Africa. *History in Africa* 32, 41–94.

Ambrose, S. 2002. Small things remembered: origins of early microlithic industries in sub-Saharan Africa. *Archeological Papers of the American Anthropological Association* 12 (1), 9–29.

Amick, D.S. & Mauldin, R.P. 1989. *Experiments in Lithic Technology*. Archaeopress, Oxford.

Amou'ou Jam, J.-P., Melingui, A., Mounkam, J. & Tchepannou, A. 1985. *Géographie: Le Cameroun*. Armand Colin, Paris.

Ardener, A. 1956. *Coastal Bantu of the Cameroon*. International African Institute, London.

Asombang, R. 1988. Bamenda in Prehistory: The Evidence from Fiye Nkwi, Mbi Crater and Shum Laka Rockshelters. Unpublished Ph.D. Thesis, Institute of Archaeology, University of London, London.

Asombang, R. 2004. Interpreting standing stones in Africa: a case study in North-West Cameroon. *Antiquity* 78 (300), 294–305.

Assoko Ndong, A. 2002. Synthèse des données archéologiques récentes sur le peuplement dans l'Holocène de la réserve de faune de la Lopé, Gabon. *L'Anthropologie* 106 (1), 135–158.

Atangana, C. 1992. Fosses d'Okolo (sud du Cameroun): fouilles et axes de recherches. *Nyame Akuma* 38, 7–13.

Auger, C.P. 1989. *Information Sources in Grey Literature*. Bowker-Saur, London.

Azevedo, M. 1982. Power and slavery in Central Africa: Chad (1890–1925). *Journal of Negro History* 67 (3), 198–211.

Bahuchet, S. 1993a. History of the inhabitants of the central African rain forest: perspectives from comparative linguistics. In: Hladick, C., Linares, O. & Hladick, A. (eds.), *Tropical Forests, People and Food. Biocultural Interactions and Applications to Development*. UNESCO/Parthenon, Paris, pp. 37–54.

Bahuchet, S. 1993b. L'invention des Pygmées. *Cahiers des Etudes Africaines* 33 (1), 153–181.

Bahuchet, S. 1996. La mer et la forêt: ethnoécologie des populations forestières et des pêcheurs du Sud-Cameroun. In: Froment, A., de Garine, I., Binam Bikoi, C. & Loung, J.F. (eds.), *Bien manger et bien vivre*. L'Harmattan, Paris, pp. 145–154.

Balfet, H., Fauvet-Berthelot, M.-F. & Monzon, S. 1983. *Pour la normalisation de la description des poteries*. Editions du CNRS, Paris.

Bastin, Y., Coupez, A. & de Halleux, B. 1983. Classification lexicostatistique des langues bantoues (214 relevés). *Bulletin des Scéances de l'Académie Royale des Sciences d'Outremer* 27 (2), 173–199.

Beleza, S., Gusmao, L., Amorim, A., Carracedo, A. & Salas, A. 2005. The genetic heritage of western Bantu migrations. *Human Genetics* 117, 366–375.

Bender, L. 2000. Nilo-Saharan. In: Heine, B. & Nurse, D. (eds.), *African Languages: An Introduction*. Cambridge University Press, Cambridge, pp. 43–73.

Biesbrouck, K. 1999. *Begyeli Forest Management in Context*. Tropenbros-Cameroon Reports 99–2. The Tropenbos-Cameroon Programme, Wageningen.

Blench, R. 1993a. Ethnographic and linguistic evidence for the prehistory of African ruminant livestock, horses and ponies. In: Shaw, T., Sinclair, P.J.J., Andah, B.W. & Okpoko, A.I. (eds.), *The Archaeology of Africa: Food, Metals and Towns*. Routledge, New York, pp. 71–103.

Blench, R. 1993b. Recent developments in African language classification and their implications for prehistory. In: Shaw, T., Sinclair, P.J.J., Andah, B. & Okpoko, A.I. (eds.), *The Archaeology of Africa: Food, Metal and Towns*. Routledge, New York, pp. 126–138.

Blench, R. 1994–1995. Linguistic evidence for cultivated plants in the Bantu borderland. *Azania* 29–30, 83–102.

Blench, R. 1999. Are the African Pygmies an ethnographic fiction? In: Biesbrouck, K., Elders, S. & Roseel, G. (eds.), *Central African Hunter-Gatherers in a Multidisciplinary Perspective: Challenging Elusiveness*. Research School for Asian, African and Amerindian Studies (CNWS), Universiteit Leiden, Leiden, pp. 41–60.

Blench, R. 2000. *Arbres sauvages et protégés de la région de l'oléoduc en Préfecture Logone Oriental, S. Tchad*. Report to ExxonMobil Corporation.

Blench, R. 2006. *Archaeology, Language and the African Past*. AltaMira Press, Lanham.

Bocoum, H. (ed.) 2002. *Aux origines de le métallurgie du fer en Afrique*. Editions UNESCO, Paris.

Bordes, F. 1961. *Typologie du paléolithique ancien et moyen*. Editions du CNRS, Bordeaux.

Bouquiaux, L., Hyman, L.M. & Voorhoeve, J. 1980. *L'Expansion Bantoue. Actes du Colloque International du CNRS, Viviers (France) — 4–16 avril, 1977*. Peeters Publishing, Leuven.

Boyd, R. 1989. Adamawa-Ubangi. In: Bendor-Samuel, J. (ed.), *The Niger-Congo Languages*. University Press of America, London, pp. 178–215.

Bradley, B. 1975. Lithic reduction sequences: a glossary and discussion. In: Swanson, E. (ed.), *Lithic Technology: Making and Using Stone Tools*. Mouton, The Hague, pp. 5–13.

Brandt, S.A. & Hassan, F. 2000. *Working Paper on Dams and Cultural Heritage Management: Executive Summary*. World Commission on Dams.

Breunig, P., Garba, A. & Hambolu, M. 2001. From ceramics to culture. Studies in the Final Stone Age Gajiganna Complex of NE Nigeria. *Berichte des Sonderforschungsbereichs 268* 14, 45–53.

Breunig, P., Neumann, K. & van Neer, W. 1996. New research on the Holocene settlement and environment of the Chad Basin of Nigeria. *African Archaeological Review* 13 (2), 111–143.

Brezillon, M. 1968. *La dénomination des objets de pierre taillée.* Editions du CNRS, Paris.

Brooks, A. 2002. Cultural contact in Africa, past and present: multidisciplinary perspectives on the status of African foragers. In: Kent, S. (ed.), *Ethnicity, Hunter-Gatherers, and the "Other": Association or Assimilation in Africa.* Smithsonian Institution, Washington, pp. 206–229.

Brooks, A.S. & Smith, C.C. 1987. Ishango revisited: new age determinations and cultural interpretations. *African Archaeological Review* 5, 65–78.

Brown, E. 1983. *Nourrir les gens, nourrir les haines.* Société d'Ethnographie, Paris.

Brown, E. 1996. *The Human Environment.* Chad Export Project, N'Djamena.

Brunk, K. & Gronenborn, D. 2004. Floods, droughts, and migrations: the effects of late Holocene lake level fluctuations and climate fluctuations on the settlement and political history in the Chad Basin. In: Krings, M. & Platte, E. (eds.), *Living with the Lake: Perspectives on History, Culture and Economy of Lake Chad.* Rüdiger Köppe Verlag, Köln, pp. 101–132.

Burnham, P. 1980. *Opportunity and Constraint in a Savanna Society: The Gbaya of Meiganga, Cameroon.* Academic Press, London.

Burnham, P. 1996. *The Politics of Cultural Difference in Northern Cameroon.* Edinburgh University Press, Edinburgh.

Burnham, P., Copet-Rougier, E. & Noss, P. 1986. Gbaya et Mkako: contribution ethno-linguistique a l'histoire de l'Est-Cameroun. *Paideuma* 32, 87–128.

Cabot, J. 1965. *Le bassin du moyen Logone.* ORSTOM, Paris.

Cahen, D. 1978a. New excavations at Gombe (ex-Kalina) point, Kinshasa, Zaire. *Antiquity* 52 (204), 51.

Cahen, D. 1978b. Vers une révision de la nomenclature des industries préhistoriques de l'Afrique centrale. *Anthropologie* (1), 5.

Cahen, D. 1982. The Stone Age in the south and west. In: van Noten, F. & Cahen, D. (eds.), *The Archaeology of Central Africa.* Akademische Druck- u. Verlagsanstalt, Graz, pp. 41–56.

Calvocoressi, D.S. & David, N. 1979. A new survey of radiocarbon and thermoluminescence dates for West Africa. *Journal of African History* 20 (1), 1–29.

Campbell, I. 2000. Environmental impact assessment, cultural property and dams in Eastern Africa. Paper presented at the International Workshop on Dams, University of Florida, Gainesville.

Chad Export Project 1999a. *Environmental Management Plan — Cameroon Portion.* ExxonMobil Corporation, Houston.

Chad Export Project 1999b. *Environmental Management Plan — Chad Portion.* ExxonMobil Corporation, Houston.

Chad/Cameroon Development Project 2003. *The Project: Development History.* Chad/Cameroon Development Project. http://www.essochad.com/Chad-English/PA/Operations/TD_History.asp. Accessed 12 September, 2007.

Chikwendu, V.E. 1998. *Cultural Succession and Continuity in SE Nigeria.* British Archaeological Reports 734, Cambridge Monographs in African Archaeology 44. Archaeopress, Oxford.

Childe, V.G. 1951. *Man Makes Himself.* New American Library, New York.

Claes, P. 1992. A propos des céramiques de Mimboman et d'Okolo. In: Essomba, J.-M. (eds.), *L'archéologie au Cameroun.* Karthala, Paris, pp. 215–227.

Clark, J.D., Cole, G.H., Isaac, G. & Kleindienst, M. 1966. Precision and definition in African archaeology. *South African Archaeological Bulletin* 21, 114–121.

Claussen, M., Kubatzki, C., Brovkin, V., Ganopolski, A., Hoelzmann, P. & Pachur, H.-J. 1999. Simulation of an abrupt change in Saharan vegetation in the mid-Holocene. *Geophysical Research Letters* 26 (14), 2037.

Clist, B. 1989. Archaeology in Gabon 1886–1988. *African Archaeological Review* 7, 59–96.

Clist, B. 1990. Des derniers chasseurs aux premiers métallurgistes: sédentarisation et débuts de la métallurgie du fer (Cameroun, Guinée Equatoriale, Gabon). In: Lanfranchi, R. & Schwartz, D. (eds.), *Paysages quaternaires de l'Afrique Centrale Atlantique.* Editions de l'ORSTOM, Paris, pp. 458–478.

Clist, B. 1991. L'Age du fer ancien: Centrafrique. In: Lanfranchi, R. & Clist, B. (eds.), *Aux origines de l'Afrique Centrale.* Centre Culturel Francaise de Libreville/Sepia, Libreville, pp. 197–201.

Clist, B. 1993. Archaeological fieldwork and labwork in Gabon during 1992. *Nyame Akuma* 39, 26.

Clist, B. 1995. *Gabon: 100.000 ans d'histoire.* Sépia, Paris.

Clist, B. 1997. Le site d'Okala, Province de l'Estuaire, Gabon, et son importance pour le compréhension du passage à la sédentarisation en Afrique Centrale. *Comptes-rendus de l'Académie des Sciences de Paris* 325, 151–166.

Clist, B. 2005. Des premiers villages aux premiers européens autour de l'estuaire du Gabon: quatre millénaires d'interactions entre l'homme et son milieu. Unpublished Ph.D. Thesis, Histoire, Arts et Archéologie, Université Libre de Bruxelles, Brussels.

Clist, B. 2006a. Mais où se sont taillées nos pierres en Afrique Centrale entre 7.000 et 2.000 bp? In: Wotzka, H.-P. (ed.), *Grundlegungen. Beiträge zur europäischen und afrikanischen Archäologie für Manfred K.H. Eggert.* Francke Verlag, Tübingen, pp. 291–302.

Clist, B. 2006b. Mise en évidence dans le nord-ouest du Gabon de la présence de l'homme au sein des forêts d'age Holocène. *Journal of African Archaeology* 4 (1), 143–152.

Commission du Bassin du Lac Tchad. 1968. *Synthèse hydrologique du Bassin du Lac Tchad (Reg 71)*. UNDP - UNESCO, Paris.

Connah, G. 1976. The Daima sequence and the prehistoric chronology of the Lake Chad region of Nigeria. *Journal of African History* 17 (3), 321–352.

Connah, G. 1981. *Three Thousand Years in Africa: Man and His Environment in the Lake Chad Region of Nigeria*. Cambridge University Press, Cambridge.

Copet-Rougier, E. 1987. Du clan à la chefferie dans l'est du Cameroun. *Africa* 57 (3), 345–363.

Cordell, D. 1985. *Dar al-Kuti and the Last Years of the Trans-Saharan Slave Trade*. University of Wisconsin Press, Madison.

Cornelissen, E. 2002. Human responses to changing environments in Central Africa between 40,000 and 12,000 B.P. *Journal of World Prehistory* 16 (3), 197–235.

Cornelissen, E. 2003. On microlithic quartz industries at the end of the Pleistocene in Central Africa: the evidence from Shum Laka (NW Cameroon). *African Archaeological Review* 20 (1), 1–24.

Courtin, J. 1962. *Recherches archéologiques et préhistoriques en pays Sara (République du Tchad). Rapport préliminaire sur la mission de 1962*. INSH, N'Djamena.

Courtin, J. 1963. *Mission dans le Sud–Ouest et l'Est du Tchad. Recherches préhistoriques et archéologiques de 1963*. INSH, N'Djamena.

Crabtree, D. 1975. Comments on lithic technology and experimental archaeology. In: Swanson, E. (ed.), *Lithic Technology: Making and Using Stone Tools*. Mouton, The Hague, pp. 104–114.

Craddock, P., Ambers, J., Hook, D., Farquhar, R., Chikwendu, V., Umeji, A. & Shaw, T. 1997. Metal sources and the bronzes from Igbo-Ukwu, Nigeria. *Journal of Field Archaeology* 24 (4), 405–429.

David, N. 1980. Early Bantu expansion in the context of central African prehistory: 4000–1 B.C. In: Bouquiaux, L. (ed.), *L'expansion Bantoue*. Vol. 3. Société d'Études Linguistiques et Anthropologiques de France 9, 609–647.

David, N. 1982a. Prehistory and historical linguistics in Central Africa: points of contact. In: Ehret, C. & Posnansky, M. (eds.), *The Archaeological and Linguistic Reconstruction of African History*. University of California Press, Berkeley, pp. 78–95.

David, N. 1982b. Tazunu: megalithic monuments of Central Africa. *Azania* 17, 43–78.

David, N. 1993. Rop rock shelter: re-excavation and reassessment. In: Andah, B., de Maret, P. & Soper, R. (eds.), *Proceedings of the 9th Congress of the Pan-African Association of Prehistory and Related Studies*. Rex Charles Publications, Ibadan, pp. 146–152.

David, N. 1998. The ethnoarchaeology and field archaeology of grinding at Sukur, Adamawa State, Nigeria. *African Archaeological Review* 15 (1), 13–63.

David, N. 2004. Watch or water towers? *Expedition* 46 (2), 30–35.

David, N. & Kramer, C. 2001. *Ethnoarchaeology in Action*. Cambridge University Press, Cambridge.

David, N.C. & Vidal, P. 1976. The central African megaliths project. *Palaeoecology of Africa* 9, 54–62.

David, N.C. & Vidal, P. 1977. The Nana-Modé village site (Sous-Préfecture de Bouar, Central African Republic) and the prehistory of the Ubanguian-speaking peoples. *West African Journal of Archaeology* 7, 17–56.

de Bayle des Hermens, R. 1975. *Recherches préhistoriques en République Centrafricaine*. Librarie C. Klincksieck, Paris.

de Maret, P. 1980. Preliminary report on 1980 fieldwork in the Grassfields and Yaounde, Cameroon. *Nyame Akuma* 17, 10–12.

de Maret, P. 1985. Recent archaeological research and dates from Central Africa. *Journal of African History* 26, 129–148.

de Maret, P. 1992. Sédentarisation, agriculture et métallurgie du Sud-Cameroun: synthèse des recherches depuis 1978. In: Essomba, J.-M. (ed.), *L'archéologie au Cameroun*. Karthala, Paris, pp. 247–262.

de Maret, P. 1994. Pits, pots and the far-west streams. In: Sutton, J.E.G. (ed.), *The Growth of Farming Communities in Africa from the Equator Southwards*. British Institute in Eastern Africa, Nairobi, pp. 318–324.

de Maret, P. 2002. L'Afrique centrale: le « savoir-fer ». In: Bocoum, H. (ed.), *Aux origines de la métallurgie du fer en Afrique*. UNESCO, Paris, pp. 123–132.

de Maret, P., Clist, B. & Mbida, C. 1983. Belgian Archaeological Mission in Cameroon: 1983 field season. *Nyame Akuma* 23, 5–6.

de Maret, P., Clist, B. & van Neer, W. 1987. Résultats des premières fouilles dans les abris de Shum Laka et d'Abeke au nord-ouest du Cameroun. *L'Anthropologie* 91 (2), 559–584.

de Vos, G. & Romanucci-Ross, L. 1975. Ethnicity: vessel of meaning and emblem of contrast. In: de Vos, G. & Romanucci-Ross, L. (eds.), *Ethnic Identity: Cultural Continuities and Change*. Mayfield, Palo Alto, pp. 363–390.

Deacon, J. 1999. *South African Heritage Legislation in Global Perspective*. Heritage Assets Management Sub-Directorate, Department of Public Works, Pretoria.

Delneuf, M., Asombang, R. & Mbida, C. 2003. *Surveillance archéologique de l'axe routier Bertoua-Garoua Bouai — Rapport Final*. IRD, Paris.

Delneuf, M., Otto, T. & Thinon, M. 2003. Occupations humaines anciennes et dynamique forestière: approche croisée en plaine Tikar. In: Froment, A. & Guffroy, J. (eds.), *Peuplements anciens et actuels des forêts tropicales*. IRD, Paris, pp. 127–156.

Deme, A. 2004. Archaeological Investigations of Settlement and Emerging Complexity in the Middle Senegal Valley. Unpublished Ph.D. Thesis, Department of Anthropology, Rice University, Houston.

Descoeudres, J.-P., Huysecom, E., Serneels, V. & Zimmermann, J.-L. 2001. *Mediterranean Archaeology 14: Aux origines de la métallurgie du fer*. Meditarch, Sydney.

Dieu, M. & Renaud, P. 1983. *Atlas linguistique de l'Afrique centrale: le Cameroun*. CERDOTOLA-DGRST, Yaoundé.

Dozon, J.-P. 1985. Les Bete: une creation coloniale. In: Amselle, J.-L. & M'bokolo, E. (eds.), *Au coeur de l'ethnie: ethnies, tribalisme et etat en Afrique*. Editions la Decouverte, Paris, pp. 49–85.

Eggert, M. 1992. The Central African rain forest: historical speculation and archaeological facts. *World Archaeology* 24 (1 [The Humid Tropics]), 1–25.

Eggert, M. 2002. Southern Cameroon and the settlement of equatorial rainforest: early ceramics from fieldwork in 1997 and 1998–1999. In: Lenssen-Erz, T., Tegtmeier, U. & Kröpelin, S. (eds.), *Tides of the desert — Gezeiten der Wüste*. Heinrich-Barth-Institut, Köln, pp. 507–522.

Eggert, M. 2005. The Bantu problem and African archaeology. In: Stahl, A. (ed.), *African Archaeology: A Critical Introduction*. Blackwell Publishing, Oxford, pp. 301–326.

Ehret, C. 1984. Historical/linguistic evidence for early African food production. In: Clark, J.D. & Brandt, S.A. (eds.), *From Hunters to Farmers*. University of California Press, Berkeley, pp. 26–36.

Ehret, C. 1993. Nilo-Saharan and the Saharo-Sudanese Neolithic. In: Shaw, T., Sinclair, P.J.J., Andah, B. & Okpoko, A.I. (eds.), *The Archaeology of Africa: Food, Metal and Towns*. Routledge, New York, pp. 104–125.

Ehret, C. 2001. Bantu expansions: re-envisioning a central problem of early African history. *International Journal of African Historical Studies* 34 (1), 5–42.

Essomba, J.-M. 1992a. Archéologie du sud du Cameroun: notes préliminaires de recherches au site du Nkometou (Mfomakap). In: Essomba, J.-M. (ed.), *L'archéologie au Cameroun*. Karthala, Paris, pp. 229–245.

Essomba, J.-M. 1992b. *Civilisation du fer et société en Afrique centrale: le cas du Cameroun méridional. (Histoire ancienne et archéologie)*. Editions l'Harmattan, Paris.

Fagg, A. 1972. A preliminary report on an occupation site in the Nok Valley, Nigeria: Samun Dukiya. *West African Journal of Archaeology* 2, 75–79.

Fagg, B. 1969. New work in West Africa: recent light on the Nok culture. *World Archaeology* 1 (1), 41–50.

Fairhead, J.D. & Green, C.M. 1989. Controls on rifting in Africa and the regional tectonic model for the Nigeria and east Niger rift basins. *Journal of African Earth Sciences* 8, 231–249.

Faraut, F. 1981. Les mboum. In: Tardits, C. (ed.), *Contribution de la recherche ethnologique à l'histoire des civilisations du Cameroun*. CNRS, Paris, pp. 159–169.

Farine, B. 1967a. Quelques outils principaux des divers faciès préhistoriques des districts de Ndjolé et de Booué. *Bulletin de la Société Préhistorique et Protohistorique Gabonaise* 7, 22–36.

Farine, B. 1967b. Nouveaux gisements préhistoriques dans les environs de Ndjolé et des portes de l'Okanda. *Bulletin de la Société Préhistorique et Protohistorique Gabonaise* 7, 14–21.

Fishman, J.A. 1989. *Language and Ethnicity in Minority Sociolinguistic Perspective*. Multilingual Matters Ltd., Clevedon.

Flynn, L., Brillanceaux, A., Brunet, M., Coppens, Y., Dejax, J., Duperon-Laoudoueneix, M., Ekodeck, K., Flanagan, K., Heintz, E., Hell, J., Jacobs, L., Pilbeam, D., Sen, S. & Djallo, S. 1987. Vertebrate fossils from Cameroon, West Africa. *Journal of Vertebrate Paleontology* 7, 469–471.

Foley, J., Coe, M., Scheffer, M. & Wang, G. 2003. Regime shifts in the Sahara and Sahel: interactions between ecological and climatic systems in Northern Africa. *Ecosystems* 6 (6), 524–532.

Garcea, E. 2004. An alternative way towards food production: the perspective from the Libyan Sahara. *Journal of World Prehistory* 18 (2), 107–154.

Gausset, Q. 1998. Historical account or discourse on identity? A reexamination of Fulbe hegemony and autochthonous submission in Banyo. *History in Africa* 25, 93–110.

Gautier, A. 1987. The archaeozoological sequence in the Acacus. In: Barich, B. (ed.), *Archaeology and Environment in the Libyan Sahara. The Excavations in the Tadrart Acacus, 1978–1983*. British Archaeological Reports 368, Cambridge Monographs in African Archaeology 23. Archaeopress, Oxford, pp. 283–312.

Goodland, R. & Webb, M. 1987. *The Management of Cultural Properties in World Bank-Assisted Projects*. World Bank, Washington.

Gosselain, O. 1995. Identités techniques. Le travail de la poterie au Cameroun méridional. Unpublished Ph.D. Thesis, Université Libre de Bruxelles, Brussels.

Gosselain, O. 1999. Poterie, société et histoire chez les Koma Ndera du Cameroun. *Cahier des Etudes Africaines* 39 (153), 73–105.

Gosselain, O. 2002. *Poteries du Cameroun méridionale. Styles, techniques et rapports à l'identité*. CNRS Editions, Paris.

Gotilogue, S. & Lanfranchi, R. 1997. Le Projet de recherche du CURDHACA sur la métallurgie du fer en la République Centrafricaine. *Nyame Akuma* 47, 14–18.

Gronenborn, D. 1998. Archaeological and ethnohistorical investigations along the southern fringes of Lake Chad, 1993 – 1996. *African Archaeological Review* 15 (4), 225–259.

Gronenborn, D. 2000. Mai-mbauji—Eine Studie über Entstehung und Wandel eisenzeitlich-historischer Fürstentümer im südlichen Tschadbecken (7./8. Jahrhundert n. Chr. bis ca. 1925). Unpublished professorial dissertation, Johann Wolfgang Goethe-Universität, Frankfurt am Main.

Gronenborn, D. 2001. Princedoms along the lakeshore. Historical - archaeological investigations on the development of complex societies in the southern Lake Chad Basin. *Berichte des Sonderforschungsbereichs 268* 14, 55–69.

Guthrie, M. 1971. *Comparative Bantu*. Gregg International, London.

Guyer, J. 1984. *Family and Farm in Southern Cameroon*. Boston University, African Studies Center, Boston.

Hartle, D.D. 1980. Archaeology east of the Niger: a review of cultural-historical development. In: Swartz, B.K. & Dumett, R. (eds.), *West African Culture Dynamics*. Mouton, The Hague, pp. 195–204.

Herbert, E. 1993. *Iron, Gender and Power: Ritual Transformation in African Societies*. Indiana University Press, Bloomington.

Hodder, I. 1982. *Symbols in Action*. Cambridge University Press, Cambridge.

Holl, A. 1993. Transition from Late Stone Age to Iron Age in the Sudano-Sahelian zone: a case study from the Perichadian plain. In: Shaw, T., Sinclair, P., Andah, B.W. & Okpoko, A.I. (eds.), *Archaeology of Africa: Food, Metals and Towns*. Routledge, London, pp. 330–343.

Holl, A. 2001. *The Land of Houlouf: Genesis of a Chadic Polity 1900 BC – AD 1800*. Museum of Anthropology, University of Michigan, Ann Arbor.

Hombert, J.-M. & Hyman, L.M. (eds.) 1999. *Bantu Historical Linguistics: Theoretical and Empirical Perspectives*. University of Chicago Press, Chicago.

Huysecom, E., Ballouche, A., Boeda, E., Cappa, L., Cisse, L., Dembélé, M., Gallay, A., Konate, D., Mayor, A., Ozainne, S., Raeli, F., Rasse, M., Robert, A., Robion, C., Sanogo, K., Soriano, S., Sow, S. & Stokes, S. 2002. Cinquième campagne de recherches à Ounjougou (Mali). *Jahresbericht SLSA 2001*, 55–113.

Inizan, M.-L., Reduron, M., Roche, H. & Tixier, J. 1995. *Préhistoire de la pierre taillée 4. Technologie de la pierre taillée*. CREP, Meudon.

Jauze, J.B. 1944. Contribution à l'étude de l'archéologie du Cameroun. *Bulletin de la Société des Etudes Camerounaises* 8, 105–123.

Jewsiewicki, B. 1989. The formation of the political culture of ethnicity in the Belgian Congo, 1920–1959. In: Vail, L. (ed.), *The Creation of Tribalism in Southern Africa*. University of California Press, Berkeley, pp. 324–349.

Joiris, D. 1994. Elements of techno-economic changes among the sedentarised BaGyeli pygmies (Southwest Cameroon). *African Study Monographs* 15 (2), 83–95.

Kadomura, H. 1984. *Natural and Man-Induced Environmental Changes in Tropical Africa*. Laboratory of Fundamental Research, Division of Environmental Structure, Hokkaido University, Sapporo.

Killick, D. 2004. What do we know about African iron working? *Journal of African Archaeology* 2 (1), 97–112.

Kinahan, J. 2000. Lessons from the joint Angolan-Namibian Lower Cunene Hydropower Scheme. Paper presented at the International Workshop on Dams, University of Florida, Gainesville.

King, T.F. 2005. *Doing Archaeology: A Cultural Resource Management Perspective*. Left Coast Press, Walnut Creek.

Kleindienst, M. 2006. On naming things. Behavioral changes in the later Middle to earlier Late Pleistocene, viewed from the Eastern Sahara. In: Hovers, E. & Kuhn, S. (eds.), *Transitions Before the Transition: Evolution and Stability in the Middle Paleolithic and Middle Stone Age*. Springer, New York, pp. 13–28.

Klieman, K. 2003a. *"The Pygmies were our Compass". Bantu and Batwa in the History of West Central Africa, Early Times to c. 1900 C.E.* Heinemann, Portsmouth, N.H.

Klieman, K. 2003b. Toward a history of pre-colonial Gabon: farmers and forest-specialists along the Middle Ogooué River, 500 BC – AD 1000. In: Reed, M. & Barnes, J. (ed.), *Culture, Ecology and Politics in Gabon's Rainforest*. The Edwin Mellen Press, Lewiston, pp. 99–115.

Kusnir, I. 1995. *Geologie, ressources minérales et ressources en eau du Tchad*. Centre Nationale d'Appui à la Recherche, N'Djamena.

Laburthe-Tolra, P. 1977. *Minlaaba, histoire et société traditionnelles chez les Beti du Cameroun Méridional*. Honoré Champion, Paris.

Lanfranchi, R., Ndanga, J. & Zana, H. 1998. New carbon 14C datings of iron metallurgy in the Central Africa dense forest. In: Eves, H., Hardin, R. & Rupp, S. (eds.), *Resource Use in the Trinational Sangha River Region of Equatorial Africa: Histories, Knowledge Forms, and Institutions*. Yale University Press, New Haven, pp. 41–50.

Langlois, O. 2004. Distributions ancienne et actuelle des décors imprimés au Diamaré (Nord-Cameroun) et a ses marges. *Préhistoire Anthropologie Méditerranéennes* 13, 109–126.

Lattanzi, G. 1999. Cultural resource management and the Internet: a touch of 'gray'. *SAA Bulletin* 17 (4). http://www.saa. org/Publications/saabulletin/17-4/saa21.html Accessed 14 October, 2007.

Lavachery, P. 1996. Shum Laka rock shelter late Holocene deposits: from stone to metal (Northwestern Cameroon). In: Pwiti, G. & Soper, R. (eds.), *Aspects of African Archaeology: Proceedings of the Tenth Pan-African Congress*. University of Zimbabwe Press, Harare, pp. 266–274.

Lavachery, P. 1998. De la pierre au métal: archéologie des dépôts holocènes de l'abri de Shum Laka (Cameroun). Unpublished Ph.D. Thesis, Faculté de Philosophie et Lettres, Université Libre de Bruxelles, Bruxelles.

Lavachery, P. 2001. The Holocene archaeological sequence of Shum Laka Rock Shelter (Grassfields, Western Cameroon). *African Archaeological Review* 18 (4), 213–248.

Lavachery, P. & Cornelissen, E. 2001. Natural and cultural spatial patterning in the late Holocene deposits of Shum Laka rock shelter, Cameroon. *Journal of Field Archaeology* 27 (2), 153–168.

Lavachery, P., Cornelissen, E., Moeyersons, J. & de Maret, P. 1996. 30,000 ans d'occupation, 6 mois de fouilles: Shum Laka, un site exceptionnel en Afrique centrale. *Anthropologie et Préhistoire* 107, 197–211.

Lavachery, P., MacEachern, S., Bouimon, T., Gouem Gouem, B., Kinyock, P., Mbairo, J., Mbida, C. & Nkokonda, O. 2005a. Cultural heritage management in Central Africa: regional survey on the Chad – Cameroon oil pipeline. *Antiquity* 79 (303). http://antiquity.ac.uk/ProjGall/maceachern/index.html Accessed 23 September, 2007.

Lavachery, P., MacEachern, S., Bouimon, T., Gouem Gouem, B., Kinyock, P., Mbairo, J. & Nkokonda, O. 2005b. Komé to Ebomé: archaeological research for the Chad Export Project, 1999–2003. *Journal of African Archaeology* 3 (2), 175–193.

Lebeuf, A.M.D., Lebeuf, J.-P., Treinen-Claustre, F. & Courtin, J. 1980. *Le gisement sao de Mdaga (Tchad): Fouilles 1960–1968.* Société d'ethnographie, Paris.

Leka, M.J. 2002. *Etude archéologique de la céramique des sites anciens et subactuelle de la plaine Tikar Sud (Nditam, Ngweu, Ngoume PK 35, Gba).* Mémoire de Maîtrise, Université de Yaoundé I.

Letouzey, R. & Fotius, G. 1985. *Carte phytogéographique du Cameroun.* Institut de la Carte Internationale de la Végétation, Toulouse.

Loumpet, G. 1998. Peuplement et environnement de l'homme en zones forestière et post-forestière du Cameroun au début du Pléistocene. In: Delneuf, M., Essomba, J.-M. & Froment, A. (eds.), *Paléo-anthropologie en Afrique centrale. Un bilan de l'archéologie au Cameroun.* Editions de l'Harmattan, Paris, pp. 161–175.

Mabulla, A.Z.P. 2000. Strategy for cultural heritage management (CHM) in Africa: a case study. *African Archaeological Review* 17 (4), 211–233.

MacDonald, K. 1996. Tichitt-Walata and the Middle Niger: evidence for cultural contact in the second millennium BC. In: Pwiti, G. & Soper, R. (eds.), *Aspects of African Archaeology: Proceedings of the Tenth Pan-African Congress.* University of Zimbabwe Press, Harare, pp. 429–440.

MacDonald, K. 1997. Korounkorokalé revisited: the *pays Mande* and the West African Microlithic Technocomplex. *African Archaeological Review* 14 (3), 161–200.

MacDonald, K. & Allsworth-Jones, P. 1994. A reconstruction of the West African macrolithic conundrum: new factory sites and an associated settlement in the Vallée du Serpent, Mali. *African Archaeological Review* 12, 105–132.

MacEachern, S. 1996. Iron Age beginnings north of the Mandara Mountains, Cameroon and Nigeria. In: Pwiti, G. & Soper, R. (eds.), *Aspects of African Archaeology: Proceedings of the Tenth Pan-African Congress.* University of Zimbabwe Press, Harare, pp. 489–495.

MacEachern, S. 1999. Report on Archaeological Survey Between Mbéré and Doba, Southern Chad, April – May 1999. Unpublished report submitted to ExxonMobil Corporation.

MacEachern, S. 2001a. Cultural resource management and Africanist archaeology. *Antiquity* 75 (290), 866–871.

MacEachern, S. 2001b. Report on Archaeological Road Survey Between Beibokoum and Doba, Southern Chad, June – July, 2000. Report submitted to ExxonMobil Corporation.

MacEachern, S. 2001c. Setting the boundaries: linguistics, ethnicity, colonialism, and archaeology south of Lake Chad. In: Terrell, J. (ed.), *Archaeology, Language, and History: Essays on Culture and Ethnicity.* Bergin & Garvey, Westport, pp. 79–101.

MacEachern, S. 2004. Ethnoarchaeology, history and culture in Mandara populations. Paper presented at the annual conference of the Society for American Archaeology. 26–30 March, 2004, Montréal.

Magnant, J.-P. 1986. *La terre sara, terre tchadienne.* Editions de l'Harmattan, Paris.

Maley, J. 1981. *Etudes palynologiques dans le bassin du Tchad et paléoclimatologie de l'Afrique nord-tropicale de 30,000 ans à l'époque actuelle.* Editions de l'ORSTOM, Paris.

Malherbe, M. 2000. *Répertoire simplifié des langues africaines.* Editions de l'Harmattan, Paris.

Marliac, A. 1973. *L'état des connaissances sur le Paléolithique et le Néolithique du Cameroun.* ORSTOM, Yaoundé.

Marliac, A. 1974. Prospection archéologique au Cameroun septentrional. *West African Journal of Archaeology* 4, 83–97.

Marliac, A. 1987. Introduction au Paléolithique du Cameroun septentrionale. *L'Anthropologie* 92 (2), 521–558.

Marliac, A. 1991. *De la préhistoire à l'histoire au Cameroun septentrionale.* ORSTOM, Paris.

Mbida, C. 1992. Fouilles archéologiques au Sud-Cameroun: résultats préliminaires de la mission de l'été 1990. *Nsi* 10–11, 6–8.

Mbida, C. 1996. L'émergence de communautés villageoises au Cameroun méridional. Etude archéologique des sites de Nkang et de Ndindan. Unpublished Ph.D. Thesis, Université Libre de Bruxelles, Bruxelles.

Mbida, C. 1998. Premières communautés villageoises au sud du Cameroun: synthèse et données nouvelles. In: Delneuf, M., Essomba, J.-M. & Froment, A. (ed.), *Paléo-anthropologie en Afrique Centrale.* L'Harmattan, Paris, pp. 202–211.

Mbida, C. 2002. Ndindan : synthèse archéologique d'un site datant de trois millénaires à Yaoundé (Cameroun). *L'Anthropologie* 106, 159–172.

Mbida, C., Asombang, R. & Delneuf, M. 2001. Rescue archaeology in eastern Cameroon. *Antiquity* 75 (290), 805–806.

Mbida, C., Doutrelepont, H., Vrydaghs, L., Swennen, R., Beeckman, H., de Langhe, E. & de Maret, P. 2001. First archaeological evidence of banana cultivation in Central Africa during the third millennium before present. *Vegetation History and Archaeobotany* 10, 1–6.

Mbida, C., van Neer, W., Doutrelepont, H. & Vrydaghs, L. 2000. Evidence for banana cultivation and animal husbandry during the first millennium BC in the forest of southern Cameroon. *Journal of Archaeological Science* 27 (2), 151–162.

McIntosh, R.J. 1993 The pulse model: genesis and accommodation of specialization in the Middle Niger. *Journal of African History* 34 (2), 181–220.

McIntosh, R.J. 2000. Social memory in Mande. In: McIntosh, R.J., Tainter, J. & McIntosh, S.K. (eds.), *The Way the Wind Blows: Climate, History and Human Action*. Columbia University Press, New York, pp. 141–180.

McIntosh, S.K. 1993. Archaeological heritage management and site inventory systems in Africa. *Journal of Field Archaeology* 20, 500–504.

Mercader, J. & Brooks, A.S. 2001. Across forests and savannas: Later Stone Age assemblages from Ituri and Semliki, Democratic Republic of Congo. *Journal of Anthropological Research* 57 (2), 197–217.

Mercader, J. & Marti, R. 1999. Archaeology in the tropical forest of Banyang-Mbo, SW Cameroon. *Nyame Akuma* 52, 17–24.

Mercader, J., Marti R., Martinez J.L. & Brooks A. 2002. The nature of 'stone-lines' in the African Quaternary record: archaeological resolution at the rainforest site of Mosumu, Equatorial Guinea. *Quaternary International* 89, 71–96.

Mercader, J., Marti, R., Wilkins, J. & Fowler, K. 2006. The eastern periphery of the Yoruba cultural sphere. *Current Anthropology* 47 (1), 173–184.

Mezop, A.L. 2002. Etude de la céramique archéologique de Wele Maroua (Est-Cameroun). Unpublished Mémoire de Maîtrise, Université de Yaoundé I.

Mitchell, P. 2000. Archaeology and the Lesotho Highlands Water Project. Paper presented at the International Workshop on Dams, University of Florida, Gainesville

Mohammadou, E. 1990. *Traditions historiques des peuples du Cameroun central*. ILCAA, Tokyo.

Mouktar Bah, T. 1993. Le facteur peul et les relations interethniques dans l'Adamaoua au XIXe siècle. In: Boutrais, J. (ed.), *Peuples et cultures de l'Adamaoua (Cameroun)*. Editions de l'ORSTOM, Paris, pp. 61–86.

Munson, P.J. 1968. Recent archaeological research in the Dhar Tichitt region of south-central Mauritania. *West African Archaeological Newsletter* 10, 6.

Muzzolini, A. 1993. Emergence of a food-producing economy in the Sahara. In: Shaw, T., Sinclair, P.J.J., Andah, B. & Okpoko, A.I. (eds.), *The Archaeology of Africa: Food, Metals and Towns*. Routledge, New York, pp. 227–239.

Mveng, E. 1971. Archéologie Camerounaise: Mvolyé. *Revue Camerounaise d'Histoire* 1, 123–127.

Ngima Mawoung, G. 2001. The relationship between the Bakola and the Bantu peoples of the coastal regions of Cameroon and their perception of commercial forest exploitation. *African Study Monographs* (suppl.) 26, 209–235.

Okafor, E.E. 1993. New evidence on early iron-smelting from southeastern Nigeria. In: Shaw, T., Sinclair, P.J.J., Andah, B. and Okpoko, A.I. (eds.), *The Archaeology of Africa: Food, Metals and Towns*. Routledge, New York, pp. 432–448.

Omi, G. 1977. *Prehistoric Sites and Implements in Cameroon: An Annex to the Interim Report of the Tropical African Geomorphology Research Project*. Nagoya University, Nagoya.

ORSTOM/IRCAM 1966. *Dictionnaire des villages de Kribi*. ORSTOM, Yaoundé.

Oslisly, R. 1993. *Préhistoire de la moyenne vallée de l'Ogoué (Gabon)*. Editions de l'ORSTOM, Paris.

Oslisly, R. & Assoko Ndong, A. 2006. *Archéologie de sauvetage sur la route Médoumane – Lalara. Vallée de l'Okano, Gabon*. Wildlife Conservation Society, New York.

Oslisly, R., Ateba, L., Betougeda, R., Kinyock, P., Mbida, C., Nlend, P. & Vincens, A. 2006. Premiers résultats de la recherche archéologique sur le littoral du Caméroun entre Kribi et Campo. In: Le Secrétariat du Congrès (ed.), *Préhistoire en Afrique / African Prehistory Acts of the XIVth UISPP Congress, University of Liège, Belgium, 2–8 September 2001*. British Archaeological Reports 1522. Archaeopress, Oxford.

Oslisly, R., Mbida, C. & White, L. 2000. Les premiers résultats de la recherche archéologique dans le sanctuaire de Banyang Mbo (Sud-Ouest du Cameroun). *L'Anthropologie* 104 (2), 341–354.

Oslisly, R. & Peyrot, B. 1992. L'arrivée des premiers métallurgistes sur l'Ogooué (Gabon). *African Archaeological Review* 10, 129–138.

Oslisly, R., Tueche, R., Kinyock, P. & Nkokonda, O. 2000. *Archaeological Reconnaissance Studies, Tchad Export Project: Kribi, Bipindi/Ndtoua, Lolodorf, Ngaoundal, Boforo and Ngan-Hi*. COTCO, Yaoundé.

Pias, J. 1970a. *La végétation du Tchad*. ORSTOM, Paris.

Pias, J. 1970b. *Les formations sédimentaires tertiaires et quaternaires de la cuvette tchadienne et les sols qui en dérivent*. ORSTOM, Paris.

Rapp, J. 1980. Fouilles 1980 dans le site Sao de Sou Blamé Radjil (Nord-Cameroun). *Bulletin de la Société d'Anthropologie du Sud-Ouest* 15, 219–228.

Rice, P. 1987. *Pottery Analysis: A Sourcebook*. University of Chicago Press, Chicago.

Rivallain, J. 1988a. Fer et forgerons dans le sud du lac Tchad à travers les écrits des premiers colonisateurs. In: Monino, Y. (ed.), *Forges et forgerons*. ORSTOM, Paris, pp. 227–240.

Rivallain, J. 1988b. Sara: échanges et instruments monétaires. In: Barreteau, D. & Tourneux, H. (eds.), *Le milieu et les hommes: recherches comparatives et historiques dans le bassin du lac Tchad*. ORSTOM, Paris, pp. 195–213.

Roset, J.-P. 1987. Paleoclimatic and cultural conditions of neolithic development in the Early Holocene of northern Niger (Aïr and Ténéré). In: Close, A.E. (ed.), *Prehistory of Arid North Africa. Essays in Honor of Fred Wendorf*. Southern Methodist University Press, Dallas, pp. 211–234.

Rowlands, M. and Warnier, J.-P. 1993. The magical production of iron in the Cameroon Grassfields. In: Shaw, T., Sinclair, P.J.J., Andah, B. & Okpoko, A.I. (eds.), *The Archaeology of Africa: Food, Metals and Towns*. Routledge, New York, pp. 512–549.

Saxon, D.E. 1982. Linguistic evidence for the eastward spread of Ubangian peoples. In: Ehret, C. & Posnansky, M. (ed.), *The Archaeological and Linguistic Reconstruction of African History*. University of California Press, Berkeley, pp. 66–77.

Ségalen, P. 1967. Les sols et la géomorphologie du Cameroun. *Cahiers ORSTOM, série pédologie* 5 (2), 137–187.

Shaw, T. 1970. *Igbo-Ukwu: An Account of Archaeological Discoveries in Eastern Nigeria*. Northwestern University Press, Evanston, IL.

Shaw, T. 1978. *Nigeria: Its Archaeology and Early History*. Thames and Hudson, London.

Shaw, T. 1993. Further light on Igbo-Ukwu, including new radiocarbon dates. In: Andah, B., de Maret, P. & Soper, R. (eds.), *Proceedings of the 9th Congress of the Pan-African Association of Prehistory and Related Studies: Jos, 1983*. Rex Charles Publications, Ibadan, pp. 79–83.

Shaw, T., Sinclair, P., Andah, B.W. & Okpoko, A.I. (eds.) 1993. *The Archaeology of Africa: Foods, Metals and Towns*. Routledge, New York.

Sinclair, P.J.J., Shaw, T. & Andah, B. 1993. Introduction. In: Shaw, T., Sinclair, P.J.J., Andah, B. & Okpoko, A.I. (eds.), *The Archaeology of Africa: Food, Metals and Towns*. Routledge, New York, pp. 1–31.

Siran, J.-L. 1980. Emergence et dissolution des principautés guerrières vouté. *Journal des Africanistes* 50 (1), 25–58.

Siran, J.-L. 1981. Elément d'ethnographie vouté pour servir à l'histoire du Cameroun central. In: Tardits, C. (ed.), *Contribution de la recherche ethnologique à l'histoire des civilisations du Cameroun*. Editions du CNRS, Paris, pp. 265–272.

Smith, A.B. 1974. Preliminary report of excavations at Karkarichinkat, Mali, 1972. *West African Journal of Archaeology* 4, 33.

Soper, R. 1985. Roulette decoration on African pottery: technical considerations, dating and distributions. *African Archaeological Review* 3, 29–52.

Stahl, A. 1991. Ethnic style and ethnic boundaries: a diachronic case study from west-central Ghana. *Ethnohistory* 38 (3), 250–275.

Stahl, A. 1993. Concepts of time and approaches to analogical reasoning in historical perspective. *American Antiquity* 58 (2), 235–260.

Stahl, A. 1994. Innovation, diffusion, and culture contact: the Holocene archaeology of Ghana. *Journal of World Prehistory* 8 (1), 51–112.

Stahl, A. 1999. Perceiving variability in time and space: the evolutionary mapping of African societies. In: McIntosh, S.K. (ed.), *Beyond Chiefdoms: Pathways to Complexity in Africa*. Cambridge University Press, Cambridge, pp. 39–55.

Stahl, A. 2005. Introduction: Changing perspectives on Africa's pasts. In: Stahl, A. (ed.), *African Archaeology: A Critical Introduction*. Blackwell Publishing, London, pp. 1–23.

Summer Institute of Linguistics 2006. *Ethnologue*. Summer Institute of Linguistics. http://www.ethnologue.com. Accessed 23 September, 2007.

Tchago, B. 1994. La métallurgie ancienne du fer dans le sud du Tchad: prospections archéologiques, sondages et directions de récherches. Unpublished Ph.D. Thesis, Département d'Histoire, Université Nationale de Cote d'Ivoire, Abidjan.

Tchago, B. 2000. *Les sites archéologiques de Oulibangala, Mban et Kollé: sondages et étude du matériel (Logine Oriental)*. COTCO, N'Djamena.

Tessmann, G. 1923. *Die Bubi auf Fernando Poo. Völkerkundliche Einzelbeschreibung eines westafrikanischen Negerstammes*. Folkwang-Verlag, Darmstadt.

Tillet, T. 1978. Recherches préhistoriques dans le sud-ouest tchadien. *Bulletin de l'IFAN* 39 (série B), 447–457.

Tillet, Th. 1983. *La paléolithique du bassin tchadien (Niger-Tchad)*. CNRS, Paris.

Treinen-Claustre, F. 1982. *Sahara et Sahel à l'Age du Fer: Borkou, Tchad*. Société des Africanistes, Paris.

UNESCO 2002. *UNESCO Cultural Heritage Laws Database*. United Nations Educational, Scientific and Cultural Organization. http://www.unesco.org/culture/natlaws/ Accessed 12 May, 2008.

van Noten, F. 1977. Excavations at Matupi cave. *Antiquity* 51 (201), 35.

van Noten, F. 1982. The Stone Age in the north and east. In: van Noten, F. & Cahen, D. (eds.), *The Archaeology of Central Africa*. Akademische Druck- u. Verlagsanstalt, Graz, pp. 27–40.

Vansina, J. 1985. Equisse historique de l'agriculture en milieu forestier (Afrique Centrale). *Muntu* 2, 5–34.

Vansina, J. 1986. Do Pygmies have a history? *SUGIA: Sprache und Geschichte in Afrika* 7 (1), 431–445.

Vansina, J. 1990. *Paths in the Rainforests: Toward a History of Political Tradition in Equatorial Africa*. University of Wisconsin Press, Madison, Wisconsin.

Vansina, J. 1995. New linguistic evidence and 'the Bantu expansion'. *Journal of African History* 36, 173–195.

Vidal, P. 1987. Activités archéologiques en Centrafrique 1986–1987. *Nsi* 2, 20–23.

Vidal, P. 1992. Au delá des mégalithes: archéologie centrafricaine et histoire de l'Afrique centrale. In: Essomba, J.-M. (ed.), *L'archéologie au Cameroun*. Karthala, Paris, pp. 133–178.

Vidal, P., de Bayle des Hermens, R. & Menard, J. 1983. Le site archéologique de l'île de Toala sur la Haute Ouham (République Centre Africaine): Néolithique et Age du Fer. *L'Anthropologie* 87 (1), 113–133.

Warnier, J.-P. 1984. Histoire du peuplement et genèse des paysages dans l'ouest Camerounais. *Journal of African History* 25 (4), 395–410.

Warnier, J.-P. 1992. Rapport préliminaire sur la métallurgie du groupe Chap. In: Essomba, J.-M. (ed.), *L'archéologie du Cameroun*. Karthala, Paris, pp. 197–210.

Williamson, K. 1993. Linguistic evidence for the use of some tree and tuber food plants in southern Nigeria. In: Shaw, T., Sinclair, P.J.J., Andah, B.W. & Okpoko, A.I. (eds.), *The Archaeology of Africa: Food, Metal and Towns*. Routledge, New York, pp. 139–143.

Williamson, K. & Blench, R. 2000. Niger-Congo. In: Heine, B. & Nurse, D. (eds.), *African Languages: An Introduction*. Cambridge University Press, Cambridge, pp. 11–42.

World Bank 1986. *Management of Cultural Property in Bank-Financed Projects*. http://wbln0018.worldbank.org/institutional/manuals/opmanual.nsf/whatnewvirt/55FA484A98BC2E68852567CC005BCBDB?OpenDocument. Accessed 4 January, 2004.

York, R.N. 1978. Excavations at Dutsen Kongba, Plateau State, Nigeria. *West African Journal of Archaeology* 8, 139–163.

Zangato, E. 1996. Étude du mégalithisme en République centrafricaine. Nouvelles découvertes de monuments à chambre dans le secteur de Ndio. *Cahiers O.R.S.T.O.M., série Sciences Humaines* 32 (3), 361–377.

Zangato, E. 1999. *Sociétés préhistoriques et mégalithes dans le nord-ouest de la République Centrafricaine*. British Archaeological Reports 768, Cambridge Monographs in African Archaeology 46. Archaeopress, Oxford.

Zangato, E. 2000. *Les occupations néolithiques dans le Nord-Ouest de la République centrafricaine*. Editions Monique Mergoil, Montagnac.

Appendix

ETA N°	Site name	UTM	Easting	Northing	Size	Artifacts observed	Approximate age	Priority for further treatment	Cultural signifi-cance
1		33 P	566549	838361	10 m²	Rouletted pottery, sandal	Recent	•	No
2		33 P	569490	840850	10 m²	Rouletted pottery	Iron Age/Recent	•	No
3		33 P	573820	845092	50x50 m	Rouletted pottery	Iron Age/Recent	•	No
4, 136	Diba I	33 P	587683	856086	5x3 m	Rouletted pottery, slag	Iron Age/Recent	••	**Yes**
5		33 P	588290	856489	8x8 m	Rouletted pottery, bottle glass, grindstone	Recent	••	No
6, 135	Diba I	33 P	589706	857121	50x50 m	Rouletted pottery, tin-ware, grindstone	Recent	••	**Yes**
7		33 P	591105	857790	125 m²	Rouletted pottery	Iron Age/Recent	•	No
8		33 P	594036	859672	8x8 m	Rouletted/map-impressed pottery	Iron Age/Recent	•	No
9		33 P	594223	859865	15x15 m	Rouletted pottery, slag	Iron Age/Recent	•	No
10		33 P	602043	865622	5x5 m	Pottery	Iron Age/Recent	•	No
11		33 P	602585	866002	15x15 m	Rouletted pottery, tin-ware, grindstone	Recent	•	No
12		33 P	603042	866328	10 m²	Rouletted/incised pottery, tin-ware	Recent	•	No
13		33 P	607115	868777	30 m²	Rouletted/mat-impressed pottery	Iron Age/Recent	••	No
14		33 P	608846	869782	10x5 m	Rouletted pottery	Iron Age/Recent	•	No
15		33 P	612616	871946	5 m²	Incised/cross-hatched pottery, slag	Iron Age/Recent	•	No
16		33 P	613826	872671	3x3 m	Rouletted/incised pottery	Iron Age/Recent	•	No
17		33 P	619961	878200	10x10 m	Mat-impressed pottery, tin-ware, laterite manuport	Recent	••	No
18		33 P	621975	879903	50x20 m	Rouletted pottery, tin-ware	Recent	••	No
19		33 P	625116	882001	5x5 m	CWR pottery, bottle glass	Recent	•	No
20		33 P	628147	884660	8 m²	Rouletted pottery	Iron Age/Recent	•	No
21		33 P	630892	887090	10x10 m	Iron slag	Iron Age/Recent	••	No
22		33 P	631205	887378	70x20 m	Rouletted/mat-impressed pottery	Iron Age/Recent	•	No
23		33 P	631412	887573	3 m²	Rouletted pottery	Iron Age/Recent	•	No
24		33 P	637670	890872	20 m²	Furnace remains, slag	Iron Age	•••	No
25, 128	Begon II	33 P	638041	894315	750 m long	Rouletted pottery, furnace remains, slag	Iron Age	•••	**Yes**
26		33 P	628221	889801	2 m²	Rouletted pottery		•	No
27		33 P	643606	899683	20 m²	Rouletted pottery		•	No
28		33 P	644183	900432	20x20 m	Rouletted pottery		•	No
29		33 P	645408	901298	200x30 m	Rouletted pottery, slag	Iron Age/Recent	••	No
30		33 P	645726	901574	5x2 m	Slag, potsherd	Iron Age/Recent	•	No
31		33 P	645933	901785	20x20 m	Slag	Iron Age/Recent	••	No
32, 108		33 P	646401	902224	5x5 m	Furnace remains, slag	Iron Age	••	No
33, 34		33 P	647115	902810	30x30 m	Slag	Iron Age/Recent	••	No
35	Bedia	33 P	649782	905245	80x100 m	Furnace remains, slag	Iron Age	•••	**Yes**
36		33 P	650072	905466	4 m²	Slag, pottery, possible furnace remains	Iron Age/Recent	•	No
37		33 P	654857	909620	10 m²	Slag	Iron Age/Recent	••	No
38		33 P	655206	909944	60 m²	Furnace remains, slag	Iron Age	•••	No
39	Kolle	33 P	655827	910597	80x30 m	Furnace remains, slag, rouletted pottery	Iron Age	•••	**Yes**
40	Kolle	33 P	656004	910720	30x30 m	Furnace remains, slag	Iron Age	•••	**Yes**
41		33 P	668320	921001	30 m²	CWR pottery		•	No
42		33 P	678733	932167	10x10 m	Incised pottery		•	No
43		33 P	679956	933417	200 m linear	Rouletted pottery	Iron Age/Recent	••	No
44		33 P	680950	934494	200 m linear	Rouletted pottery		•	No
45		33 P	690342	942538	75x50 m	Furnace remains, slag	Iron Age	••	No
46	Beboura	33 P	691179	942800	1500 m linear	Rouletted pottery, slag	Recent	•••	**Yes**
47		33 P	696571	943044	10 m²	Furnace remains, slag	Iron Age/Recent	•	No
48		33 P	697964	943865	4 m²	Rouletted pottery		•	No
49		33 P	697811	943549	5 m²	Rouletted pottery, bottle glass	Recent	•	No
50		33 P	701401	944992	80 m²	Rouletted pottery, slag	Iron Age/Recent	••	No
51		33 P	571754	844244	20 m²	Rouletted pottery	Iron Age/Recent	•	No
52		33 P	574671	852160	20 m²	Rouletted pottery, bottle glass	Recent	•	No
53		33 P	593002	865941	10 m²	Possible biface		•	No
54		33 P	592680	865847	10x10 m	Rouletted pottery, slag	Iron Age/Recent	•	No
55		33 P	592106	865701	20x20 m	Rouletted/incised pottery	Iron Age/Recent	•	No
56	Ouliban-gala	33 P	591114	865423	50 m²	Lithics, rouletted pottery, slag, grindstone fragment, bottle glass	Stone Age/Iron Age/recent	••	**Yes**
57		33 P	590466	865256	10 m²	Rouletted pottery, slag	Iron Age/Recent	•	No
58		33 P	590014	864897	200x50 m	Rouletted pottery, tin-ware	Recent	•	No

Appendix A *(continued)*. Sites in Chad. (Priority for further treatment, •: low; ••: medium; •••: high).

ETA N°	Site name	UTM	Easting	Northing	Size	Artifacts observed	Approximate age	Priority for further treatment	Cultural significance
59		33 P	608471	873069	5x5 m	Slag		●	No
60		33 P	608918	873835	20x10 m	Slag, rouletted pottery	Iron Age/Recent	●	No
61		33 P	610083	874864	50x20 m	Rouletted pottery, tin-ware, bottle glass	Recent	●	No
62		33 P	611243	877853	20 m^2	Rouletted/incised pottery	Iron Age/Recent	●	No
63		33 P	611243	877853	800x100 m	Mat-impressed/rouletted pottery	Iron Age/Recent	●	No
64		33 P	617511	888091	10x10 m	Rouletted pottery, slag	Iron Age/Recent	●	No
65		33 P	619252	888332	10 m^2	Incised pottery, slag	Iron Age/Recent	●	No
66		33 P	622230	889238	300x50 m	Mat-impressed pottery, slag	Iron Age/Recent	●●	No
67		33 P	624882	889629	10x10 m	Slag, plain pottery	Iron Age/Recent	●	No
68		33 P	629354	890978	20 m^2	Furnace remains, slag	Iron Age	●●	No
69	**Mban I**	33 P	630432	891808	100 m^2	Furnace remains, slag	Iron Age	●●	**Yes**
70		33 P	630749	891994	6 m^2	Slag	Iron Age/Recent	●●	No
71-72		33 P	632946	893673	100 m^2	Furnace remains, slag	Iron Age	●●●	No
73		33 P	634175	893905	5 m^2	Slag		●	No
74		33 P	652515	909746	50 m^2	Tombs	Recent	●●●	**Yes**
75	**Kolle-Kagopal**	33 P	655992	913131	150 m^2	Furnace remains, slag	Iron Age	●●●	**Yes**
76		33 P	656535	913767	8 m^2	Slag	Iron Age/Recent	●●	No
77		33 P	658136	915305	200x100 m	Mat-impressed and incised pottery	Iron Age/Recent	●	No
78		33 P	672291	940760	30 m^2	Pottery, slag	Iron Age/Recent	●●	No
79		33 P	673099	941895	20 m^2	Rouletted pottery		●	No
80		33 P	684141	939785	40 m^2	Rouletted pottery	Iron Age/Recent	●●	No
81	**Kome Aeroport**	33 P	693578	943010	13x9 m	Pottery, charcoal	Iron Age/Recent	●●	**Yes**
82	**Kome Aeroport**	33 P	692797	944303	11x8 m	Pottery, charcoal	Iron Age/Recent	●●	**Yes**
83	**Begada**	33 P	696240	943060	8x6 m	Pottery, other debris, charcoal	Iron Age/Recent	●●	**Yes**
84	Begada	33 P	691735	949911	6x4 m	Pottery, lithics, charcoal	Iron Age/Recent	●	No
85	**Begada**	33 P	692401	943060	17x5 m	Pottery, slag, iron, shell, bone	Iron Age/Recent	●●●	**Yes**
86	**Kome Base**	33 P	691587	942934	35x28 m	Pottery, lithics, charcoal	Iron Age/Recent	●●●	**Yes**
87	**Kome Base**	33 P	692436	943003	6x3.5 m	Pottery	Iron Age/Recent	●●	**Yes**
88	**Kome Base**	33 P	692163	942999	5x3 m	Charcoal, stone fragment	Iron Age/Recent	●●●	**Yes**
89	Kome Base	33 P	690783	942679	7x4 m	Charcoal, stone fragment		●	No
90	Kome Base	33 P	687686	941508	8x3 m	Charcoal, stone fragment		●	No
91	Kome Base	33 P	687005	940891	6x4 m	Pottery, lithics, charcoal	Iron Age/Recent	●	No
92	KomeBase	33 P	686232	939996	9x4 m	Pottery, charcoal	Iron Age/Recent	●	No
93	**Begada**	33 P	691269	942828	9x6 m	Pottery, charcoal	Iron Age/Recent	●●	**Yes**
94	**Kome Base**	33 P	692209	943000	11x6 m	Pottery, charcoal	Iron Age	●●●	**Yes**
95	**Bolobo**	33 P	680730	934254	42x35 m	Pottery, lithics, charcoal	Iron Age/Recent	●●	**Yes**
96	**Bolobo**	33 P	680312	933828	37x24 m	Pottery, lithics, charcoal	Iron Age/Recent	●●	**Yes**
97	**Mayongo**	33 P	679441	932908	450x305 m	Pottery, lithics, charcoal	Iron Age	●●●	**Yes**
99	Kaba	33 P	663244	916883	17x8 m	Pottery, possible furnace fragment	Iron Age/Recent	●	No
100	Kaba	33 P	663053	916727	14x6 m	Pottery	Iron Age/Recent	●	No
101	Kaba	33 P	662945	916639	9x5 m	Pottery	Iron Age/Recent	●	No
102	**Beto**	33 P	671446	923572	25x12 m	Pottery	Iron Age	●●●	**Yes**
103	Kaba	33 P	661219	915232	5x3 m	Lithics		●	No
104	Kolle	33 P	657155	911709	18x7 m	Pottery	Iron Age/Recent	●	No
105	Kolle	33 P	656166	910843	6x4 m	Lithics		●	No
106	Ouao	33 P	653968	908902	12x8 m	Pottery	Iron Age/Recent	●	No
107	**Kaba**	33 P	662356	916157	35x7 m	Pottery, charcoal	Iron Age	●●●	**Yes**
109	**Kouloulou**	33 P	643115	899306	24x12 m	Pottery	Iron Age/Recent	●●	**Yes**
110	**Ouao**	33 P	655174	909968	5x4 m	Pottery, charcoal	Iron Age/Recent	●●	**Yes**
111-118	**Ouao**	33 P	654812	909651	3x3 m	Pottery, charcoal	Iron Age/Recent	●●●	**Yes**
119-120	**Bedia**	33 P	650614	905937	29x27 m	Pottery, lithics, charcoal, slag	Iron Age/Recent	●●●	**Yes**
121	**Bedia**	33 P	650194	905566	10x7 m	Pottery, lithics, charcoal	Iron Age/Recent	●●	**Yes**
122	**Koundja I**	33 P	640689	902664	18x16 m	Pottery, charcoal	Iron Age/Recent	●●	**Yes**
123	Koundja I	33 P	646176	902003	4x3 m	Pottery, charcoal	Iron Age/Recent	●	No
124	**Begon II**	33 P	639011	892563	28x17 m	Pottery	Iron Age/Recent	●●●	**Yes**

Appendix A *(continued)*. Sites in Chad. (Priority for further treatment, ●: low; ●●: medium; ●●●: high).

ETA N°	Site name	UTM	Easting	Northing	Size	Artifacts observed	Approximate age	Priority for further treatment	Cultural significance
125	Begon II	33 P	638485	894716	12x9 m	Pottery, lithics, slag	Iron Age/Recent	●	No
126	**Begon II**	33 P	638380	894535	11x8.5 m	Pottery, lithics, slag, bone, charcoal	Iron Age/Recent	●●	**Yes**
127	**Begon II**	33 P	638116	894366	29x17 m	Pottery, charcoal, slag, shell	Iron Age/Recent	●●●	**Yes**
129	Beguelka	33 P	633464	889683	13x8 m	Pottery	Iron Age/Recent	●	No
130	**Beguelka**	33 P	632443	888642	12x8 m	Pottery, charcoal	Iron Age/Recent	●●	**Yes**
131	**Bendjabo**	33 P	625077	881958	11x7 m	Pottery	Iron Age/Recent	●●	**Yes**
132	Bekao I	33 P	614330	873027	8x6 m	Pottery	Iron Age/Recent	●	No
133	Bembar	33 P	599884	864077	7x5 m	Pottery	Iron Age/Recent	●	No
134	**Ma-Bin**	33 P	594907	860418	11x9 m	Pottery, lithics	Iron Age/Recent	●●	**Yes**
137	**Diba I**	33 P	587412	855907	18x13 m	Pottery, lithics	Iron Age/Recent	●●	**Yes**
138	**Diba I**	33 P	585877	854894	27x14 m	Pottery, lithics	Iron Age/Recent	●●	**Yes**
139	**Diba I**	33 P	585811	854859	25x12 m	Pottery, lithics	Iron Age/Recent	●●	**Yes**
140-141	Diba I	33 P	585700	854822	20x18 m	Pottery, lithics	Iron Age/Recent	●●	No
142	**Woum**	33 P	585117	854413	26x17 m	Pottery, lithics	Iron Age/Recent	●●	**Yes**
143	**Baibakoum**	33 P	582215	851670	31x13 m	Pottery, lithics	Iron Age/Recent	●●	**Yes**
144, 151	Baibakoum	33 P	580710	850422	19x6 m	Pottery, lithics	Iron Age/Recent	●●	No
145	Mbaissaye	33 P	576529	847252	8x5 m	Pottery, lithics	Iron Age/Recent	●	No
146	Koumao	33 P	569727	841097	12x6 m	Pottery	Iron Age/Recent	●	No
147	Mbikouni	33 P	568550	839819	45x20 m	Pottery, lithics, hoe	Iron Age/Recent	●	No
148	Bitoye II	33 P	567348	838834	29x12 m	Pottery	Iron Age/Recent	●	No
149	Camp de Mbere	33 P	559462	836210	21x15 m	Pottery, lithics	Iron Age/Recent	●	No
150	**Diba II**	33 P	587087	855080	12x7 m	Lithics (quartz)	Late Stone Age	●●	**Yes**
152	Mbaissain	33 P	574322	845570	8x5 m	Pottery, rock	Iron Age/Recent	●	No
153	Bingo	33 P	566946	838556	5x3 m	Pottery	Iron Age/Recent	●	No
154	Mbikom	33 P	566823	838472	4.5x3 m	Pottery, lithics	Iron Age/Recent	●	No
155	Gaitao	33 P	564435	837140	4x2 m	Pottery	Iron Age/Recent	●	No
156	Mboura	33 P	564166	837061	4x 2.5 m	Pottery	Iron Age/Recent	●	No
157	Bitoye II	33 P	564115	837045	3x2 m	Pottery, grindstone	Iron Age/Recent	●	No
158	Sakara	33 P	563674	836914	4x2.5 m	Pottery, pot handle	Iron Age/Recent	●	No
159	Sakara	33 P	561931	836603	4.5x3 m	Pottery	Iron Age/Recent	●	No
160	Bitoy I	33 P	560805	836423	3x2 m	Pottery, lithics	Iron Age/Recent	●	No
161	Mbere	33 P	560582	836384	4x3 m	Pottery, grindstone	Iron Age/Recent	●	No
162	Mbere	33 P	559044	836238	4x2 m	Lithics		●	No
163	**Mbere**	33 P	569446	840791	12x9 m	Pottery, lithics, charcoal	Iron Age/Recent	●●●	**Yes**
164	**Missi Madji**	33 P	695763	944029	40x35 m	Slag, tuyère and furnace fragments	Iron Age	●●●	**Yes**
165	**Ngon Mbang**	33 P	361793	942886	1000x700 m	Pottery, slag, furnace fragments	Iron Age/Recent	●●●	**Yes**
166	**Begon II Chef du Village**	33 P	639406	893154	155x75 m	Slag, tuyère and furnace fragments	Iron Age	●●●	**Yes**
167	**Karmankass**	33 P	658304	960707	400x200 m	Pottery, flakes	Iron Age	●●●	**Yes**
168	Doba	33 P	702801	948131	400x200 m	Pottery	Iron Age/Recent	●	No
169	Madjo	33 P	703066	948813	700x62 m	Pottery	Iron Age/Recent	●	No
170	**Maikery**	33 P	670458	941040	25x15 m	Furnace fragments	Iron Age/Recent	●●	**Yes**
171	Bebedjia	33 P	666943	965762	200x20 m	Pottery	Iron Age/Recent	●	No
172	Bengoro	33 P	671476	932355	275x200 m	Pottery	Iron Age/Recent	●	No
173	**Badila**	33 P	318814	924863	20x10 m	Furnace fragments	Iron Age	●●●	**Yes**
174	Moundouli 2	33 P	640140	951663	300x10 m	Pottery	Iron Age/Recent	●	No
175	**Bekia**	USR	337901	940953	300x150 m	Furnace fragments and pottery	Iron Age	●●●	**Yes**
176	Begada	USR	364651	940572	200x150 m	Pottery	Iron Age/Recent	●	No
177	Miadoum	USR	340805	942206	500x200 m	Pottery	Iron Age/Recent	●	No
178	**Miadoum**	USR	341528	941119	500x250 m	Furnace fragments and pottery	Iron Age	●●●	**Yes**
179	Begada	USR	364835	942167	500x250 m	Pottery	Iron Age/Recent	●	No
180	Mbaga-Kome	USR	365450	942666	100x100 m	Pottery	Iron Age/Recent	●	No
181	Begada	USR	363631	939656	200x200 m	Pottery	Iron Age/Recent	●	No
183	Mbanga	USR	364561	941966	300x100 m	Pottery	Iron Age/Recent	●	No
185	**Begada**	USR	363779	940812	300x200 m	Pottery	Iron Age/Recent	●●●	**Yes**
186	Ndaba	USR	366617	941105	300x200 m	Pottery	Iron Age/Recent	●	No
187	Begada	USR	364586	939699	180x120 m	Pottery	Iron Age/Recent	●	No
188	**Dodang**	USR	366872	944773	500x300 m	Pottery	Iron Age	●●●	**Yes**

Appendix A *(end).* Sites in Chad (Priority for further treatment, ●: low; ●●: medium; ●●●: high).

ETA N°	Site name	Discovery	Geo. System UTM	Easting	Northing	Zone	Conservation	Site type	Priority*	Artifacts observed	Post discovery treatment/ monitoring
2/163	Mbere	PC survey	33 P	569490	840850	Pipeline	Buried site	DAH(s)	●●●	Rouletted pottery, lithics	Data recovery (excavations): 4 m² excavated (1 pit feature)
4/136	Diba I	PC survey	33 P	587683	856086	Pipeline	Surface site	DAS	●●	Rouletted pottery, slag	Data recovery (excavations): 29 m² excavated (living floor) and 4 m² (pit feature)
6/135	Diba I	PC survey	33 P	589706	857121	Pipeline	Surface site	DAS	●●	Rouletted pottery, tin-ware, grindstone	Data recovery (excavations): 25 m² excavated (living floor)
25/128 + 127	Begon II	PC survey	33 P	638041	894315	Pipeline	Buried site	DAH(s)	●●●	Rouletted pottery, furnace remains, slag, shell	Data recovery (excavations): 20 m² excavated (1 living floor and 2 pit features)
35	Bedia	PC survey	33 P	649782	905245	Pipeline	Buried site	IWH(s)	●●●	Furnace remains, slag	Data recovery (excavations): 12 m² excavated (4 furnaces and 1 slag heap)
36/121	Bedia	PC survey	33 P	650072	905466	Pipeline	Buried site	DAS(s)	●●	Slag, pottery, possible furnace remains	Data recovery (excavations): 4 m² excavated (1 pit feature)
37/111-118	Ouao	PC survey	33 P	654857	909620	Pipeline	Buried site	DAH(s)	●●	Pottery, slag	Data recovery (excavations): 29 m² excavated (7 pit features)
38/110	Ouao	PC survey	33 P	655206	909944	Pipeline	Buried site	DAH(s)	●●●	Furnace remains, slag, pottery	Data recovery (excavations): 4 m² excavated (1 pit feature)
39	Kolle	PC survey	33 P	655827	910597	Pipeline	Buried site	IWH(s)	●●●	Furnace remains, slag, rouletted pottery	Data recovery (excavations): 24 m² (pottery horizon and 2 furnaces)
40	Kolle	PC survey	33 P	656004	910720	Pipeline	Buried site	IWH(s)	●●●	Furnace remains, slag	Data recovery (excavations): 24 m² (6 furnaces)
46	Beboura	PC survey	33 P	691179	942800	Pipeline	Surface site	DAS	●●●	Rouletted pottery, slag	Data recovery (excavations): 68 m² (living floor, 5 blacksmithfurnaces)
56	Ouliban-gala	PC survey	33 P	591114	865423	Road	Buried site	DAH(s)	●●	Lithics, rouletted pottery, slag, grindstone fragment, bottle glass	Data recovery (excavations): 450 m² excavated (living floor)
69	Mban I	PC survey	33 P	630432	891808	Road	Buried site	IWH(s)	●●	Furnace remains, slag	Data recovery (excavations): 20 m² excavated (5 furnaces)
74		PC survey	33 P	652515	909746	Road	Surface site	Modern tombs	●●●	Tombs	Avoidance
75	Kolle-Kagopal	PC survey	33 P	655992	913131	Road	Buried site	IWH(s)	●●●	Furnace remains, slag	Data recovery (excavations): 16 m² excavated (4 furnaces)
81	Kome Aeroport	Monitoring of clearing activities	33 P	693578	943010	Pipeline	Buried site	CH(s)	●●	Pottery, charcoal	Data recovery (excavations): 4 m² excavated (living floor)
82	Kome Aeroport	Monitoring of clearing activities	33 P	692797	944303	OFDA	Buried site	CH(s)	●●	Pottery, charcoal	Data recovery (excavations): 4 m² excavated (living floor)
83	Begada	Monitoring of grading activities	33 P	696240	943060	Pipeline	Buried site	CH(s)	●●	Pottery, other debris, charcoal	Data recovery (excavations): 6 m² excavated (living floor)
85/87	Begada	Monitoring of trenching activities	33 P	692401	943060	Pipeline	Buried site	DAH(s)	●●●	Pottery, slag, iron, shell, bone	Data recovery (excavations): 4 m² excavated (living floor)
86	Kome Base	Monitoring of grading activities	33 P	691587	942934	Pipeline	Buried site	DAH(s)	●●●	Pottery, architectural features	Data recovery (excavations): 2 m² (living floor)
88/94	Kome Base	Monitoring of trenching activities	33 P	692163	942999	Pipeline	Buried site	DAH(s)	●●●	Pottery, stone fragments	Data recovery (excavations): 4 m² excavated (1 pit feature)
93	Begada	Monitoring of trenching activities	33 P	691269	942828	Pipeline	Buried site	CH(s)	●●	Pottery, charcoal	Data recovery (excavations): 4 m² excavated (1 pit feature)
95	Bolobo	Monitoring of trenching activities	33 P	680730	934254	Pipeline	Buried site	DAH(s)	●●	Pottery, lithics, charcoal	Data recovery (excavations): 6 m² excavated (living floor)
96	Bolobo	Monitoring of trenching activities	33 P	680312	933828	Pipeline	Buried site	DAH(s)	●●	Pottery, lithics, charcoal	Data recovery (excavations): 2 m² (1 pit feature)
97	Mayongo	Monitoring of trenching activities	33 P	679441	932908	Pipeline	Buried site	DAH(s)	●●●	Pottery, slag, lithics, charcoal	Data recovery (excavations): 4 m² excavated (living floor)

Appendix B *(continued).* Site treatments in Chad (CH: Ceramic horizon; CS: Ceramic scatter; DAH(s): Diverse artefact horizon(s); DAS: Diverse artefact scatter; IWH(s): Iron working horizon(s); Priority*: Priority for further treatment, ●: low; ●●: medium; ●●●: high).

ETA N°	Site name	Discovery	Geo. System UTM	Easting	Northing	Zone	Conser- vation	Site type	Priority*	Artifacts observed	Post discovery treatment/ monitoring
102	Beto	Monitoring of trenching activities	33 P	671446	923572	Pipeline	Buried site	CH(s)	●●●	Pottery	Data recovery (excavations): 6 m² excavated (1 pit feature)
107	Kaba	Monitoring of trenching activities	33 P	662356	916157	Pipeline	Buried site	CH(s)	●●●	Pottery, charcoal	Data recovery (excavations): 4 m² (1 pit feature)
109	Kouloulou	Monitoring of grading activities	33 P	643115	899306	Pipeline	Buried site	CH(s)	●●	Pottery	Intentional backfill of the trench
119-120	Bedia	Monitoring of trenching activities	33 P	650614	905937	Pipeline	Buried site	DAH(s)	●●●	Pottery, lithics, charcoal, slag	Data recovery (excavations): 8 m² excavated (2 pits)
122	Koundja I	Monitoring of trenching activities	33 P	640689	902664	Pipeline	Buried site	CH(s)	●●	Pottery, charcoal	Data recovery (excavations): 4 m² excavated (1 pit feature)
124	Begon II	Monitoring of grading activities	33 P	639011	892563	Pipeline	Buried site	CH(s)	●●●	Pottery	Intentional backfill of the trench
126	Begon II	Monitoring of trenching activities	33 P	638380	894535	Pipeline	Buried site	DAH(s)	●●	Pottery, lithics, slag, bone, charcoal	Data recovery (excavations): 4 m² excavated (1 pit feature)
130	Beguelka	Monitoring of trenching activities	33 P	632443	888642	Pipeline	Buried site	CH(s)	●●	Pottery, charcoal	Data recovery (excavations): 4 m² excavated (1 pit feature)
134	Ma-Bin	Monitoring of grading activities	33 P	594907	860418	Pipeline	Surface site	DAS	●●	Pottery, lithics	Intentional backfill of the trench
137	Diba I	Monitoring of grading activities	33 P	587412	855907	Pipeline	Surface site	DAS	●●	Pottery, lithics	Intentional backfill of the trench
138-141	Diba I	Monitoring of grading activities	33 P	585811	854859	Pipeline	Surface site	DAS	●●	Pottery, lithics	Intentional backfill of the trench
142	Woum	Monitoring of grading activities	33 P	585117	854413	Pipeline	Surface site	DAS	●●	Pottery, lithics	Intentional backfill of the trench
143	Baibokoum	Monitoring of grading activities	33 P	582215	851670	Pipeline	Surface site	DAS	●●	Pottery, lithics	Intentional backfill of the trench
150	Diba II	Monitoring of trenching activities	33 P	587087	855080	Pipeline	Buried site	DAH(s)	●●	Pottery, lithics	Data recovery (excavations): 6 m² excavated (1 pit feature)
164	Missi Madji	PC survey	33 P	695763	944029	OFDA	Buried site	IWH(s)	●●●	Slag, tuyère + furnace fragments	Data recovery (excavations): 10 m² excavated (2 furnaces, 1 slag heap)
165	Ngon Mbang	PC survey	33 P	692145	943152	Pipeline	Buried site	DAH(s)	●●●	Pottery, slag, furnace fragments	Data recovery (excavations): 25 m² excavated (living floor)
166	Begon II Chef du Village	PC survey	33 P	639406	893154	Pipeline	Buried site	IWH(s)	●●●	Slag, tuyère + furnace fragments	Data recovery (excavations): 10 m² excavated (2 furnaces, 1 slag heap)
167	Karman- kass	PC survey	33 P	658304	960707	OFDA	Buried site	DAH(s)	●●●	Pottery, flakes	Site avoidance, monitoring and data recovery: 12 m² excavated (living floors)
170	Maikery	PC survey	33 P	670458	941040	OFDA	Buried site	IWH(s)	●●	Furnace fragments	Data recovery (excavations): 6 m² excavated (2 furnaces)
173	Badila	PC survey	33 P	318814	924863	Pipeline	Buried site	IWH(s)	●●●	Furnace fragments	Data recovery (excavations): 4 m² excavated (1 furnace)
175	Bekia	PC survey	33 P	688111	940977	OFDA	Buried site	IWH(s)	●●●	10 iron-smelting furnaces, slag, pottery	Data recovery (excavation): 8 m² excavated (2 furnaces)
178	Miandoum	PC survey	33 P	671581	941109	OFDA	Buried site	IWH(s)	●●●	Furnace fragments, pottery	Data recovery (excavation of the only feature in the ROW): 4 m²
185	Begada	PC survey	33 P	694067	941090	OFDA	Surface site	DAS	●●●	Pottery, slag, furnace fragments, houses	Avoidance
188	Dodang	PC survey	33 P	697056	945022	OFDA	Buried site	DAH(s)	●●●	Pottery, slag	Data recovery (3 test trenches in the flowline ROW): 30 m² (living floor)

Appendix B *(end)*. Site treatments in Chad (CH(s): Ceramic horizon(s); CS: Ceramic scatter; DAH(s): Diverse artefact horizon(s); DAS: Diverse artefact scatter; IWH(s): Iron working horizon(s); Priority*: Priority for further treatment, ●: low; ●●: medium; ●●●: high).

Date #	Site code	Village	Context	Laboratory #	Age bp	Calibrated age (2 sigma)
RC 57	ETA 006/135	Diba I	Settlement	Beta 175340	Modern	NA
RC 58	ETA 025/127–128	Begon II	Furnace 1 (80 cm)	Beta 175341	1000 ± 40 bp	AD 970 – AD 1040
RC 59	ETA 035	Bedia	Furnace 2	Beta 175342	980 ± 40 bp	AD 1000 – AD 1170
RC 60	ETA 040	Kolle	Furnace 2	Beta 175343	1000 ± 80 bp	AD 900 – AD 1190
RC 61	ETA 040	Kolle	Furnace 4	Beta 175344	620 ± 80 bp	AD 1260 – AD 1440
RC 62	ETA 046	Beboura	Settlement: square A6 (15–20 cm)	Beta 175345	150 ± 60 bp	AD 1650 – AD 1950
RC 63	ETA 056	Oulibangala	Trench B (20 cm)	Beta 163965	Modern	NA
RC 64	ETA 069	Mban I	Furnace 1 (40 cm)	Beta 163966	3160 ± 70 bp	BC 1540 – BC 1280
RC 65	ETA 069	Mban I	Furnace 2 (50 cm)	Beta 163967	380 ± 40 bp	AD 1430 – AD 1630
RC 66	ETA 069	Mban I	Furnace 1 (60 cm)	Beta 175346	940 ± 40 bp	AD 1020 – AD 1210
	ETA 069	Mban I	Furnace 1 (65 cm)	Beta 169033	1020 ± 50 bp	AD 890 – 1160
RC 67	ETA 075	Kagopal	Furnace 4 (55 cm)	Beta 163968	670 ± 40 bp	AD 1270 – AD 1400
RC 68	ETA 088/094	Komé Base	Settlement: pit feature (100 cm)	Beta 185377	540 ± 60 bp	AD 1300 – AD 1450
RC 69	ETA 097	Mayongo	Settlement: square A5 (70 cm)	Beta 185378	1890 ± 40 bp	AD 50 – AD 230
RC 70	ETA 097	Mayongo	Settlement	Beta 187029	Modern	NA
RC 71	ETA 102	Beto	Settlement	Beta 185379	1030 ± 40 bp	AD 960 – AD 1040
RC 72	ETA 107	Kaba	Settlement	Beta 185380	830 ± 40 bp	AD 1160 – AD 1270
RC 73	ETA 164	Missi Madji	Furnace 1 (55 cm)	Beta 187930	1240 ± 40 bp	AD 685 – AD 890
RC 74	ETA 165	Ngon Mbang	Settlement	Beta 185381	120 ± 50 bp	AD 1660 – AD 1950
RC 75	ETA 165	Ngon Mbang	Settlement/square A4 (25 cm)	Beta 187931	240 ± 60 bp	AD 1500 – AD 1950
RC 76	ETA 166	Begon II (chef du village)	Furnace 16 (30 cm)	Beta 185382	880 ± 50 bp	AD 1030 – AD 1260
RC 77	ETA 166	Begon II (chef du village)	Furnace 20 (20 cm)	Beta 185384	900 ± 40 bp	AD 1030 – AD 1250
RC 78	ETA 166	Begon II (chef du village)	Furnace 20 (30 cm)	Beta 187932	930 ± 60 bp	AD 1000 – AD 1250
RC 79	ETA 166	Begon II (chef du village)	Furnace 16 (50 cm)	Beta 185283	1070 ± 40 bp	AD 980 – AD 1020
RC 80	ETA 167	Karmankass	Settlement: test pit II (130 cm)	Beta 187933	1600 ± 130 bp	AD 130 – AD 670
RC 81	ETA 167	Karmankass	Settlement: test pit I (205 cm)	Beta 185385	1510 ± 70 bp	AD 410 – AD 660
RC 82	ETA 173	Badila	Furnace 1 (70 cm)	Beta 163963	910 ± 40 bp	AD 1030 – AD 1230
RC 83	ETA 173	Badila	Furnace 2 (55 cm)	Beta 163964	890 ± 70 bp	AD 1010 – AD 1270
RC 84	ETA 175	Bekia	Furnace 6	Beta 187934	1040 ± 50 bp	AD 970 – AD 1160
RC 85	ETA 188	Dodang	Square A6 (15 cm)	Beta 187935	640 ± 50 bp	AD 1280 – AD 1420

Appendix C. Radiocarbon dates in Chad.

ECA N°	Site name	UTM	Easting	Northing	Size (m x m)	Artifacts observed	Approximate age	Priority*	Cultural significance
1		33 N	559165	836376	2x2	Grinding stones	Indeterminate	●	None
2		33 N	558761	836463	20x20	Pottery	Iron Age	●	None
3	Mbaiboum	33 N	557153	835749	30x20	Flaked stone fragments, pottery	Iron Age	●●	None
4		33 N	556741	835522	100x30	Flaked stone fragments	MSA/LSA	●	None
5		33 N	555070	834428	30x30	Flaked stone fragments	MSA/LSA	●	None
6		33 N	550268	830781	250x30	Flaked stone fragments, grinding stones	Iron Age	●	None
7		33 N	549670	830304	100x30	Flaked stone fragments, pottery	Iron Age	●	None
8		33 N	544000	825631	200x30	Grinding stones, pottery, flaked stone fragments, slag	Iron Age	●	None
9		33 N	539117	822664	200x30	Flaked stone fragments, pottery, grinding stone	Iron Age	●	None
10		33 N	538273	822234	6x3	Pottery	Indeterminate	●	None
11		33 N	536882	821530	5x8	Grinding stones	Indeterminate	●	None
12		33 N	536497	821059	20x20	Pottery, slag, tuyère fragments	Iron Age	●	None
13		33 N	535548	819886	20x20	Flaked stone fragments	MSA/LSA	●	None
14		33 N	534526	818626	5x8	Grinding stones, wooden tools	Indeterminate	●	None
15	Mbong	33 N	533268	817048	30x30	Standing stones	Neolithic/Iron Age	●●●	None
16		33 N	532804	816477	100x30	Flaked stone fragments	MSA/LSA	●	None
17		33 N	532546	816156	3x3	Standing stones	Neolithic/Iron Age	●	None
18		33 N	528126	811612	100x100	Flaked stone fragments	MSA/LSA	●	None
19		33 N	527409	811149	1x1	Pottery	Iron Age	●	None
20		33 N	527139	810983	5x5	Pottery, grinding stones	Iron Age/Recent	●	None
21		33 N	517827	808737	4x4	Pottery	Iron Age/Recent	●	None
22		33 N	518592	808583	1x1	Grinding stones	Indeterminate	●	None
23		33 N	519148	808512	10x10	Pottery	Iron Age/Recent	●●	None
24	Bemboyo	33 N	519520	808551	200x60	Pottery, slag, flaked stone fragments, possible funeral pits	Iron Age	●●●	High
25		33 N	519872	808617	20x20	Flaked stone fragments	MSA/LSA	●	None
26		33 N	520127	808640	100x60	Pottery, flaked stone fragments	Iron Age	●	None
27		33 N	521064	808780	50x50	Flaked stone fragments	MSA/LSA	●	None
28		33 N	521446	808839	50x50	Flaked stone fragments	MSA/LSA	●●●	None
29		33 N	522833	809003	100x30	Flaked stone fragments	MSA/LSA	●●●	None
30		33 N	508421	802038	5x5	Pottery	Iron Age/Recent	●	None
31		33 N	508769	802292	100x100	Flaked stone fragments, pottery	Iron Age	●	None
32		33 N	509468	802790	50x50	Flaked stone fragments	MSA/LSA	●●	None
33		33 N	512187	804721	20x5	Pottery, flaked stone fragments	Iron Age	●●●	None
34		33 N	515434	807037	50x20	Flaked stone fragments	MSA/LSA	●●	None
35		33 N	500474	796375	150x30	Flaked stone fragments, cores, one scraper	MSA/LSA	●	None
36		33 N	505178	797162	250x30	Pottery, grinding stone, one flaked stone fragment	Iron Age	●	None
37		33 N	504762	799434	200x100	Pottery, flaked stone fragments, discoidal core	Iron Age	●	None
38		33 N	505722	800125	5x5	Grinding stones	Indeterminate	●	None
39		33 N	488746	791484	10x1	Pottery, flaked stone fragments	Iron Age	●	None
40		33 N	489157	791651	1x1	Flaked stone fragments	MSA/LSA	●	None
41		33 N	489390	791738	100x100	Flaked stone fragments	MSA/LSA	●	None
42		33 N	499088	795448	10x10	Flaked stone fragments	MSA/LSA	●	None
43	Sokorta Manga	33 N	481423	788525	50x30	Flaked stone fragments, pottery, tuyère fragments	MSA/LSA	●●●	High
44		33 N	482141	788859	60x20	Pottery, flaked stone fragments	Neolithic/Iron Age	●	None
45		33 N	476508	786389	10x10	Flaked stone fragments	MSA/LSA	●	None
46		33 N	478968	787540	1x1	Grinding stone	Indeterminate	●	None
47	Djaoro Mbama	33 N	471805	784184	60x20	Slag, tuyère fragments, furnace remains	Iron Age	●●●	High
48		33 N	473343	784914	20x20	Flaked stone fragments	MSA/LSA	●	None
49		33 N	474859	785619	20x20	Flaked stone fragments	MSA/LSA	●	None
50		33 N	476041	786116	20x20	Flaked stone fragments	MSA/LSA	●	None
51		33 N	463505	780367	3x3	Slag, tuyère fragments, furnace remains	Iron Age/Recent	●●	None
52		33 N	465876	781647	200x30	Slag, tuyère fragments, eroded pottery	Iron Age/Recent	●	None
53		33 N	469170	782989	5x5	Pottery	Iron Age/Recent	●	None
54		33 N	454024	770148	30x5	Pottery, grinding stones, slag	Iron Age/Recent	●	None
55		33 N	454350	770483	30x5	Pottery	Iron Age/Recent	●	None
56		33 N	454581	770724	250x10	Pottery, flaked stone fragments	Iron Age	●●	None
57		33 N	450130	766712	20x10	Pottery	Iron Age/Recent	●	None
58		33 N	451213	767617	5x1.5	Pottery	Iron Age/Recent	●	None
59		33 N	444273	759800	100x50	Pottery, including 3 buried pots	Recent	●●●	None

Appendix D *(continued)*. Sites in Cameroon (Priority*: Priority for further treatment, ●: low; ●●: medium; ●●●: high).

ECA N°	Site name	UTM	Easting	Northing	Size (m x m)	Artifacts observed	Approximate age	Priority*	Cultural significance
60		33 N	420538	725104	20x20	Architectural remains, European tinware	Recent	●	None
61		33 N	439783	754085	500x30	Architectural remains, pottery	Recent	●	None
62		32 N	601058	322458	1x1	Pottery	Iron Age/Recent	●	None
63		32 N	603723	325306	2x2	Flaked stone fragments	LSA	●	None
64		32 N	603986	325811	1x1	Pottery	Iron Age/Recent	●	None
65		32 N	602181	323663	2x2	Pottery	Iron Age/Recent	●	None
66		32 N	625992	337894	1x1	Flaked stone fragments	MSA/LSA	●	None
67		32 N	619555	334563	3x3	Pottery	Iron Age/Recent	●	None
68	**Ndtoua Rockshelter**	32 N	635456	338648	12x5	Pottery, flaked stone fragments	Iron Age/Recent + Neolithic/ Iron Age + LSA + MSA	●●●	**High**
69		32 N	636208	338563	3x3	Pottery	Iron Age/Recent	●	None
70		32 N	610324	329759	1x1	Pottery	Iron Age/Recent	●	None
71		32 N	614246	331592	2x1	Pottery	Iron Age/Recent	●	None
72		32 N	615018	331867	1x1	Iron latch, pottery, slag	Recent	●	None
73	Ndoumba Kanga	33 N	304941	540538	1x1	Pottery, flaked stone fragments	Neolithic/Iron Age	●	None
74	Ndoumba Kanga	33 N	305479	540640	3x4	Pottery	Iron Age	●●	None
75		33 N	303897	540312	20x10	Pottery	Iron Age	●	None
76	Yong River	33 N	301776	539913	2x2	Pottery	Iron Age	●	None
77	Yong River	33 N	301244	539810	20x30	Pottery, flaked stone fragments	Iron Age	●	None
78	Yong River	33 N	300184	539594	10x20	Pottery	Iron Age	●	None
79	Mbinang	33 N	298362	539244	5x10	Pottery, flaked stone fragments	Late Stone Age/Iron Age	●●	None
80	Mbinang	33 N	299151	539402	100x30	Pottery, slag, smoking pipes	Iron Age	●●	None
81	**Mbinang**	33 N	299674	539510	20x30	Pottery, flaked stone fragments	Iron Age	●●●	**High**
82		33 N	293547	538318	2x5	Pottery	Iron Age	●	None
83		33 N	292741	538145	5x20	Pottery	Iron Age	●	None
84	**Koukony**	33 N	285229	536286	650x30	Pottery, flaked stone fragments, slag	LSA + Neolithic/Iron Age	●●●	**High**
85	Koukony	33 N	282702	535706	15x5	Pottery	Iron Age	●	None
86	Koukony	33 N	282287	535671	3x3	Pottery	Iron Age	●	None
87	Koukony	33 N	286043	536435	100x30	Pottery, slag, smoking pipes	Iron Age	●●	None
88	Tara Plage	32 N	600225	321550	100x30	Pottery, flaked stone fragments, modern glass	Iron Age/Recent	●●	None
89		33 N	291216	537861	5x5	Pottery	Iron Age/Recent	●	None
90		33 N	289961	537590	3x3	Pottery	Iron Age/Recent	●	None
91		33 N	276693	535127	30x30	Pottery	Iron Age/Recent	●	None
92		33 N	275830	534953	30x50	Pottery, smoking pipes	Iron Age/Recent	●	None
93	**Ewankang**	33 N	261755	531414	300x30	Pottery, flaked stone fragments	Iron Age/Recent	●●●	**High**
94		33 N	310834	542425	10x10	Pottery	Iron Age/Recent	●	None
95		33 N	309246	542066	30x30	Pottery	Iron Age/Recent	●	None
96		33 N	308858	541968	50x30	Pottery	Iron Age/Recent	●	None
97		33 N	311359	542750	1x1	Pottery	Iron Age/Recent	●●	None
98		33 N	311775	543070	10x10	Pottery	Iron Age/Recent	●	None
99		33 N	311858	543136	10x10	Pottery	Iron Age/Recent	●	None
100		33 N	312239	543533	10x10	Pottery	Iron Age/Recent	●	None
101	Biombe (PS3)	33 N	314005	546613	500x100	Pottery, grinding stones	Iron Age/Recent	●	None
102	Biombe	33 N	314420	551007	200x30	Pottery	Iron Age/Recent	●	None
103	Biombe	33 N	313844	549991	100x30	Pottery	Iron Age/Recent	●	None
104	Koukony	33 N	289961	537590	20x30	Pottery	Iron Age/Recent	●	None
105	Koukony	33 N	282146	535672	120x30	Pottery	Iron Age/Recent	●	None
106	Ebaka	33 N	313674	547591	60x30	Pottery	Iron Age/Recent	●	None
107	Sakoundji	33 N	316062	556364	10x10	Pottery	Iron Age	●	None
109	Mbete	33 N	317332	557795	2x5	Pottery	Recent	●	None
110		32 N	605576	327695	100x30	Pottery	Iron Age/Recent	●	None
111	Bambo	33 N	319014	559461	6x30	Pottery	Iron Age/Recent	●	None
112		32 N	608036	328822	10x10	Pottery	Iron Age/Recent	●	None
113	Bambo	33 N	319468	559689	5x30	Pottery	Iron Age/Recent	●	None
114		32 N	611811	330413	50x30	Pottery	Iron Age/Recent	●	None
115	Bambo	33 N	320003	560371	10x30	Pottery	Iron Age/Recent	●	None
117	Ndoumba Kanga	33 N	307212	541477	100x30	Pottery, slag, tuyères	Iron Age	●●	None
118		32 N	620898	335427	25x5	Pottery	Iron Age/Recent	●	None
119	**Belabo SOCOPAO**	33 N	312206	543487	30x600	Pottery, tuyères, slag	Iron Age	●●	**High**
120		32 N	626641	338018	40x30	Pottery	Iron Age/Recent	●	None
121	Ebaka	33 N	314016	547070	30x200	Pottery, tuyère	Iron Age/Recent	●	None

Appendix D *(continued).* Sites in Cameroon (Priority*: Priority for further treatment, ●: low; ●●: medium; ●●●: high).

ECA N°	Site name	UTM	Easting	Northing	Size (m x m)	Artifacts observed	Approximate age	Priority*	Cultural significance
122		32 N	628055	338246	10x10	Pottery	Iron Age/Recent	●	None
123	Ebaka	33 N	313495	547764	30x300	Pottery	Iron Age/Recent	●	None
124	**Makoure**	32 N	630383	338387	100X10	Furnaces, slag	Iron Age	●●●	**High**
125	Yebi	33 N	313717	549869	5x3	Pottery, slag	Iron Age	●●	None
126		32 N	660140	341272	25x30	Pottery	Iron Age/Recent	●	None
127		33 N	321658	562032	1x2	Modern tomb	Recent	●●●	**High**
128		32 N	659009	340780	20x15	Pottery	Iron Age/Recent	●	None
129	Biombe	33 N	314292	550461	20x3	Pottery	Iron Age/Recent	●●	None
130	**Dombe**	32 N	605536	327675	11x2	Pottery, stone tools (in 2 pits)	Neolithic/Iron Age	●●●	**High**
133	Mbaki	33 N	322021	570789	10x5	Pottery	Iron Age	●●	None
134	Bidjocka	32 N	665682	345371	2x2	Pottery	Iron Age/Recent	●	None
135	Mbaki	33 N	322205	567987	10x3	Pottery, slag	Iron Age	●●	None
136	Bidjocka	32 N	671194	350611	3x3	Pottery	Iron Age/Recent	●	None
137	Mbaki	33 N	321896	571207	50x30	Pottery	Recent	●	None
138	**Bissiang**	32 N	613491	331415	35x3	Pottery, stone tools (in 2 pits)	Neolithic/Iron Age	●●●	**High**
139		33 N	321493	571791	250x30	Pottery	Recent	●	None
141	Lom II	33 N	319107	579929	20x30	Pottery	Recent	●	None
143		33 N	319029	580421	3x3	Pottery	Recent	●	None
144	Ndtoua	32 N	640965	338676	3x3	Pottery	Iron Age/Recent	●	None
145	Goyoum	33 N	318818	581794	10x100	Pottery	Recent	●	None
146	**Bidou II**	32 N	620320	335062	15x3	Pottery (in 2 pits)	Neolithic/Iron Age	●●●	**High**
148		32 N	645314	339435		Pottery	Iron Age/Recent	●	None
149	Goyoum	33 N	321541	574214		Pottery	Iron Age/Recent	●	None
150	Grand Zambi	32 N	643194	339184	3x3	Pottery	Iron Age/Recent	●	None
151	Goyoum	33 N	321504	574936		Pottery	Iron Age/Recent	●	None
152	Grand Zambi	32 N	641734	338835	20x30	Pottery	Iron Age/Recent	●	None
153	Lom II	33 N	319505	582949	10x20	Pottery	Recent	●	None
154	Bifoum	32 N	653700	339971	10x18	Pottery, slag	Iron Age/Recent	●●	None
155	Lom II	33 N	320607	583565	10x20	Pottery, hammerstone	Iron Age	●●	None
157	**Lom II**	33 N	321792	584567	100X30	Pottery	Neolithic/Iron Age	●●	**High**
158	Mbikiliki	32 N	670915	350392	200X30	Pottery, slag, glass	Recent	●	None
159	Lom I	33 N	323399	590646	10x30	Pottery, tuyères	Iron Age	●	None
160		32 N	666852	346890	30x50	Pottery	Iron Age/Recent	●●	None
161	Lom I	33 N	331691	597203	25x30	Pottery	Iron Age/Recent	●	None
162	Ndtoua	32 N	642127	338930	2x2	Pottery (in 1 pit)	Neolithic/Iron Age	●	None
163	Lom I	33 N	332741	597539	20x20	Pottery, slag, tuyères, bricks	Iron Age/Recent	●●●	None
164	**Ndtoua**	32 N	642925	339124	30x3	Pottery, charcoal (in 6 pits)	Neolithic/Iron Age	●●●	**High**
165	Pangar	33 N	340938	611131		Pottery	Recent	●	None
166	Grand Zambi	32 N	648009	339628		Pottery (in 1 pit)	Neolithic/Iron Age	●	None
167	Pangar	33 N	341398	613288		Pottery	Recent	●	None
168	Mbikiliki	32 N	671925	351182		Pottery, tuyère, slag, grinding stone	Iron Age	●	None
169	Pangar	33 N	341872	614160	30x80	Pottery	Iron Age	●●	None
170	Koampboer	32 N	707983	368174		Pottery	Iron Age/Recent	●●	None
171	**Pangar**	33 N	345933	617024	30x600	Pottery	Iron Age/Recent	●●	**High**
172	Bikoue I	32 N	706186	368170	25x25	Pottery, flaked stone fragments	Iron Age	●	None
173	**Pangar**	33 N	346715	617331	500x30	Pottery, grinding stone	Iron Age/Recent	●●	**High**
174	Bikoue I	32 N	706315	368191	20x30	Pottery, possible flaked stone fragments	Iron Age	●●	None
175	Lom I	33 N	322932	591852	30x50	Pottery	Iron Age/Recent	●	None
176	Bikoue-Si	32 N	707082	368284	100x15	Possible flaked stone fragments	Late Stone Age	●●●	None
177	**Lom I**	33 N	323328	592208	30x10	Isolated polished axe	Neolithic/Iron Age	●●●	**High**
178	**Mvile**	32 N	678019	355982	12x2	Slag, tuyères	Iron Age/Recent	●●	**High**
179	Lom I	33 N	324032	592831	30x100	Pottery	Recent	●	None
180	Mvile	32 N	677000	355107	1x1	Pottery (in a refuse pit)	Neolithic/Iron Age	●	None
181	Lom I	33 N	328361	595591	30x700	Pottery, slag, stone artifacts	Iron Age	●●●	None
182	**Bikoka**	32 N	676051	354359	30x200	Pottery (in several refuse pits)	Neolithic/Iron Age	●●●	**High**
184	Bikoue-Si	32 N	707983	368174	100x30	Possible flaked stone fragments, 1 potsherd	Iron Age	●●●	None
185	**Lom I**	33 N	338468	602355	30x100	Pottery	Iron Age/Recent	●●	**High**
186	**Bikoue-Si**	32 N	708687	368077	50x30	Possible flaked stone fragments, pottery	Iron Age	●●●	**High**
187	Lom I	33 N	340012	604678	30x150	Pottery	Iron Age/Recent	●	None
188	Bikoue-Si	32 N	709223	368033	25x30	Pottery	Iron Age/Recent	●	None
189	Lom I	33 N	340317	608313	30x50	Pottery	Iron Age/Recent	●	None
190	Madong II	32 N	695342	362836		Pottery	Recent	●	None
191	Lom I	33 N	341935	614208	30x600	Pottery	Recent	●	None

Appendix D *(continued)*. Sites in Cameroon (Priority*: Priority for further treatment, ●: low; ●●: medium; ●●●: high).

ECA N°	Site name	UTM	Easting	Northing	Size (m x m)	Artifacts observed	Approximate age	Priority*	Cultural significance
192	**Bikoue II Rockshelter**	32 N	709409	368021	5x5	Pottery, flaked stone fragments	LSA + Neolithic/Iron Age	●●●	**High**
193	Pangar	33 N	345072	616676	30x20	Pottery	Iron Age/Recent	●	None
194	Mikan I	32 N	712215	367937		Pottery	Iron Age	●	None
195	Pangar	33 N	347243	617534	30x50	Pottery	Iron Age/Recent	●	None
196	Angonfeme	32 N	734502	375333		Pottery	Iron Age/Recent	●	None
197	Pangar	33 N	348245	618482	30x100	Pottery	Iron Age/Recent	●	None
198		32 N	710049	368201		Pottery, flaked stone fragments	Iron Age	●	None
199	**Pangar**	33 N	357720	623683	30x200	Pottery, flaked stone fragments	Neolithic/Iron Age	●●●	**High**
200	**Minkan I**	32 N	713506	368865	30x200	Pottery, flaked stone fragments, grinding stones	Iron Age	●●	**High**
201	Mararaba	33 N	358197	624111		Pottery	Iron Age/Recent	●	None
202	Nkoelon	32 N	756538	396229		Slag	Iron Age/Recent	●	None
203	Mararaba	33 N	359498	626294	30x10	Pottery	Recent	●	None
204	Nkolnlong	32 N	745373	383169	20x45	Pottery (possibly in pits)	Neolithic/Iron Age	●●	None
205	Mararaba	33 N	364058	631880		Pottery	Recent	●	None
206	Nkolnlong	32 N	746070	383674		Pottery	Recent	●	None
207	Mararaba	33 N	368128	640898		Pottery	Iron Age/Recent	●	None
208	**Bikoka**	32 N	692017	362083	30x150	Potsherds (in refuse pits)	Neolithic/Iron Age	●●	**High**
209	Tapare	33 N	371631	652692	250x30	Pottery	Iron Age	●●	None
210		32 N	762188	407034		Pottery	Iron Age/Recent	●	None
211	Dang-patou	33 N	369802	650165		Pottery	Recent	●	None
212		32 N	756091	389431		Pottery	Iron Age/Recent	●	None
213	Dang-patou	33 N	368606	648563	200x30	Pottery	Iron Age	●●	None
214		32 N	753501	387584		Pottery, slag	Iron Age/Recent	●	None
215	Douafo	33 N	376059	659095		Pottery	Recent	●	None
216	**Ngoumou**	32 N	757803	398458	1x1	Pottery (in a pit)	Neolithic/Iron Age	●●●	**High**
217	Douafo	33 N	375917	658891	150x30	Pottery, grinding stones	Iron Age	●●	None
218	Ngoumou	32 N	763543	411387		Pottery	Iron Age/Recent	●	None
219		33 N	374147	656084		Furnace fragments, slag	Recent	●	None
220	**Ngoumou**	32 N	758102	399017	50x30	Furnace fragments, slag	Iron Age	●●	**High**
221	Mabele	33 N	376918	660189		Grinding stone fragments	Indeterminate	●	None
222	Ngoumou	32 N	758036	399339	20x10	Pottery	Neolithic/Iron Age	●●	None
223	Mabele	33 N	376670	659921		Pottery, grinding stone	Iron Age	●	None
224	**Obokoue**	32 N	761217	403473	2x2	Pottery (in a refuse pit)	Neolithic/Iron Age	●●●	**High**
225	**Kongolo**	33 N	386938	673740	4x2	Pottery	Recent	●●	**High**
226	Angon II	32 N	763809	417974		Pottery	Iron Age/Recent	●	None
227	Kongolo	33 N	391391	679761	20x20	Pottery	Iron Age	●●	None
228	**Binguela II**	32 N	763626	413808	2x2	Pottery (in pit)	Neolithic/Iron Age	●●●	**High**
229	Konde	33 N	396792	687218	100x30	Pottery, slag, flaked stone fragments	Iron Age	●●	None
230	Angon II	32 N	763836	417019		Pottery (in pit)	Neolithic/Iron Age	●	None
231		33 N	401974	694314	600x30	Pottery, slag, tuyères	Iron Age	●●	None
232	Ekabita	32 N	780212	447702		Pottery	Iron Age/Recent	●	None
233		33 N	406531	700755		Pottery, slag, tuyères	Iron Age/Recent	●	None
234		32 N	764288	420979		Furnace fragments	Iron Age/Recent	●	None
235		33 N	406127	700130		Pottery	Iron Age/Recent	●	None
236	**Zoatoupsi**	32 N	764378	421466	2x2	Pottery (in refuse pit)	Neolithic/Iron Age	●●●	**High**
237	Ndamboura	33 N	422829	728067	260x30	Pottery	Iron Age/Recent	●	None
238	Nkometou	32 N	781016	448508	10x10	Pottery	Iron Age/Recent	●	None
239	Mbarang	33 N	429193	736709	400x30	Pottery, hammerstones, grinding stones	Iron Age/Recent	●●	None
240	Nkometou	32 N	783081	449910		Pottery	Iron Age/Recent	●	None
241	Beka Petel	33 N	436531	749283	10x7	Pottery	Iron Age/Recent	●	None
242	**Ozom**	32 N	768430	433055	25x2	Pottery (in 4 pits)	Neolithic/Iron Age	●●●	**High**
243	**Beka Petel - Gamboro**	33 N	435968	748473	200x30	Pottery, flaked stone fragments	Neolithic/Iron Age + Iron Age/Recent	●●●	**High**
244	Nkometou	32 N	783844	450159		Pottery	Recent	●	None
245	Beka Petel	33 N	435323	747410	5x2	Pottery	Iron Age	●	None
246	Essong Missang	32 N	785207	451162		Pottery, slag, tuyères	Recent	●	None
247		33 N	438709	753419		Pottery	Iron Age/Recent	●	None
248	**Essong Missang**	32 N	786575	452674	12x2	Pottery (in 2 refuse pits)	Neolithic/Iron Age	●●●	**High**
249		33 N	439187	754087		Pottery	Iron Age/Recent	●	None
250	**Leboudi**	32 N	769142	433992	35x10	Pottery (in pits), flaked stone fragments (on surface)	MSA + Neolithic/ Iron Age	●●●	**High**
251	Nyasse Soukol	33 N	441303	756540		Pottery	Recent	●	None

Appendix D *(continued)*. Sites in Cameroon (Priority*: Priority for further treatment, ●: low; ●●: medium; ●●●: high).

ECA N°	Site name	UTM	Easting	Northing	Size (m x m)	Artifacts observed	Approximate age	Priority*	Cultural significance
252	Afan-Essele	32 N	795242	463017		Pottery	Recent	●	None
253	Nyasse Soukol	33 N	443973	759560		Pottery	Recent	●	None
254	Afan-Essele	32 N	795493	463349		Pottery	Recent	●	None
255	**Seka**	33 N	449813	765571	500x30	Pottery, flaked stone fragments	Neolithic/Iron Age	●●●	**High**
256		32 N	793964	461394	120x20	Pottery, flaked stone fragments	Iron Age	●●	None
257	Seka	33 N	449601	766224		Pottery, grinding stones	Iron Age/Recent	●	None
258		32 N	794477	462029	30x30	Pottery, flaked stone fragments	Iron Age	●●	None
259	Seka	33 N	450603	767100	100x30	Pottery, grinding stones, flaked stone fragments	Neolithic/Iron Age	●●	None
260	Ebot	32 N	773905	440451		Pottery, slag	Iron Age/Recent	●	None
261	Seka	33 N	451301	767691	200x30	Pottery, grinding stones, polished stone tools fragments	Neolithic/Iron Age	●●	None
262	**Ebot**	32 N	773876	440812	20x2	Flaked stone fragments, pottery	LSA	●●	**High**
263	Nangarou	33 N	453015	769076		Pottery, flaked stone fragments	Iron Age	●	None
264	**Yegue Assi**	32 N	774274	441718	2x1	Iron smelting furnace fragments	Iron Age	●●●	**High**
265	**Lesouaka**	33 N	453972	770075	100x30	Pottery, flaked stone fragments, polished stone tools fragments	Neolithic/Iron Age	●●	**High**
266	**Yegue Assi**	32 N	774454	442326	10x2	Pottery (in 2 refuse pits), hammerstone and slag (on the graded surface)	Neolithic/Iron Age	●●●	**High**
267		33 N	455851	772207	500x30	Pottery, grinding stones	Iron Age	●●	None
268	Nkolnlong	32 N	752517	386999		Pottery, slag	Iron Age/Recent	●	None
269		33 N	466149	781812		Pottery	Iron Age/Recent	●	None
270	Nkometou	32 N	776044	444514		Pottery, slag	Iron Age	●	None
271	Sokorta Manga	33 N	480008	788019	30x50	Pottery	Recent	●	None
272	**Ezezang**	32 N	777424	445411	300X30	Flaked stone fragments (in layer), pottery (in refuse pits and in layer)	LSA + Neolithic/ Iron Age	●●●	**High**
273	Elig Mebenga	32 N	763561	411370		Pottery	Iron Age/Recent	●	None
275	Zoatoupsi	32 N	764234	420675	60x30	Furnace fragments, slag, pottery	Iron Age	●●	None
277	Yandea	33 N	486643	790661		Pottery	Iron Age/Recent	●	None
279	**Ongot**	32 N	764062	426075	2x2	Pottery, iron (in a pit)	Iron Age	●●●	**High**
281	**Ngoya**	32 N	772288	438140	1x2	Modern tomb	Recent	●●●	**High**
283	Leboudi	32 N	768056	432563		Pottery	Iron Age/Recent	●	None
291	**Mvog Dzigui**	32 N	776568	444866	1x2	Modern tomb	Iron Age/Recent	●●●	**High**
295	Nkometou	32 N	781987	449192	25x25	Pottery	Recent	●	None
299	Mvomdoumba	32 N	797345	466107	5x2	Possible flaked stone fragments	Iron Age/Recent	●	None
300	Nzon	33 N	435949	748446	5x5	Pottery	LSA	●	None
301		32 N	801342	471602	20x5	Pottery, slag	Recent	●	None
303	Nkoayos	32 N	806077	477454	10x2	Pottery	Iron Age/Recent	●	None
305	**Nkoayos**	32 N	807296	478974	150x30	Pottery, flaked stone fragments	Recent	●●●	**High**
307		32 N	810145	482515	300X30	Pottery, slag	Iron Age/Recent	●●	None
309	Ndjore	32 N	811317	484065	50x30	Pottery, slag	Iron Age/Recent	●	None
311	Ndjore	32 N	811828	484485	25x3	Pottery	Iron Age/Recent	●	None
313		32 N	812636	485257	20x5	Pottery	Iron Age/Recent	●	None
315	**Ndjore**	32 N	813952	486490	200x30	Pottery, slag, human bones (in 8 pits)	Iron Age/Recent	●●●	**High**
317	**Ndokoa**	32 N	817479	490938	30x2	Pottery (in pits), flaked stone fragments (on surface)	Iron Age/Recent	●●●	**High**
319	**Kondengui**	32 N	826585	495742	5x2	Pottery	Iron Age	●●●	**High**
321	**Bikoto**	32 N	830813	496658	300x30	Pottery, slag, flaked stone fragments	Iron Age/Recent	●●	**High**
323	**Zili**	32 N	831268	496786	2x2	Pottery, slag (in pit)	Iron Age/Recent	●●●	**High**
325		33 N	181148	500954	2x2	Pottery (in pit)	Iron Age/Recent	●	None
327		33 N	191012	506178	2x2	Pottery, slag (in pit)	Iron Age	●	None
329	**Doumba**	33 N	191537	506384	1x1	Pottery, slag (in pit)	Iron Age/Recent	●●●	**High**
331		33 N	194906	508137	10x10	Pottery	Iron Age/Recent	●	None
333	**Nanga Eboko**	33 N	210912	514378	30x350	Pottery, flaked stone fragments (in 3 pits)	Iron Age/Recent	●●●	**High**
335	**Meyang**	33 N	243403	528403	22x3	Pottery, flaked stone fragments (in 3 pits)	Neolithic/Iron Age	●●●	**High**
337		33 N	249422	529156	2x2	Pottery (in pit)	Neolithic/Iron Age	●	None
339		33 N	252492	529698	2x2	Pottery (in pit)	Iron Age/Recent	●	None
400	Koleya	33 N	435949	748446	150x30	Pottery	Iron Age/Recent	●	None
401	Mgbata	33 N	432904	743413	40x20	Grinding stones fragments	Indeterminate	●	None
402	Mgbata	33 N	432630	742930	85x65	Grinding stones fragments	Recent	●	None
403	Mbarang	33 N	430153	738494	10x10	Pottery	Recent	●	None
404	Ndamboura	33 N	425737	732089	3x3	Pottery, clay smoking pipes	Iron Age/Recent	●	None
405	Ndamboura	33 N	424957	731031	5x5	Grinding stones fragments	Indeterminate	●	None
406		33 N	419179	722965	100x30	Pottery	Iron Age/Recent	●	None
407		33 N	418752	722259	50x30	Pottery, slag, grinding stones	Iron Age/Recent	●	None
408		33 N	418176	721290	25x15	Pottery	Iron Age/Recent	●	None

Appendix D *(end)*. Sites in Cameroon (Priority*: Priority for further treatment, ●: low; ●●: medium; ●●●: high).

ECA No.	Site name	Discovery	UTM	Easting	Northing	KP	Conserva-tion	Site Type	Artifacts observed	Priority*	Site treatment
24	Bemboyo	PC survey	33 N	519520	808551	231	Buried site	DAH(s)	Pottery, slag, flaked stone fragments, possible funeral pits	●●●	Data recovery (excavations)
43	Sokorta Manga	PC survey	33 N	481423	788525	273	Buried site	DAH(s)	Flaked stone fragments, pottery, tuyère fragments	●●●	Data recovery (excavations)
47	Djaoro Mbama	PC survey	33 N	471805	784184	285	Buried site	IWH	Slag, blowpipe fragments, furnace remains	●●●	Narrowing of the ROW + data recovery (excavations)
68	Ndtoua Rockshelter	PC survey	32 N	635456	338648	1025	Buried site	DAH(s)	Pottery, flaked stone fragments	●●●	Data recovery (excavations)
81	Mbinang	Monitoring of grading activities	33 N	299674	539510	610-612	Buried site	DAH(s)	Pottery, flaked stone fragments	●●●	Narrowing of the ROW
84	Koukony	Monitoring of grading activities	33 N	285229	536286	622	Buried site	DAH(s)	Pottery, flaked stone fragments, slag	●●●	Intentional backfill of the trench
93	Ewankang	Monitoring of trenching activities	33 N	261755	531414	647	Buried site	DAH(s)	Pottery, flaked stone fragments	●●●	Narrowing of the ROW + data recovery (excavations)
119	Belabo SOCOPAO	Monitoring of grading activities	33 N	312206	543487	594-595	Surface site	DAS	Pottery, blowpipes, slag	●●	Narrowing of the ROW
124	Makouré	Monitoring of grading activities	32 N	630383	338387	1037	Buried site	IWH	Furnaces, slag	●●●	Narrowing of the ROW + data recovery (excavations)
127		PC survey	33 N	321658	562032	571	Surface site	Modern tomb	Modern tomb	●●●	Narrowing of the ROW
130	Dombè	Monitoring of trenching activities	32 N	605536	327675	1060	Buried site	Ceramic aggregate	Pottery, stone tools (in 2 pits)	●●●	data recovery (excavations)
138	Bissiang	Monitoring of trenching activities	32 N	613491	331415	1051	Buried site	DAH(s)	Pottery, stone tools (in 2 pits)	●●●	Data recovery (excavations)
146	Bidou II	Monitoring of trenching activities	32 N	620320	335062	1040	Buried site	Ceramic aggregate	Pottery (in 2 pits)	●●●	Data recovery (excavations)
157	Lom II	Monitoring of grading activities	33 N	321792	584567	545	Buried site	CH	Pottery	●●	Narrowing of the ROW + data recovery (excavations)
160	Bidjouka	Monitoring of grading activities	32 N	666852	346890	992	Surface site	CS	Pottery	●●	Monitoring of trenching activities
164	Ndtoua	Monitoring of trenching activities	32 N	642925	339124	1025	Buried site	CH	Pottery, charcoal (in 6 pits)	●●●	Intentional backfill of the trench
171	Pangar	PC survey (clearing)	33 N	345933	617024	498	Surface site	CS	Pottery	●●	Narrowing of the ROW
173	Pangar	PC survey (clearing)	33 N	346715	617331	497	Surface site	DAS	Pottery, grinding stone	●●	Narrowing of the ROW
177	Lom I	Monitoring of trenching activities	33 N	323328	592208	536	Surface site	LS	Isolated polished axe	●●●	Data recovery (artefact collected)
178	Mvile	Monitoring of grading activities	32 N	678019	355982	980	Buried site	IWH	Slag, blow pipes	●●	Narrowing of the ROW
182	Bikoka	Monitoring of trenching activities	32 N	676051	354359	970	Buried site	CH	Pottery (in several refuse pits)	●●●	Intentional backfill of the trench
185	Lom I	Monitoring of trenching activities	33 N	338468	602355	517	Surface site	CS	Potsherds	●●	Intentional backfill of the trench
186	Bikoue-Si	Monitoring of grading activities	32 N	708687	368077	944	Buried site	DAH(s)	Possible flaked stone fragments, pottery	●●●	Narrowing of the ROW
192	Bikoue II Rockshelter	PC survey	32 N	709409	368021	945	Buried site	DAH(s)	Pottery, flaked stone fragments	●●●	Narrowing of the ROW
199	Pangar	Monitoring of grading activities	33 N	357720	623683	485	Buried site	DAH(s)	Pottery, flaked stone fragments	●●●	Narrowing of the ROW + data recovery (excavations)
200	Minkan I	Monitoring of trenching activities	32 N	713506	368865	939	Buried site	DAH(s)	Pottery, flaked stone fragments, grinding stones	●●	Intentional backfill of the trench
208	Bikoka	Monitoring of trenching activities	32 N	692017	362083	970	Buried site	CH	Pottery (in refuse pits)	●●	Intentional backfill of the trench
216	Ngoumou	Monitoring of trenching activities	32 N	757803	398458	882	Buried site	Ceramic aggregate	Pottery (in a pit)	●●●	Data recovery (excavations)
220	Ngoumou	Monitoring of grading activities	32 N	758102	399017	880	Buried site	IWH	Furnace fragments, slag	●●	Narrowing of the ROW
224	Obokoue	Monitoring of trenching activities	32 N	761217	403473	875	Buried site	Ceramic aggregate	Pottery (in a refuse pit)	●●●	Data recovery (excavations)

Appendix E *(continued)*. Site treatment in Cameroon (CH: Ceramic horizon; CS: Ceramic scatter; DAH(s): Diverse artefact horizon(s); DAS: Diverse artefact scatter; IWH: Iron working horizon; LS: Lithic scatter; Priority*: Priority for further treatment, ●: low; ●●: medium; ●●●: high; ROW: Right-of-way).

ECA No.	Site name	Discovery	UTM	Easting	Northing	KP	Conser-vation	Site Type	Artifacts observed	Priority*	Site treatment
225	**Kongolo**	PC survey	33 N	386938	673740	425	Buried site	CH	Pottery	●●	Data recovery (excavations)
228	**Binguela II**	Monitoring of trenching activities	32 N	763626	413808	864	Buried site	Ceramic aggregate	Pottery (in pit)	●●●	Data recovery (excavations)
236	**Zoatoupsi**	Monitoring of trenching activities	32 N	764378	421466	857	Buried site	Ceramic aggregate	Pottery (in refuse pit)	●●●	Data recovery (excavations)
242	**Ozom**	Monitoring of trenching activities	32 N	768430	433055	843-847	Buried site	Ceramic aggregate	Pottery (in 4 pits)	●●●	Data recovery (excavations)
243	**Beka Petel - Gamboro**	Monitoring of grading activities	33 N	435968	748473	335	Buried site	DAH(s)	Pottery, flaked stone fragments	●●●	Data recovery (excavations)
248	**Essong Missang**	Monitoring of trenching activities	32 N	786575	452674	815	Buried site	Ceramic aggregate	Pottery (in 2 refuse pits)	●●●	Data recovery (excavations)
250, 285	**Leboudi**	Monitoring of trenching activities	32 N	769142	433992	842	Buried site	Ceramic aggregate	Pottery (in pits), flaked stone fragments (on surface)	●●●	Data recovery (excavations and surface collection)
255	**Seka**	Monitoring of grading activities	33 N	449813	765571	312	Buried site	DAH(s)	Pottery, flaked stone fragments	●●●	Narrowing of the ROW
262	**Ebot**	Monitoring of trenching activities	32 N	773876	440812	834	Surface site	LS	Flaked stone fragments, pottery	●●	Intentional back-fill of the trench
264	**Yegue Assi**	Monitoring of trenching activities	32 N	774274	441718	833	Buried site	IWH	Iron smelting furnace fragments	●●●	Intentional back-fill of the trench
265	**Lesouaka**	Monitoring of grading activities	33 N	453972	770075	305	Buried site	DAH(s)	Pottery, flaked stone fragments, polished stone tools fragments	●●	Intentional back-fill of the trench
266	**Yegue Assi**	Monitoring of trenching activities	32 N	774454	442326	832	Buried site	Ceramic aggregate	Pottery (in 2 refuse pits), hammer-stone and slag (on the graded surface)	●●●	Data recovery (excavations)
272	**Ezezang**	Monitoring of trenching activities	32 N	777424	445411	827	Buried site	DAH(s)	Flaked stone fragments (in layer), pottery (in refuse pits and in layer)	●●●	Data recovery (excavations)
279	**Ongot**	Monitoring of trenching activities	32 N	764062	426075	854	Buried site	DAH(s)	Pottery, iron (in a pit)	●●●	Data recovery (excavations)
281	**Ngoya**	Monitoring of grading activities	32 N	772288	438140	846	Surface site	Modern tomb	Modern tomb	●●●	Narrowing of the ROW
291	**Mvog Dzigui**	Monitoring of grading activities	32 N	776568	444866	829	Surface site	DAS	Modern tomb	●●●	Narrowing of the ROW
305	**Nkoayos**	Monitoring of trenching activities	32 N	807296	478974	782	Buried site	CH	Pottery, flaked stone fragments	●●●	Intentional back-fill of the trench
315	**Ndjore**	Monitoring of trenching activities	32 N	813952	486490	772	Buried site	CH	Pottery, slag, human bones (in 8 pits)	●●●	Data recovery (excavations)
317	**Ndokoa**	Monitoring of trenching activities	32 N	817479	490938	777	Buried site	DAH(s)	Pottery (in pits), flaked stone fragments (on surface)	●●●	Data recovery (excavations)
319	**Kondengui**	Monitoring of trenching activities	32 N	826585	495742	755	Buried site	Ceramic aggregate	Pottery	●●●	Data recovery (excavations)
321	**Bikoto**	Monitoring of trenching activities	32 N	830813	496658	752	Buried site	Ceramic aggregate	Pottery, slag, flaked stone fragments	●●	Intentional back-fill of the trench
323	**Zili**	Monitoring of trenching activities	32 N	831268	496786	751	Surface site	DAS	Pottery, slag (in pit)	●●●	Data recovery (excavations)
329	**Doumba**	Monitoring of trenching activities	33 N	191537	506384	723	Buried site	DAH(s)	Pottery, slag (in pit)	●●●	Data recovery (excavations)
333	**Nanga Eboko**	Monitoring of trenching activities	33 N	210912	514378	702	Surface site	CS	Pottery, flaked stone fragments (in 3 pits)	●●●	Data recovery (excavations)
335	**Meyang**	Monitoring of trenching activities	33 N	243403	528403	666	Buried site	DAH(s)	Pottery, flaked stone fragments (in 3 pits)	●●●	Data recovery (excavations)

Appendix E *(end)*. Site treatment in Cameroon (CH: Ceramic horizon; CS: Ceramic scatter; DAH(s): Diverse artefact horizon(s); DAS: Diverse artefact scatter; IWH: Iron working horizon; LS: Lithic scatter; Priority*: Priority for further treatment, ●: low; ●●: medium; ●●●: high).

Date N°	Site Code	Village	Context	Laboratory #	Age bp	Calibrated age (2 sigma)
RC 1	ECA 024	Bemboyo	Bemboyo 1/I-K 13 (20–30 cm)	Beta 182529	modern	
RC 2	ECA 024	Bemboyo	Bemboyo 3/C5 (40–50 cm)	Beta 182530	90 ± 70 bp	
RC 3	ECA 043	Sokorta Manga	D10 (20–40 cm)	Beta 182531	830 ± 40 bp	AD 1155 – AD 1275
RC 4	ECA 043	Sokorta Manga	O60 (20–40 cm)	Beta 182532	1040 ± 40 bp	AD 960 – AD 1040
RC 5	ECA 047	Djaoro Mbama	Furnace A/C4 (40–60 cm)	Beta 182533	1950 ± 60 bp	BC 60 – AD 215
RC 6	ECA 047	Djaoro Mbama	Slag heap/ (40–60 cm)	Beta 182534	1980 ± 70 bp	BC 165 – AD 155
RC 7	ECA 047	Djaoro Mbama	Below furnace A/C10 (125–145 cm)	Beta 182535	2010 ± 60 bp	BC 170 – AD 115
RC 8	ECA 047	Djaoro Mbama	Furnace B/(30–40 cm)	Beta 182536	1770 ± 80 bp	AD 75 – AD 430
RC 9	ECA 047	Djaoro Mbama	Pit feature/(120–130 cm)	Beta 182537	1880 ± 60 bp	AD 5 – AD 255
RC 10	ECA 068	Ndtoua	C6 (20–30 cm)	Beta 182538	700 ± 60 bp	AD 1225 – AD 1400
RC 11	ECA 068	Ndtoua	C6 (170–180 cm)	Beta 182539	5490 ± 70 bp	BC 4460 – BC 4225
RC 12	ECA 068	Ndtoua	C6 (80–90 cm)	Beta 182540	1920 ± 70 bp	BC 55 – AD 245
RC 13	ECA 068	Ndtoua	C6 (40–50 cm)	Beta 182541	1910 ± 60 bp	BC 40 – AD 240
RC 14	ECA 084	Koukony	Trench (-100 cm)	Beta 182542	1690 ± 70 bp	AD 215 – AD 535
RC 15	ECA 093	Ewankang	A1 (20–30 cm)	Beta 182543	400 ± 50 bp	AD 1425 – AD 1635
RC 16	ECA 124	Makouré	A2 (40–60 cm)	Beta 182544	2210 ± 60 bp	BC 395 – BC 100
RC 17	ECA 125	Yébi	Trench (20–40 cm)	Beta 182545	240 ± 60 bp	AD 1500 – AD 1695
RC 18	ECA 130	Dombé	Pit B (80–120 cm)	Beta 182546	2540 ± 60 bp	BC 815 – BC 420
RC 19	ECA 130	Dombé	Pit A (40–80 cm)	Beta 182547	2440 ± 60 bp	BC 785 – BC 390
RC 20	ECA 138	Bissiang	Pit A	Beta 182548	2550 ± 60 bp	BC 820 – BC 425
RC 21	ECA 138	Bissiang	Pit B (80–110 cm)	Beta 182549	2770 ± 70 bp	BC 1105 – BC 805
RC 22	ECA 146	Bidou II	Pit (-75 cm)	Beta 182550	1530 ± 70 bp	AD 400 – AD 655
RC 23	ECA 160	Bidjouka	Pit E (60 cm)	Beta 182551	1580 ± 80 bp	AD 325 – AD 640
RC 24	ECA 160	Bidjouka	Pit A (80 cm)	Beta 182552	1480 ± 70 bp	AD 425 – AD 670
RC 25	ECA 163	Lom I	B1-C1 (20–30 cm)	Beta 182553	270 ± 70 bp	AD 1470 – AD 1950
RC 26	ECA 199	Pangar	C4 (20–30 cm)	Beta 182554	920 ± 120 bp	AD 885 – AD 1295
RC 27	ECA 216	Ngoumou	Pit (-50 cm)	Beta 182555	2000 ± 40 bp	BC 60 – AD 85
RC 28	ECA 224	Obokouc	Pit (20–40 cm)	Beta 182556	330 ± 50 bp	AD 1445 – AD 1660
RC 29	ECA 228	Binguela II	Pit A (40–60 cm)	Beta 182557	1590 ± 60 bp	AD 350 – AD 610
RC 30	ECA 228	Binguela II	Pit B (40–60 cm)	Beta 182558	1670 ± 70 bp	AD 230 – AD 545
RC 31	ECA 228	Binguela II	Pit D (80–100 cm)	Beta 182559	1630 ± 70 bp	AD 250 – AD 585
RC 32	ECA 236	Zoatoupsi	Pit (120–140cm)	Beta 182560	2170 ± 70 bp	BC 390 – BC 40
RC 33	ECA 242	Ozom	Pit (40–60 cm)	Beta 182561	1550 ± 70 bp	AD 385 – AD 645
RC 34	ECA 243	Beka Petel	A1 (90–100 cm)	Beta 182562	870 ± 60 bp	AD 1025 – AD 1275
RC 35	ECA 243	Beka Petel	A1 (00–30 cm)	Beta 182563	750 ± 70 bp	AD 1170 – AD 1315
RC 36	ECA 248	Essong Missang	Pit B (20–40 cm)	Beta 182564	1420 ± 60 bp	AD 540 – AD 690
RC 37	ECA 250	Leboudi	Pit A (100–120 cm)	Beta 182572	2140 ± 110 bp	BC 400 – AD 80
RC 38	ECA 272	Ezezang	Pit D (80–100 cm)	Beta 182565	2120 ± 70 bp	BC 375 – AD 30
RC 39	ECA 272	Ezezang	Pit M (40–60 cm)	Beta 182566	2410 ± 60 bp	BC 775 – BC 385
RC 40	ECA 272	Ezezang	Unit K (00–20 cm)	Beta 182567	2220 ± 70 bp	BC 400 – BC 80
RC 41	ECA 272	Ezezang	Unit K (20–40 cm)	Beta 182568	2260 ± 40 bp	BC 395 – BC 95
RC 42	ECA 272	Ezezang	Unit K (40–60 cm)	Beta 182569	2210 ± 40 bp	BC 385 – BC 180
RC 43	ECA 279	Ongot	Pit A (145–165 cm)	Beta 182570	2240 ± 100 bp	BC 515 – BC 45
RC 44	ECA 279	Ongot	Pit A (85–105 cm)	Beta 182571	1410 ± 60 bp	AD 545 – AD 700
RC 45	ECA 315	Ndjoré	Pit C (80–100 cm)	Beta 182573	1930 ± 60 bp	BC 50 – AD 230
RC 46	ECA 315	Ndjoré	Pit D (60–100 cm)	Beta 182574	2020 ± 60 bp	BC 180 – AD 95
RC 47	ECA 315	Ndjoré	Pit E (40–60 cm)	Beta 182575	1810 ± 60 bp	AD 75 – AD 385
RC 48	ECA 315	Ndjoré	Pit B (40–60 cm)	Beta 182576	1870 ± 40 bp	AD 45 – AD 230
RC 49	ECA 315	Ndjoré	Pit B: skeleton (120–135 cm)	Beta 182577	modern	
RC 50	ECA 317	Ndokoa	Pit (60–80 cm)	Beta 182578	1980 ± 80 bp	BC 180 – AD 225
RC 51	ECA 323	Zili	Pit (170–190 cm)	Beta 182579	2630 ± 70 bp	BC 910 – BC 560
RC 52	ECA 329	Doumba	Pit (163–183 cm)	Beta 182580	2020 ± 60 bp	BC 180 – AD 95
RC 53	ECA 333	Nanga Eboko	Pit E (20–60 cm)	Beta 182581	2190 ± 60 bp	BC 390 – BC 60
RC 54	ECA 333	Nanga Eboko	Pit F (20–60 cm)	Beta 182582	2040 ± 80 bp	BC 350 – AD 120
RC 55	ECA 335	Meyang	Pit C (100–120 cm)	Beta 182583	2360 ± 60 bp	BC 755 – BC 365
RC 56	ECA 335	Meyang	Pit B (60–80 cm)	Beta 182584	2110 ± 60 bp	BC 360 – AD 20

Appendix F. Radiocarbon dates in Cameroon.

Abbreviations

CEP	Chad Export Project
CHM	Cultural Heritage Management
COTCO	Cameroon Oil Transportation Company S.A.
CTF	Central Treatment Facility
EEPCI	Esso Exploration and Production Chad, Inc.
EMP	Environmental Management Plan
ESA	Early Stone Age
FSO	Floating Storage and Offloading
KP	Kilometer Post
LSA	Later Stone Age
MSA	Middle Stone Age
OC	Operations Center
OFDA	Oilfield Development Area
PRS	Pressure-Reducing Station
PS	Pump Station
SOCOPAO	Société Commerciale des Ports Africains
TOTCO	Tchad Oil Transportation Company S.A.